The Crisis of French Symbolism

ALSO BY LAURENCE M. PORTER

The Renaissance of the Lyric in French Romanticism

The Literary Dream in French Romanticism: A Psychoanalytic Interpretation

Aging in Literature (with Laurel Porter)

Critical Essays on Gustave Flaubert

"The Interpretation of Dreams": Freud's Theories Revisited

The Crisis of
French Symbolism

LAURENCE M. PORTER

Cornell University Press

ITHACA AND LONDON

First published 1990 by Cornell University Press.

International Standard Book Number 0-8014-2418-6
Library of Congress Catalog Card Number 89-45976

Printed in the United States of America

Librarians: Library of Congress cataloging information appears on the last page of the book.

♾ The paper used in this publication meets the minimum requirements of the American National Standard for Permanence of Paper for Printed Library Materials Z39.48–1984.

For Anne Elizabeth Channing Porter, poet

Contents

Preface

Studies of French Symbolism have successfully described what distinguishes each of its major poets from the others. Baudelaire is typically presented as a precursor of the movement. Mallarmé appears to be the one indisputably "symbol-*ist*" poet: he systematically deploys a limited vocabulary of recurring metaphors as the main materials for poetry. He therefore provides the most obvious inspiration for such later poets as Rilke, Yeats, Valéry, and Claudel. Verlaine and Rimbaud seem to announce two diverging branches of later poetry, the one musical and imagistic, the other kaleidoscopic and surrealistic. Critics have provided incisive readings of the major poems by these French Symbolists; only Verlaine has been somewhat neglected.

All four poets lived close together in time and space. In this book I explore what else they share. What do they really have in common? Why do we see them as a group? How are they related to the poetic movements that preceded and followed them?

To answer these questions I subject traditional histories of the nineteenth-century French lyric to scrutiny; invoke as a heuristic device Roman Jakobson's categories for describing the act of communication; and distinguish a "first Symbolism" of crisis which lasted from 1851 to around 1875—the period on which I focus—from a second or "high Symbolism" that flourished till about 1925 and prepared the way for Modernism in Latin America, England, and the United States.

I argue that the poetry of the first third of the nineteenth century in France was a form of Neoclassicism that revived and refined traditional genres; that the middle third of the century was the true Romantic period, when the inherited codes and contexts of poetry were called into question; and that the overlapping latter half of the century was shaped by the crisis that erupted when the Symbolists questioned the linguistic vehicle of poetry and the very act of communication. A loss of faith in the ability of language to signify threatened the existence of poetry in the minds of the people who were creating it.

The major French Symbolists focused on different cruxes of difficulty along the axis of communication. Mallarmé subverted the idea of inspiration (the link between sender and message); Verlaine vehemently mistrusted language itself; Baudelaire found that to make contact with his audience was impossible, or worse yet, pointless; and Rimbaud felt his audience to be attentive but irrevocably hostile. I discuss these poets in the order in which I have just described them rather than chronologically, for I wish to shift emphasis away from the diachronic notion of a chronological development within the Symbolist "movement" to the synchronic concept of the problematics of communication. I thereby imply that all four poets evolved in parallel. The chapters concentrate, in order, on the conception, encoding, transmission, and reception of the poetic message. All four poets experienced difficulties in all four areas, but the relatively greater emphasis that each gave to one area in particular constitutes a main component of his personal style.

Such stances were partly deliberate, reflecting the poets' urgent need to "make it new," not merely by reshaping the perceptions of their audience, as the Romantics had tried to do, but by revolutionizing that audience's presuppositions about the reliability of communication. André Gide spoke sensitively on this issue in the preface to his anthology of French poetry when he identified "the extraordinary novelty that Baudelaire brought to the field of poetry.... It was an unprecedented revolution to no longer yield oneself up to the lyric flow; to resist facile 'inspiration,' rhetorical laxity, the domination of outmoded words, images, and conventions; to treat the Muse like a recalcitrant being who had to be subdued rather than trusted, with one's mind and critical faculties in abeyance."[1]

The Symbolists resolved their crisis by inventing a new genre, the

1. André Gide, *Anthologie de la poésie française* (Paris: Gallimard, 1949), p. x.

prose poem, through which Baudelaire, Rimbaud, and Mallarmé achieve ironic self-consciousness and escape from the aporia of "l'incommunicabilité" at war with an urgent sense of vocation. Here two clarifications are in order. First, their elliptical, unconventional syntax, hermetic vocabulary, and enigmatic frames of reference obviously make Mallarmé's and Rimbaud's prose poems hard to understand and thus add to the difficulties of communication. But such features are intended to challenge us to become initiates. The verbal vehicles of these poems resist interpretation. The message of the prose poems, however, is that virtual (apparent) authorial control over language has been reaffirmed, and that in various ways communication between the poet and his ideal audience (as distinguished from us, the empirical readers) has become less problematical. Second, I do not claim that prose poems could come into being only after the crisis of the Symbolist verse poems had run its course. In Baudelaire's career, and even more in Mallarmé's, the periods of composition of verse and of prose poems overlap. Problem and solution coexist for a long time.

Any book on Symbolist poetry which treats individual authors should give Mallarmé pride of place. The chapter I devote to him, however, is relatively brief. So many great critics have treated him in exhaustive detail and his laments about poetic sterility are so well known that my task is greatly simplified: to examine neglected bodies of evidence (notably, the manuscript variants and the surviving fragments of "Pour un tombeau d'Anatole") and to situate him in the context of my overall argument. The movement that he ultimately led, "high Symbolism," and the very way in which he led it, through the inspirational improvisations offered at his Tuesday-evening *cénacle* in Paris, reflect a renewed faith in communicability which lies beyond the province of my study.

The fundamental question to be answered at the outset is whether Jakobson's model for the communicative act is still valid, and if so, in what sense; or whether it has become hopelessly outdated. Ross Chambers explains that

> in adapting the communicational triangle of addresser-addressee-referent he inherited from Bühler, Jakobson inherited also a dualistic and representational ("words-and-things") view of language in which discourse represents a pre-existing world and simultaneously is available as a tool of "expression" to human subjects who are similarly thought of as autonomous from the linguistic system. We are learning, however, to turn this conception on its head, and to understand language as a

signifying system (and discourse as a signifying practice), asking not
how it "represents" the world and "expresses" human subjects, but how
it produces meanings, given that [as Derrida says] "il n'y a pas de hors-
texte."[2]

My answer is that I do not invoke Jakobson's categories to "explain"
Symbolist poetry. Instead, I deploy them as a heuristic device to show
how the "words-and-things" system still current in the second half of
the nineteenth century raised problems for the greatest French Symbolists when they came to realize that they were *not* independent of
language and that language was *not* a reliable tool of expression. In
my view, Modernism represented a step backward from this insight,
which was widely rediscovered only in the 1960s.

All translations in this book are mine. To translate is to interpret.
To expose the presuppositions and orientations of my approach
clearly in this way should help others to relate their critical stances to
my own.

Many kind, indulgent people have helped inspire this book and
guided its development. At Harvard University, Paul Bénichou's un-
pretentious yet dazzling seminar on Mallarmé in the fall of 1958 first
revealed to me the excitement of close encounters with hermetic Symbolist texts and awakened the ambition to write about them someday.
René Jasinski's Baudelaire seminar two years later offered a model
combination of magisterial erudition and humanistic sensibility. As
nuclei of the various chapters gradually formed from 1978 on, valuable suggestions were offered by Ross Chambers, Robert Greer
Cohn, A. C. Goodson, Herbert Josephs, Susan Noakes, Marshall Olds,
and Laurel Porter, who enhanced the entire study with her keen
stylistic sensitivity. Ursula Franklin, Virginia La Charité, and Eléonore
Zimmermann shared their work on Mallarmé at particularly critical
moments, helping to shape my insights. Robert L. Mitchell's invitation
to write a chapter on Rimbaud for a collection of essays and Robert
Greer Cohn's rich book on Rimbaud, which appeared just at that time,
were also important stimuli. In the final stages, Marshall Olds offered
a superb reading, which had a strong constructive influence, for Cornell
University Press. And although I cannot approach his luminous insight and theoretical mastery, Ross Chambers has had the greatest

2. Ross Chambers, "An Address in the Country: Mallarmé and the Kinds of Literary
Context," *French Forum*, 11 (May 1986), 205.

effect of all on my understanding of Symbolist poetry through the
wealth of wonderfully subtle, elegant, illuminating studies that have
established him as the finest Baudelaire critic of our time. His un-
stinting support always provided heartwarming encouragement.

In recent years, Michigan State University gave crucial support
through an All-University Research Initiation Grant that provided a
term off for research in the fall of 1987; further All-University Research Grant funds during the summer of 1988 paid for a research
assistant, Debora V. Traas, whose competence and resourcefulness
were exceptional. I am indebted to Ohio State University Press for
permission to use the text that constitutes about a fourth of Chapter
5, and to Michael Riffaterre, editor of the *Romanic Review*, for permission to incorporate in Chapter 2 an essay that appeared in that
journal in November 1985. Working with Cornell University Press
has been a delight, thanks to the empathic solicitude and unfailing
courtesy of my editor, Bernhard Kendler. Barbara H. Salazar lavished
expert attention on the typescript; and so far as ensuring factual
accuracy, appropriate diction, clarity, and coherence is concerned, my
copy editor, Martha Linke, has truly been my coauthor. Together,
she and Ms. Salazar provided the best editing I have experienced in
thirty years.

LAURENCE M. PORTER

East Lansing, Michigan

The Crisis of French Symbolism

Chapter 1

The Crisis of French Symbolism

The history of the nineteenth-century French lyric needs to be redefined. The very discredit into which diachronic approaches have fallen during the eras of Structuralism and Poststructuralism allows the assumptions that have informed these approaches to survive unchallenged in the collective preconscious of literary critics. We may consider literary history no longer worthy of consideration; we may divert our attention from it; but it will still survive subliminally, intact, and insulated from the salutary influence of competing ideas. Since we each have a personal history and pass through an organic life cycle, we shall always be compelled on some level to project the historical and organic metaphors onto other phenomena such as literature.

The prevailing scheme for structuring the history of nineteenth-century French poetry divides the century into three periods: Romanticism, an undifferentiated transitional phase, and Symbolism. Lacking the conceptual "home" of an identified literary movement, some major mid-century poets are neglected, while others are reft from their historical context so that they may be presented as precursors of Modernism rather than as representatives of their own times.

The French Romantics are perceived as revolutionary innovators. This perception has been shaped by the largely unexamined assumption that since literature reflects society, the French Revolution must have engendered radical transformations of literature. It touched off a quarter century of exhausting wars and internecine political strife that crippled developments in the arts. Overall, the first third of the nineteenth century was marked by the profoundly reactionary social movements of the Empire and the Restoration. During this time, literature reacted as well, retreating to a prerevolutionary Neoclassicism. We tend to overlook this fact in part because our perception of the French Romantics is unconsciously influenced by our awareness of the innovative poetic practice of the English writers Coleridge, Wordsworth, and Blake. Consequently, we assume that all Romantics of any stature must have transformed literature, and we dismiss Alphonse de Lamartine and Alfred de Vigny as minor poets when on close examination they seem to have added little to the established traditions of verse. Even those critics who might hotly deny so disparaging an evaluation seldom take the time to write defenses of these poets. Lamartine appears a belated elegist (nobody considers the turbulent epic *La Chute d'un ange*) and Vigny a nostalgic advocate of the Neoclassic Stoic that went out of fashion after Napoleon I and David.

The poetry of Lamartine, Vigny, and the early Victor Hugo actually represents an unrecognized Neoclassicism. The eighteenth century, having lost the sense of the lyric, settled down to telling stories in rhymed verse. The early French "Romantics" innovated through reaction, returning to the genres of the Renaissance. From their viewpoint, what we today think of as Neoclassicism was coextensive with French art and French tradition since the early sixteenth century (the Baroque being a fascinating minor deviation). As John Porter Houston has observed, "For much of the nineteenth century in France, formal aesthetic questions continued frequently to be conceived according to basic assumptions of neoclassicism (imitation, unity of detail, symmetry)."[1]

It has become a misleading commonplace to say that French Romanticism broke down conventional generic categories. True, the first third of the nineteenth century witnessed the birth in France of the historical novel (inspired by Sir Walter Scott), the "conte fantastique" (created by Charles Nodier and then given a great impetus by trans-

1. John Porter Houston, *French Symbolism and the Modernist Movement: A Study of Poetic Structures* (Baton Rouge: Louisiana State University Press, 1980), p. 2. For an authoritative overview of the entire Symbolist phenomenon, with discussions of its aesthetic and philosophical underpinnings, see *The Symbolist Movement in the Literature of European Languages*, ed. Anna Balakian (Budapest: Akadémiai Kiado, 1982), pts. I–II, pp. 15–123.

lations of E. T. A. Hoffmann), and the melodrama (Guilbert de Pixérécourt). The Rousseauistic (self-justifying) confession also blossomed into a genre. But the notion of a breakdown of genres does not explain what was happening in French lyric poetry up until at least 1830. In 1828, for example, Emile Deschamps's influential preface to his *Etudes françaises et étrangères* invoked the concept of genre rather than of a Romantic revolt against Classicism in order to explain the evolution of poetry in his day. Deschamps suggested that writers had surveyed existing genres and then chosen to devote themselves to those that had not already been overexploited: "The Lyric, Elegiac, and Epic being the weak areas in our former poetry ... it is therefore in them that the energies of the poetry of today were destined to be focused. Therefore, Victor Hugo revealed his talents in the Ode, Lamartine in the Elegy, and Alfred de Vigny in the 'Poëme.' "[2] The generic subtitles the early French Romantics frequently employed indicate that they themselves thought of their lyric poems in terms of traditional genres. In sum, they conceived of their achievements in the lyric as a culmination of Neoclassicism, and they saw themselves as rejuvenating traditional forms with new ideas just as André Chénier before them had claimed to do. (One thinks of the quintessentially Romantic painter Delacroix's indignant rejection of that label when he protested: "Je suis un pur classique.") They achieved novelty through a crystallization of generic self-consciousness; they revived the lyric genres by recentering them on metaphors that summed up the essence of each. Lamartine used the metaphor of the echo to subsume the traditional elegiac pattern of appeal and response; Vigny condensed the manifold heroic actions of the epic into a sculptural shorthand of assertive and submissive bodily attitudes and gestures, thus moving the short narrative poem toward the lyric; and Hugo telescoped the spatial sublime of the ode into the "metaphor maxima" (the juxtaposition of two nouns such as "monde châtiment" or "l'Hydre univers") to form a kernel of revelation replacing the optimistic but rhetorical, verbose, and thus diluted prophecies of the eighteenth-century visionary ode. These revivals formed a literary parallel to the political developments of the time, specifically the Restoration.[3]

2. Emile Deschamps, *Etudes françaises et étrangères* (Paris: A. Levavasseur, 1828), pp. 12–13.

3. See Laurence M. Porter, *The Renaissance of the Lyric in French Romanticism: Elegy, "Poëme," and Ode* (Lexington, Ky.: French Forum, 1978), pp. 11–14.

The codes (systems of widely understood and generally accepted references and meanings) of the elegy, short narrative poem, and ode, moreover, presume social solidarity. The elegiac poet has been isolated by loss and grief, but not by estrangement from society: he appeals for sympathy from others, who unquestionably share his values. The short narrative relates a socially significant event from the perspective of a shared heritage of history and tradition. Vigny deplores war, the injustice of the Old Testament God, the decline of the aristocracy, and society's lack of appreciation for poets, but he adopts the stance of a would-be reformer (or reactionary) working within the system. The encomiastic quality of the ode also presumes a community of values. The choice of such a genre takes for granted the facility of inspiration, the formality and elegance of diction, reference, and subject, and an attentive reception by a public in harmony with the poet and his or her values. Surveying the history of French poetry during the first two-thirds of the century, Théodore de Banville claimed that the ode had come to dominate the mainstream of French poetry.[4]

According to the consecrated, unexamined categories of traditional literary history, French poets of the middle third of the century fall into the chronological cracks between Romanticism and Symbolism. Like all awkward exceptions to a general scheme, they are accommodated by special labels—Théophile Gautier and Banville by "L'Art pour l'Art"; Charles-Marie Leconte de Lisle and José María de Heredia by "Parnasse"—which reduce them to oddities and remove them from serious consideration. Baudelaire fits in uneasily as a transitional figure between Romanticism and Symbolism. Others, including Tristan Corbière, Jules Laforgue, Arthur Rimbaud, and le comte de Lautréamont (and on these poets much good work *has* been done) have been considered interesting mainly as harbingers of the twentieth-century ironic tradition, of Surrealism, or of Modernism.

In fact, poets such as Corbière, Lautréamont, and Laforgue were the true Romantics: only around mid-century did a real revolutionary departure from conventional genres, diction, and theme occur. Hugo waited until 1854 to claim "j'ai mis un bonnet rouge au vieux dictionnaire" (I have set a [revolutionary's] red cap on the old dictionary).

---

4. Théodore de Banville, *Petit Traité de poésie française* (Paris: Charpentier, 1891 [1872]), p. 158: "L'ode, je le répète une dernière fois, a absorbé tous les genres poétiques ... elle est devenue toute la poésie moderne."

In the work of these poets, as well as in that of Leconte de Lisle and Maxime Du Camp (*Chants modernes*, 1855), the code and context of traditional lyrics are affected.[5] Romanticism proper retains the familiar poetic vehicles but changes their message, dramatizing a poet standing apart from society. Such a condition of literature is illustrated perfectly by Lautréamont's *Poésies*, which take an old form—the aphorism modeled after Pascal and Vauvenargues—and reverse its conventional wisdom.

The simplest of the familiar and therefore readily available ways of reshaping and subverting traditional themes was to shift from the tone of encomium to that of satire. To the dominant discourse declaring that whatever is, is right, the Romantics retorted with a counterdiscourse or oppositional narrative.[6] This truculent mode of expression extended eventually to their vocabulary as well as their themes and led to the interjection of familiar and coarse locutions into what had traditionally been a solemn situation. Hugo claims to transform language, but the real changes in diction come with Corbière and Laforgue. The most obvious symptoms of this upheaval were the appearance of a major new genre, the prose poem; the reemergence of satire; and the de-euphemization of metaphor, which reversed the previous tendency of this master trope of the lyric to make the unpleasant pleasant.[7]

Lautréamont—in fact rather timidly—transforms the encounter between poet and reader from a didactic to a sexual one that claims to be neither useful nor pleasant. Even when the Romantic poet withdraws, however, even when society does not heed him or her, the poet's reaction is to forge better weapons and then reenter the fray, denouncing indifference, mediocrity, and complacency. (The Flaubert of *Bouvard et Pécuchet* is still very much a Romantic.) Even a mutually aggressive, negative relationship remains a relationship. A bad object

5. For a discussion of the terms "code" and "context" as used in linguistics, see Roman Jakobson's influential *Studies on Child Language and Aphasia* (The Hague: Mouton, 1971), pp. 41–48, 54–55, 61, and 67–73; his "Linguistics and Poetics," in *Selected Writings* (The Hague: Mouton, 1981), 3 vols., III, 18–27; and the famous "Closing Statement: Linguistics and Poetics," in Thomas A. Sebeok, ed., *Style in Language* (Cambridge, Mass.: M.I.T. Press, 1960), pp. 350–77.

6. See Richard Terdiman, *Discourse and Counterdiscourse: The Theory and Practice of Symbolic Resistance in Nineteenth-Century France* (Ithaca, N.Y.: Cornell University Press, 1985), and Ross Chambers, *Mélancolie et opposition: Les Débuts du modernisme en France* (Paris: Corti, 1987).

7. On this last point see Laurence M. Porter, "Modernist Maldoror: The De-euphemization of Metaphor," *L'Esprit Créateur*, 18 (Winter 1978), 25–34.

seems better than none. Wrestling with his loathsome God, Lautréamont still enjoys intimacy. In opposing convention, Romantic literature remains bound to it, engaged in an unending dialogue with
accepted values and continually revitalizing them—like Hercules' hy-
dra—through the very act of contestation.

In the Romantic system, then, values have become problematical,
but the act of communication still has not. As Houston has explained,
pre-Symbolist poetry in general is characterized by

> great clarity in rhetorical situations, by which I mean the relationships
> among author, speaker, person or thing addressed, subject matter, and
> reader, or whatever combination of them is relevant. This clarity is
> demonstrable on the levels of syntax, vocabulary, and figurative lan-
> guage.... A noteworthy stylistic aspect of romantic lyric is the reader's
> ability to distinguish between concrete and figurative language or to
> recognize the simultaneous presence of both.... we can perceive the
> poem's reference as general, exemplary, or particular.[8]

The actual transition from Romanticism to Symbolism was provoked
by the problems raised by Romanticism's Neoplatonic worldview,
which assumed that there were identifiable transcendent referents for
language.

In practice, Symbolism is ordinarily defined either too narrowly or
too broadly: as a general tendency of *La Belle Epoque* (1880–1914) or
as the systematic, pervasive use of a restricted vocabulary of symbols
in poetry. Standard definitions of Symbolism in dictionaries and en-
cyclopedias tend merely to list some of the writers—and sometimes
the painters and musicians—of the latter years of the nineteenth century, without defining what they may have had in common, as though
the movement lacked definitive or even characteristic traits. It is therefore not surprising that literary historians have not agreed on who
the Symbolists were. Attempts to identify and categorize them seem
to follow at least four major tendencies. The first claims that Baudelaire was a precursor and that after him Symbolism divided into
two "branches," the musical and the metaphoric, dominated respectively by Paul Verlaine and Stéphane Mallarmé.[9] A second view dis-

---

8. Houston, *French Symbolism and the Modernist Movement*, pp. 7–8.

9. See Thomas A. Kovach, "A New Kind of Poetry: Hofmannsthal and the French
Symbolists," *Comparative Literature*, 37 (Winter 1985), 50n, 51; and *The Oxford Companion
to French Literature*, ed. Joyce M. H. Reid (Oxford: Clarendon, 1976), s.v. "Symbolism,"
pp. 603–4.

cerns two different branches: the free-form, alogical creations of Rimbaud and the intellectual,, stringently formalistic verse of Mallarmé, an opposition echoed in the twentieth century by Paul Valéry ("a poem should be a festival of the intellect") and André Breton ("a collapse of the intellect").[10] A third view would also include Corbière and Laforgue as Symbolists, presumably in order to give two fine neglected poets their due by sheltering them under the umbrella of an overarching movement in literary history.[11] A fourth perspective extends the Symbolist period to the mid-1920s and embraces such twentieth-century figures as Paul Claudel, Guillaume Apollinaire, and Valéry.[12] Only Mallarmé appears on everyone's list; Verlaine, Baudelaire, Rimbaud, and Valéry are each omitted by some formulation. And those critics who try to characterize the poetic practice of the Symbolist authors, in addition to merely enumerating them, almost inevitably divide these authors into two opposing groups.

One wonders, then, what if anything the representatives of those contrasting persuasions share. Musicality? Only Verlaine really demonstrates this characteristic, and indeed the last famous French poet able to produce verse consistently appropriate for a musical setting was Guillaume de Machaut (1300–1377). The late-nineteenth-century composers Claude Debussy, Henri Du Parc, and Gabriel Fauré, through the magisterial achievement of their art songs, were mainly responsible after the fact for giving Symbolist poets the reputation of being musicians. Mallarmé's "Un coup de Dés" adopts a system of notation analogous to that of the musical score insofar as the spatial disposition of the words on the page suggests an attribute comparable to pitch and the type size suggests an attribute comparable to intensity (loudness). But this is an isolated experiment, and to call it musical is to confuse graphic notation, a feature of both poetry and music, with the arrangement of sounds in relation to one another at a given moment and also over time, a feature of music alone. Synesthesia? This quality is prominent only in Baudelaire and in his non-Symbolist master Théophile Gautier. Symbols? The essence of the symbolism of all periods as we have traditionally understood it is that its metaphors are organized into a system. But surely one finds a greater

10. See Hugo Friedrich, *The Structure of Modern Poetry, from the Mid-Nineteenth to the Mid-Twentieth Century* (Evanston, Ill.: Northwestern University Press, 1974), p. 109.

11. See Houston, *French Symbolism and the Modernist Movement*, pp. 59–83 and passim.

12. See James R. Lawler, *The Language of French Symbolism* (Princeton: Princeton University Press, 1969), pp. vii–ix and passim.

density of symbols in William Blake, John Donne, and Maurice Scève
than in Rimbaud or Verlaine. Baudelaire uses allegory and simile
more often than metaphor, although it is on his symbolism that I
focus later in this book. And Rimbaud's poetry is more striking in its
effects of disjunction than of coherence. Only Mallarmé deploys a
limited and tightly organized vocabulary of metaphors as the main
materials for his poetry. Must we then limit French Symbolism to
Mallarmé?

The view I am advocating would replace the traditional division of
the nineteenth-century French lyric into the phases of Romanticism/
transitions/Symbolism with a division into Neoclassicism/Romanti-
cism/Symbolism. One could schematize it as follows:

Mode	Neoclassicism	Romanticism	Symbolism
Vehicles	Conventional	Conventional	Original
Codes	Conventional	Original	Original
Metalanguage	Affirmative	Questioning	Negating

In epistemological terms, the Romantics assailed the absurdity and
errors of existing institutions, seeking to reform them or replace them
with others. The Symbolists saw all institutions as relative to time and
place and circumstance and therefore as delusional. The rationale for
the Symbolists' departure from tradition was most clearly expressed
by Schopenhauer in Book III of *The World as Will and Idea*, where he
summed up a current of thought widespread in the nineteenth
century:

> Time, space, and causality are that arrangement of our intellect by virtue
> of which the *one* being of each kind which alone really is, manifests
> itself to us as a multiplicity of similar beings, constantly appearing and
> disappearing in endless succession. The apprehension of things by
> means of and in accordance with this arrangement is *immanent* knowl-
> edge; that, on the other hand, which is conscious of the true state of
> the case, is *transcendental* knowledge. The latter is obtained *in abstracto*
> through the criticism of pure reason, but in exceptional cases it may
> also appear intuitively.[13]

Vigny had anticipated this contrast of two forms of knowledge in
his ironically titled "Les Oracles," referring to ambitious men who

13. Arthur Schopenhauer, *The World as Will and Representation*, 3 vols. (London:
Routledge & Kegan Paul, 1948), I, 224.

scatter their thoughts to the winds of political debate instead of trying
to crystallize, in solitude, the diamond of pure poetry. So the poet's
mission is to see beyond the flux of appearances in order to apprehend
the essential. Baudelaire articulated these aspirations clearly in his
article on Hugo in 1861: "tout est hiéroglyphique.... Or, qu'est-ce
que le poète (je prends le mot dans son acception la plus large), si ce
n'est un traducteur, un déchiffreur?" (Everything is a hieroglyph....
Now, what is a poet [I am taking the word in its broadest possible
meaning] if not a translator, a decipherer?).[14] Through the imagination Baudelaire tried to apprehend universal analogy, "ou ce qu'une
religion mystique appelle la *correspondance*."[15] Elsewhere he defined
the experience of revelation in quasi-Schopenhauerian terms: "Dans
certains états de l'âme presque surnaturels, la profondeur de la vie
se révèle tout entière dans le spectacle, si ordinaire qu'il soit, qu'on a
sous les yeux. Il en devient le Symbole" (In certain almost supernatural
states of the soul, the depths of existence are entirely revealed in the
spectacle, however ordinary it may be, you have before your eyes. It
becomes the Symbol [of those depths]).[16]

Seeking transcendence, the Symbolists abandoned both Neoclassic
tradition and Romantic opposition, but as poets they remained tied
to the use of language, a system of conventions which prima facie
seemed hardly susceptible of attaining or even becoming the vehicle
for a vision of transcendence. To evade this aporia, they adopted one
of three main solutions. Two had already been tried by the Romantics
and by earlier poets as well.

The first solution, the age-old doctrine of Cratylism, postulated that
language in and of itself, as a divine creation, bears an ultimate signification. Its shape and sound constitute the outward and visible sign
of an inward and invisible transcendence. In addition to graphemes,
etymology, homonymy, and onomatopoeia supposedly hold clues to
primordial meanings. This tradition runs through Rousseau to Nodier
and of course Mallarmé, whose speculations on the expressive forms

14. Charles Baudelaire, "Réflexions sur quelques-uns de mes contemporains: Victor
Hugo," in his *Oeuvres complètes*, ed. Yves Le Dantec and Claude Pichois, 2 vols. (Paris:
Gallimard, 1975–76), II, 129–41 (p. 133); hereafter cited in text and notes as *OC*.

15. Baudelaire to Alphonse Toussenel, January 21, 1856, in his *Correspondance*, ed.
Claude Pichois, 2 vols. (Paris: Gallimard, 1973), I, 336.

16. Baudelaire, *Fusées* XI (frag. 17), *OC* I, 659. This passage and the two previous
quotations from Baudelaire are all cited by Henri Peyre, *Qu'est-ce que le Symbolisme?*
(Paris: Presses universitaires de France, 1974), pp. 44–46.

of letters and typography are well known.[17] The rapid development of historical linguistics in the nineteenth century, as it traced Western languages back to an Indo-European root, encouraged belief in Cratylism. Some poets believed that one could "purify" language by using it so that it more closely reflected its origins. Mallarmé had urged: "Donner un sens plus pur aux mots de la tribu" (Give a purer meaning to the words of the tribe). In his "Suite à une réponse à un acte d'accusation," Hugo for one had earlier expounded an almost mystical concept of language; in passages dated from 1830 to 1864 and collected in the *Postscriptum de ma vie* he repeatedly emphasizes the necessity of fusing form and matter—a notion echoed by Banville in his *Petit Traité de poésie française* of 1872.[18] Hugo, however, finally confronted the unbridgeable gap between language and the transcendent in the last ten pages of his unfinished visionary poem "Dieu," one still too little known. After presenting ten successive and ever more refined depictions of God by winged beings whom the poet encounters during an imagined ascension toward Heaven—a progress that metaphorically asserts his claim of being in contact with a realm of higher knowledge—the poet capitulates:[19]

> Le mot noir est un grain de cendre dans la brume,
> O gouffre, et le mot blanc est un flocon d'écume,
> L'infini ne sait point ce qu'on murmure en bas;
> ....
> Pourquoi chercher les mots où ne sont plus les choses?
> Le vil langage humain n'a pas d'apothéoses.

(The black word is a speck of ash in the fog, / O abyss, and the white word is a trace of foam, / The infinite is unaware of what is murmured below; / Why seek words where there are no things? / Vile human language has no apotheoses.)[20]

For ten more pages the conclusion of the poem expatiates on the inadequacy of language, and the last word is an angelic command to the poet: "Silence!" Hugo complied by not completing the last two of the projected ten sections of the poem.

17. See Gérard Genette, *Mimologiques: Voyages en Cratylie* (Paris: Seuil, 1976), especially the chapters on Nodier and Mallarmé.
18. Banville, *Petit Traité*, pp. 262–63; see also Margaret Gilman, *The Idea of Poetry in France* (Cambridge: Harvard University Press, 1957), p. 233.
19. See Porter, *Renaissance of the Lyric*, pp. 100–106.
20. Victor Hugo, *La Légende des siècles; La Fin de Satan; Dieu* (Paris: Gallimard, 1962), pp. 1066, 1104.

If a direct attack on the transcendent by means of words seemed bound to fail, there remained the hope that the beyond could be intuited, suggested, indirectly evoked. So Baudelaire referred to poetry as a "magie suggestive," and Banville called poetry "this sorcery by means of which ideas are infallibly communicated to us in a certain way by words which do not express them."[21] And Mallarmé of course declared, "*Nommer* un objet, c'est supprimer les trois-quarts de la jouissance du poëme qui est faite de deviner peu à peu: le *suggérer*, voilà le rêve. C'est le parfait usage de ce mystère qui constitue le symbole" (To *name* an object is to suppress three-quarters of the enjoyment of the poem, which consists in guessing little by little: to *suggest* it, that is my dream. The symbol is constituted by the flawless practice of this mystery/ministry).[22] In practice, such an enterprise must steer a treacherous course between the Scylla of obscurity and the Charybdis of preciosity based upon periphrasis and allusion. In the latter instance the flash of insight achieved in guessing the answer to a riddle may masquerade as a window on transcendence.

After abandoning the prophetic statements of frankly visionary literature or the alternative of suggestion, the poet is reduced to a third possibility: to despair of the success of the communicative process altogether, since only the transcendent is worth communicating and since the poet's verbal vehicle must be the antithesis of transcendence. Such despair is what characterizes Symbolism proper—or more precisely, the first or crisis period of Symbolism as opposed to the optimistic "second Symbolism" of the mid–1880s on—as distinguished from Romanticism. Romanticism preserved a robust optimism about its ability to apprehend an ultimate truth and to communicate it, be it only eventually and to only a happy few. Although Hugo abandoned his attempt to depict God verbally, he persisted till the end of his life—for another quarter century—in his attempts to describe the reverberations of Providence in human history. In advance, he scheduled his posthumous publications at five-year intervals so as to ensure the greatest possible impact for his revelations. But all the major Symbolist poets in France underwent a crisis of loss of faith in the communicative process. They experienced what the French call "l'incommunicabilité"—the difficulty or impossibility of mutual under-

21. Banville, *Petit Traité*, p. 291, cited in Gilman, *Idea of Poetry in France*, p. 236.
22. Stéphane Mallarmé, "Réponses à des enquêtes sur l'évolution littéraire," in *Oeuvres complètes*, ed. Henri Mondor and G. Jean-Aubry (Paris: Gallimard, 1956), p. 869.

standing. (Before, during, and after the apogee of Symbolism, of course, this motif is commonplace in larval form as the *quiproquo* of comic theater; it receives thematic development in plays such as Alfred de Musset's *Fantasio* and in the theater of the absurd.) Eléonore Zimmermann and Claude Cuénot come to mind as two critics with a keen sense of this unifying principle in French Symbolism. Cuénot, for example, has said that "Verlaine is modern in his effort to express the inexpressible, and in that respect he is indeed a disciple of Baudelaire and a kindred spirit to Rimbaud and Mallarmé.... The magnificent generation of poets that followed Baudelaire owes its greatness to this almost despairing attempt."[23]

Mallarmé, Verlaine, Baudelaire, and Rimbaud all encounter hindrances to communication at all points along the axis running from sender to receiver: inspiration is elusive, the words available for embodying a transcendent poetic vision are conventions, and the potential audience remains indifferent or alien. Symbolist poetry is a poetry of failure. But each poet chooses to dramatize only one particular problem as insoluble, while merely stating or implying solutions to the others.

Thus the relationship with a Muse—a dramatized figuration of inspiration—is problematic in the verse poems of Verlaine, Baudelaire, and Rimbaud, who depict their respective lyric personae as being afflicted, dominated, or disgusted by the (often supernatural) female Other. But Mallarmé's personae can achieve no relationship at all with this figure, who flees and eludes them. Given the problem that only the conventional tokens of human language are available to convey the unique and transcendent poetic vision, Mallarmé, as we have seen, resorts to Cratylism, finding in the shape of letters and in the sound and etymology of words innate meanings deeper than the conventional signifieds. Baudelaire denounces the vacuity of words ("tel est du globe entier l'éternel bulletin" [such is the tedious news bulletin of the entire planet]) as a reflection of our spiritual emptiness without God.[24] Rimbaud violently distorts conventional prosody and tortures

23. Claude Cuénot, "Situation de Paul Verlaine," *L'Information littéraire*, 9 (May–June 1957), 106–10 (p. 109); and Eléonore M. Zimmermann, "Mallarmé and Rimbaud in Crisis," in Mary Ann Caws, ed., *Writing in a Modern Temper: Essays on French Literature and Thought in Honor of Henri Peyre*, Stanford French and Italian Studies, vol. 23 (Stanford: Anma Libri, 1984), pp. 102–16.

24. For detailed comments on the influence of the great seventeenth-century French preachers (Bossuet, Bourdaloue, Massillon) on Baudelaire's poetry, see Jean Starobinski, "Les Rimes du vide," *Nouvelle Revue de Psychanalyse*, 11 (1975), 133–44. This influence

the lexicon with glaring neologisms. But only Verlaine literally erases all human discourse by inserting into his lines words denoting musical tones and nonhuman noises that appear to function autonomously and not merely as an element of a description, as does the howling city street in Baudelaire. And while other poets may have trouble reaching their audiences or may at times be reduced to talking to themselves, only Baudelaire must seemingly forfeit all self-expression in his messages in order to attract the attention of an audience, by bribing potential hearers with a narcissistic image of themselves. Finally only Rimbaud—in the early verse—imagines an audience that is attentive but so hostile and overwhelming that he must assassinate it or flee it, or both.

So each French Symbolist impresses a distinctive, personal stamp upon the common theme that the unreliability of language and communication makes it difficult to be a poet even when one does not have to endure alienation from an unappreciative society. And the poetic dark night of the soul eventuated differently for each of them. Mallarmé ultimately regained faith in the existence of an absolute signification that could be verbally conveyed to a public: most of his surviving notes for the totalizing "Livre" (the poetical parts must have been burned after his death by his daughter, at his request) involved counting the house of the potential future audiences for public readings. Verlaine relapsed into a dilutely confessional neo-Romanticism with his collections of anecdotes about "My Hospitals" and "My Prisons." Baudelaire turned to writing self-critical prose poems that brilliantly disparaged his past hopes. And Rimbaud, of course, abandoned poetry: the most authentic and consequently, for those of us who cherish the chimera of lyricism, the most dismaying solution to the communicative crisis.

We have still to establish the place of French Symbolism in literary history: exactly when did it occur, and why then? No clear-cut historical events delineate a Symbolist period as the fall of Napoleon in 1815 and the promulgation of the Second Empire in 1851 may be said to have defined Romanticism in France.[25] The first use of the term "Symbolist" to characterize a literary movement seems attrib-

---

is obvious elsewhere, for instance in *Les Paradis artificiels,* although it has never received adequate critical attention.

25. See, e.g., *Romantisme et politique, 1815–1851,* Colloque de l'Ecole Normale Supérieure de Saint-Cloud, 1966 (Paris: Colin, 1969).

utable to the obscure Gustave Kahn in 1886, long after most of the
major poetry of that movement in France had been written.

One may attempt to establish a period in literary history in at least
five ways: each is based on a discrete presupposition and each leads
to results markedly different from those reached by the other meth-
ods.[26] In order of increasing comprehensiveness, these possible criteria for periodization are:

1. The publication of formal artistic manifestos proclaiming a new
   school of writing.
2. The publication (or more precisely, the period of composition)
   of literary masterpieces, subjectively identified.
3. The span of the productive careers of leading authors in the
   movement in question.
4. Decisive historical events.
5. General currents of ideas; the zeitgeist.

To invoke the first criterion apropos of Symbolism would produce
narrow and misleading results indeed. Like Realism, whose leading
self-proclaimed exponent was the now forgotten writer Champfleury,
Symbolism was launched by a now obscure figure, Jean Moréas, who
published the movement's first manifesto in the September 18, 1886,
issue of Le Figaro. Moréas advocated a nonrhetorical poetry based on
suggestion rather than statement, a poetry that employs metaphor as
the chief organizing principle and seeks a "musicality" not dependent
on regular rhythm and rhyme. In that same year he published four
issues of an ephemeral review, Le Symboliste. One could also mention
the short-lived Revue wagnérienne, which from 1885 to 1887 nurtured
the myth of the German composer (who was known to most readers and contributors only through piano reductions of his scores and
salon recitals of a few highlights) as a pretext for advocating an all-
encompassing art, the Gesamtkunstwerk. By September 14, 1891, Moréas announced that "Symbolism" had died and had been replaced
by "L'Ecole romane." From this perspective, French Symbolism considered as a self-conscious literary movement would span only the
period 1885–91. Moreover, none of the major poets later known as
Symbolists adopted the label for themselves. Verlaine, for example,

26. For a discussion of the problems of periodization in literary history, see Laurence
M. Porter, "The Present Directions of French Romantic Studies, 1960–1975,"
Nineteenth-Century French Studies, 6 (Fall 1977–Winter 1978), 1–20, esp. 3–6.

vehemently rejected it in a poem whose third stanza begins "A bas le symbolisme, mythe / Et termite" (Down with Symbolism, [it's] a myth and a termite [three times a myth]).[27] On the other hand, Proust's *Le Temps retrouvé*, posthumously published in 1926, still proclaimed a specifically "Symbolist" aesthetic of organic unity as the key shaping principle for art.[28]

To use the publication of "masterpieces" as the determining criterion for the time span of a movement begs the question of which authors to include. If one begins with the first number of *Le Parnasse contemporain*, which gathered together the early efforts of many Symbolists and was roughly contemporaneous with the publication of Verlaine's first collections of verse, the starting point for Symbolism is 1866 and the terminus perhaps in 1898 with the appearance of "Un coup de Dés." But if one chooses to include Baudelaire as a Symbolist, the publication date of the first edition of *Les Fleurs du Mal* pushes the movement back to 1857. To consider all of Baudelaire's productive career would stretch the movement back to 1841. (If he "becomes" a Symbolist later, when and why?) Looking ahead, one might wish to include Apollinaire's *Alcools*, published in 1913, and Valéry's *Charmes* of 1926. To end with the death of Valéry would bring us up to 1945, creating a Symbolist movement that lasted for over a century.

Those who use historical events as a convenient demarcation tend to agree on the advent of the Franco-Prussian war in 1870 as the starting point of Symbolism, and on World War I (i.e., until either 1914, 1918, or 1919) as the movement's end. Such dating, of course, excludes most of Verlaine's most interesting poetry and all of Baudelaire's. James Lawler, for example, adopts the period 1870–1920, but as he acknowledges, its breadth precludes any definition other than that of chronological coincidence. He simply says, "I take the term 'Symbolism' primarily in a historical sense, as applying to a group of writers who brought rare intensity to the practice of their art. They had no common doctrine or exclusive techniques." Thus he in part justifies the inclusion of Apollinaire (the question of whose "Symbol-

27. Paul Verlaine, "La Ballade de l'Ecole Romane" (*Invectives*, IX), in *Oeuvres poétiques complètes*, ed. Yves Le Dantec and Jacques Borel (Paris: Gallimard, 1962), p. 908.
28. René Wellek, "The Term and Concept of Symbolism in Literary History," in *Actes du V' Congrès de l'Association Internationale de Littérature Comparée* (Belgrade, 1967), ed. Nikola Banasevic (Amsterdam: Swets & Zeitlinger, 1969), pp. 275–92. This article also appeared in *New Literary History*, 1 (1969/70), 249–70, and was reprinted in Wellek, *Discriminations* (New Haven: Yale University Press, 1970), pp. 90–121.

ism" I myself pondered for a long time) because "he partakes of
Symbolism chronologically."[29]

Finally, if one seeks to equate Symbolism with a general current in
the history of ideas, one may well agree with René Wellek that "it is
better to think of 'symbolism' in a wider sense: as the broad movement
in France from Nerval and Baudelaire to Claudel and Valéry," as an
intellectual current spanning an enormous variety of theories. Referring to Europe as a whole, Wellek recommends that we "call the period
of European literature roughly between 1885 and 1914 'symbolism,'
...an international movement which radiated originally from
France."[30] These suggestions are reasonable enough, but they abandon the attempt to define precisely what Symbolism was, on the assumption that no single definition could encompass it. In relation to
the pan-European tradition, this view is undoubtedly true. Yet I believe that Baudelaire and Mallarmé, for instance, share characteristics
not found in Gérard de Nerval, Claudel, and Valéry. Without cir-
cumscribing the rich variety of their poetry, we must nonetheless seek
what the songlike Verlaine, the cerebral Mallarmé, the tempestuous
Rimbaud, and the grim moralizer Baudelaire may have in common.

To sever the Gordian knot of historical complexity, and to uncover
a single generative principle of Symbolism, the strict constructivist
view ordinarily takes the concept "symbol-ism" at face value. Accordingly, Symbolism is defined as a movement that systematically deploys
a strictly limited repertoire of recurring metaphors as the primary
materials for poetry. A Symbolist poem proper would be tightly organized around a central presiding metaphor. Typical of this view is
a recent article in *Comparative Literature:* "It is the central role played
by metaphor that shows the poem's affinity with French Symbolism.
Metaphor, rather than being a more or less effective ornament...is
here liberated from any specific reference point and becomes instead
the structuring principle of the whole poem. It is precisely this metaphoric structure which has been shown [sic] to be one of the most
characteristic features of French Symbolist poetry."[31]

This position presents at least two major problems. First, it would
make Mallarmé the only late-nineteenth-century Symbolist poet—a
not unreasonable proposition but one that sacrifices the concept of a

29. Lawler, *Language of French Symbolism*, pp. vii, ix.
30. Wellek, "Term and Concept of Symbolism," pp. 287, 291.
31. Kovach, "New Kind of Poetry," p. 57.

literary movement—while failing to provide a rationale for the exclusion of such writers as William Blake, Maurice Scève, and the English Metaphysical poets from the ranks of the "Symbolists." Second, the concept of "symbol" itself has been hopelessly confused in our everyday usage. Consider the three contrasting concepts of the "symbol" which can be inferred from definitions of symbolism found in respected dictionaries:

1. [Symbolism is] "the representation of things by use of symbols" (*Webster's New International Dictionary*, 2d ed.).
2. [A Symbolist is] "any of a group of chiefly French artists and writers of the late 19th century who expressed their ideas and emotions indirectly through symbols" (*American Heritage Dictionary*).
3. [The symbol] "seeks to express the secret affinities of things with our soul" (*Nouveau Petit Larousse illustré*, 1952).

In other words, the essence of the symbol has been variously identified with a means of representation, or signifier; the nature of the content, or the signified; and the relationship between signifier and signified.

Philip Wheelwright is the critic who has done most to offer a clear definition of the symbol as a signifier "standing for some larger meaning or set of meanings which cannot be given, or not fully given, in perceptual experience itself." He first distinguishes the "steno-symbols" of logic and mathematics, which have an unvarying, universally intelligible signified, from "tensive symbols," which are "neither entirely stipulative nor entirely exact."[32] He then identifies five types of tensive symbols: (1) the presiding metaphor of a particular poem; (2) a metaphor repeated and developed by an individual poet and having special significance for that person; (3) a metaphor that acquires new life by being renewed in fresh contexts as it is passed from poet to poet; (4) a metaphor significant for an entire cultural group; and (5) an archetype significant for humanity in general. It seems obvious that the second and third types are literary "symbols" as we usually understand them.[33] In a later work, Wheelwright identifies the characteristics of such literary symbols: semantic congruity (an appropriate connection between tenor and vehicle, a feature that

32. Philip Wheelwright, *Metaphor and Reality* (Bloomington: Indiana University Press, 1962), p. 92.
33. Ibid., pp. 92–110.

the steno-symbol need not possess), polysemy, soft focus, and a contextual variability that does not thereby sacrifice "a strong affinity of
meaning" among separate instances of use.[34] This listing of traits, like
"Aristotle's" (i.e., Tasso's) three unities of ancient Greek drama, provides a helpful, retrospective normative guide. Yet the Symbolist poets
themselves did not work out such categories, nor did they discuss
them as basic for their concept and praxis of poetry. Indeed, Henri
Peyre for one claims that Symbolism died out because "the movement
had not been based upon a sufficiently solid philosophical or aesthetic
system of thought."[35]

    Yet French Symbolism possessed a powerful aesthetic heritage, run-
ning from Kant to Coleridge to Poe to Baudelaire.[36] By emphasizing
the autotelic nature of poetry, its detachment from social and intersubjective concerns, this heritage enormously increased the burden
on a conventional language that was expected to convey unique and
unconventional thought while remaining intelligible. According to
Kant in *The Contemplation of the Beautiful*, genius always creates something unique and detached from reality, through the free play of the
whole being. In the individual, autonomous, and unpredictable judg-
ment of taste that responds to the beautiful object, "no rule or pre-
scription, but only that which cannot be subsumed under rules and
concepts, i.e., the supersensible substrate of all our faculties, serves
as a subjective standard."[37] Shedding its referents, poetry in this tradition becomes self-reflexive, focused on the poet and poetry.[38]

    34. Philip Wheelwright, "The Archetypal Symbol," in Joseph Strelka, ed., *Perspectives in Literary Symbolism*, The Yearbook of Comparative Criticism, 1 (University Park: Penn-
sylvania State University Press, 1968), pp. 214–43, esp. 214–22. Bernard Weinberg
expresses a similar ambition to distinguish among different types of symbols, but his
suggested typology is cruder and less useful than Wheelwright's. See Weinberg, *The
Limits of Symbolism: Studies of Five Modern French Poets* (Chicago: University of Chicago
Press, 1966), pp. 6–7.
    35. Peyre, *Qu'est-ce que le Symbolisme?* p. 154.
    36. Such, at least, is the conventional wisdom. Actually, Poe corroborated and fo-
cused Baudelaire's aesthetics and poetic practice more than he inspired it. Baudelaire's
thought was formed before he discovered Poe. See W. T. Bandy, "Baudelaire et Edgar
Poe," *Revue de littérature comparée*, 41 (April–June 1967), 180–94, esp. p. 194. In Chapter
4 I briefly discuss how the radical shifts of emphasis in Baudelaire's Poe criticism mirror
his own changing preoccupations.
    37. Karl Jaspers, *Kant* (New York: Harcourt, Brace, 1962 [1957]), pp. 78–81.
    38. An unsuccessful attempted refutation of this idea is instructive. In *The Limits of
Symbolism*, Weinberg protests concerning Mallarmé's "L'Après-Midi d'un faune": "The
playing on pipes, they say, must stand for the making of poetry, and inspiration must
necessarily be poetic inspiration. Both of these are gratuitous assumptions; if they are
signs, they are general signs, belonging only to the reader's general conceptions of

In earlier times the topics of the poet and poetry had been com-partmentalized. Poets discussed their poetry in their prefaces, in in-vocations to the Muse in odes and epics, and in asides to the audience asserting that even the most famous heroes and rulers were dependent on the poet, because unless they had been celebrated in literature, even their greatest feats and achievements would be forgotten. Ro-mantic writers at times devote entire poems to the topic of being inspired—as in Musset's "Nuit de Mai," Vigny's "L'Esprit pur," and Hugo's "Ibo"—but these poems function as liminal or concluding pieces in a collection or series. In and of themselves, these series are still subject to the law of metonymic association; they are presented as telling a story. Symbolism, in contrast, provides a new sort of or-ganization by presenting the poetic act in connection with a cluster of associations (notably those derived from Catholic ritual, from one of the other arts, or from the physical action of writing or printing itself). At the same time, the poet's inspiration becomes spatially de-mythologized. In Romanticism and early Symbolism, the poet's access to a higher knowledge is symbolized by a glance or movement in an unusual direction—upward or through an opening ("Elévation"; "Les Fenêtres")—or by a breaking through ("Le Bateau ivre"; "Le Pitre châtié"). In mature Symbolism the procedure for depicting the arrival of inspiration becomes much more radical: the poet does not simply focus on subjects apart from the material world; he deploys a vocab-ulary of catastrophe, void, and negation which sweeps that world entirely away. Only the locus of the poetic vision itself remains. The self-reflexive quality of this vision may be suggested by metaphors of mirrors (frequent in Baudelaire and Mallarmé) and reflections on the water (a subtler device characteristic of Rimbaud). Scenes described are often illusions (Baudelaire), unseeable (Mallarmé), or shattered (Rimbaud). Such descriptions generate the pervasive vagueness that Wheelwright calls "soft focus." In compensation, each signifier be-comes many signifiers with many signifieds, the latter becoming ap-parent only as the reader proceeds from one context to the next.

poetry and to his wish to read the poem as a poem about poets; they have no specific function as particular signs within the poem, and there is no particular justification within the poem for reading them as such" (pp. 168–69). Weinberg assumes that a symbol indicates identity, but it indicates only analogy. Both poet and faun try to recreate and "perpetuate" experience by means of an artistic medium. The faun an-nounces this purpose at the outset and attempts it first by music and then by narration, before abandoning the attempt at artistic recuperation in favor of recuperation through the dream.

Mallarmé, moreover, realized that language could be detached from its conventional function of labeling and enriched not only horizontally but also vertically: through homonyms (cygne [the bird]/Cygne [the constellation]/signe [the signifier]), etymologies (l'âme = soul/ breath), and embedded words (l'ex*il*[e] inut*ile*)—to select examples from only one sonnet. Such devices generate Wheelwright's "plurisignation" (polysemy).

Familiar considerations such as the foregoing, which have been directed to the general reader rather than to the specialist, point out that Symbolist poetry acquires a more markedly self-referential character than earlier verse had possessed. But these considerations also have the adverse effect of reinforcing the conventional view that Mallarmé's poetry is a privileged locus of semantic richness, a view that elevates him above his contemporaries. We end up with a quasi-Aristotelian hierarchy based on privation, according to which the other Symbolists are held to be inferior to Mallarmé because their poetry possesses fewer attributes. Such a conclusion fails to explain how the other poets may differ from each other, why they remain of interest in their own right, and what a symbol-poor figure such as Verlaine may share with a symbol-rich figure such as Mallarmé. To arrive at an explanation, we must make a fresh start.

The unifying concept that can best explain French Symbolism is provided by Roman Jakobson's model of the act of linguistic communication.[39] Jakobson postulates an axis running from sender to receiver and characterizes it as follows:

$$\text{SENDER} \longrightarrow \text{MESSAGE} \longrightarrow [\text{CONTACT}] \longrightarrow \text{RECEIVER}$$

The message is comprehensible because sender and receiver share a code and context. Romanticism, as I claim above, questioned the then current code and context.

French Symbolism carried this skepticism further. Instead of merely challenging the audience's preconceptions regarding what poetry should say, and how, Symbolism disrupted the very communicative axis linking sender to message to receiver, thus calling into question the possibility of any communication whatsoever. The French Symbolist movement, then, was neither a coterie nor a system, but a crisis. Each poet in turn passed through it and went on. I suggest that for

39. See above, n. 5.

Baudelaire the crisis lasted from 1851 to 1858; for Verlaine, from 1863 to 1874; for Mallarmé, from 1864 to 1869 (but prolonged artificially for fifteen years by his relative poetic inactivity and momentarily revived during the preparation of the first edition of his collected *Poésies* in 1887); and for Rimbaud, from 1869 to 1875 or 1877, depending on when one believes he abandoned poetry.

Before commenting on these crises in detail, I must slightly modify Jakobson's model. Jakobson employs the term "contact" to designate the essential contiguity of message and receiver, the fact that a message must reach its receiver and must be heard and understood in order to be a message. One can object that the notion of contact is secondary or even otiose, since any emission of a message assumes an attempt to get attention. But the attention-getting or "phatic" function of language obviously exists and is significant, as is the redundancy or reduplicative back-up that, according to some linguists, fills up half the typical verbal message. On a lexical level—if we consider the message *in* the poem rather than the message *of* the poem—we can identify certain segments of language in an appropriate context as communicating exclusively an appeal for attention (e.g., naming the intended recipient of the message at the outset). Moreover, poets do not take for granted that the message *of* the poem will achieve contact either. For them its reception is always problematical. Since poets couch their words in the form of imaginative literature, the potential decoder must be familiar with an extra, unusual number of linguistic conventions above and beyond those of everyday language. Writing poetry constitutes a marked choice of formality, since the act of reading is a highly ritualistic one that—unlike ordinary conversation—cannot be readily undertaken at the same time as other activities; and it entails play rather than practicality (leisure is required for its reception) since its referents are not real. For all these reasons the poet needs an elite audience, and the *captatio benevolentiae*, the appeal for the public's goodwill, is an inescapable fact of poetic life.

What must be added to Jakobson's model (as its obvious asymmetry suggests) is the link between the sender and the message. I mean what linguists might call "poetic competence," what classical rhetoric called *inventio*,[40] what poets call inspiration, and what I shall call—for reasons

40. *Inventio* is the art of finding and elaborating on a subject. For a fine general essay on the critical categories of rhetoric, see Roland Barthes, "L'Ancienne Rhétorique: Aide-mémoire," *Communications*, 16 (1970), 172–229.

of eurhythmy and euphony—the "concept": finding new things to talk about or (more often than not) new ways to talk about the familiar, or both. Linguists do not need to consider the concept. They can assume that the referent is a given and that the sender's assured linguistic competence enables him or her to encode it automatically. Choosing from among the available resources of language to achieve the intended effect is the sender's only intellectual problem. There is always an identifiable best answer, but usually any of several solutions is functional. You need not find a fresh, ingenious way to ask me to pass you the salt or tell you the time in order to have a valid claim on my attention. Poets, however, must seek their referents (they are creating imaginative literature). Even when these referents *are* givens, as in the epic poem, they must still be encoded in a way that differs enough from previous versions to justify our harkening once again to the same story. Obvious indices of the importance of the concept for lyric poets are their traditional appeals for inspiration and their habitual personifications of inspiration, usually in the form of a Muse figure.

Romanticism had already aggravated the difficulty of achieving both concept and contact by its cult of originality, by insisting on radically unfamiliar codes and contexts that broke with tradition (so visionary insight rather than mere competent craftmanship was needed to discover them) and that consequently risked baffling or alienating the public. Symbolism heightened the challenge to the reader by choosing the frustration of communication as its generative idea or matrix.[41]

Therefore it is misleading to single out Mallarmé, as Wellek has done, as being "the first poet radically discontent with the ordinary language of communication."[42] Verlaine, for one, was equally discontent, independently and at about the same time, and we should keep clearly in mind the passage from Hugo's "Dieu" quoted above. The problem is that communication involves more than just a grammar and lexicon, more than a vehicle. Jakobson's categories allow us to "unpack" the notion of language as a dynamic event, as an exchange. Thus, instead of accepting Mallarmé as the Symbolist poet par excellence, or the only true French Symbolist poet, we have a method

41. On this conception of the matrix or "structure of the given" apparent only in the perturbations it generates in the text, see Michael Riffaterre, *Semiotics of Poetry* (Bloomington: Indiana University Press, 1978), p. 13 and passim.

42. Wellek, "Term and Concept of Symbolism," p. 288.

for contrasting him with his great contemporaries without losing sight of the characteristics they all share.

The next four chapters develop these distinctions, presenting them in a conceptual rather than a chronological order by proceeding along the axis of communication from sender to receiver. The result is a synchronic view of the crisis phase of French Symbolism, approximately from 1851 to 1875. My starting point, then, is the link between sender and message—the concept—as problematized by Mallarmé. Mallarmé finds the concept itself defective or lacking. His frequent use of symbols connoting poetic sterility is well known. What has yet to be studied, however, is the consistency with which he revised his poems to reinforce this symbolism, particularly during his metaphysical crisis of the middle 1860s, and again in 1887 while he prepared the first collected edition of his verse.[43] In the major poems, for which few variants survive, the same tendency can be observed in Mallarmé's treatment of the Muse figure, used simultaneously to evoke and to negate the idea of inspiration; in his elimination of titles, which by identifying a pretext (the thought or event presented as having occasioned a poem) refer nondiscursively to the inspiration for the poem they introduce; and in his erasure, attenuation, or negation as well of the figure of a creator whose activities seem analogous to the poet's. Near the end of his career, however, Mallarmé regained his faith in inspiration and entered the mainstream of the "second Symbolism" in the 1880s, during an era of manifestos and at the height of the Wagner craze. Transcendence no longer appeared empty, and the poet planned a series of public readings to enlighten his compatriots.

Verlaine's crisis was a loss of faith in the capacity of words themselves to signify. His sense of the treacherous absurdity of words (the raw materials for the message), which informs his later work, is anticipated by "L'Angoisse," "Cauchemar," and other pieces in the Poèmes saturniens. This mistrust culminated in the Fêtes galantes. Words become increasingly devalued as this collection unfolds. First, silence is invoked as the ultimate meaning. Next, the names of musical notes literally invade the text at the expense of conversation. Then the language of lovers is satirized: what should be the occasion for the most intimate communication becomes a dialogue of the deaf speaking

---

43. Compare Hugo Friedrich's remark in Structure of Modern Poetry that "as of 1865, Mallarmé very conspicuously uses the word néant in passages whose themes [i.e., subjects] were expressed earlier by such words as azure, dream, ideal" (p. 93).

in clichés. Finally, the lyric self replaces the trite, conventional lovers of the earlier poems in such a way as to become directly implicated in the breakdown of language. "Colloque sentimental" concludes the collection by dramatizing a failure of dialogue worthy of the theater of the absurd. After this volume, Verlaine escapes the impasse of the meaninglessness of language through the relatively simple solution of invoking musicality, producing the songlike "mood poem" (John Porter Houston's expression) in *Romances sans paroles,* where impressionistic notation and the formal virtuosity of original rhythm and sound structure create the impression of replacing words without actually, of course, doing so. The technical mastery of the collection already conceals a thematic retreat. The issue of signification is now evaded rather than called into question.

Unlike Verlaine, Baudelaire trusts in the power of the word to signify. His Symbolist crisis springs from his loss of faith in the power of his message to reach and influence an audience. This uncertainty, caused in part by the collapse of liberal ideals as a result of the coup d'état of 1851, was reinforced by his condemnation for offending public morals with his art, in 1857. His letters and early art criticism reveal what André Gide sensitively identified as Baudelaire's singular yearning to draw closer to the reader.[44] But from around 1851 on, this desire is greatly intensified by despair and desperation. For the next seven years his verse deploys phatic devices, and in particular apostrophe, even more frequently and in more varied fashion than in the elegiac tradition of appeal from which he derives; indeed, he uses these devices obsessively. He multiplies conative expressions (in Jakobson's terms, those that indicate that the hearer or reader is implicated in the reception of the message—in particular, second-person pronouns and possessive adjectives) as if to seduce an absent or indifferent Other, in order to assure himself an ideal (understanding, sympathetic) audience. But because he envies the self-sufficing plenitude of the Other, whom he confuses with the mother-imago, the loved woman, or God, Baudelaire's poet-persona often turns on the implied audience or dramatized interlocutor in a sadistic assault when he finally makes contact with them. At the end of his Symbolist crisis, Baudelaire returns to a more thoroughly allegorical, totalizing discourse, where his own personal drama becomes distanced through

44. André Gide, *Anthologie de la poésie française* (Paris: Gallimard, 1949), pp. xli–xlii.

generalization and rhetorical ornament. Without resolving the cycle of love/hate, the keenly self-critical prose poems unmask Baudelaire's strategy of pursuing the love object, the public/mistress/mother, while keeping it at a distance.

For Rimbaud contact is both a given and a problem. Doubts about winning and keeping his audience's attention do not trouble him. His difficulty is that this audience is hostile, alertly disapproving, and intrusive. From his early poems on, he imagines an inimical public that mocks and enslaves, and whose presence inspires a generalized inhibition. Rather than seek to placate, he counterattacks with fantasies of massacre and cataclysm. But in his early poems, even after his fantasized foes have been overcome, their corpses still clog his verse. Soon realizing that mere defiance traps one into a relationship of opposition with that which one defies, Rimbaud seeks a more authentic autonomy by constructing an unstable and hence undefinable identity. This instability is frequently based on a device that Hugo Friedrich has characterized as "crossfade," constructed with two interwoven and inextricable frames of reference such as the land and sea in "Marine"[45] (to be distinguished, for example, from Verlaine's superficially similar but actually impressionistic efforts such as "L'Echelonnement des haies"). Overt metaphors, which offer a hostile audience the lever of interpretability, are replaced by a metonymic debris from the shattered object of representation, only glimpses of whose origins remain visible. Then from "Mémoire" on, Rimbaud increasingly introduces metaphors of the eye into his work, thus contemplating his own message and transforming himself into its receiver, creating a short circuit that obviates the Other and prepares the poet's ultimate complete detachment from his audience when he stops writing altogether.

The Orphic role of the poet and the totalizing power of poetic language were recuperated by Modernist optimism and its French equivalents. Apollinaire's early poetic selves, before World War I, may be suffused with shame, confusion, and self-doubt, but from the beginning, they are still magicians. Valéry, Claudel, and St.-John Perse all seize the world and shape it to their will. They all possess superior knowledge. Their poetic acts are a success. From the Symbolists of the first, crisis phase, they inherit a radical skepticism about language

45. Friedrich, *Structure of Modern Poetry*, p. 61.

as an instrument of transcendence per se (even Claudel presents himself as only a *simia Dei*). But while poetic language is not for them a Holy Grail, it *is* an enchanted sword. By wielding it, they aim to win through to Meaning. And they trust in their ability to initiate an audience. Thus they prove true descendants of the late—but not the early—Mallarmé.

Chapter 2 _____

Mallarmé's Disappearing Muse

I

The erasure of inspiration in Mallarmé's mature verse is familiar to his readers. Where the Romantics celebrate poetic fecundity, Mallarmé evokes the difficulty of writing. But what has not been studied is the way he creates that difficulty for himself. His struggle to express the inexpressible is voluntarily assumed, not forced on him. His casual verse and his nearly single-handed creation (for the better part of a year) of the fashion magazine *La Dernière Mode* provide ample proof of his facility. In his early verse, where he is content with conventional subjects, Mallarmé often summons the Muse at will, while choirs of angels descend to echo his sentiments.

During Mallarmé's metaphysical crisis at Tournon in the middle 1860s, and again though less strongly in 1887 as he prepared the first collected edition of his verse, he experienced a *prise de conscience* regarding his role as a poet which led him to strengthen the self-negating tendencies already prominent in his verse. On each occasion he rewrote several poems, and most of his rewriting makes the virtual axis of communication (i.e., the literary representation of the attempt at communication) seem more tenuous. Or to be more precise, when he reshapes a single major poem, as he did extensively with "L'Après-Midi d'un faune," "Prose pour des Esseintes," and "Hérodiade" at various periods from the 1860s till the end of his life,[1] he appears preoccupied with the inner logic, clarity, and coherence of expression demanded by the unique circumstantial drama of the individual poem. But both the Tournon crisis and the assembling of his *oeuvre* two decades later afforded him an overview that brought the dilemmas of the communicative act to the forefront of his concerns. The resulting retouches are limited in scope but more consistent than the extensive revisions of longer individual poems. As early as 1866 (the year Mallarmé composed "Hérodiade"), the latter often reflect faith in the possibility of a totalizing discourse. Thus Mallarmé's revisions of the longer poems, made with seeming self-confidence, contradict the image of poetic sterility and frustration which he seeks to evoke and to intensify through his localized alterations in the shorter poems. Form follows function here. The longer the text, the greater the poet's apparent optimism concerning his powers of creation. In contrast, the shorter, nonexpansive variants of the shorter poems often reflect an overarching theoretical preoccupation with communicability.

As an author's revisions offer the surest clue to his or her intentions (even overt, discursive statements of purpose must be considered less definitive than the concrete evidence of variants), it is these we should examine. Although the variants I concentrate on may appear mar-

---

1. Illuminating examinations of the Tournon crisis can be found in Leo Bersani, *The Death of Stéphane Mallarmé* (Cambridge: Cambridge University Press, 1982), pp. 1–47, and in Walter A. Strauss's fine, unjustly neglected *Descent and Return* (Cambridge: Harvard University Press, 1970), pp. 81–139. Still well worth reading are the comments on Mallarmé's *échec* in Jean-Pierre Richard, *L'Univers imaginaire de Mallarmé* (Paris: Seuil, 1961), pp. 431–37. See also pp. 603–5, where Richard demystifies Mallarméan "transcendence."

A rich, impeccably scholarly study of the drama of the anxiety of influence is found in Austin Gill, *The Early Mallarmé*, vol. II: *Youth and Young Manhood: Early Poems* (Oxford: Clarendon, 1986). Gill studies the influence of Hugo, Banville, and Baudelaire on Mallarmé, showing how Mallarmé's admiration for Baudelaire turned rather suddenly into parody in the spring or summer of 1862 as he came to feel that Baudelaire's talent had become exhausted. See especially Gill's comments on Mallarmé's "L'Enfant prodigue," pp. 165–75. Once the emulation of illustrious precursors no longer provides an unquestioned source of inspiration, the origination of one's own ideas becomes problematical.

From 1887, evidence that Mallarmé rewrote to attenuate suggestions of inspiration in his poems appears in twenty-one variants, plus one each from 1883 and 1885. After the 1860s, Mallarmé's correspondence no longer reflects theoretical aesthetic investigations (which now are found, instead, in his writings on the theater, especially during 1885 and 1886) but rather reflects concerns about the technical and financial side of the production of his books. For reasons expounded immediately below, the extensive variants of the "Faune," "Hérodiade," and "Prose pour des Esseintes" published by Henri Mondor, Gardner Davies, and others will not be studied here.

ginal—because they do not allow us to reconstruct the fictive drama of the genesis of individual poems, they are in fact central to my primary interest here, namely, the sharpening focus of Mallarmé's self-imposed struggle with inspiration.

Before approaching the variants, we must specify precisely what inspiration is for Mallarmé and why he chooses to represent it as lacking. The best evidence of his intentions appears in his correspondence between January 1864 and February 1869, when he was most deeply preoccupied with aesthetic problems. Critics tend to act as if hypnotized by Mallarmé's letter to his closest friend, Henri Cazalis, on May 14, 1867, in which he announced: "Je viens de passer une année effrayante: ma Pensée s'est pensée, et est arrivée à une Conception pure [var. divine]...je suis maintenant impersonnel et non plus Stéphane que tu as connu—mais une aptitude qu'a l'Univers spirituel à se voir et à se développer, à travers ce qui fut moi" (I have just spent a terrifying year: my Thought has been thought, and has reached a pure [var. divine] Conception.... I am now impersonal, no longer the Stéphane you knew—but an aptitude that the spiritual Universe has for perceiving and unfolding itself, through what used to be me).[2] Explicitly or implicitly, critics usually take this letter to represent the sudden outcome of a spiritual crisis reflecting Mallarmé's discovery of Hegelian thought. Such a dramatic view of Mallarmé's intellectual evolution has been fostered by lacunae in our evidence, by the absence of his letters for the whole of 1867 up until this particular text addressed to Cazalis. We have no idea how his thought unfolded during the preceding four and a half months. In the context of his total correspondence, however, the hypothetical Hegelian adventure assumes its proper and at best minor place.

Taken by itself, the famous passage in the letter to Cazalis might suggest that Mallarmé felt he had come into contact with an ultimate supersensory reality and would henceforth serve as its passive conduit, rather as Milton had felt that he was writing at the dictation of God. But in this letter Mallarmé's careful change of the word "divine" to "pure"—and his removal of the word "Dieu" in general from the poems written in 1866 and 1867—reveals instead that his thinking

---

2. Stéphane Mallarmé, *Correspondance*, 11 vols., ed. Lloyd James Austin, Henri Mondor, and Jean-Pierre Richard (Paris: Gallimard, 1959–85), I, 240, 242. This work, which is indispensable for all serious students of Mallarmé, will hereafter be cited in both text and notes as *Corr.*

reflects what Guy Michaud calls "a metaphysics of Nothingness and Absence, which is rather a refusal of metaphysics."[3]

Lloyd James Austin long ago attributed this atheistic metaphysical position to the influence of Hegel. Since the pages of Mallarmé's copy of Hegel appear to have remained uncut until his death, one would have to invoke a probable source of Hegelian influence in conversations between Mallarmé and his friend Eugène Lefébure, who exchanged visits with him in April and June 1866 and to whom he had been writing since at least the beginning of 1865. Villiers de l'Isle-Adam may also have helped introduce Mallarmé to Hegelianism. And Hegel's *Encyclopedia of Philosophical Sciences* may have inspired much of Mallarmé's speculation about the Absolute in the late 1860s. But Mallarmé mentions Hegel by name, in writing, only once. And as Jacques Derrida has convincingly argued, Mallarmé presents only a "simulacrum" of either Platonic or Hegelian idealism. The referent of his poetic activity is not a transcendent realm of Ideas or of a dialectical process; rather, he presents us with the spectacle of "mimicry imitating nothing," creating only the mirage of a corresponding reality. Thus for Mallarmé inspiration derives not from the apprehension of some "external" metaphysical truth or process but from his own inner mental processes. His subject is the totalizing structures of illusion we create for ourselves and the irrepressible hope—even in the poet who sees through them—that they might be true.[4]

3. According to Guy Michaud, as paraphrased in *Corr.* I, 242, n. 3.

4. Jacques Derrida, "The Double Session," in *Dissemination*, trans. and ed. Barbara Johnson (Chicago: University of Chicago Press, 1981 [French ed., 1972]), pp. 181–207. Louis Wirth Marvick corroborates Derrida's view; see his *Mallarmé and the Sublime* (Albany: State University of New York Press, 1986). After exhaustively studying the use of the word "sublime" in Mallarmé's prose (it does not occur in the poetry), Marvick concludes that Mallarmé "uses the word 'sublime' in a less than superlative sense, to describe the setting or preparation for the advent of the ideal—an advent that never, strictly speaking, takes place" (see chap. 12, pp. 97–140; this observation appears on p. 156).

On the much-debated Mallarmé-Hegel question, see also Lloyd James Austin, "Mallarmé et le rêve du livre," *Mecure de France*, 317 (January 1953), 81–108, who invokes as the most probable paratext, not Augusto Véra's three volumes of translations with commentary but Edmond Schérer's "Hégel et l'hégélianisme," *Revue des Deux Mondes*, 31 (February 1861), 813–56; Jean-Pierre Richard, *L'Univers imaginaire de Mallarmé* (Paris: Seuil, 1961), pp. 229–30, 231–33 (where he provides a bibliography on this question), 277–78, 452–55, and passim; John Porter Houston, *Patterns of Thought in Rimbaud and Mallarmé* (Lexington, Ky.: French Forum, 1986), pp. 97–100 and passim. More recently Janine D. Langan has devoted a careful and, wisely, inconclusive book to Hegel's influence on Mallarmé: see *Hegel and Mallarmé* (Lanham, Md.: University Press of America, 1986); chap. 2, pp. 18–40, provides the background. Elsewhere

A constant of Mallarmé's mature thought is that finding inspiration is difficult for him, not because he has nothing to say but because of his great ambitions for literature. He speaks of being able to treat superficial subjects easily. In January 1864, for instance, he writes to Cazalis that "avant de prendre la plume, il fallait, pour conquérir un moment de lucidité parfaite, terrasser ma navrante Impuissante [*sic*]. Il [the poem "L'Azur"] m'a donné beaucoup de mal, parce que bannissant mille gracieusetés lyriques et beaux vers qui hantaient incessamment ma cervelle, j'ai voulu rester implacablement dans mon sujet" (*Corr.* I, 103: Before taking up the pen, in order to win a moment of perfect lucidity, I had to wrestle down my heartbreaking powerlessness. I had a great deal of trouble with it ["L'Azur"], because, banishing a thousand pretty lyrical touches and fine lines that were haunting my brain without respite, I tried to remain implacably focused on my topic). He restated the same view playfully thirty-one years later in the well-known lines "Ainsi le choeur des romances / A la lèvre vole-t-il / Exclus-en" (Thus the chorus of romantic ballads flies to your lips. Exclude them).[5] He himself announces the end of his uncompromising search for the Ideal in a letter to Cazalis on March 3, 1871: "Je redeviens un littérateur pur et simple. Mon oeuvre n'est plus un mythe" (*Corr.* I, 342: I'm becoming an ordinary literary writer once again. My work is no longer a myth). Planning seriously to attempt to establish himself in Paris and anticipating the birth of his second child in a few months, he foresaw the need for more revenue than a *lycée* teacher could command. Thenceforth he would divide his efforts between remunerative literary tasks and the composition of the supreme *Livre*.[6] He began speaking of plans to write a play, short stories, and literary criticism.

Langan draws parallels between Hegelian ideas, "Prose pour des Esseintes," and "Un coup de Dés." To my mind, however, Julia Kristeva provides the most incisive examination of the question; see *La Révolution du langage poétique* (Paris: Seuil, 1974), pp. 534–40, and the good bibliography (pp. 534–35, n. 29). Kristeva believes that Mallarmé uses Hegelian tags freely for poetic ends; negativity in the German philosopher is integrated into a system, but "Mallarmé's negativity always remains elusive" (p. 535).

5. Stéphane Mallarmé, *Oeuvres complètes*, ed. Henri Mondor and G. Jean-Aubry (Paris: Gallimard, 1956), p. 73. Unless I have noted otherwise, subsequent page references are to this edition (cited as *OC*). No Mallarmé scholar, however, can afford not to consult the magnificent critical edition of the *Poésies* by Carl Paul Barbier and Charles Gordon Millan (Paris: Flammarion, 1983 [*Oeuvres complètes*, I; 3 vols. planned]), hereafter cited in text and notes as Barbier. See, for example, the comments on Mallarmé's January 1864 letter to Henri Cazalis, Barbier, p. 153.

6. Jacques Scherer's edition of *Le "Livre" de Mallarmé* (Paris: Gallimard, 1957), which

Only in 1985, however, with the publication of the full text of his letter of December 20, 1866, to Armand Renaud, could the extent of his self-confidence and totalizing poetic ambitions be known. He explained: "J'ai infiniment travaillé cet été, à moi d'abord, en créant, par la plus belle synthèse, un monde dont je suis le Dieu,—et à un Oeuvre qui en résultera, pur et magnifique, je l'espère. *Hérodiade*. . . . Tout est ébauché, je n'ai plus que la place de certains poèmes intérieurs à trouver, ce qui est fatal et mathématique. Ma vie entière a son *idée*, et toutes mes minutes y concourent. Je compte publier le tout d'un bloc" (I've worked enormously this summer, first of all on myself, by creating, through the most marvelous synthesis, a world of which I am the God—and on a Work that will result from this, a pure and splendid one, I expect. *Hérodiade* [will be a pillar of the total edifice I have conceived]. . . . Everything is sketched out; all I need do now is to decide on where certain poems should go in the interior, which is inevitable and mathematical. My whole life has its *idea*, and every minute I have contributes to it. I intend to publish the whole thing at once).[7] Such self-assured statements are not rare for Mallarmé. At another moment he even claimed: "Tout est si bien ordonné en moi, qu'à mesure, maintenant, qu'une sensation m'arrive, elle se transfigure et va d'elle-même se caser dans tel livre et tel poème" (Everything is so well arranged within me that nowadays as an impression strikes me, it becomes transfigured and spontaneously finds a home in a particular book and a particular poem). And in the same letter he claimed that such inspiration was potentially universal: "Tout homme a un Secret en lui, beaucoup meurent sans l'avoir trouvé, et ne le trouveront pas parce que morts, il n'existera plus, ni eux" (Every man has a Secret within himself; many die before they discover it, and they

---

mainly contains only disappointing arithmetical calculations, is misleading because it does not take into account Mallarmé's explicit identification of his "Hérodiade" as part of this projected work. Nor does he realize that Mallarmé's daughter undoubtedly destroyed his unpublished manuscripts at his death, as Mallarmé had requested in his will. On the latter point see Henri Mondor, *Vie de Mallarmé* (Paris: Gallimard, 1941), p. 801. In *The Aesthetics of Stéphane Mallarmé in Relation to His Public* (Rutherford, N.J.: Fairleigh Dickinson University Press, 1976), Paula Gilbert Lewis relates the surviving notes for "Le Livre" to Mallarmé's aesthetic thought throughout his life; see esp. pp. 15–44, 64, 157–58, 175–76, and 201.

7. *Corr.* XI, 21, 22. Partially published in *Corr.* V, 199–200. Georges Poulet, notably, recognized in *La Distance intérieure* (Paris: Plon, 1952) that Mallarmé had known exactly what he was about from age twenty on.

will not discover it because, once they are dead, neither it nor they will exist any more).[8]

The difficulty, then, is first to be able to withdraw sufficiently from the distractions of life to make contact with this inner Secret: "Il m'est si difficile," Mallarmé complained, "de m'isoler assez de la vie pour sentir, sans effort, les impressions extraterrestres, et nécessairement harmonieuses que je veux donner, que je m'étudie jusqu'à une prudence qui ressemble à de la manie" (It is so hard for me to cut myself off from life enough to be able to feel the unworldly and necessarily harmonious impressions that I wish to impart, that I study myself to the point of a prudence that seems like a fixation).[9] Having done so, he must still strive to render the resulting impressions in detail: "Il est, en effet, si difficile de faire un vers quand on l'a dans l'âme; qu'est-ce, lorsqu'il faut le faire longtemps après avoir oublié ce qui eût pu le faire naître" (Indeed, it is so difficult to write a line of poetry when you have it in your soul; what is it like, then, when you have to write it after having forgotten what might have brought it forth?).[10]

The notion of inspiration becomes undermined for Mallarmé, however, primarily because he knows that there is no metaphysical ground or origin for inspiration. That is why he writes that in working on "Hérodiade," "en creusant le vers à ce point, j'ai rencontré deux abîmes, qui me désespèrent. L'un est le Néant... et je suis encore trop désolé pour pouvoir croire même à ma poésie et me remettre au travail, que cette pensée écrasante m'a fait abandonner... nous ne sommes que de vaines formes de la matière, mais bien sublimes pour avoir inventé Dieu et notre âme" (Delving into verse to that extent, I encountered two abysses, which drive me to despair. One of them is Nothingness [the other being his ill-health]... and I am still too despondent to be able even to believe in my poetry and to take up again the work which that crushing thought led me to renounce... we are no more than empty shapes of matter, but quite sublime for having invented God and our soul). So he dreams of a work that would celebrate the "glorious lie" of conscious matter frantically hurling itself toward an ideal that it knows does not exist.[11] To realize this dream Mallarmé sets himself a twofold goal, which he describes lucidly to

8. Mallarmé to Théodore Aubanel, July 16, 1866, *Corr.* I, 222.
9. Mallarmé to Aubanel, January 3, 1866, *Corr.* I, 195.
10. Mallarmé to Catulle Mendès, late April 1866, *Corr.* I, 213.
11. Mallarmé to Cazalis, late April 1866, *Corr.* I, 207–8.

Villiers de l'Isle-Adam: "Il me reste la délimitation parfaite et le rêve intérieur de deux livres, à la fois nouveaux et éternels, l'un tout absolu 'Beauté,' l'autre personnel, les 'Allégories somptueuses du Néant,' mais (dérision et torture de Tantale), l'impuissance de les écrire" (What I have left is the perfect outline and the inner dream of two books, both new and eternal, one entirely absolute "Beauty," the other personal, "Sumptuous Allegories of the Void," but [ridiculousness and tantalizing torment] the inability to write them).[12] Mallarmé cannot depict absolute beauty in words because words are not absolute and because what is beautiful in his vision is the absolute purity of non-being. When the idealized figure exemplified by Hérodiade is circumscribed by verse and by narrative structure (albeit a narrative of absolute refusal), she has compromised herself and is already fallen away from grace.

Mallarmé cannot seriously depict the personal drama of human self-deception either, because he has always already seen through its delusions; he cannot suspend disbelief long enough to give them a solemn fictive existence. By equating protagonist with poet automatically and without nuance, as we critics tend unthinkingly to do when treating the Symbolist or modern poetry so often focused on the creative act, we miss much of that poetry's irony and humor. Mallarmé mocks his own vulnerability to the temptation either to pursue or to evade the phantom of the Ideal; he embodies this besetting weakness in his fictional personae. When his faun tries to determine the ontological status of his nymphs, as Hans-Jost Frey points out, "meaning introduces an absence into their presence, because through it they now refer to what they are not. Meaning undermines the presence of things.... Language [here] means the wish to overcome language."[13] So we must recognize, for example, that in part the faun is

---

12. Mallarmé to Villiers de l'Isle-Adam, September 24, 1867, *Corr.* I, 259.

13. Hans-Jost Frey, "The Tree of Doubt," in *Stéphane Mallarmé: Modern Critical Views*, ed. Harold Bloom (New York: Chelsea House, 1987), pp. 142, 145. I highly recommend this compelling, lucid deconstructionist commentary. Eileen Souffrin-Le Breton's solid article, "The Young Mallarmé and the Boucher Revival," in *Baudelaire, Mallarmé, Valéry: New Essays in Honor of Lloyd James Austin*, ed. Malcolm Bowie, Alison Fairlie, and Alison Finch (Cambridge: Cambridge University Press, 1982), pp. 283–313, attempts to demystify the duality of the nymphs (a topic that has inspired much metaphysical commentary) by reminding us how much Mallarmé's decor resembles those of Boucher and how Boucher's "Pan et Syrinx," showing two naked, interlaced nymphs surprised by a faun, was probably the major external inspiration for Mallarmé's poem. This argument is weakened, however, when we realize that during revisions from 1862 through 1864 Mallarmé vacillated between Boucher and Lancret (see Barbier, p. 111).

the naive butt of a joke, the figuration of our unwitting lust for the void. Artistic proclivities aside, he reminds one more than anything of that other faun figure, Mephistopheles, duped and beguiled by the phantoms he pursues during Goethe's Classical Walpurgis Night.

On a smaller scale, a conventional reading of "Le Pitre châtié"—another appeal to the Muse—has solemnly declared that "the [clown's] grease-paint becomes in itself the symbol at once of all the inadequacy of the poet's calling, and also of its royal splendor and its sacred mission"; this poet/clown would be a traitor for having abandoned his calling (by leaping through the wall of his circus tent instead of continuing to perform in front of the public).[14] True, the poet figure learns that he cannot transcend himself, but we must not forget that in entertaining the public as he did, he was inevitably ridiculous and that Mallarmé as implied author dissociates himself from the "faithful" performer-poet who remains under the tent (like Baudelaire's old soldier in "La Cloche fêlée") as well as from the hubristic one who breaks out of it. Likewise in "L'Azur," the speaker is not Mallarmé, but again a dupe whose melodramatic tone makes him at least slightly comical. To take him too uncritically is to view him through the lens of a "Romantic" reading similar to that of Rousseau's misprision of "Le Misanthrope." Although Mallarmé shared the experience of "impuissance," he hears his desperate protagonist ranting "par une exclamation grotesque d'écolier délivré" (with the grotesque shout of a schoolboy when the bell rings), while he himself stands back calm and detached to calculate the effect of every word.[15]

One could make similar comments on a number of other early and apparently equally self-dramatizing poems. In "Le Sonneur," for example, Mallarmé describes a monk mournfully grumbling prayers in

---

It becomes weaker still when we realize how amused Mallarmé would have been by all this erudition, for a common secondary meaning of "nymphes" in French is the labia minora of the vulva. Separating two nymphs whom the gods have joined together means phallic penetration.

For a general study of the Muse figure in poetry see Robin Skelton, *The Poetic Pattern* (Berkeley: University of California Press, 1956). For a rich classical reading of "L'Après-Midi d'un faune," see Robert Greer Cohn, *Toward the Poems of Mallarmé* (Berkeley: University of California Press, 1965), pp. 13–30.

14. See Lloyd James Austin, "Mallarmé's Reshaping of 'Le Pitre châtié,'" in *Order and Adventure in Post-Romantic French Poetry* (New York: Harper & Row, 1973), pp. 56–71. The quotation appears on p. 63.

15. At the time, Mallarmé believed, and was inspired by, Poe's myth of the perfectly controlled, premeditated poetic composition. See Mallarmé's detailed comments on "L'Azur" in his letter to Cazalis of January 1864, *Corr.* I, 103–5.

Latin (an incomprehensible language, like that of hermetic poetry) and futilely pulling the bell-rope in hopes of making the Ideal peal forth. The text forthrightly announces, "Je suis cet homme" (I am that man, p. 36). But the concluding invocation to Satan gives the game away. Mallarmé, who does not believe in a transcendent supernatural but whose great model and precursor had to be Baudelaire, tries out both the Romantic pose of the despairing artist and the Platonic idealism that holds that there really is an Absolute "up there." In doing so he makes himself more keenly aware of what he wishes to discard.

In other words, Mallarmé calls into question not inspiration per se but the irrepressible, instinctive tendency to hypostatize inspiration, to conceive it as coming from a supernatural Beyond rather than from within ourselves. The paradox of the literary endeavor for Mallarmé is that beauty consists in the idea of an absolute, which does not itself exist; it is analogous to the imaginary numbers of mathematics. To render this paradox, he will depict a Muse figure (inspiration, our intermediary with Beauty, personified) but show her only vanishing, fading, elusive, an error of our fabulous senses. Her theater is the expanse of water or ice, or the white page, figuring the myth of the unattainable origin.

At other times Mallarmé conflates this mythic origin with the Muse by rendering it as an empty womb, refusing to give birth (to "produce" Beauty); thus he reverses traditional gender roles so that it is the male poet casting his seed into the matrix of inspiration who would fecundate the Muse rather than, as in the conventional image, she who fecundates him. And in either situation, in describing the setting of the quest for inspiration, Mallarmé effectively erases it. Were we to attempt literally to sketch the scenes his verse evokes, we would be left with only the invisible: white on white, transparency in darkness, a blank page, sometimes with one surviving detail to convey the mocking presence of absence.

Two-thirds of Mallarmé's rewritings in manuscript involve references to poetic inspiration (the origin of poetry in terms of the communicative act), and nearly all of them make it more precarious or erase it altogether. It is primarily in what I have termed the "concept" that he inscribes disruption of the axis of communication. In what forms does such disruption appear? Poetry can refer non-discursively to its concept by identifying a pretext (the thought or event presented as having given rise to a poem), often plainly announced, indeed, in the title; by presenting a creator whose activities are analogous to those of the poet; or by introducing inspiration personified in the form of a Muse figure. Erasing, attenuating, or negating these features strengthens the impression of a poetic sterility that blocks progress along the communicative axis running from the person of the poet to the enunciation of a message. In analyzing ordinary human verbal communication, linguists habitually take for granted linguistic "competence"—the ability to speak or write. But for any poet, poetic competence—that is, the ability to create—always is at issue, if only because even the most prolific writer dreads losing his or her special gift (the writer is after all continually surrounded by people who lack such a gift and who are immersed in sterile routines, like so many cautionary figures), and because nearly all experiences of creativity themselves lack the exhilarating intensity of the rare moments of unadulterated inspiration which are granted us. Living as a poet, for Mallarmé at any rate, meant nearly always living below the peak.

In Mallarmé's poetry, as in the ancient traditions on which it draws (at first seriously but soon after parodically), the Muse figure is ordinarily female and supernatural. Femaleness signifies otherness in the male-dominated conventions of official high art which Symbolism brings to a paroxysm. And the Muse, whose femaleness is a symptom of the gender categories imposed in order to structure our overall experience of the world, is a perfect exemplar of the habit of "thought by sexual analogy" denounced by feminists.[16] Mallarmé, instead of associating the Muse with the positive spiritual values that typify a Beatrice, Laura, or Marguerite, implicitly connects her to the pejorative patriarchal construct of femininity, embodying negativity, lack of meaning, irrationality, chaos, and darkness—"in short, non-Being." "If patriarchy sees women as occupying a marginal position within the symbolic order," Toril Moi explains, "then it can construe them as the *limit* or borderline of that order. From a phallocentric point of view, women will then come to present the necessary frontier between man and chaos; but because of their very marginality they will also

---

16. See Mary Ellmann, *Thinking about Women* (New York: Harcourt, Brace, 1968), pp. 6–8. Mallarmé's own unvarnished sexism and that of his intellectual milieu, the male salon, is exposed by Kristeva, *Révolution du langage poétique*, pp. 452–55. Another noteworthy discussion of this topic appears in Penny Florence, *Mallarmé, Manet, and Redon—Visual and Aural Signs and the Generation of Meaning* (Cambridge: Cambridge University Press, 1986). See the Derridean chapter 5, "Gender-in-Signification," pp. 127–39.

always seem to recede into and merge with the chaos of the outside."[17] One recalls the apparition of Nerval's Aurélia withdrawing to her star or fading back into the garden where she appeared. Mallarmé repeatedly dramatizes such merging with the primordial chaos of non-being as a submerging: the supernatural aquatic female glimpsed momentarily then dives beneath the surface of a lake or sea. Needless to say, her negative aspects serve also as a vehicle for the poet's own projected sense of powerlessness.

In Mallarmé's earliest poems inspiration appears conventionally as a celestial vision. Thus his "Cantate pour la première communion" unequivocally announces its pretext in the title. Then a choir of angels bringing inspiration from the beyond is summoned and instructed to perform, as it might have been in an eighteenth-century ode:

> Chantez—célébrez tous en choeur
> La joie et le bonheur
> Des enfants de la terre.   [p. 4]

(Sing—celebrate all in chorus / The joy and the happiness / Of the children of earth.)

Even so early in Mallarmé's career, however, the inadequacy of human inspiration may be suggested through the etymological meaning of "enfants," those who cannot yet speak. Here angels must do so for humanity. But at least the articulate angelic replacements are readily available. More accurately, the angels, whose sex is unspecified (they are not necessarily the female "Other" of the male poet, sources of something from beyond or outside himself), function not as Muse figures but rather as dramatizations of the topos of inexpressibility (a "timeless theme," i.e., a traditional motif recurring in many countries and periods, through which the poet elaborates on conventions and dispenses with the need for being inspired). All the stanzas of this early poem stop short, as if inspiration had failed.[18]

Until the completion of parts of "Hérodiade" in 1867 (to the extent that this work of a lifetime ever was completed), Mallarmé used titles to disclose his poems' sources of inspiration at the outset. Such a

17. Toril Moi, *Sexual/Textual Politics: Feminist Literary Theory* (London: Methuen, 1985), pp. 166–67.

18. For background on the angel figure, see Ursula Franklin, "Segregation and Disintegration of an Image: Mallarmé's Struggle with the Angel," *Nineteenth-Century French Studies,* 12 (Fall 1983–Winter 1984), 145–67.

practice creates icons of inspiration unproblematically accorded as soon as one sits down to write. Titles present the initial impetus as a "given." In "Hérodiade," however, the title has already become a mask. The allusion to the biblical story with its historico-legendary topic conceals a self-referential drama involving a Muse figure, one who refuses to permit the approach of other beings or to make contact with materiality. She requires the spectacle of herself in the mirror, however, in order to acquire an identity. Thus Mallarmé underlines the fact that she is not an absolute origin and that to seek such an origin (a definitive meaning, interpretation, or source) is to open up the prospect of unending semiosis. When the severed head of Saint John the Baptist is brought to her, so that, perhaps, he may define her with his gaze and thus confirm her beauty, his dead eyes are blind; nor would Hérodiade have wished it any other way. The poet can rejoin her, can accede to her ideal realm, only by annihilating the corporeal. The poem's concluding section, the "Cantique de saint Jean" (which Mallarmé may have finished only near the time of his death), celebrates the aftermath of the suicidal union of the poet figure with inspiration, a union whereby this poet achieves "salvation"— literally the last word of the text. But this and the projected middle section of the poem, which was to have described how the virginal Muse made contact with reality by encountering the saint's gaze, were not released during Mallarmé's lifetime. His apparent dissatisfaction with his conception of how inspiration could commune with the poet prevented Mallarmé from realizing the greatest poetic project of his life.[19] Although the surviving sketches of the middle section on the union of woman and saint show that mere narcissism is not the only meaning of the poem, non-narcissistic segments were not published.

Having struggled with his metaphysical crisis in this fashion, Mallarmé reached an impasse. It is not surprising that he nearly stopped publishing poetry for fifteen years, from the late 1860s to 1883. When he resumed, he largely eliminated titles, except for those that are self-referential ("Prose pour des Esseintes") or commemorative ("Tombeaux"). The unstated metonymy of the latter makes the act of commemoration itself (writing the poem) into the monument, into an act of homage attesting to the powers of the person rendering it.

19. On Hérodiade's narcissism, see Gardner Davies, *Mallarmé et le rêve d'"Hérodiade"* (Paris: Corti, 1978), pp. 37–39, 62, and 294. Mary Ellen Wolf goes over the same ground with modish terminology in *Eros under Glass: Psychoanalysis and Mallarmé's "Hérodiade"* (Columbus: Ohio State University Press, 1987), pp. 21–27 and 40–41.

Not that the notation of inspiration altogether disappears. Mallarmé's erasures of his former references to it leave traces that preserve the full import of his poems while simultaneously enriching them. The reader is thus engaged in a meditative enterprise required to recuperate their import. Specifically, Mallarmé, like the writers of classical antiquity, conceived of inspiration as the *furor poeticus* resulting from the encounter of the human and the divine (at this point we must recall that he is dramatizing a delusion, depicting something he knows does not exist). The terms of that encounter are spelled out, for example, in the original title "Sainte Cécile jouant sur l'aile d'un chérubin" ("Saint Cecilia Playing Music on a Cherub's Wing," December 5, 1865), where the presence of an angel allows a human to make music. The revised title "Sainte" ("Female Saint," 1883) condenses the two terms into a one-word oxymoron: the human and divine are completely fused. Moreover, the original title refers to a stained-glass window, a luminous point of intersection between transcendent externality and the human space within. The pane makes these spaces mutually visible through the very act of separating them. (The analogy holds even if this pane is in fact translucent rather than transparent, for it still allows an intimation of the spiritual to penetrate.) The abridged title of the final version erases the stained-glass window, but it can be inferred from the words "fenêtre" (l. 1) and "vitrage" (l. 9), which remain in the text of the poem.

Like other major symbols, the Muse can be double-edged, representing the power and mystery of creativity or its frustration. Just as Shiva functions either to create or to destroy, just as the lion may figure either Christ or Satan, so the supernatural female of Symbolism can represent either the source (or vehicle) of the inspiration that brings the transcendent within reach of the poet or else the self-sufficing, unattainable ideal in and of itself and the inarticulateness that overwhelms the poet confronting this ideal. In the course of his career Mallarmé progresses toward an ever more pessimistic treatment of the Muse. He begins with the convention according to which the spiritual presence of the Muse not only facilitates but almost compels a poetic response, as in "Sa fosse est creusée": "la vierge se fait ange / Pour éblouir nos yeux, avant d'aller à Dieu! / Nous voulons l'admirer" (p. 6: the virgin makes herself into an angel / To dazzle our eyes, before going to God! / We wish to admire her). But he soon telescopes the opposite extremes of expressivity and incommunicability into the figure of a Muse who deliberately evades the poet.

Insofar as we identify with him, her elusiveness functions as a powerful phatic device to rivet our attention. Finally, in the "Sonnet en -yx" (the 1887 version) a further metonymic dislocation prevents us from assuming the Muse's control of inspiration any more than we could take for granted her availability to Mallarmé's poet-persona.

We can best appreciate this ultimate transformation in the light of revisions Mallarmé made in various other poems, revisions that all enhance the impression of "incommunicabilité." The following list, which examines twenty-nine of these variants, reveals how Mallarmé calls into question every point along the axis of communication, although he focuses on the concept in particular. The evidence is scant—few corrected manuscripts by Mallarmé survive—but telling.

In the list below, the first page reference is to the earlier version of any given poem, reproduced at the end of the Pléiade edition. The second page reference indicates where in that edition the definitive published version can be found.

1.–2. "La Prière d'une mère" (pp. 1388 and 12, no dates).

> [Dieu] Qui lança le soleil en sa route embrasée
> Et créa tout d'une pensée!

([God] Who cast the sun forth on its flaming way / And created everything with a thought!)

becomes

> Qui lança le soleil en la voûte éternelle
> De son regard faible étincelle.

(Who cast the sun forth into the eternal vault / Like a dim spark from His gaze.)

The reference to God's creating everything through the power of thought—an activity analogous to and serving as a model for poetic creativity—has been eliminated. The effect is to replace a suggestion of the idea of inspiration, which seemingly brings forth poems *ex nihilo* or from a transcendent domain, with the idea of craftsmanship employing existing materials. In the same poem the mother's entreaty runs as follows (pp. 1388 and 13):

> Donne à notre prière une aile
> Pour qu'elle s'envole à ton coeur

>Comme le parfum qui révèle
>Au matin l'aubépine en fleur!

(Give wings to our prayer, / So that it may fly to your heart / Like the perfume that reveals / The flowering hawthorn to the morn.)

Revised, the last two lines become

>Comme le frais parfum que mêle
>Aux brises, l'aubépine en fleur!

(Like the fresh scent that the flowering hawthorn mingles with the breezes!)

In the initial version, the poem as prayer, like the perfume revealed to the morning by the flowering hawthorn tree, aims to inspire the heart of God (who functions here as audience) with tenderness. This active role for the poem as vehicle of inspiration dwindles when "mêle" replaces "révèle." The contact of the prayer with God is still recorded, but the reinforcing parallel—the contact of the perfume-as-message with the dawn—has disappeared together with its hint of Romantic panpsychism, a world-system that guaranteed the contact.

3–6. In "Le Sonneur" (pp. 1428–29 [1862] and 36 [1866]).

>Cependant que la cloche, enivrant sa voix claire
>A l'air plein de rosée et jeune du matin
>Invite la faucheuse à chanter pour lui plaire
>Un Angélus qui sent la lavande et le thym

(While the bell, whose bright voice becomes intoxicated / With the morn's youthful, dew-laden air, / Invites the woman reaping to sing for his pleasure / An Angelus scented with lavender and thyme)

becomes

>Cependant que la cloche éveille sa voix claire
>A l'air pur et limpide et profond du matin
>Et passe sur l'enfant qui jette pour lui plaire
>Un angélus parmi la lavande et le thym

(While the bell awakens its bright voice / In the pure, deep, and limpid
morning air / And passes over the child who tosses off for his pleasure
/ An angelus among the lavender and thyme)

Here the notion of inspiration conveyed in the first version by
"enivrant" (suggesting an altered state of consciousness) is attenuated by being displaced to the air, described as "pur" and
"profond"—qualities associated with the transcendent ideal. The air
now is merely juxtaposed with the bell, a poet-surrogate (for it emits
a "song" that rises toward heaven), rather than imbibed by it. Next
the bell takes over the role of inspiration from the clear air, but its
specific solicitation of the second poet figure, conveyed by the verb
"invite," has been removed. This figure itself is transformed from
someone who collects, binds, and stores to someone who does not.
That is, he has no "product" (in French, collections of verse often
are called "gleanings"). The Angelus, the poem experienced as the
emanation of sound, was at first associated with the aromatic plants
of the harvest fields, which emanate fragrant odors. Thus the
Angelus as poem becomes further associated with a concrete
achievement—the gathering of the harvest itself. In the final version,
this connotation of permanence is replaced by one of transience.
The poetic response itself has become devalued: "angelus" loses its
capital letter and is "tossed off" rather than "sung." That both the
harvester and the child respond to the bells with a prayer heightens
in both versions the contrast between them and the third poet-
persona, the ineffectual monk who throughout the remaining stanzas
helplessly struggles to call forth the voice of the ideal. Finally, in line
12 that voice loses its capital letter of the original ("la Voix"/"la voix")
as if to render the Ideal more remote and inaccessible for the eponymous character: no longer is it necessarily contained within the
sound he faintly hears. What remains from one version to the next is
his frustration, and a mocking invitation to transcendence—the bell-
rope—which can actually lead only to death by hanging. (In universal symbolism, moreover, being suspended between earth and sky
implies blocked psychic development.)

7. "Brise marine" (pp. 1432 [1865] and 28 [1866]). Line 7, "Du
papier qu'un cerveau châtié me défend" (A sheet of paper forbidden
to me by a chastened mind) becomes "Sur le vide papier que la blan-
cheur défend" (On the blank paper defended by [its] whiteness). The
absence of inspiration now is caused by an external rather than an

internal obstacle. Therefore the problem of achieving creativity has become absolutely rather than relatively insoluble.

8. The change of title from "Sainte Cécile jouant sur l'aile d'un chérubin (Chanson et image anciennes)" (1865) to "Sainte" (1883), in addition to producing the effects mentioned above, removes from the definitive version of the poem the mention of artistic creation ("jouant"), its supernatural origin ("l'aile d'un chérubin"), and its historical dignity ("anciennes").

9. In the first two lines of an untitled poem (pp. 1500 [undated] and 75 [1885]), "De l'Orient passé des Temps / Nulle étoffe jadis venue" (No fabric that formerly came / From the Orient of bygone days) becomes "Quelle soie aux baumes de temps / Où la Chimère s'exténue" (What silken fabric in the perfumed time / Where the Chimera is sinking into exhaustion). The final version suppresses the exotic place of origin of the fabric—"l'Orient"—together with the very idea of origination ("jadis venue"). Traces of both are, however, preserved in the metonymically displaced "soie" (i.e., in the name of the material that replaces the object—a cloth—made from it). "Soie" as homonym for the subjunctive "soit" juxtaposed with "quelle" adds a nuance of modal uncertainty, in and of itself and also by hinting at the phrase "quelle que soit" (whatever may be).

10–13. "Le Guignon" (pp. 1410 [1862] and 28 [1887]). In stanza 2, ". . . Leurs bannières / Où passe le divin gonflement de la mer" (. . . Their banners / Swollen by the divine breath of the sea) becomes

> Un noir vent sur leur marche éployée pour bannières
> La flagellait de froid tel jusque dans la chair,
> Qu'il y creusait aussi d'irritables ornières.

(A sinister wind spread over their march like banners / Whipped them with cold cutting right to the flesh, / Hollowing out furrows of soreness there.)

In the original version, the divine breath of inspiration. (To Mallarmé, moreover, any fabric suggests a text because, according to its etymology, a "text" is "something woven," and any white fabric suggests the white page awaiting poetic inspiration as the sail awaits the wind.) In the revision, inspiration becomes intangible. The physical banners have been replaced by a wind that is cold, painful, and sinister rather than divine. "Creusait," referring to the hollows dug in the marchers'

puckered flesh by the inclement weather, further connotes an absence
of inspiration. Like a barren field, the poets' physical substance yields
nothing, although it is endlessly tilled by the implied metaphorical
plow of the wind. "Toujours avec l'espoir de rencontrer la mer" (with
the abiding hope of reaching the sea), the added line in stanza 3,
removes the poet figures far from the sea as source of inspiration:
they were next to it in stanza 2 of the original. The hypothetical failure
of creativity, which still holds out the possibility of a compensatory
Icarian renown, is transformed into a definitive failure when in stanza
5 "Leur défaite" (Their defeat) replaces "S'il sont vaincus" (If they
are conquered). And in stanza 11 the Muse figure as well as the poet
becomes indirectly degraded when "Le Guignon," who in the first
version rode behind the undifferentiated "mendieurs d'azur" (beggars
for the Beyond), now accompanies the new characters, "Amants" (suggesting the poet and his Muse). Further, he no longer transforms a
lone "superbe nageur" (proud swimmer) into a "fou crotté" (muddy
madman) but the "blanc couple nageur" (white pair of swimmers) into
a "bloc boueux" (muddy lump).

14–16. "Placet futile" (pp. 1415 [1862] and 30 [1887]). The original
title was "Placet" (an appeal to a superior). The importance of the
poem as message diminishes when the self-referential "petition" of
the title is devalued as "frivolous." In line 3 of the same poem Mallarmé revises "Mais je suis un poète" (But I am a poet) to "J'use mes
feux" (I expend my fires [of ardent desire]). Specific designation of
the lyric self as creative artist has been eliminated, and the suggestion
of futility ("use" = "wear out, consume") superimposed. The second
tercet of the same poem changes "et Boucher...Me peindra" (and
Boucher...will paint me) to "pour qu'Amour...M'y peigne" (So that
Cupid...may paint me there). The historical artist Boucher has been
replaced by a mythological abstraction, and the substance of the act
of artistic creation has been weakened by being presented as optative
rather than assertoric—as the object of a wish rather than as a stated
fact. Thus the potential creation of the work of art undergoes a twofold shift from reality to fantasy.

17–18. "Le Pitre châtié" (pp. 1416–17 [1864] and 31 [1887]). Originally the entire poem consisted in an apostrophe addressed to the
"Muse" (named in the direct address of lines 3 and 14 of this sonnet),
whose name and association with the lyric self ("moi, ton pitre" [I,
your clown]; l. 3) disappear from the poem.

19–20. "Aumône" (pp. 1434–37 [1862, 1864, 1866] and 39–40

[1887]). Originally titled "Haine du pauvre" ("Hatred of the Poor Man," a deliberately ambiguous phrase), the poem later introduced personified audiences as dedicatees in the versions of 1864 ("A un mendiant"/"To a Beggar") and 1866 ("A un pauvre"/"To a Poor Man") but then eliminated that reference in the definitive title, which instead implies that we the literary audience are the beggars (the poem we consume is the alms we have asked), since now no other recipient is named in the title. As "alms" are usually only a minute sum that the donor will not miss, the poet disparages both us and himself with a form of higher sarcasm (literally or verbally giving people what they want while knowing the gift to be worthless). In all four versions, however, the poet does serve as a source of inspiration for the beggar by offering him the money that may allow him a greater freedom of choice and action. All the versions thus satirize the Romantic convention that the poet functions as a Muse for society.

21–24. "Autre éventail de Mademoiselle Mallarmé" ("Another of Miss Mallarmé's Fans," pp. 1474–75 [1884] and 58 [1887]). In both versions the third stanza evokes the trembling awakening of space stirred by the fan. But three notations of order and self-control in the original are replaced by an experience of disorientation and alienation in the definitive text. The earlier poem (emphasis added to both versions) reads:

> *Vaste jeu!* voici que frissonne
> L'espace comme un grand baiser
> Qui *fier* de *n'être* pour personne
> Ne *sait* jaillir ni s'apaiser

(*Vast game!* Now space shivers / Like a great kiss / That, *proud* of *being* destined for no one, / *Is unable* either to spring forth or to calm itself.)

And in 1887 it reads

> *Vertige!* voici que frissonne
> L'espace comme un grand baiser
> Qui, *fou* de *naître* pour personne,
> Ne *peut* jaillir ni s'apaiser.

(*Vertigo!* Now space shivers / Like a great kiss / That, *crazed* from having been *born* for no one, / *Can* neither spring forth nor calm itself.)

"Vaste jeu!" "fier," and "ne sait," which all allow for the possibility of control, become "Vertige!" "fou," and "ne peut," which do not. The last of these changes replaces the *pour-soi* with the *en-soi* (the self-determining entity with one passively subject to exterior influence). In a further movement toward the concrete, "n'être" gives way to its homonym "naître" to transform the original dyad of non-being/control into one of being/loss of control. In both versions, of course, Mallarmé erects the facade of impersonality that is characteristic of his mature work, through his typical device of replacing the perceiver by that which is perceived. The personified figure of space serves thus as a metonymy for the poet observing the scene and projecting his impressions on it.

25–26. In "Victorieusement fui" ("Having Triumphally Fled," pp. 1486–87 [1885] and 68 [1887]), the original mention of poetic immortality achieved through an implied contact with audiences of the future ("vaincre le tombeau" [to conquer the grave]; l. 4) and the designation of "le poète" (l. 6) himself are erased, although their scattered traces remain in the first and last words of the opening quatrain: "Victorieusement fui . . . mon absent tombeau."

27–29. "Le Tombeau d'Edgar Poe" (pp. 1493 [1876] and 70 [1887]). Mallarmé initially removes an explicit reference to the poetic message. In line 2, "Le Poète suscite avec un hymne nu," the word "hymne" is superseded by "glaive" (The Poet raises up with a naked hymn/sword). At the same time the countermessage of the anti-selves (traditional base and villainous foils to the noble poet in the conventional moralizing ode) has become stronger.[20] In both versions these adversaries accuse Poe of having found inspiration in drunkenness. Their charge is stated in a typically precious periphrasis: "le sortilège bu / Dans le flot sans honneur de quelque noir mélange" (Magic imbibed / in the dishonorable tide of some sinister brew). But Mallarmé's revision turns their accusations from thoughts ("Tous pensèrent entre eux" [All thought to themselves]; l. 7) to shouts ("Proclamèrent très haut" [They loudly proclaimed]). The second stanza, however, puts forward a counterexample through which the ontological—or one might better say verbal—status of the poet's message is strengthened. In a chiasmic movement of thought that the French would call a

20. For a discussion of these traditional figures of lyric villainy, see Laurence M. Porter, *The Renaissance of the Lyric in French Romanticism: Elegy, "Poëme," and Ode* (Lexington, Ky.: French Forum, 1978), pp. 97–98.

"chassé-croisé," the ignorant viewpoint of Poe's detractors yields to the enlightened viewpoint of a fellow poet. Both versions use Poe's tombstone to symbolize what remains after his death, the poetic *oeuvre*. In the first version the *oeuvre* is sinister, its critics perdurable; in the definitive version these terms are reversed: the *oeuvre* has become permanent and its critics sinister. The first version goes:

> *Sombre* bloc à jamais chu d'un désastre obscur,
> Que ce granit du moins montre à jamais sa borne
> Aux *vieux* vols du blasphème épars dans le futur.

(*Dark* block forever fallen from a mysterious disaster, / May this granite [Poe's tombstone], if nothing else, forever mark the bounds / Of the *ancient* flights of blasphemy [calumny] scattered throughout the future.)

Compare the definitive version:

> *Calme* bloc ici-bas chu d'un désastre obscur,
> Que ce granit du moins montre à jamais sa borne
> Aux *noirs* vols du Blasphème épars dans le futur.

(*Tranquil* block fallen here below from a mysterious disaster, / May this granite, if nothing else, forever mark the bounds / Of the *sinister* flights of Blasphemy scattered throughout the future.

These variants strengthen the virtual communicative axis in two ways, both by glorifying the message and condemning a hostile audience and by switching the site of the event from an indefinite time to a definite place. Mallarmé's exceptionally clear use of value-laden terms here probably derives from his awareness that this poem was destined for a foreign audience. Indeed, he even helped translate it into English.

The greatest number of Mallarmé's significant variants that undermine communication appear in the heavily revised "Sonnet allégorique de lui-même" of 1868, republished without title in 1887.[21] This poem has been studied by numerous critics. Michel Grimaud has cogently summed up the reasoning adduced to support various critical interpretations, and Michael Riffaterre has convincingly demon-

---

21. *Documents Stéphane Mallarmé*, ed. Carl Paul Barbier (Paris: Nizet, 1973), IV, 41. The Pléiade text of the "Sonnet en -yx" is slightly inaccurate for the earlier version.

strated that it is a poem about nothingness.[22] My interest, however, is how it became such a poem. For there are degrees of nothingness in literature, if not in logic or in physics.

Many of the variants discussed above illustrate how Mallarmé dislocated the communicative axis by erasing references to it. But his negations in the "Sonnet en -yx" are more complex and profound. He disrupts the process of virtual inspiration in the poem by context dislocation, by denying us a network of associations that form part of the cultural code that ensures communicability and that we ordinarily take for granted. Let us consider a homey example of such dislocation. If out of the blue you were to say, "How about them Tigers?" most North Americans would assume that you were referring to the American Baseball League pennant race and the favorable prospects of the Detroit-based team rather than to a zoo, a safari, or a toy store. Yet your conversational partner could quickly adjust to these latter possibilities, since they still form part of a communality of real or imagined experience. But if your next words were "They're extinct," you would shift the frame of reference from a rule-governed victory to a mysterious defeat and from a familiar social ritual to an unknown disaster and an unknown species. Mallarmé does something similar. Specifically, in a predictable lyric poem, the supernatural female either helps the male poet triumph by mediating between him and the ideal or else triumphs herself as an epiphany of that ideal. In the "Sonnet en -yx," however, Mallarmé shows her to be both inaccessible and defeated.

The original title, "Sonnet allégorique de lui-même" (1868), evokes a parthenogenetic fecundity. When the poem reappears untitled in print in 1887, the idea of an intersection has been preserved in the rare rhymes themselves. The chiasmic "-yx" implies the meeting of poet and Muse, an inside contacting an outside at a window ("la croisée" suggested by the X-shape), while the rhyme "-or" evokes the sunlight that illuminates the pane—particularly since the first occurrence of this rhyme is in the word "lampadophore" (lamp-bearer).

An 1868 letter to Cazalis specifies that the inspiration for the "Sonnet en -yx" had come from within itself rather than from something external. "Il est inverse, je veux dire que le sens, s'il y en a un (mais

---

22. See Michel Grimaud, "Les Mystères du *Ptyx:* Hypothèse sur la remotivation psychopoétique à partir de Mallarmé et Hugo," *Michigan Romance Studies*, 1 (1980), 98–162; and Michael Riffaterre, *Semiotics of Poetry* (Bloomington: Indiana University Press, 1978), pp. 12–19.

je me consolerais du contraire grâce à la dose de poésie qu'il renferme, ce me semble) est évoqué par un mirage interne des mots mêmes." (It is inverse; I mean that the signification, if there is any [but I would feel consoled if the opposite were true, owing to the dose of poetry I think it contains], is evoked by an internal mirage of the words themselves).[23] Even in the first version of this sonnet Mallarmé contrasted "poetry" with communication and declared his aim of obliterating any trace of external inspiration. The final version, nevertheless, takes this minimalist enterprise further:

Sonnet allégorique de lui-même (1868)

La Nuit approbatrice allume les onyx
De ses ongles au pur Crime, lampadophore,
Du Soir aboli par le vespéral Phoenix
De qui la cendre n'a de cinéraire amphore

Sur des consoles, en le noir Salon: nul ptyx,
Insolite vaisseau d'inanité sonore,
Car le Maître est allé puiser de l'eau du Styx
Avec tous ses objets dont le Rêve s'honore.

Et selon la croisée au Nord vacante, un or
Néfaste incite pour son beau cadre une rixe
Faite d'un dieu que croit emporter une nixe

En l'obscurcissement de la glace, décor
De l'absence, sinon que sur la glace encor
De scintillations le septuor se fixe.

("Sonnet: An Allegory of Itself." The approving Night illuminates the onyx of its nails [the stars] / In the sight of pure Crime, the lamp-bearer / Of the Evening abolished by the Phoenix of twilight, / Whose ashes have no funerary urn // On the sideboards, in the dark Living Room: no ptyx [a word that Mallarmé gleefully believed to exist in no known language], / An unusual vessel of sonorous vacuity, / For the Master has gone to draw water from the Styx, / With all his objects with which the Dream celebrates itself. // And next to the vacant window facing North, an inauspicious gold [in order to provide a subject] / For its handsome frame, incites a scuffle / Caused by a god whom a water sprite thinks to carry off // In the darkening of the mirror, a scene / Of absence, were it not that in the mirror still / The septet of scintillations [the seven stars of the Big Dipper, a celestial ptyx the end of whose handle points to the North Star, the still center of the revolving heavens] has come to a halt.)

23. Mallarmé to Cazalis, July 18, 1868, *Corr.* I, 278; also in *OC*, p. 1489.

[Untitled, 1887; pp. 68–69]

Ses purs ongles très haut dédiant leur onyx,
L'Angoisse, ce minuit, soutient, lampadophore,
Maint rêve vespéral brûlé par le Phénix
Que ne recueille pas de cinéraire amphore

Sur les crédences, au salon vide: nul ptyx,
Aboli bibelot d'inanité sonore,
(Car le Maître est allé puiser des pleurs au Styx
Avec ce seul objet dont le Néant s'honore).

Mais proche la croisée au nord vacante, un or
Agonise selon peut-être le décor
Des licornes ruant du feu contre une nixe,

Elle, défunte nue en le miroir, encor
Que, dans l'oubli fermé par le cadre, se fixe
De scintillations sitôt le septuor.

(Its pure nails dedicating their onyx very high, / Anguish, this midnight,
supports, a lamp-bearer, / Many a twilight dream burned by the Phoenix
/ Whom no funerary urn gathers // On the credenzas, in the empty
living room; no ptyx, / Abolished knick-knack of sonorous vacuity / [For
the Master has gone to draw tears from the Styx / With this single object
with which the Void celebrates itself]. // But near the vacant window
facing north, a gold / Is in its death agonies, next perhaps to a scene /
Of unicorns rearing fiery against a water sprite, // She, a defunct nude
[or: cloud] in the mirror, although, / In the oblivion sealed by the frame,
/ Suddenly the septet of scintillations comes to a halt.)

Providing the pretext for the first version, night erases the material
world, whose spectacle might otherwise tempt one to a mundane art
of unimaginative representation. The repetition of the word "mirror"
("glace," which also can mean a sheet of ice) recalls the narcissistic
world of Hérodiade, where only one's own reflection grants identity,
and Beauty claims to be utterly self-sufficient. But the very darkness
paradoxically reveals a vision of absence in the remote stars, the constellation of the Big Dipper, which imaginatively serves to draw water
(or later, tears), and the North Star, which remains a fixed point of
reference in a changing world. Negative as it already is, this version
of inspiration becomes even more tenuous in the final version. An act

of light-giving ("allume") yields to a static light-supporting ("soutient"). "La Nuit" is replaced by "l'Angoisse," the effect night produces
in the lyric self. And the etymological source of the word "Angoisse,"
angustia (a narrow place), reinforces the general effect of a narrowing
focus in the second version. The cosmic setting, which would seem
to offer a vast panorama from which to derive inspiration, is severely
restricted by a number of synergistic devices. The added word "minuit" covertly reinscribes the vanished "Nuit" letter for letter in the
poem. But in so doing, it replaces the broad field of the night sky by
a point in space (the nadir of the noonday sun), and the long hours
of darkness by one moment in time. Mallarmé creates a sense of
further restriction by eliminating the words "approbatrice," connoting
an inclusive acceptance, and "allume," anticipating a broadening of
light. All in all, the spectacle no longer greets the poet with open arms,
so to speak, but now offers only the narrowest access. Already concerned with concentration in the first version, Mallarmé limited the
semantic field through the awkward technique of synonymy, through
uncharacteristic redundancies in lines three and four: "soir . . . vespéral; cendre . . . cinéraire." The final version deploys synonymy more
discreetly via Mallarmé's more usual mature devices of etymological
undertone and homophony. "Dédiant" derives from the root "digi-
tus," meaning "finger"; "onyx" comes from a Greek word for "claw"
(a beast's or bird's fingernail); and "maint" itself echoes the sound of
"la main" (hand). These three details—the homonymic dream-hand,
the stars as fingernails, and the extended arm of the lamp-bearer—
all simultaneously limn the single posture of a hieratic ritual cele-
brant consecrating herself while she preserves the memory of the vanished sun.

Mallarmé heightens the tension between the human and the cosmic
by eliminating the supernumeraries of the first stanza ("le pur Crime"
and "le Soir aboli") with their distracting Baudelairean resonances.
Although the adjective "pur" strongly suggests that Mallarmé does
not associate this crime with the human dimension, purity does not
exclude humanity, and it occurs in apparent harmony with the cosmic
Night, Evening, and Phoenix as the sacred immolator of the sun. So
the term "crime" threatens to confuse a human reaction of horror
with the celestial drama. But in the final version, "l'angoisse" appears
in sharp focus as a poetic fixation on the vestiges of the past contrasted
with the impassive, inexorable progression of the natural cycle. The
new negative verb "ne recueille pas" now emphasizes the disparity

between human and cosmic. The ashes from the sunset, from the self-sacrifice of the Phoenix, cannot be preserved. And since the verb "recueille" is closely related to the noun "recueil" (collection of poems), Mallarmé implies that the cosmic drama cannot be captured by poetry either.

Mallarmé's reworking of the second stanza further refutes the notion that poetry can replace reality by forming a memory that might compensate for material loss. "Consoles," the word for the furniture in the first version, had hinted at such a consoling compensation, as it does in the sonnet "Tout Orgueil fume-t-il du soir." The new term, "crédences," suggests the utter disappearance of the sun in several ways: first, through association with sudden death (the Italian *credenza* was a sideboard where meals could be tasted to ensure they were not poisoned); second, through the idea of an expected but missing formal display (the modern "crédence" is a fancy sideboard used to display silver or gold dishes that gleam like celestial bodies); and third, since a "crédence" can also designate a table bearing the elements of the Mass, the absence of a *ptyx* or communion chalice here implies a religious ceremony that has been nullified. That is, it suggests the failure of communication between the supernatural and the human.

The remaining changes in the second stanza further associate the *ptyx* with the erasure of inspiration, as a womb both empty and also irrevocably absent. It is linked no longer to "le Rêve," a possible source of poetry, but to "le Néant." The phrase "aboli bibelot" applied to the *ptyx* provides an onomatopoetic rendering of "inanité sonore." Semantically it designates something of no importance, something that no longer exists (a twofold "inanity"), while phonetically it resonates (is "sonorous") through the echoing *b*'s, *l*'s, and *i*'s, like Shakespeare's tale told by an idiot, full of sound and fury, signifying nothing. At the same time, through apophany (a shift from one vowel to another), "bibelot" evokes a phantom *biblio*, the absent, burned, or uncreated book. The typographical boundary of the parentheses added in lines 7 and 8 debars the *ptyx* from the real world. And by making it the only object pridefully acknowledged by the Void, rather than one of several objects belonging to the Master (a poet figure), Mallarmé reveals the *ptyx* to be a *mise en abyme* (an internal reduplication) of the empty room from which it came, while both *ptyx* and room signify the poet's mind, devoid of inspiration.

In the definitive version, the *ptyx* serves to draw tears rather than water from the Styx. The new phrase "puiser des pleurs" again cancels the process of poetic creativity by subtly reversing it. Whether one weeps or writes poetry, emotions move from "inside" to "outside" during their expression. But in Mallarmé's poem the Master draws inward the tears that had already been shed, as if he were making a gesture of suppression rather than of expression. In contrast, the original wording "puiser l'eau," conceals the homophony "l'ô." The latter constitutes a marked choice for direct address used only in the poetic apostrophe and thus signifies the recuperation of inspiration from what had been oblivion—the river Styx, a stream one cannot cross twice. Finally, the form of the letter *o* in itself suggests the vanished sun as well as the zero or "Néant" that cancels it.

What points most unequivocally to Mallarmé's project for erasing inspiration from this text is a dramatic reversal of sexual roles in both versions and a decisive change of mythological reference in the second one. The original had evoked "une rixe / Faite d'un dieu que [*sic*] croit emporter une nixe." A nixie is a water sprite. Conjuring up her bucolic world, the phallocratic imagination thinks of an Arcadia of legalized rape (to a God/male, all is permitted) where Pan seizes Syrinx only to lose her at once as she undergoes a metamorphosis into a stand of reeds. (Or, of course, we recall Mallarmé's own afternoon faun, whose desired nymphs likewise elude him.) To commemorate her, and by way of compensation for himself, Pan cuts the reeds to make them into his rustic flute so that Syrinx's vanished body now inspires not lust but art. In Mallarmé's sonnet, however, it is the Muse, inferred from the supernatural female, who as an active feminine principle attempts to carry off a god, a transcendent "meaning" captured by inspiration. The issue of the struggle remains uncertain. But in the final version the nixie, again unequivocally the aggressor, is sharply repulsed. Unicorns breathe fire at her, and she dies.

To understand the full import of this vignette, one must recall the traditional linking of woman and unicorn in legend. The latter could be captured only by a virgin, who would sit in the forest until the beast came to lay its head on her lap and be charmed to sleep. This motif often further symbolized the incarnation of Christ, the Word made flesh. But for Mallarmé it connotes the Idea embodied in words— an impossibility. His unicorns reject the supernatural woman; the *unio mystica* of inspiration fails. The very multiplicity of the creatures here suggests a diffuse, ill-defined goal. Concomitantly, the frame ("cadre") is no longer characterized as "beau." As a result, a note of complacent artistic self-consciousness—and the accompanying suggestion that what the frame surrounds is a privileged, aesthetic domain where the poet's visions appear—also vanishes from the poem.

In the first version of the sonnet, after the Muse figure disappears the poet presents a septet of lights reflected in the vacant mirror with a conjunction that implies that they might form an exception to, a replacement for, or even a compensation for her absence: "décor / De l'absence, *sinon que* sur la glace encore..." (A scene of absence, *were it not that* in the mirror still...). The second version moves the Muse not only out of sight but out of mind, replacing "absence" with "oubli." And a new conjunction dismisses the possibility of reviving inspiration: "Elle, défunte nue en le miroir, *encor / Que*" (She, a defunct nude/cloud in the mirror, *although* [emphasis added]). The Muse— and "elle" is a homonym for her "aile" (wing) of inspiration—has died *even though* the celestial *ptyx* of the Big Dipper gleams in the mirror. Not only the meaning of the conjunction but also the abrupt enjambment of half of it brutally dissociates the stellar vision from any possibility of an earthly effect.

Both versions of the poem deploy a traditional Renaissance symbolism of the mirror and the empty chalice to suggest the vanity of the material world. Nevertheless, by placing the verb "se fixe" in final position in the first version, Mallarmé hints at some higher permanence accessible through poetry, some "compte total en formation" (the optimistic phrase from the conclusion of his great final poem, "Un coup de Dés"). The second version attenuates this impression of an ultimate stability by moving "se fixe" back one line. "Le septuor," now in final position, still evokes the music of the spheres, but the words suggesting the presence of an observer who might hear that music—"obscurcissement" and "décor de l'absence"—have been removed.

The relatively extensive variants of the "Sonnet en -yx" provide an unusual opportunity to observe in action Mallarmé's erasure of inspiration. They confirm the impression produced by his revisions of other verse poems, whose subjects derive largely from the drama of frustrated union with the Muse. Having studied how this drama is reflected locally by lexical change in the revisions, we can now consider its pervasive effects in other poems, how it influences poetic structure and affects the Muse figure itself. But because it is necessary to recognize the willfulness and calculation with which Mallarmé creates his own difficulties as a poet, we should first examine his thirteen prose poems, where his ironic treatment of inspiration throws these characteristics into sharp relief. Although the first six were composed in 1864, during the metaphysical crisis of Tournon, they reveal a stance toward poetic creativity which contrasts radically with the stance in the verse poems composed at the same time. The early prose poems anticipate the optimism of the last twenty years of Mallarmé's career, an optimism openly expressed in the last seven prose poems.[24]

I I

"Le Phénomène futur," the first of these poems in the published order (all appear in OC, pp. 269–89, except for "Conflit," which is on pp. 355–60), depicts an exhausted world near the end of time. Even its colors are pale and faded. This poem is contemporaneous with the verse "Le Pitre châtié," in which the clown flees the prison of his tent and performance in quest of an ideal inspiration (a situation reminiscent of Baudelaire's prose poem "Le Fou et la Vénus," 1862). In "Le Pitre châtié," the artificial light of the performance (artistic creation) is overwhelmed by the natural light of the sun, which exposes the naked semblance of the clown's body, sooty with makeup, as woefully pale and inadequate to convey the ideal. One thinks of "Don du poème." But in the prose poem the tent of illusion becomes the site of revelation: it rises as if from nowhere before the weary crowd, having been evoked with a confident verbal gesture ("monte"); the setting sun announces an approaching supernatural vision, in the tradition of visionary romanticism; and streetlights come on, transforming the crowd's tired faces. In short, the decadent world dims, but the poetic vision emerges to supplant it. The onlookers' dead eyes catch fire and they forget their everyday existence (p. 270). The process of transformation is not only narrated here but also symbolized. The glorious woman of yesteryear, miraculously preserved, rises like Venus with the salt of the primordial sea still on her legs. "A la place du vêtement vain, elle a un corps" (Instead of a useless/empty garment, she has a body). And the poets of the future who see her all become inspired.

24. Detailed interpretations of and background to the prose poems appear in Ursula Franklin, *An Anatomy of Poesis: The Prose Poems of Stéphane Mallarmé*, North Carolina Studies in the Romance Languages and Literatures, no. 16, (Chapel Hill: University of North Carolina Press, 1976), and Robert Greer Cohn, *Mallarmé's Prose Poems: A Critical Study* (Cambridge: Cambridge University Press, 1987). Cohn emphasizes the pervasive, often implied sensual presence of the anonymous female principle or female entity, or both, in the text (pp. 9–11, 74, 90–91, and 94–95).

Even the etymological meaning of the first word of the title, "phé-nomène," connotes an appearance, an epiphany rather than an eva-sion or a retreat. The poem offers a plenitude of inspiration in the full, jutting breasts of the ideal woman. The "montreur des choses passées" (exhibitor of things past), the masterful poet figure, effort-lessly gathers a crowd and dominates memory, the mother of the Muses.

In the second poem, "Plainte d'automne," the old-fashioned tune the barrel organ plays again suggests access to memory, that indis-pensable source of poetry. The original title, "L'Orgue de Barbarie," designated the musical instrument, the subject of the poem. The later title, however, evokes autumn, the pretext, together with the poetic response, "plainte" (a term whose secondary meaning is a specific poetic genre, the lament).

"Frisson d'hiver" likewise represents both pretext (winter) and re-sponse (the shivering) in the title. The woman in "Frisson d'hiver" is presumably Maria Gerhard, who was soon to marry Mallarmé (this text is unusually autobiographical). Her presence compensates for the absence of another Maria, Mallarmé's sister, who had died at age thirteen. Inspiration flows from the poet to the woman (as in some poems of Baudelaire) rather than the reverse, as he invites her to "pense...contemple." In each of the five major paragraphs of the text, a rhetorical question summons and silences her simultaneously. But she also functions as an available, an effective, and even a pos-sessive Muse. Her utterance is provoked by the poet's mention of a potential rival Muse, the naked phantom of the unknown woman who once might have contemplated her beauty in their mirror. Loving old things, she is associated with Mnemosyne (goddess of memory, mother of the Muses); she has already dictated to her poet a line praising "choses fanées" (withered things); and the poet will rest his head in her lap in order to speak to her for hours, generating an imaginary world superseding the exterior landscape, which is erased by the snow that blurs contours and the cold that chases other people from the scene. The fourfold parenthetical refrain with variations, mentioning the spider webs shadowing the windows, constitutes an obsessive ges-ture of artistic self-consciousness, an allusion to the (woven) text ob-scuring the objective world, a tissue of dark words blocking the light, an index of sterile hypercreativity which the poet tries to ignore.

"Le Démon de l'analogie" more directly refers to an unwanted excess of inspiration, a haunting phrase that will not go away: "Des paroles inconnues chantèrent-elles sur vos lèvres, lambeaux maudits

d'une phrase absurde?" (p. 272: Did unknown words sing on your
lips, accursed shreds of an absurd utterance?). Nor is such inspiration
experienced only by the poet: the rhetorical question suggests that
others may have shared his experience. The supernatural presence
of the silent angel wing in the verse poem "Sainte," a wing whose
feathers noiselessly play a stringed instrument, becomes a voice of
unknown origin in the prose poem. The text's verbal repetition seems
to connote the blockage of inspiration: "La Pénultième est morte, elle
est morte, bien morte, la désespérée Pénultième" (pp. 272–73: The
Penult has died; she is dead, quite dead, that desperate Penult). Here
the "penultimate" designates the Muse, for it is she who arrives just
before the ultimate, the creation of a poem. Nul, the penultimate
syllable of the word "pénultième" itself, is associated by Mallarmé with
the string of a musical instrument which has broken as the Muse has
died. In this poem, then, Mallarmé is inspired by the very death of
inspiration. Like Baudelaire, he wanders through Paris; but while the
older poet does so to seek inspiration (e.g., in "Le Soleil"), Mallarmé
encounters inspiration willy-nilly. He wakes from his reverie with a
start to find himself in front of a display of ancient instruments and
stuffed birds corresponding to the associative decor of his own poem.

"Pauvre enfant pâle" again evokes a misunderstood poet figure, the
homeless beggar boy singing for his supper, overflowing with inspiration although, like a victim of Baudelaire's "guignon" (jinx), unheard. In the poem "La Pipe," smoking a pipe brings to the poet's
mind memories of the previous winter and thus reveals to him the
plenitude of involuntary memory. Involuntary memory is evoked all
the more strongly because Mallarmé's title inevitably recalls two plausible intertexts, Alphonse Rabbe's "La Pipe" (1825), usually considered
the first clearly identifiable French prose poem (although Mallarmé
may not have known of it), and Baudelaire's verse poem "La Pipe."[25]
As in the verse poem "Toute l'âme résumée" (p. 73), the rising whorls
of smoke suggest the effortless production of a text, spun out on the
poet's breath.

With the exceptions of "Un spectacle interrompu" (1875?) and
"Conflit" (published in 1895), all the prose poems written after the
Tournon period date from the secondary crisis period of 1885–1888,
during which Mallarmé collected, revised, published, and reacted to
the reception of his complete verse. The early "Réminiscence" in

25. See Franklin, Anatomy of Poesis, pp. 11, 84–85.

particular was extensively rewritten at this time. Eleven of the thirteen prose poems, in other words, appear to have been stimulated by an aesthetic *prise de conscience*. The post-Tournon prose poems continue to counterbalance the verse by dramatizing an abundance or super-abundance of inspiration rather than its absence or scarcity.

The action in both versions of "Réminiscence" takes place during the hour before a circus show begins—that is, in a moment of poten-tiality. Appropriately, then, the tone of the poem is optimistic. And the title suggests that the poet can recall the experience at will, that inspiration remains readily available to him. "Un spectacle inter-rompu" attempts to transcribe an anecdote from the viewpoint of the ideal rather than the real. If this procedure could be generalized, as Mallarmé hopes and intends, anything could become grist for the poetic mill. In this instance a bear in a vaudeville or similar show, performing with a mime, suddenly interrupts his routine to stand up and place one paw on the actor's shoulder. He is distracted and lured offstage with a piece of raw meat. Others in the audience saw only the danger to the human actor and imagined that the bear was think-ing of reducing him to its own level (to raw meat). But Mallarmé saw in the incident the operation of an anagogic principle that links as-piration to the ideal and that could transform reality: he imagines the bear as curious to learn the secrets of human wisdom and insight from his companion, to rise to the human level. So as he watched, he felt serene, rather than concerned for the human actor, "car ma façon de voir, après tout, avait été supérieure, et même la vraie" (p. 276: for my way of seeing things, after all, had been better, and even the correct one). Not only is the poetic vision here imbued with certitude but it potentially has the power to redirect the attention of ordinary humans from the material to the ideal by showing them how to rein-terpret the details of everyday experience like a poet: such vision incarnates the anagogic principle par excellence.

"La Déclaration foraine" describes a journey to the country with a woman who functions, in effect, as a portable Muse. It is she who initiates the couple's visit to a fairgrounds, and she who mounts a platform, obliging the poet to produce some verse praising her to the public that has flocked to the spectacle. Having paid the old man at the entrance, who will benefit from the elegant couple's charity, the crowd must now be made to feel that they have had their money's worth. The woman herself simply stands there "sans supplément de danse ou de chant." To paraphrase Kierkegaard's dictum concerning the God of Love, Mallarmé's Muse does not herself sing, but all others get their songs from her. After the poet has declaimed his sonnet, he must switch from verse to prose in order to interpret the poem to the uncomprehending crowd. The prose medium has helped to dramatize the experience of inspiration by embedding a doubly foreign (verse rather than prose; an English sonnet rather than a French) inspired message within a doubly quotidian context (prosaic in both senses of the word). Such embedding suggests an epiphany, in the literary sense of a second voice intervening to enunciate a transcendent message with a purity and intensity greater than those of ordinary speech and even of ordinary poetic diction.

In "Le Nénuphar blanc" the poet's relationship with his Muse becomes even more effortless, fruitful, and fortuitous. Drifting in a boat, he reaches his destination without knowing it, at the estate of a lady friend of a friend, whom he does not yet know and to whom he is supposed to introduce himself. Still hidden from the nearest path by a curtain of reeds, he hears an "imperceptible noise" (note the oxymoron combining voice and silence), wonders whether the lady exists only in his thoughts or really is present; feels separate from her yet with her all at once; and retreats, unseen, with an imaginary trophy. The verbal medium itself becomes a source of inspiration, as the etymological undertone of one word produces a subsequent situation or event. "Tôt" (soon) from *tostus*, burned, leads to a notation of the time, a "flaming July"; the root of the word "avirons" (oars), *virer* (turn about), leads to the retreat of the poet.[26] The language of courtly love that runs through the text evokes a rule-governed quest that must prove successful if one adheres to the rules; the poet feels sure of being able to reach the desired object—the Muse—but elects not to. More precisely, by not looking at the unknown woman, the poet transmutes the real into the ideal, as he has already done by different means in "Un spectacle interrompu." Thus he makes nearly anything capable of generating inspiration.

Ultimately, the opening of the final prose poem, "Conflit," specifies that Mallarmé had long ago banished chance inspirations from his thought: now he rigorously selects stimuli to his creativity, through acts of will. This discipline contrasts with the abandon of the eponymous character of the earlier poem "L'Ecclésiastique": a priest in the Bois de Boulogne, blindly subjugated by the rebirth of nature in

26. See ibid., p. 138.

spring and thinking himself unobserved, rolls wildly downhill, covering his cassock with sticky stems and leaves. Mallarmé hates spring, when nature creates, overwhelming the poet and enslaving him with ungovernable animal impulses. Here the priest serves as a scapegoat to discharge the instincts unacceptable to the poet, who must remain a deliberate, conscious artist.

So at the very moments in his career, around 1864 and 1887, when Mallarmé covertly banishes inspiration from his verse poems, depicting a virginal, elusive Muse who refuses to entangle herself in the sticky materiality of words or in a union with the poet, in the prose poems he describes situations of abundant or even excessive inspiration. During the earlier period, in 1864, this contrast may reflect a certain mistrust of prose as being too facile because it lacks the disciplines of regular rhythm and rhyme. Sometime around 1870 or shortly thereafter, however, as Mallarmé began to enjoy some success, starting with the triumph of an assignment to Paris, the distinction between verse and prose became less important to him.[27] Perhaps he no longer required the external, material support of the elegant and elite medium of rhyming verse in order to feel like a poet. The playful, punning title "Prose pour des Esseintes," in a poem that includes some of the fullest rhymes in French literature, suggests this new orientation. Mallarmé can now smile at the tricks of his trade, by exaggerating them. This latter poem, moreover, shares with several of the prose poems ("Le Phénomène futur," "La Déclaration foraine," "Un spectacle interrompu") a dramatized, uncomprehending audience. Their presence—necessitating a switch from verse to prose in the second poem—implies a latent desire to communicate with a public broader than an elite of poets and therefore signals a move away from the youthful, disdainful stance of "Hérésies artistiques—L'Art pour tous" (1862) toward publicity projects for Le Livre.

But above all, the paradoxical contrast between Mallarmé's dramatization of the difficulties of inspiration in the verse poems and his almost parodic suggestions of the ease of inspiration in the prose poems written at the same time illustrates the emotional phenomenon known to psychotherapists as "splitting the ambivalence." For example, we all wish to be brave, powerful, and admired; but we also all fear danger, pain, and death. In the traditional phallocratic literary epic, the male assumes all the resolve, and the woman is left to worry

27. See ibid., p. 93.

and weep. Mallarmé, during his periods of crisis, was torn between pride in his gifts as a poet and doubts about his capacity to create. This inner conflict itself becomes a powerful source of inspiration as he sharpens and intensifies his vision by polarization, embodying its uncertainties in the verse and its countervailing hubris in the prose.

III

The problematics of inspiration in Mallarmé's other verse poems and in related texts from the latter half of his career should now be more accessible. Mallarmé reverses the gender roles of traditional lyric poetry, which themselves had constituted a covert reversal of the conventional opposition of active male and passive female. Earlier poets, that is, presented themselves as passive, inspired by an active Muse. The Romantic Musset, for example, asks his Muse for a kiss. Presumably, she will comply. Thus his poem will arise from something the fictive female gives to him, something with which she impregnates him. But in Mallarmé's "L'Azur," it is the poet who must give something to a fictive female if there is to be a poem. The feminine Idea pathetically entreats her chosen poet for adornment, and he in turn helplessly complains that "ma cervelle, vidée / Comme le pot de fard gisant au pied d'un mur, / N'a plus l'art d'attifer la sanglotante idée" (p. 38 [1864]: my brain, empty as the jar of makeup lying at the base of a wall, no longer knows the art of prettifying the sobbing idea). Likewise in "Don du Poëme" ("Gift of the Poem" [ca. 1865]), the initial movement is from the poet to the female Other. She does not bring something to him; he brings his verse to her. This gift, however, is offered not as the overture to a conventional attempt at seduction (she has just given him a baby) but from a sense of reciprocity.

    This reversal of direction represents Mallarmé's response to a paradox. Mallarmé wishes to treat the difficulty of finding inspiration, and the limited, precarious, and ultimately illusory nature of whatever inspiration finally may be offered. Yet the poetic statement that inspiration is hard to find must itself have a source of inspiration. The poem's very existence presupposes such a source. But to announce the inspiration first would vitiate the statement that it is difficult to find. So what Mallarmé will do, especially in his mature period, is to invert the order of events in many of his poems: only at or near the end does the genesis of his inspiration emerge. The resulting structure is similar to that of the sonnet or other short poems that terminate with a *pointe*, a pithy one-line paradox that the remainder of the poem has prepared for. Although the poet conceives the *pointe* first, he introduces it with what is actually a subsequent elaboration of other ideas. The original title of "Don du Poëme," for example was "Le Jour," thus daybreak is the pretext. The second title, "Poème nocturne," masked the pretext by replacing it with the effect it had produced, the sudden awareness that the "Don du Poëme" was nocturnal, artificial, and inferior.

Similarly, in "L'Après-Midi d'un faune," composed during the decade before its appearance in 1876, the only pretext is the poet/faun's own mental experience, which he seeks to recreate. Instead of the Muse summoning art, art here attempts to summon the woman. She appears as the goal of art rather than as the mediatrix whose presence engenders art. The faun awakens to feel desire's full force. Its distraction prevents him from realizing any artistic substitute. Via art he attempts to reverse the process of inspiration, to return from sublimation to the original object of desire. First the landscape becomes the source of music, but music cannot represent (a limitation figured earlier by the flight of the nymphs as the faun begins to play his pipes). Next he attempts narration. He wishes the landscape to become a pretext that will reconstitute the nymphs. But the possibility that the nymphs might have been real is erased by an ellipsis: "Réfléchissons ... / ou si les femmes dont tu gloses / Figurent un souhait de tes sens fabuleux!" (p. 50: Let us reflect... / [Did I really encounter them] or do the women whom you are glossing figure a wish of your fabulous senses!). "Gloser" means to explain an obscure text by paraphrasing it with more intelligible words: to apply the term to the nymphs covertly transforms them into a text already produced by the faun. Woman in this setting is if anything inspiration's enemy rather than its ally. The faun himself—part goat, part man, and part minor god— is a liminal figure, a trickster like the carrion-eating fox or crow of American Indian myth, who cuts across categories and mediates between them. He is a personification of Carnival. Specifically, in the literary perspective of the ancient eclogue, the faun is at once traditional and unreal, a Dionysiac figure of uncontrolled natural lust and an Apollonian figure of cultural, artistic restraint, an embodiment of the signifier with shifting, unstable meanings who incarnates the ontological uncertainty of the verbal medium of poetry.

A more subtle, condensed example of how the Muse becomes an

effect rather than a cause occurs in "Salut" (1893), the occasional poem whose title is both a beginning (a toast) and an ending (salvation); its first word, "rien," is both etymologically something (from Latin *rem*) and at the same time literally nothing. This poem uses its "landscape" to create the Muses (plural, for Mallarmé is toasting many poets here, and each needs a Muse) as the string of bubbles in the champagne glass evokes the trace left by a disappearing troupe of sirens (the elusive supernatural females) on the surface of the water. Their physical position, "mainte à l'envers" (many a one upside down), serves as an icon of how Mallarmé has literally stood on its head the sequence (1) inspiration and (2) poem. And the last line, "Le blanc souci de notre toile" (p. 27: The white concern of our sail) finally reveals the confrontation of the poet and the blank page (here presented as a sail "swelled" by the breath of inspiration) as the point of departure. But from the first word, "Salut," a fully accomplished speech act has already been represented.

Finally, Mallarmé juxtaposes the exhibition of his own hypercreativity with the announcement of sterility (the absence of the Muse) by verbal repetitions and echoes that simultaneously depict emptiness (only something hollow can resonate) and plenitude (he demonstrates the power to spin out more words at will). The fourfold exclamation "L'azur!" at the end of the poem of that name is the most obvious example, but elsewhere often enough an echo will accompany the notation of silence and absence:

> ... Que vêt parmi l'ex*il* inut*ile le* Cygne [p. 68]
> Le *flanc enfant* d'une sirène [p. 76]
> Triste*ment dort* une *mandore* [p. 74]

(... That amid his futile exile the Swan dons. / The childlike hip of a siren. / Sadly sleeps a mandorla [an archaic musical stringed instrument] with [its] hollow music-making void.)

And of course in the sonnet "Le vierge, le vivace, et le bel aujourd'hui" (built on rhymes that share only one vowel sound among them) a sequence of key words in the quatrains describing the impossibility of taking flight (in verse) ironically contains embeddings of inspiration itself in its Dionysian aspect: "*ivre* ... *givre* ... se dé*livre* [the second syllable as a whole, of course, presents the product of inspiration, the book] ... *vivre*" (pp. 67–68: intoxicated, frost, frees itself, to live).

The hyper-rich rhymes of the ironically titled "Prose pour des Esseintes" are an extreme example of the contrast between the regularity of repeated sounds and the formlessness of inexpressibility. This relatively long poem contains exceptional accumulations of phonemic equivalences, not only in the rhymes but also in the recurrence of sounds in key words, such as the "plri/iprl" echo in "Hyperbole" at the beginning of the poem and "Pulchérie" at the end. (The etymologies of these words connote aspects of the poetic venture: "hyperbole," a casting beyond, suggests the venture of the mind ranging beyond its own confines; "pulchérie," from Latin "pulcher," evokes the trace or impression of beauty remaining behind to attest to the poetic venture.) As Malcolm Bowie has pointed out, the "prl" sounds recur together on fourteen other occasions (notably, in "spirituel"), and elsewhere assonance and homophony are used extensively.[28] As in the examples just cited from other poems, sounds echo with particular density at the moments when verbal expression appears most inadequate:

> Oh! *sache l'esprit de litige*
> A *cette* heure *où nous nous taisons,*
> Que *de lis* mu*lti*ples *la tige*
> G*randissait trop pour nos raisons.* [p. 56]

(Oh! disputatious minds should know / In this hour when we keep silence, / That the stems of a multitude of lilies / grew too much for our reason[s].)

It is impossible to render justice to the complexity of this sonic network without a long and tedious description that would enumerate the four *r*'s of line 4 and the *s*'s in the second syllables of lines 1 and 2 and in the third syllables of lines 3 and 4, and so forth. The point is that the closer language comes to reproducing cosmic order through the interplay of its own repetitions, the more it loses its particularity and fades into a homophonic blur, suggested for example by the threefold vowel echo "*Anastase*" in the one word spoken by the Muse figure in this poem. The materiality of the word, as phoneme and grapheme, simultaneously supports and undermines its claim to serve as an instrument of transcendence. Thus Mallarmé mimes his lucid, hopeless

---

28. Malcolm Bowie, *Mallarmé and the Art of Being Difficult* (Cambridge: Cambridge University Press, 1978), pp. 25–89, esp. 54–71. Kristeva gives a richly detailed phonemic analysis of "Prose pour des Esseintes" in *Révolution du langage poétique*, pp. 239–63.

aspirations. And on the explicit, thematic level, in the two places where the poet seems most ardently to proclaim the ideal, he also most forcefully denies the usefulness of words in attaining it (i.e., in stanza 6, line 4, and stanza 10, line 2).[29]

In "Prose pour des Esseintes" the poet strolls with his female companion through a magical landscape, comparing its enchantments to hers (stanza 3). What seems at first like an act of insipid gallantry actually functions more profoundly, to reverse the direction of inspiration so that it will fail to find a voice. Instead of serving as a catalyst that releases the verbal flux of the poet's landscape, the Muse operates as a sort of black hole into which all the attributes of that landscape are drawn and absorbed by comparison with her. The next four stanzas repeatedly stress the unbridgeable gulf between the natural spectacle and words: the poet and his Muse contemplate it with a "double / Inconscience" (a twofold lack of awareness); the site "ne porte pas de nom" (bears no name); the flowers swell "sans que nous en devisions" (without our chatting about them); and each flower (vision) is separated from the garden (its setting) by a luminous outline. The poet's companion smiles enigmatically, declining even to look at the same vision the poet sees, no matter how exalted he becomes (stanza 9). In other words, she remains intact and autonomous, rather than serve as a womblike vehicle where the poet's imaginings may be made flesh. Only when she emerges from her own ecstasy at the end of the poem does she utter a word that signifies resurrection and eternity, and even then it is only after the poet has specified clearly that her *énoncé* has no referent: "ce pays n'exista pas" (that land did not exist). Thus she expresses the principle of inspiration, but without any limiting and tangible content. Such content, like the flowers grown too large to be dealt with by discursive reason, would, by eliminating possibilities, itself become a letter that killed (the "trop grand glaïeul," the last word in the poem, literally means "gladiolus" but is derived from *gladius*, "sword") rather than the spirit that gives life.[30] As Mallarmé announced in his essay on *Hamlet* the following year (1886; p. 300), "il n'est point d'autre sujet, sachez bien: l'antagonisme de [*sic*] rêve chez l'homme avec les fatalités à son existence départies par le malheur" (there is no other subject, know this well: the antagonism

29. Bowie, *Mallarmé and the Art of Being Difficult*, p. 27.

30. Marshall Olds provides a good, thorough reading of this poem in *Desire Seeking Expression: Mallarmé's "Prose pour des Esseintes"* (Lexington, Ky.: French Forum, 1983).

of dream in humanity with the inexorable facts misfortune has distributed to our existence [in other words, the ultimate fact of cosmic irony]). The universe was not designed to respond to our hopes and desires, including those of capturing it in words. Here Mallarmé's thought has changed little from 1864, when he said in *Symphonie littéraire* that no verbal expression could be adequate for Beauty, only silence (p. 262).

In the famous sonnets "Surgi de la croupe et du bond" and "Une dentelle s'abolit," the possibility of communion between male and female principles, between poet and Muse, is negated. The second quatrain of "Surgi de la croupe" appears to be a prosopopoeia spoken by some undefined spirit of the air:

> Je crois bien que deux bouches n'ont
> Bu, ni son amant ni ma mère,
> Jamais à la même Chimère,
> Moi, sylphe de ce noir plafond! [p. 74]

(I surely believe that no two mouths, / Neither her lover's nor my mother's, / Have ever drunk from the same Chimera, / I the sylph of this dark ceiling!)

From "amant" to "Moi" the phantom of the absent, unfulfilled lips has been ironically evoked by the presence of eight *m*'s in thirteen syllables. Not only does one pronounce these sounds by bringing the lips together and protruding them slightly as in kissing or drinking from a fountain (the major organ of articulation here reduplicates that implied by the phrase "deux bouches") but the two rounded open loops of the letter *m* themselves suggest the two lips drawn in profile. Mallarmé stressed the symbolism of letters in his idiosyncratic textbook *Les Mots anglais*. Of *M* he observes: "M traduit le pouvoir de faire, donc la joie, mâle et maternelle; puis, selon une signification venue de très loin dans le passé . . . la rencontre, la fusion" (p. 960: *M* translates the power to do, therefore joy, both male and maternal; then, according to a meaning derived from a very distant past . . . a meeting, a fusion). The context of darkness and the transparent, fragile glass vase near the ceiling which never holds a liquid suggests that the sylph is not one of the mythological figures commonly painted on ceilings at the time but rather the globe of a candelabra that refuses to give birth to a flower = candle flame. Such a flame itself commonly betokens inspiration, which, the sylph laments, has never been shared by the Muse, his mother, and the poet who is her lover. He remains unconceived. "Une dentelle s'abolit" similarly discloses an absent bed and the overpowering light of the sun, which, as in "Don du Poëme," completely overwhelms the feeble, artificial human inspiration symbolized by the lamp. Only from the empty, sterile, and impossible womb formed by the resonance chamber of an archaic musical instrument could a true poet (serving here as a metonymic representation of his productions, the poems) possibly be born.

In other poems that Mallarmé wrote throughout most of his career, the Muse actively flees the poet. She withholds her siren song, averts her face, and plunges wordlessly back into the watery element whence she came, to be unborn. By describing her flight, the narrative line of such poems depicts not the realization of inspiration but rather the continual, inexorable retreat that makes inspiration less and less possible. In "L'Après-Midi d'un faune," for example, not only do the two nymphs who have been momentarily captured slip from the satyr's grasp, but neither the performance of music nor the recitation of verse can summon them back again. In "A la nue accablante tu," "Un coup de Dés," "Salut," and elsewhere, the Muse proves equally elusive.

In "Salut" (p. 27) the Muse figures are multiplied because we are in the presence of an entire banquet table full of poets, who each require one: "Telle loin se noie une troupe / De sirènes mainte à l'envers" (Such, far off, does a troupe of sirens drown itself, many a one upside down). We can detect a punning undertone, since "en vers" alludes to the lines of poetry where these supernatural females have indeed just been mentioned; the sirens' position, upside down as they dive, hints at the indecisive conclusion to the search for the inspiration that they embody. The quest concludes "en queue de poisson," a French idiom meaning "indeterminately," since the fishtail is the last visible part of the diving sirens. In this particular poem, of course, the speaker's contact with a sympathetic and comprehending audience of fellow-poets compensates for the absence of the Muse.

For all that, it is essential to insist that Mallarmé does not settle for the facile solution of a poetry of negation. When the void that engulfs his Muses closes upon itself, negation has gone full circle. It then forms itself into what Mallarmé often describes as an empty womb, by virtue of which the Muse is simultaneously present through synecdoche and absent through the metonymic dislocation of being unconceived. The empty womb is variously figured by the mirror, the empty vessel, the celestial illusion of the Big Dipper, the trough of a wave, or the oxymoronic "creux néant musicien."

As "Salut" shows, Mallarmé invoked the Muse nearly all his life, although in this late poem he does so in a playfully self-referential way. At the same time, however, he evolves away from this traditional figure of inspiration considered as separate from but somehow belonging to the poet. The paradigmatic form of his new, "Museless" poetry is the "Tombeau" or commemorative poem—for Gautier, Poe, Baudelaire, or Verlaine—in which the male poet replaces the female Muse as source of inspiration and, like her, has been erased and effaced by death. It is difficult to date Mallarmé's turn away from the personified Muse with precision, but one could speculate that it occurred during the winter of 1872–73, when "Toast funèbre" was conceived. In that poem, the agonized golden monster (the recollection of Gautier's resplendent career, combined with grief at his loss) is contained within Mallarmé's thoughts (symbolized by the empty glass he raises for a toast) just like the sirens of "Salut," rather than dramatized as external to the poet. Mallarmé even disclaims the hope of magically recalling Gautier's shade. If he could, the phantom would only obscure the deceased writer's glory, for "le splendide génie éternel n'a pas d'ombre" (glorious, undying genius casts no shadow), and imbue the surviving poets with a nostalgia that would distract them from their "ideal [1. intellectual; 2. pure] duty."[31]

The altered role of the Muse in Mallarmé's poetry of this time appears to reflect his growing self-confidence and sense of his range as a writer. Late in 1871, he left Sens and successfully established himself in Paris (a move whose cultural significance is indicated by a singularity of the French language, in which "province" is used to mean "not-Paris," with the implication that anywhere else is a kind of limbo.) Soon he was becoming friends with Manet, Zola, and other luminaries of culture. By 1874 he had founded, edited, and managed a fashionable magazine, La Dernière Mode. His contacts with London and his translations suggest that by the next year he had begun to acquire an international reputation as a writer. By then, when he was

31. For a rich, wide-ranging discussion of the symbolism of the imagination in Mallarmé, see James R. Lawler, "Mallarmé and the 'Monstre d'or,'" in The Language of French Symbolism (Princeton: Princeton University Press, 1969), pp. 3–20. Lawler chooses "Toast funèbre" as his point of departure.

still only thirty-three, Mallarmé's mature prose style was formed,[32] and he had proven his competence in several fields of literary endeavor.

A pivotal moment reflecting the changed role of the Muse in Mallarmé's poetic practice occurs in the sonnet "Sur les bois oubliés" dated November 2, 1877.[33] Here the Muse *asks* for inspiration instead of granting it: "Pour revivre il suffit qu'à tes lèvres j'emprunte / Le souffle de mon nom murmuré tout un soir" (p. 69: To live again I need only borrow from your lips / The breath of my name murmured throughout the evening). Writing this poem to console a recent widower on the day after "le Jour des morts" (the French equivalent of All Saints' Day), Mallarmé dictates this speech to the man's deceased wife. The quotation marks surrounding the poem reveal its ventriloquistic character. The poet rather than a Muse becomes the ostensible source of the words. And the order in which the attributes of the departed person are evoked—"mon Ombre . . . mon doigt . . . mon nom"—once again reverses the conventional order of inspiration (pretext) and poem. The presence of the female ghost (i.e., of the supernatural female) is followed by her agency (she raises the lid of her coffin with her finger so that she can emerge from it to visit her husband) and then by the thought of her ("my name"). So the cause of the poem, remembrance of the dead, comes last; its effect, her virtual presence, precedes. The palindrome "mon nom" and the phonic echo "mur/mure" further reveal this text as a self-reflexive drama where the poet has overtly assumed the power and the functions of the Muse.

One of the richest sources for studying this new mode of expression dramatized as emanating not from the Muse but from the poet is found in the 202 fragments editorially titled "Pour un tombeau d'Anatole" (dating, presumably, from 1879).[34] Anatole, Mallarmé's only son, was born in 1871. At seven he fell seriously ill with rheumatic

32. See Norman Paxton, *The Development of Mallarmé's Prose Style* (Geneva: Droz, 1968), pp. 50, 56, and passim.

33. In the details of the discussion that follows, I rely heavily on Ross Chambers's fine "Parole et poésie: 'Sur les bois oubliés . . .' de Mallarmé," *Poétique*, 37 (1979), 56–62.

34. Mallarmé, *Pour un tombeau d'Anatole*, ed. Jean-Pierre Richard (Paris: Seuil, 1961); for an English translation together with the French original, see Paul Auster, *A Tomb for Anatole* (San Francisco: North Point Press, 1983). In the following discussion the numbers in parentheses refer to the editorial numbers of the fragments so that the reader can easily use either of the two editions cited here.

fever, and after half a year's painful illness he died. To commemorate
him, Mallarmé began sketching an ambitious poem.

In this work there is no mythified Muse to provide inspiration.
Mallarmé instead presents the contact between male and female principles, and the resulting creation of a child, as a given from the outset:
"enfant sorti de nous deux—nous montrant notre idéal, le chemin"
(1: a child who emerged from both of us, showing us our ideal, the
way). Here it is not the female Other as Muse who refuses to offer
anything to the poet but the poet and Muse together who decide to
"be silent": "père et mère se promettant de n'avoir pas d'autre enfant"
(17: father and mother promising each other to have no other child).
This child has been forced back into the womb of death (5) but did
emerge from it for a time, leaving a trace. Thus—ill in the spring and
dead in the fall—he has followed the trajectory of the solar hero whom
Mallarmé found at the core of all myths (3); a wave carried him off
(183); thus he has been assimilated to the natural cycle and has associated the poet with it. His sickness placed him simultaneously in a
state of being and of non-being (2). On this occasion, Mallarmé had
to face the natural cycle and the vanishing of life intimately and
directly; he could not simply contemplate such a confrontation as an
abstraction. He is proud that the progress of civilization—faith in
which he again seems to recapture—has internalized the desire for
immortality instead of projecting it on externality in the primitive
forms of mummification and monuments; "egypte [sic] ancienne—
embaumements . . . cryptes—tout ce changement jadis barbare et ma-
tériel extérieur—maintenant moral et en nous" (27–28: Ancient
Egypt, embalmings . . . crypts, all this change, formerly barbarous, material, external; today moral and within us).

The triumph of the mental life in this series of sketches (unlike,
say, "Don du Poëme," where the imaginative product appears pitifully
inadequate in the face of real existence) means that the poet can will
to reunite himself with his lost child through words: "ce mot—qui
nous confond tous deux—nous unit enfin" (26: this word, which
blends us together, unites us at last). The child will not die until the
poet who thinks of him has died. Memories of the survivors constitute
a "tribut vivifiant pour lui" (114: a vivifying tribute to him). Our
thoughts make him live: "nous lui rendons vie / en nous faisant pen-
seur" (119: we restore him to life by making ourselves into thinkers).
The poet can know, can reflect on, death for his child, who was too

young to understand it, and can therefore preserve the child's memory: "trop enfant pour de telles choses / je le *sais,* c'est en cela que *son être* est perpétué" (36: too much a child for such things; I *know,* it is in that that *his being* is perpetuated). We recall the faun's unrealizable wish to "perpetuate" the nymphs through thought; to seek them again he must take refuge in the dream (involuntary thought) rather than continue the futile search in the domain of art (voluntary thought). Here, in contrast, Mallarmé not only can recapture Anatole through voluntary thought but can perhaps improve on him as well: "transmuer en esprit pur?" (188: transmute into pure spirit?); "Que ma pensée lui fasse une vie plus belle plus pure" (191: Let my thought make him a life more beautiful, more pure).

Paradoxically, this poem describing the omnipotence of thought (in the domain of thought), a quasi-Orphic affirmation, never was finished, whereas the poems concerning the erasure of inspiration were sufficiently inspired for Mallarmé to complete them. He wrote several other "Tombeaux" successfully; that "Pour un tombeau d'Anatole" remained incomplete suggests that Mallarmé did not want closure, for it would have symbolically killed the lost child, locking him into a rigid system of words. Moreover, in this poem he realizes more clearly than he had in "Sur les bois oubliés," written two years earlier, that inspiration is not everything: it cannot bring the dead to life or ensure happiness.

The great importance of the supreme work, "Un coup de Dés jamais n'abolira le Hasard," which concluded Mallarmé's career, is that it shows rather than tells the vanity of "inspiration," of depending passively on the visitation of something from outside the self. Mallarmé's experiments with typography in this poem not only make one aware of virtual space but also emphasize by contrast the blank page, which provides the background for these experiments. The white space represents ultimate nothingness, against which the traceries of our illusions—or their residue in the form of printed words on a page—are projected.

Mallarmé had experimented with varying his graphemes even when he was in secondary school. Thereafter, his continuing interest in typography is manifested in various ways throughout his mature work: he frequently mentioned spatial form in his essays; he used italics to distinguish remembered dream from waking reality in "L'Après-Midi d'un faune"; and he meditated on the type styling for "Hérodiade." The heightened sensitivity to spatial form in "Un coup de Dés" appears to have derived from two main sources: Mallarmé's discovery of ballet, around 1885–86, and, about the same time, his negative reaction to what he saw as the blindly adulatory French response to Wagner.[35] In the essay "Ballets" (1886), Mallarmé saw the movements of the dancer as reflecting the ideal dance of the constellations. The dancer combines inspiration and expression; she is not a woman who dances but pure suggestive poetry writing itself without words or scribe (pp. 303, 309, 304). By replacing an art of time—literature—with an art of space, Mallarmé discovers a forum where relationships can be instantly perceived. Theater per se he finds too coarse, and music alone too vague (p. 335). Wagner's revival of primitive legends is too concrete, Mallarmé believes, and the example of his art has taken us only halfway up the sacred mountain of the Muses (whose summit we never may reach).[36] By 1895, in a radical change of attitude, Mallarmé had come to believe that everything contained the potential for generating inspiration—"tout, au monde, existe pour aboutir à un livre" (everything, in the world, exists to end up as a book)—and that the supreme Book would be achieved by a "total expansion" of the letter in space.[37] In other words, inspiration now comes from within. Projected outward by the poet's mind, it imposes order on externality, as Orpheus' music imposed order on stones and savage beasts.

To realize this ideal in "Un coup de Dés" and to free his text from the binding sequential constraints of syntax, Mallarmé devised multiple ambiguities of word arrangement, capitalization, and syntax, while suppressing punctuation. (He had already used this last procedure in earlier poems, creating a number of "two-way" lines linkable either to what precedes or to what follows in the text.) Thus the reader is obliged to become the organizer of the text, to become imaginatively involved. Mallarmé's indeterminacy, that is, has a didactic function: "The author disappears from the text; he figuratively and literally vacates the print. There is no argument, no point of view, no opinion to accept or reject, no message to be decoded, no experience to share, and no exchange to enjoy.... The text is a fiction, it cannot be experienced or enacted, only its reading is reality." One can read it

35. For Mallarmé's discovery of the ballet, see Paxton, *Development of Mallarmé's Prose Style*, p. 99.
36. Stéphane Mallarmé, "Richard Wagner: Rêverie d'un poëte français" (July 1885), *OC*, pp. 544–46.
37. "Le Livre, instrument spirituel," *OC*, pp. 378–80.

starting at any point; forward or backward; by signatures, rectos, or versos.[38] As the poet must project significance upon the blank screen of phenomena—if only the awareness that there is no significance— the reader must project significance onto the blank screen of the poem, thus participating in the poet's existential dilemma of the permanent, irremediable loss of a transcendent inspiration by taking responsibility for being himself the source of inspiration.

So the question is how to survive without an external Muse, how to function as an artist without relying on infusions of meaning from a transcendent exterior source. In an important commentary on Mallarmé's note "Mimique" (p. 310 [1886]) on the pantomime "Pierrot assassin de sa femme," Jacques Derrida points out that in this text Mallarmé conceives an art free from origins, from an external impetus: "The Mime imitates nothing. And to begin with, he doesn't imitate. There is nothing prior to the writing of his gestures. Nothing is prescribed for him. No present has preceded or supervised the tracing of his writing. His movements form a figure that no speech anticipates or accompanies. They are not linked with *logos* in any order of consequence."[39] Similarly, we could add, the only *event* of "Un coup de Dés" is the hypothetical gesture of casting forth, after which, as Mallarmé specifies, "nothing will have taken place except the place" (where the gesture occurred), and this place itself is an undifferentiated chaos.

---

38. Virginia La Charité, *The Dynamics of Space: Mallarmé's "Un coup de Dés jamais n'abolira le Hasard"* (Lexington, Ky.: French Forum, 1987), pp. 20, 27, 29, 45–46, 105– 6, and 166. Citations are from pp. 106 and 166. Pp. 156–75 contain an informed discussion of the various aleatory readings possible for this poem, which strikingly recall Pierre Boulez's flexible instructions to his performers. On this poem see also the magisterial readings by Robert Greer Cohn, *Toward the Poems of Mallarmé*, and by Gardner Davies, *Mallarmé et le rêve d'"Hérodiade."* A useful review of the recent criticism on this poem appears in Bonnie J. Isaac, "'Du fond d'un naufrage': Notes on Michel Serres and Mallarmé's 'Un Coup de dés,'" in Bloom, *Stéphane Mallarmé*, pp. 167–83.

The expansion of the letter in space goes beyond the creation of a quasi-symphonic score in "Un coup de Dés": during Mallarmé's last years he demythologized the white page (still bound to the notion of inspiration because it inevitably suggests its absence) by inscribing poetry on previously used or utilitarian surfaces, or both. He wrote verses on fans, candy wrappers, and jugs of calvados, and as addresses on letters to his friends. The addresses, in octosyllabic quatrain form, were collected in an 1894 chapbook edition and are today known as *Les Loisirs de la poste*. For reliable texts of the occasional verse see Barbier's edition of the *Poésies*, cited in n. 5, above. Marian Sugano is examining this topic in an interesting work in progress. See also the luminous article by Ross Chambers, "An Address in the Country: Mallarmé and the Kinds of Literary Context," *French Forum*, 11 (May 1986), 199–215, esp. 199–201.

39. Derrida, *Dissemination*, pp. 194–95.

To privilege a certain site would be to hypostatize, through metonymic and often through metaphoric connection as well, the phenomenon that occurs there. Christ may be born only of a virgin. The
poem connected to an ideal meaning can be conceived only on the
white page. To play spatially on the page's surface—and even more
to replace it with other and "profane" surfaces such as envelopes,
fans, and gift wrappings, as Mallarmé did in his last years—is to
promote the poetic gesture to priority over its supposed origin, which
withers away like the stump of an umbilical cord. For Mallarmé (who
lost his mother at age five and his beloved sister at age fifteen) as for
most of us, the primordial sacred surface is the dream-screen, the
blurry expanse of the nursing mother's breast filling the sated infant's
field of vision as it falls asleep.[40] To break free of the hypnotic fascination of this subliminal surface is finally to become one's own imaginative origin, which each successive gesture perpetually renews.

40. See Henri Vermorel, "Les Chemins de la création dans l'oeuvre de Stéphane
Mallarmé," *Revue française de psychanalyse*, 44 (1980), 59–97, updating Charles Mauron,
Des métaphores obsédantes au mythe personnel (Paris: Corti, 1963); and Bertram D. Lewin's
pioneering "Sleep, the Mouth, and the Dream Screen," *Psychoanalytic Quarterly*, 15
(1946), 419–34. See also his "Inferences from the Dream Screen," *International Journal
of Psycho-analysis*, 29 (1948), 224–31.

Chapter 3 ⸺⸺⸺⸺⸺⸺⸺⸺⸺⸺⸺⸺⸺

Verlaine's Subversion of Language

Verlaine has been neglected in recent years. The brevity of his poems; their songlike, informal diction; their paucity of metaphor and allusion; and their lack of those intellectual themes that are commonly held to characterize true "Symbolism"—from the beginning, all these features have tempted critics to judge his verse agreeable but minor. His alcoholism and the poetic decline of his final fifteen years, which he spent as a sodden derelict, have reinforced the trend to slight or to dismiss his work. Until recently even critics who have looked closely at his poems have tended to obscure our sense of the evolution of Verlaine's poetry by treating it in terms of what they perceive to be general, overarching tendencies such as "fadeur" (insipidity) or "naiveté,"[1] to say nothing of the all too familiar "musicality." A fine recent collection of French essays is disparagingly titled *La Petite Musique de Verlaine*.[2] Once one has described Verlaine's "music" by counting syllables and noting repetitions of sounds, there seems to be little more to say.[3] Like Lamartine, he has been damned with faint praise.

1. See James Lawler, *The Language of French Symbolism* (Princeton: Princeton University Press, 1969), chap. 2, "Verlaine's 'Naiveté,'" pp. 21–70; and Jean-Pierre Richard, *Poésie et profondeur* (Paris: Seuil, 1955), "Fadeur de Verlaine," pp. 165–85.

2. *La Petite Musique de Verlaine* (Paris: SEDES [for the Société des Etudes Romantiques], 1982).

3. For more sophisticated studies of Verlaine's "musicality," however, see Nicolas Ruwet, "Blancs, rimes, et raisons: Typographie, rimes, et structures linguistiques en poésie," *Revue d'esthéthique*, 1/2 (1979), 397–426; and Eléonore M. Zimmermann, *Magies*

If one seriously addresses the question of Verlaine's musicality, it seems intuitively obvious that repetition and regularity are more "musical" than their absence. In actual music composed before the modern era, a high percentage of the measures occur more than once—only one-third or one-quarter of the total may be different—whereas in a literary work few if any sentences are repeated. Zola need use the same sentence only half a dozen times in a long novel such as *La Bête humaine* before critics start comparing it to a Wagnerian leitmotif. A modest amount of repetition in literature, then, has the same effect as the considerable amount of repetition in music. The phrases that echo frequently in a poem such as Verlaine's "Soleils couchants" attract all the more attention because they do not belong to a conventional pattern of recurrence in a fixed form such as the rondeau or the ballade.

No one, however, has yet done a statistical study to determine whether Verlaine deploys obvious forms of repetition—rich rhyme, internal rhyme, anaphora, epiphora, refrains, reduplication of single words, alliteration, and assonance—more frequently than less "musical" poets. Baudelaire and Mallarmé, in fact, seem to use more rich rhymes than does Verlaine; Baudelaire more often repeats lines. Nor has anyone done an empirical study to determine whether poems identified as "musical" by naive and by sophisticated audiences actually contain more repetitive devices than do other poems. No one, in short, has rigorously characterized "musicality" in language in linguistic terms. And no one who wishes to ascribe "musicality" to the verse of Verlaine and the other Symbolists has come to terms with the fact that all these poets were lamentably illiterate and incompetent as composers, as performers, and even as passive listeners to music.[4] While awaiting the outcome of the empirical and statistical studies of the future, we can best treat the problem of literary "musicality" by recognizing that "musicality" serves merely as a metaphor for the relative prominence of phonemic and verbal repetition; for allusions to, evocations of, and descriptions of things musical; for the foregrounding of

---

de Verlaine: Etude de l'évolution poétique de Paul Verlaine (Paris: Corti, 1967), pp. 11, 20–27, 65, and passim. A detailed data base for such studies has recently been provided by Frédéric S. Eigeldinger, Dominique Godet, and Eric Wehrli, comps., *Table de concordances rythmique et syntaxique des Poésies de Paul Verlaine: "Poèmes saturniens," "Fêtes galantes," "La Bonne Chanson," "Romances sans paroles"* (Geneva: Slatkine, 1985).

4. Henri Peyre, "Poets against Music in the Age of Symbolism," in Marcel Tetel, ed., *Symbolism and Modern Literature: Studies in Honor of Wallace Fowlie* (Durham, N.C.: Duke University Press, 1978), pp. 179–92.

rhythm, which is the essence of music; for vagueness of denotation; and for the suppression of overt narrative progression. (These last two traits often figure together in descriptions of that critical artifact called "literary impressionism.") Taken all together, these features do not help to distinguish Verlaine's poetry from that of many of his contemporaries.

One can obtain a more fruitful definition of Verlaine's "musicality" by observing what I consider to be a primary rule in literary criticism: once you have singled out a certain motif or a feature for analysis, seek its polar opposite. It is not the motif of "musicality" alone but the structure formed by thesis (here, "musicality"), antithesis (whatever for Verlaine may seem opposed to "musicality"), and the relationship between them which characterizes the creative individuality of the poet. This structure defines his imagination (in linguistic terms, his poetic "competence") and its expression (in linguistic terms, his poetic "performance") in a way that one isolated element such as "musicality," shared by many poets, could not possibly do.

Mistrusting the act of communication, each of the major French Symbolist poets focuses his principal suspicion on one particular, discrete point along the axis of communication. What Verlaine's good early verse does is to call into question the signifying capacities of the verbal medium itself. He fears lest the very ground of his utterances be meaningless or at least vitiated by the way it is ordinarily treated. The problem is not merely that he finds words inadequate to treat transcendent subjects (Mallarmé's difficulty) but rather that he finds words unreliable, period. Since he still wishes to write poetry, he has no recourse other than to exalt the "je ne sais quoi," the "imprécis," and to expatiate upon the topos of inexpressibility.

Antoine Adam, a noted critic of Verlaine, does not take the poet's antilinguistic stance too seriously. He invokes the testimony of Edmond Lepelletier, who saw Verlaine daily at the time of his early publications and claimed that lyrical expressions of love and sadness in the *Poèmes saturniens* and the *Fêtes galantes* were mere poses in a person interested primarily in dogmatic poetics. He cites two lines from "Aspiration" (1861) to suggest that the critique of love language in ensuing collections may derive as much from misogyny as mistrust of communication: "Loin de tout ce qui vit, loin des hommes, encor / Plus loin des femmes" (p. 15: Far from all that lives, far from men, and yet / Farther from women). Referring specifically to the *Fêtes galantes*, Adam claims: "This poetry of an all-embracing melancholy dimension is, however, meant to be a game.... The poet amuses himself.... Baudelaire's sober doctrine [in Verlaine's "A Clymène"] becomes a pretext for subtle combinations of hues and fragrances. The enjambments that set off the ironical charge of a phrase, and the rhymes—profuse, unusual, employed in a hundred original ways—these are part of the fun."[5]

But in an interpretation similar to my own, Jacques-Henry Bornecque, who studied this crucial collection in much more detail, maintains that it traces a sequence of moods declining toward pessimism and despair. Verlaine contaminates with his own sadness the playful Regency world (1715–23) into which he had hoped to escape. His other writings of the same period include many macabre pieces that express his disgust with his contemporaries. Bornecque observes, "In those verse or prose pieces that are not 'fêtes galantes,' Verlaine does not disguise his feelings: he gives free rein to his peevishness as to his anguish, regularly and obviously swinging between aggressive bitterness and the despairing detachment which is the ebb tide of the former."[6] He cites many examples, notably the sinister short story "Le Poteau," which reveals a certain affinity with Baudelaire's "Vin de l'assassin." The death of Verlaine's beloved Elisa Moncomble four days before the composition of the first two "Fêtes galantes" seems decisive. Bornecque characterizes the collection as the work of a convalescent—a convalescent, one could add, with nothing to live for.

Sensitive though he is to Verlaine's moods, Bornecque overlooks the poet's mistrust of language, so characteristic of the Symbolist crisis. Unlike the other major French Symbolist poets, Verlaine focuses this mistrust on the linguistic medium itself, instead of on the acts of conceiving and communicating a message. He subverts the notion of the essential "humanness" of language by playfully (and of course figuratively) replacing human speakers with nonhuman ones. And by making utterances flatly contradict the situations to which they refer, Verlaine challenges our assumption that language provides reliable information. Many instances can be found in the prose works, particularly the *Mémoires d'un veuf*. There "Bons bourgeois" describes a family quarrel: after an exchange of insults, "la parole est à la vaisselle

5. See Antoine Adam, *The Art of Paul Verlaine* (New York: New York University Press, 1963), pp. 63, 70, and 84.
6. See Jacques-Henry Bornecque, *Lumières sur les "Fêtes galantes" de Paul Verlaine* (Paris: Nizet, 1959), pp. 50–59, 76–89, 97–103, and 109–10. This quotation appears on p. 50.

maintenant" (now the crockery [which the family members start throwing at each other] does the talking). Afterward the lady of the house excuses herself to her visiting country relative by saying "CELA N'ARRIVE JAMAIS" (that never happens). "Ma Fille" cancels its own language when after an idealized description the narrator announces, "Heureusement qu'elle n'a jamais existé et ne naîtra probablement plus!" (Fortunately she never lived and probably will not be born in the future!). In another story, Pierre Duchâtelet has a conversation with his wife in which he lies to conceal his imminent departure for a ten-day mission to a battle zone; on his return he finds a letter saying simply, "Monsieur—Adieu pour toujours" (Sir: Farewell forever). And if we read allegorically, considering the hand as the writer's instrument (cf. George Sand's "L'Orgue du Titan"), we could even say that artistic self-expression destroys its subject and is itself doomed to a sudden death. Such an interpretation illuminates Verlaine's tale "La Main du Major Muller" (from *Histoires comme ça*), where the preserved hand that had to be amputated after a duel comes to life, poisons its owner, and then quickly rots.

The most compelling corroborative evidence for Verlaine's dour linguistic self-consciousness, however, comes from the master article of all his literary criticism (and one that should be much better known): his response to another great Symbolist poet, Baudelaire. This piece appeared in the November 16, 1865, issue of *L'Art*. Of three individual lines cited as models, two treat nonverbal communication: "Le regard singulier d'une femme galante" (the odd glance of a promiscuous woman) and "Un soir l'âme du vin chantait dans les bouteilles" (One evening the soul of the wine was singing inside the bottles). From the five wine poems, in other words, the one line that Verlaine cites is one that gives a voice to a nonhuman entity. And from the "Tableaux parisiens" section, likewise, Verlaine singles out this passage:

> Et, voisin des clochers, écouter en rêvant
> Leurs hymnes solennels emportés par le vent
> . . . .
> Je verrai l'atelier qui chante et qui bavarde.

(And, next to the bell towers, to listen dreamily / To their solemn hymns carried off by the wind / . . . / I shall see the workshop singing and chattering.)

After beginning the essay with the declaration that "le public est un enfant mal élevé qu'il s'agit de corriger" (the public is a badly brought up child: you have to chastise it), Verlaine gives as examples of appropriate behaviors instances of silencing: the poem "Semper eadem" with its repeated "Taisez-vous!" (Quiet!) and elsewhere the command to the beloved, "Sois charmante, et tais-toi" (Be charming, and be still). Far more is at stake here than mere playfulness.[7]

Whereas narrative and drama represent what is meaningful to at least several people or to a collective culture, the lyric represents what is meaningful to only one person. Poetry is half a conversation, a soliloquy or apostrophe to a being that is nonhuman, absent, or dead, and therefore incapable of responding in words. When we say "Rose, thou art sick," we don't expect an answer. In those instances where the interlocutor is not suppressed, poetry becomes "dramatic lyric" that shades into theater. In the lyric situation, where the single speaking voice is the norm, Verlaine sometimes imposes one of two marked choices. Either he uses free direct discourse—a conversation that does not identify the speakers—to multiply the sources of meaningfulness to the point where each interferes with the other and they blur; or else he introduces nonverbal elements so as to subvert meaningfulness at its source; or he does both at once, as in the paradigmatic "Sur l'herbe" of the *Fêtes galantes*.

When Verlaine does depict the normal one-sided conversation, he undermines its meaningfulness as much as he can without sacrificing coherence. He tries to express his radical skepticism regarding the power of words to signify by undermining their status and seeming to replace them with something else. For him this something else is musicality: not a flight into a balmy vagueness, but the cutting edge of his satiric attack on the verbal ground of our relationships. By using uncommon "rythmes impairs" (five-, seven-, nine-, eleven-, or thirteen-syllable lines) instead of the octosyllables, decasyllables, or alexandrines that were to dominate French poetry through the 1920s, Verlaine again makes a "marked choice"; he selects a form of expression that violates our expectations through the absence or the excess of a certain quality. He foregrounds the supreme musicality of rhythm at the expense of the other elements of poetry. Since the essence of music lies in rhythm more than in melody, harmony, intensity, or

7. See Paul Verlaine, *Oeuvres en prose complètes*, ed. Jacques Borel (Paris: Gallimard, 1972), pp. 77–79, 82, 57, 154–61, and 599–612.

timbre, a poetry that calls attention to its rhythm makes that element a rival of the verbal poetry rather than its adjunct. Similarly, from the *Fêtes galantes* on, internal rhyme and assonance become more common in Verlaine's poetry, constituting a marked choice of sound repetition in excess of what one would ordinarily expect and thus suggesting, once again, an antiverbal musicality. More obviously, of course, words seem to become ancillary in Verlaine's texts when he uses them to denote, connote, or describe music and the visual arts.[8] He subverts language by using words to evoke indefinable states of vagueness and confusion; to designate situations in which the words themselves are trivial, insincere, or absurd; and to characterize acts whereby words cancel themselves or serve to impose silence. To produce a mere catalogue of such devices would be a facile and not very enlightening exercise. But as it happens, examining them in context can illuminate the structure of individual collections of verse and clarify the trajectory of Verlaine's entire career.

The section titled "Melancholia" in Verlaine's first collection of verse, the *Poèmes saturniens* (1867), presents the dilemma of the breakdown of signification thematically, by depicting the lyric self's nostalgia for a past time when love language was still meaningful. Distancing himself from his nostalgia in the last section of the *Poèmes saturniens*, the lyric self shifts to a parody of love language from "La Chanson des ingénues" on; such parody persists to the end of the *Fêtes galantes* (1869). As the historical Verlaine strives to return to a conventional life, *La Bonne Chanson* (1870) transiently adopts a conventional, affirmative poeticizing. The *Romances sans paroles* (1872) revert to undermining signification, but they show rather than tell. A supreme discursive *prise de conscience* affirming vagueness and musicality as the highest poetic goals appears in "L'Art poétique" of 1874 (published only when *Jadis et naguère* appeared in 1882). This statement itself, however, is subverted by verbal excess, for there is a fundamental paradox in specifying how to be allusive.

Verlaine's Symbolist crisis, then, as I would define it, lasted from 1866 to 1874. After his conversion in prison, he seems to have become dedicated to betraying his earlier self. He reverts to a wholly conventional prosodic practice and to a thematic questioning, typical of Romanticism, of the codes and contexts of traditional beliefs rather than

8. See the classic theoretical statement by Calvin S. Brown, *Music and Literature: A Comparison of the Arts* (Athens: University of Georgia Press, 1948).

a questioning of the efficacy of the communicative process itself. Some thirty-two poems from his earlier years, previously unpublished in collections, appear in the later collections (notably in *Jadis et naguère*, which contains twenty-seven of them) but without exception they lack the critical bite of those already published—the reason Verlaine had set them aside in the first place. A few pieces in *Parallèlement* (1889), composed probably between 1884 and 1889, again present a lyric self alienated from love and his own words and sinking into a preoccupation with mere physicality. But these poems appear superficial; they degenerate into self-parody; and they convey none of the fundamental questioning of signification characteristic of Verlaine's "Symbolist" period. Verlaine's 1890 article "Critique des *Poèmes saturniens*"[9] rejected everything he had written before *Sagesse* in 1881—in other words, nearly everything most critics still find important:

> L'âge mûr a, peut avoir ses revanches et l'art aussi, sur les enfantillages de la jeunesse, ses nobles revanches, traite des objets plus et mieux en rapport, religion, patrie, et la science, et soi-même bien considérée sous toutes formes, ce que j'appellerai de l'élégie sérieuse, en haine de ce mot, psychologie. Je m'y suis efforcé quant à moi et j'aurai laissé mon oeuvre personnelle en quatre parties bien définies, *Sagesse, Amour, Parallèlement*—et *Bonheur* [1891].... Puis, car n'allez pas prendre au pied de la lettre mon 'Art poétique' de *Jadis et Naguère*, qui n'est qu'une chanson, après tout,—JE N'AURAI PAS FAIT DE THEORIE. [pp. 1073–74]

(The age of maturity, and art as well, can take its revenge, its noble revenge, on the childishness of youth; it treats subjects closer and more appropriate to itself, religion, the fatherland, science, and itself examined carefully in every form, what I shall term the serious elegy, out of hatred for that word, psychology. As for me, I have striven to do so and I shall have left my personal work in four distinct parts, *Wisdom, Love, In Parallel*—and *Happiness*.... Moreover, for don't take literally my "Art of Poetry" in *Formerly and Not So Long Ago*, which is only a song, after all—I SHALL HAVE CREATED NO THEORIES.)

With that disclaimer, Verlaine's self-betrayal was consummated. It had begun with the distribution of a "prière d'insérer" (publicity flier) for

---

9. Paul Verlaine, "Critique des *Poèmes Saturniens*," *Revue d'Aujourd'hui*, 3 (March 15, 1890), reproduced in Verlaine, *Oeuvres poétiques complètes*, ed. Yves Le Dantec and Jacques Borel (Paris: Gallimard, 1962). Unless I have indicated otherwise, all subsequent references to Verlaine are from this edition and appear in the text, identified by page number only.

Sagesse in 1881, describing him as "sincèrement et franchement revenu aux sentiments de la foi la plus orthodoxe" (p. 1111: having sincerely and openly returned to the most orthodox sentiments of religious faith), including support of attempts to restore the monarchy.

Written from the time he was fourteen, Verlaine's earliest surviving poems reflect his admiration for the grandiosity of Victor Hugo. But from 1861 on (when he was seventeen) he initiates a thematic critique of poeticism in the manner of Musset and the late Romantics such as Corbière and Laforgue. "Fadaises" presents a series of conventional lover's homages in rhyming couplets (in French this sort of versification is called "rimes plates," "plates" also designating what is trite and inexpressive), with a surprise ending revealing that all of these compliments have been addressed to Lady Death.[10] The title ("Insipidities") already dismisses the import of the verses that follow; the *pointe* of the conclusion dismisses life itself: "Et le désir me talonne et me mord, / Car je vous aime, ô Madame la Mort!" (p. 16: And desire spurs me on and bites me, / For I love you, O Mistress Death!). To equate love with death is a typically Romantic gesture. If the title works in conjunction with this equation to undermine the conventionality of the earlier verses, then Verlaine has done little new. But if the title can be held to dismiss the concluding Romantic cliché, as well as those clichés that the Romantic cliché is dismissing (with the implied topos of *vanitas vanitatum*), then Verlaine's world-weariness extends to and contaminates the verbal medium itself. Whether it actually does so, however, we cannot tell for certain from the text alone. But in the context of Romantic practice this poem stands out because Romantic poems do not usually appear under titles that make their protests, as well as the targets of those protests, seem frivolous from the outset. They do not do so, that is, until the ironic poetry of Corbière and Laforgue.

Additional albeit equally ambiguous evidence that Verlaine early adopted a skeptical attitude toward Romanticism appears in the early poem that most specifically comments on poetic creation, the "Vers dorés" of 1866 (p. 22). There he claims that poetry should be impersonal: "maint poète / A trop étroits les reins ou les poumons trop gras" (many a poet / Has loins too narrow or lungs too fat); only those

---

10. In his informative edition of Verlaine's *Poésies* (Paris: Imprimerie Nationale, 1980), Jacques Décaudin refers to "Fadaises" as "an anticipatory 'Fête galante,' which capsizes in anguish and the death wish, a poem of loneliness and sadness" (p. 10).

who "se recueillent dans un égoïsme de marbre" (commune with themselves within an egoism of marble) are great. At first this statement seems simply to belong to the "second Romanticism" of Gautier or De Lisle, standing in opposition to the earlier belief that "Gefühl ist alles." But like the title of "Fadaises," the term "égoïsme" again renders suspect Verlaine's homage to the "Neoclassic Stoic."

After the prologue, the first section of the *Poèmes saturniens*, titled "Melancholia," expresses a nostalgic faith in the charms of past love: "Et qu'il bruit avec un murmure charmant / Le premier *oui* qui sort des lèvres bien-aimées!" ("Nevermore," p. 61: And how it rustles with a charming murmur / The first *yes* that leaves beloved lips!).[11] But this vision must not become too precise: in "Mon Rêve familier" the idealized woman speaks with the voice of the beloved dead "qui se sont tues" (who have fallen silent), but of her name the poet remembers only that it is "doux et sonore / Comme ceux des aimés que la vie exila" (p. 64: sweet and resonant / Like the names of loved ones whom life exiled). In the present time of narration, however—or more accurately, of lyricization—artistic self-consciousness begins to intrude. A poem such as "Lassitude," for example, seems initially only to echo the Baudelairean taste for the illusion of love when it asks the beloved: "fais-moi des serments que tu rompras demain" (make me promises that you will break tomorrow; see, e.g., Baudelaire's "L'Amour du mensonge"). But Baudelaire never really loses faith in art, and Verlaine does. His epigraph from Luis de Góngora, "a batallas de amor campos de pluma" (for battles of love, fields of feathers), suggests by juxtaposition that not only the content of professions of love but perhaps even their verbal vehicle is false. The double meaning of *pluma*, feathers for lying on or writing with, implies that the falsity of the beloved's specious assurances may extend to and contaminate the verbal medium itself, where the cradling regularity of the verses reflects the sensuous pleasure of the caresses that the woman lavishes

11. Décaudin, *Poésies*, sees the title of the first poem in the collection, "Votre âme est un paysage choisi," as a clue to the meaning of the entire collection: these are "paysages intérieurs" (p. 19). This observation is congruent with John Porter Houston's identification of the "mood poem" as Verlaine's greatest original creation (see below, n. 24). For a sprightly interpretation of the two poems titled "Nevermore" in the *Poèmes saturniens*, see Jefferson Humphries, *Metamorphoses of the Raven: Literary Overdeterminedness in France and in the South since Poe* (Baton Rouge: Louisiana State University Press, 1985), pp. 60–68. Humphries reads the second poem as "an allegory of its own inadequacy" (p. 67).

on the lyric self. Such a possibility, farfetched as it may initially seem, emerges blatantly in the poem "L'Angoisse" in the same section.

> Nature, rien de toi ne m'émeut, ni les champs
> Nourriciers, ni l'écho vermeil des pastorales
> Siciliennes, ni les pompes aurorales,
> Ni la solennité dolente des couchants.
>
> Je ris de l'Art, je ris de l'Homme aussi, des chants,
> Des vers, des temples grecs et des tours en spirales
> Qu'étirent dans le ciel vide les cathédrales,
> Et je vois du même oeil les bons et les méchants.
>
> Je ne crois pas en Dieu, j'abjure et je renie
> Toute pensée, et quant à la vieille ironie
> L'Amour, je voudrais bien qu'on ne m'en parlât plus.
>
> Lasse de vivre, ayant peur de mourir, pareille
> Au brick perdu jouet du flux et du reflux,
> Mon âme pour d'affreux naufrages appareille.   [p. 65]

(Nature, nothing in you moves me, neither the nurturant fields, / Nor the crimson echo of Sicilian pastorals, / nor the splendor of dawn, / Nor the plaintive ceremony of the sunsets. // I laugh at Art, I laugh at Man as well, at songs, / Poetry, Greek temples and the spiraling towers / That the cathedrals stretch forth into the sky, / And I see the virtuous and wicked as the same. // I don't believe in God, I abjure and forswear / All thought, and as for that old irony, / Love, I'd rather you not speak to me of it at all. // Wearied of living, afraid of dying, like / The lost brig, a plaything of the ocean's ebb and flow, / My soul is being rigged for fearsome shipwrecks.)

The poet rejects art, the very activity that defines him, and its products of music and verse. He surrenders himself to the rocking, delusive movement of the alexandrine verses like a lost ship. This "musicality," this hypnotic empty signifier, is reinforced by the pervasive additional regularity of verbal parallelisms. The first stanza is built around four successive clauses beginning in "ni"; the second begins by repeating "je ris de" and then lists four items each of which is preceded by "des"; the last verse of this stanza pairs "les bons et les méchants." The third stanza deploys a fourfold anaphora of "je" associated with what the poet abjures. More verbal parallels in lines 9 ("j'abjure et je renie"), 12 ("lasse de vivre, ayant peur de mourir"), and 13 ("du flux et du reflux")—the last with an internal rhyme—create a countercurrent of soothing regularity beneath the explicit textual meanings of the negation of nature, art, God, and love. Ultimately, of course, such denials and a passive yielding to rhythmic flux lead to the same thing: the ultimate disaster for which the lyric self prepares in the last line; the loss of a personal identity, which can be expressed and maintained only through words.

Generally, then, during the course of the "Melancholia" section of the *Poèmes saturniens* the poet affirms that words once had a transcendent meaning that they now have lost: they expressed the eternity of love (see "Le Rossignol," pp. 73–74). As "Lassitude" reveals, the poet prefers this willfully recreated illusion to the reality of sexual fulfillment in the present. But the illusion can be sustained not by specific words themselves but only by the *idea* of words, just as the name of the beloved in "Nevermore" can be preserved only as a general impression. Finally, in "L'Angoisse" the despairing poet will reject all talk about love—remembered, potential, or allusive—to surrender himself to the rocking rhythm of the hemistiches. Thus the self comes to be suspended between life and death, as it is more specifically in the concluding lines of "Chanson d'automne":

> Et je m'en vais
> Au vent mauvais
> Qui m'emporte
> Deçà, delà,
> Pareil à la
> Feuille morte.   [p. 73]

(And I go off / On the evil wind / That carries me / Here and there / Like the / Dead leaf.)

For the historical Verlaine, alcoholism achieved a similar compromise between suicide and survival, preserving him as much as possible in a blurry, dreamy swoon that did not threaten immediate self-annihilation but offered the one advantage of that state—relief from pain. Such a narcissistic retreat into the self effaces the disappointments of the exterior world. And the incursions of the other arts into Verlaine's poetry obscure the meretricious words with which one attempts to communicate with that world. Not only is this poetry opposed to commitment—expressing "l'amer à la bouteille" rather than "la bouteille à la mer"—it also is anti-impressionist. For real impressionism opens itself to sensory experience; it does not exploit such experience as a narcotic.

The following section of the *Poèmes saturniens*, titled "Eaux-fortes" (engravings), moves away from the verbal toward the visual. But at the same time the relative impersonality of these descriptive poems added to the frequent marked choice of "rythmes impairs" makes them more nearly "musical" than the ordinary poem, in a context that allows us to recognize such musicality as antiverbal. "Croquis parisien" has one five-syllable line amid three decasyllabic lines in each stanza; "Cauchemar" has lines of seven and three syllables; "Marine" has five-syllable lines. These are the first three of five poems in this section. When Verlaine returns to conventional versification in the last two, he preserves the titles that suggest works of visual art: "Effet de nuit" and "Grotesques." And as if to offset the return to rhythmical conventions, he treats subjects that make explicit his feelings of alienation: outcasts rejected by the elements and menaced with imminent death.

To the "musicality" of a marked choice of an unusual rhythm (pentasyllables again), the first of the "Paysages tristes," "Soleils couchants," adds the "musicality" of an exceptional amount of repetition. In sixteen lines there are only four rhymes—two in each group of eight lines. Line 3 is the same as line 5; 11 is the same as 16. The expression "soleils couchants" appears four times as well as in the title, while the word "défilent" occupies the first three of five syllables in lines 13 and 14.

Moreover, the flux of transition subverts the stability essential to allow representation, and this poem is liminal on many levels. Both dawn and sunset, passages between darkness and light, are evoked. The poem's beach stands between sea and land, as its dream stands between waking and sleeping and its phantoms between life and death. Furthermore, these diverse states interpenetrate. The poem literally begins with a weak dawn light that suggests a sunset; in the last eight lines this natural setting, in turn, becomes the stage for "d'étranges rêves" associated only by simile with the setting suns. The event of the title, "setting suns," has been twice displaced, first to dawn and then to dream. The apparent history of the poem's composition thus moves backward: instead of the title serving as the pretext for the poem, the poem becomes, as it were, the pretext for the title. This multiplication of perspectives makes any particular sequence of associations appear arbitrary. The constellation of associations comes to seem rather like a musical theme that could equally well be played cancrizans (backward) or inverted. Verlaine is well aware of his poems' resistance to interpretation, as we can see in the sardonic self-glossing

of stanzas 8 through 10 of "Nuit du Walpurgis classique," the fourth
poem in "Paysages tristes":

> —Ces spectres agités, sont-ce donc la pensée
> Du poète ivre, ou son regret, ou son remords,
> Ces spectres agités en tourbe cadencée,
>   Ou bien tout simplement des morts?
>
> Sont-ce donc ton remords, ô rêvasseur qu'invite
> L'horreur, ou ton regret, ou ta pensée,—hein?—tous
> Ces spectres qu'un vertige irrésistible agite,
>   Ou bien des morts qui seraient fous?—
>
> N'importe! ils vont toujours, les fébriles fantômes. [p. 72]

(These agitated ghosts, now are they the thoughts / Of the drunken
poet, or his regrets, or his remorse, / These ghosts stirred up in a
rhythmical rabble, / Or are they quite simply the dead? // Now are they
your remorse, day-dreamer courted / By horror, or your regrets, or
your thoughts, eh? All / These ghosts agitated by an irresistible vertigo,
/ Or else might they be dead people gone mad? // No matter! They're
moving still, the feverish phantoms.)

The tenor of the poem, visionary Romantic disorder, is negated by
its triply Apollonian vehicle: the orderly alexandrines, the allusion to
classical ancient Greece in Goethe's *Faust,* part II, and the regular
French (rather than unkempt English) gardens of Le Nôtre, "correct,
ridicule, et charmant" (proper, ridiculous, and charming). These
words conclude and define the poem while repeating the last line and
a half of stanza 1. The implied author retains a bit of playfulness by
breaking the frame rather than affirming it, for example in the first
stanza, when an excess of regularity creates dislocation because the
vision is described as "un rhythmique [*sic*] sabbat, rhythmique, ex-
trêmement / Rhythmique" (p. 71: A rhythmical Sabbath, rhythmical,
extremely / Rhythmical). The word "extremely" forces the word
"rhythmical" beyond the end of the line in an enjambment that disrupts rhythm. And again, at the beginning of stanzas 6 and 7, the
word "s'entrelacent" (embrace) applied to the dancing specters literally obliges one stanza to carry over a sentence from the previous one.
Thus, contrary to the classical norm, according to which each stanza
contains one neat, complete sentence, these stanzas run over into each
other, swept up in the grotesque, promiscuous dance of the dead.
    It would be tempting to assume that Verlaine's mockery of con-

ventional prosody in his Walpurgis Night functions to enhance by contrast his unconventional prosody, and that the latter's "musicality" offers us a haven of nonreferential innocence by challenging the false primacy of words. But Verlaine will not allow this impression to stand. The ensuing Saturnian poems will assail the innocence—both verbal and nonverbal—associated with love language and then insinuate this now-debased language into the "musical" world of purity so as to threaten the reassuring connotations of the orderly repetitions of "musicality" itself. The first move in Verlaine's parodic enterprise can be observed in "La Chanson des ingénues" of the section "Caprices." From the outset, these ingénues are faced with extinction because they inhabit "les romans qu'on lit peu" (novels that are seldom read). Are they actual young women or sentences ("la phrase," of feminine grammatical gender in French) in the text? The second stanza, beginning "Nous allons entrelacées" (p. 75), introduces a series of sentences that Verlaine has "interlaced" into one monstrously long sentence by replacing periods with semicolons for the remaining seven stanzas of the poem. The portrait of the ingénues also becomes textually "interlaced" with other suspect depictions of innocence, for the first phrase with which they characterize themselves—"Et le jour n'est pas plus pur / Que le fond de nos pensées" (And the daylight is no purer / Than the depths of our thoughts)—parodies Hippolyte's equivocal protestation to his father in Racine's *Phèdre* (IV, 2). The assaults of suitors are repulsed by "les plis ironiques / De nos jupons détournés" (the ironic folds / Of our averted skirts). These folds, ostensibly protective owing to the extra density of material that they interpose between female and male, also suggest both the folds of the female sexual organs and partially hidden thoughts. Such "pensers clandestins" emerge in the last two lines, where the ingénues imagine themselves as the future lovers of libertines. These young women were initially interchangeable from one novel to another. Now they have proven interchangeable in the roles of innocence and experience as well. They are unmasked as empty signs whose meaning is not innate or even fixed, but arbitrary and unstable.

"Sérénade" and "Nevermore," near the end of the collection, intimately link the lulling reassurance of "musicality" to the falsity of words. "Sérénade" stresses rhythm by employing the unusual alternation of ten- and five-syllable lines we have already observed in "Croquis parisien." The poem recalls the Baudelairean quasi-pantoum (see "Harmonie du soir," where the second and fourth lines of each stanza become the first and third lines of the next), except that it uses stanzas rather than lines to achieve its lulling effect: the first of seven quatrains is also the fourth, and the second reappears as the seventh. The poem displays many other Baudelairean motifs: the beloved's onyx eyes, the Lethe of her breast, the Styx of her dark hair, her "parfum opulent." But Verlaine condenses Baudelaire's alternatives of adoration and sadistic assault into single lines: the poem as "chanson" is both "cruelle et câline" (cruel and cajoling); the woman is "Mon Ange! — ma Gouge!" (My Angel! — my Whore!) Such laconism appears flippant, as if Verlaine were suggesting that he could easily replicate Baudelaire's tricks. The anticlimactic platitude of the poet's supreme appeal for contact—"Ouvre ton âme et ton oreille au son / De ma mandoline" (open your soul and your ear to the sound / Of my mandolin)—plus the humbleness of his instrument add up to a pungent satire of lyrical conventions and a devaluation of lyricism itself, both in the modern sense of an emotional effusion and in the medieval sense of a poem designed to be accompanied by music. Above all, Verlaine writes a gay mockery of heterosexual romance.

"Nevermore" again adopts a Baudelairean device by repeating the first line of a five-line stanza at its end. Given an appropriate context, repetition above and beyond the ordinary in the lyric usually creates a reassuring world of regularity and stability. In Verlaine's poem the motif of repetition introduced by the versification reflects the psychic condition of the subject: the lyric self's aging heart will attempt to rebuild and readorn the past monuments of its hymns. But the fundamental falsity of existence has now extended its domain to encompass prayer as well as love: "Brûle un encens ranci sur tes autels d'or faux.... Pousse à Dieu ton cantique.... Entonne, orgue enroué, des Te Deum splendides" (Burn a rancid incense on your altars of false gold.... Heave your canticle to God.... Thunder forth, hoarse organ, splendid Te Deums). Other voices join the poet's in chorus in a pseudo-elegiac movement, but only to mingle the ludicrous with the noble: "Sonnez, grelots; sonnez, clochettes; sonnez, cloches!" (Ring, sleigh bells; ring, hand bells; ring, bells!). And at the end, the almost breathless recital of Baudelairean motifs in condensed form—an impatient and halfhearted reenactment—robs them of the tragic grandeur they had in the original: "Le ver est dans le fruit, le réveil dans le rêve, / Et le remords est dans l'amour: telle est la loi" (The worm is in the fruit, awaking in the dream, / And remorse is in love: such is the law). Finally, the title "Nevermore," connoting the irretrievable uniqueness of an experience, is undercut from the beginning, for not only does it echo the refrain of Poe's "Raven," it has also been previously used in the *Poèmes saturniens* themselves.

The concluding poems just before the Epilogue are, in the manner of Parnassianism, intrinsically false. The notes to the Pléiade edition misleadingly claim that Verlaine tried to profit from the current vogue of Leconte de Lisle (considered, as recently as the early years of the twentieth century, to be the second greatest poet of nineteenth-century France, after Victor Hugo) and that he was untrue to himself by imitating Leconte de Lisle; but the Epilogue clearly shows that Verlaine's homage of imitation is once again ironic. He mocks the specious sublimity of the Parnassian pantheon and neo-Hellenism by casting himself in the role of one of "les suprêmes Poètes / Qui vénérons les Dieux et qui n'y croyons pas" (we supreme Poets / Who venerate the gods and don't believe in them). The following lines that reject inspiration in favor of effort are obviously ironic and parody the movement of "l'Art pour l'Art" (headed by Théophile Gautier) as well as the Parnassian school of Leconte de Lisle: "A nous qui ciselons les mots comme des coupes / Et qui faisons les vers émus très froidement." (Here's to us who chisel words like goblets / And write emotional verse quite in cold blood.) The truculence of Verlaine's parody, sharp as that of the young Rimbaud, has long been underestimated.

Verlaine's sense of the absurdity of language culminates in the *Fêtes galantes*. More radically than before he attacks the notion that language is the proud, unmatched achievement of humanity. He deprives humans of speech and bestows it on nonhuman entities. By means of cacophony, he further assails the assumption that what is poetic is what is harmonious. By having the names of musical notes invade the poems, he refutes the belief that only what is verbal signifies. Finally, his satire of love language in this collection undermines the conventional association of intensity with originality by stressing the conventional rhetorical nature of expressions of intense love feelings.[12]

According to J. S. Chaussivert in his fine study of the *Fêtes galantes*,[13] the twenty-two poems in this collection are arranged in a cyclothymic movement, a mood swing rising to and then falling away from a manic

---

12. See Pierre Martino, *Verlaine* (Paris: Boivin, 1951), pp. 71–72 and note.

13. J. S. Chaussivert, "Fête et jeu verlainiens: *Romances sans paroles. Sagesse*," in *Petite Musique de Verlaine*, pp. 49–60.

episode. The first two poems express a certain sadness and hesitation before the lyric self embarks on the adventure of the festival. The latter, Chaussivert continues, affords an opportunity for what Mikhail Bakhtin calls "carnival," episodic, ritualized, socially sanctioned transgression. The very title conveys this notion insofar as "galant" refers to flirtation and sex outside of marriage. (In classical French parlance, a "femme sensible" has had one lover; a "femme galante" has or has had several.) For Chaussivert, the poem "En bateau" sums up the irresponsible mood that colors the entire collection:

> C'est l'instant, Messieurs, ou jamais,
> D'être audacieux, et je mets
> Mes deux mains partout désormais! [p. 115]

(This is the time, Sirs, if ever there was one, / To be audacious, and I'm going to put / My two hands everywhere from now on!)

Poems 3 through 19 depict this "phase where flirtatious playfulness fully unfolds,"[14] while the last three are impregnated with a postorgiastic melancholy.

Beneath the mounting and ebbing excitement of the festival, however, the *Fêtes galantes* follows a different trajectory, a steady devaluation of the word which is unaffected by the climax of the carnival mood. First, in "Clair de lune" and "Pantomime," Verlaine invokes a silence that supplants conversation. Then music invades and disrupts the fragmented conversation of "Sur l'herbe." Intensifying these shifts in the discourse of an unchanging set of characters in *style direct libre* (a sequence of conversational remarks whose speakers are unidentified), the more radical kaleidoscopic shifts of characters in "Fantoches" and "En bateau" totally destroy narrative coherence. "Mandoline" then simultaneously dehumanizes the lovers and strips them of significant discourse while attributing such discourse to things.[15] Next, "Lettre," "Les Indolents," and "Colombine" show rather than tell (as "Mandoline" had done) that the language of lovers is a set of empty signifiers. But although these poems leave declarations of passion

---

14. Chaussivert, "Fête et jeu verlainiens," p. 49.
15. For a fuller discussion see Laurence M. Porter, "Text versus Music in the French Art Song: Debussy, Fauré, and Verlaine's 'Mandoline,'" *Nineteenth-Century French Studies,* 12 (Fall 1983–Winter 1984), 138–44; and the companion article (with musical examples) "Meaning in Music: Debussy and Fauré as Interpreters of Verlaine," *Topic: A Journal of the Liberal Arts,* 35 (1981), 26–37.

unanswered, or reject or banish them, they do so in a lighthearted vein. Beneath the superficial frivolity of the concluding poems, "L'Amour par terre" and "Colloque sentimental," however, the tone turns serious; and the lyric self, having been introduced as a personified observer, now becomes implicated in the failure of the language of love.[16]

The title *Fêtes galantes* itself calls into question the primacy of words by evoking Watteau's painting of the same name. And the tone of the frolicking masquers in the first poem, "Clair de lune," clashes with their message: "l'amour vainqueur et la vie opportune" (conquering love and a life of opportunity). For they celebrate love "in a minor key." They themselves are "quasi tristes," as is the moonlight in which they gambol. That moonlight mingles with their songs in the second stanza and then supersedes human words in the third with its omnipotent nonverbal message: "Qui fait rêver les oiseaux dans les arbres / Et sangloter d'extase les jets d'eau" (p. 107: Which makes the birds dream in the trees / And the fountains sob with ecstasy). The birds become silent and immobilized; the inanimate fountains take on inarticulate human feelings in response to the moon's message. To be sure, in ordinary poetic prosopopoeia and apostrophe a real-life verbal exchange between two living, waking, neighboring human beings

---

16. See Georges Zayed, "La Tradition des 'Fêtes galantes' et le lyrisme verlainien," *Aquila: Chestnut Hill Studies in Modern Languages and Literatures*, 1 (1968), 213–46. This rich, sensitive article, which deserves to be much better known, shows how common the term "fêtes galantes" and its associated *commedia dell'arte* figures were before and during Verlaine's time. Zayed celebrates this collection as Verlaine's masterpiece and mentions as sources Victor Hugo's "Fête chez Thérèse" (often mentioned by others), "Passé," and "Lettre"; Théophile Gautier's *Poésies diverses* of 1835; and Théodore de Banville's "Fête galante" in *Les Cariatides*. But none of the twenty-seven examples cited from precursors contains any direct discourse, which so typifies the imagination of Verlaine. Compare, e.g., Gautier's "Le Banc de Pierre" in the first *Parnasse contemporain* of 1866 with the "Colloque sentimental":

> Ce qu'ils disaient la maîtresse l'oublie;
> Mais l'amoureux, coeur blessé, s'en souvient,
> Et dans le bois, avec mélancolie,
>   Au rendez-vous, tout seul, revient.

(What they used to say, the mistress forgets; / But the man who loved her, with a wounded heart, remembers; / And all alone, with melancholy mein, to the grove / Where they used to meet, returns.)

Zayed, like Bornecque, stresses the presence of the memory of Elisa Moncomble: see pp. 237–45.

becomes an exchange between only one such human being and an addressee who could not actually respond. But one side of a conversation nevertheless remains. By the end of "Clair de lune," however, the singing humans have been swept from the stage, and nature is left to commune wordlessly with itself.

The second poem, "Pantomime," removes words from people altogether, except for the unspecified voices that Colombine hears in her heart. Each of the four stanzas presents a discrete character, totally cut off from the others in the present time of lyricization. People recapture words in the third poem, "Sur l'herbe," but in a context-free *style direct libre* that recalls Apollinaire's "Lundi rue Christine." We cannot say precisely how many speakers are involved or who is saying what. At least four persons must be present because the text mentions "Mesdames" and "Messieurs" in direct address. Three individuals are specified: an abbé, a marquis, and the dancer La Camargo. Dashes reveal that at least two are talking. But Verlaine is not particular about the distribution of their lines. A variant of the initial verse had no dash at mid-line to indicate a change of speaker, whereas one appears in the definitive version. Lines 7 through 11 suggest at least three male speakers, although theoretically any of them could be women. The free-floating conversation consists of insults and bantering flattery. We cannot tell whether the final five syllables ("Hé! bonsoir, la Lune!") constitute a facetious address to a celestial body or a comic sexual reference to an earthly one. ("Je vois la lune" in familiar parlance means "I see somebody's bare ass.") As if all these features did not make the poem sufficiently incoherent, a series of musical notes invades it twice. Even as music the two series remain ambiguous. Both begin with an ascending major triad but finish unresolved, one ending on the double dominant, the other on the dominant. And as the added emphasis in the text cited below indicates, in the middle stanza the musical notes homophonically invade their immediate context. Their innate musicality elicits a further "musical" response in the form of the marked repetitions of assonance and alliteration. The musical term "croche" (eighth note) is embedded here as well. And the stability of individual signifiers is further weakened by homonyms of the rhyme—*si* and *l'une*—inserted in stanzas 2 and 3:

> L'abbé divague.—Et toi, marquis,
> Tu mets de travers ta perruque.

—Ce vieux vin de Chypre est exquis
Moins, Camargo, que votre nuque.

—Ma flamme... *Do, mi, sol, la si.*
L'*abb*é, ta noirceur se dévoile!
—Que je meure, Mesdames, *si*
Je ne vous dé*croche* une étoile!

—Je voudrais être petit chien!
—Embras*sons* nos bergères *l'une*
Après l'autre.—Messieurs, eh bien?
—*Do, mi, sol.*—Hé! bonsoir, *la Lune.*

(The Abbé is rambling.—And you, Marquis, / You put your wig on
crooked. / —This old wine from Cyprus is exquisite, / Less, Camargo,
than your nape. // —My love... Do, mi, so, la si. / Abbé, your evil scheme
is exposed! / —I hope to die, ladies, if / I don't bring down a star for
you! // I'd like to be a little dog! / —Let's kiss our shepherdesses one /
After the other.—Well, gentlemen? / —Do, mi, so—Hi there! Good
evening, Moon.)

Less radical, "A la promenade" exploits the semantic connotations
of embedded homophony to underline the tone of pleasurable insincerity imposed on love language:

Trompeurs exquis et coquettes char*mantes,*
Coeurs tendres, mais affranchis du ser*ment,*
Nous devisions délicieuse*ment*...   [p. 109; emphasis added]

(Exquisite deceivers and charming coquettes, / Tender hearts, but freed
from our vows, / We chatted deliciously...)

Both rhymes in this stanza end in a syllable that is a form of the verb
mentir, to lie. This stanza, the middle one of five, is framed by notations
of nonverbal communication far more significant than words, which
thus are once again depreciated. The first stanza describes the indulgent, complicitous "smile" of the landscape; the last ends by conjuring up the provocative pout of a flirtatious mouth. Because words
have been repressed, the suggestiveness of the sexual challenge in
such details is all the broader. But predictably "La moue assez clé*mente*
de la bouche" (the rather lenient pout of the mouth) again contains
a homonym of the verb *mentir*.

"Dans la grotte" further devalues words by superimposing banality
on insincerity. The poem consists entirely of a tissue of clichés de-

scending to what even in this context is an anticlimax, and the third line of each quatrain, an alexandrine among octosyllables, presents the objective correlative of the rhetorical excess that pervades the poem. In the first stanza the lover announces, "Là! je me tue à vos genoux!" (There! I'll kill myself at your knees!). The fearsome Hyrcanian tiger seems a lamb next to his cruel Clymène. But he moderates his outburst in the second stanza. His sword, which has felled so many heroes, *will* end his life. Not only has the act been safely postponed to an indefinite future but metonymy separates the potential suicide from the instrument of his death (he now says "my sword will kill me" rather than "I shall kill myself). This substitution of the instrument for the agent implies that the lover is now at some distance from the act and also that he has a choice of possible ways to do himself in— or indeed he might choose not to kill himself at all. And so, as we could have predicted, in the third stanza the hero prudently concludes he does not need a sword; did not love pierce his heart with sharp arrows the moment the beloved woman's eye shone on him? The equivocal device of a rhetorical question, whose vehicle expresses uncertainty while its tenor conveys certitude, brings the poem full circle from despair to flirtation.

Obsession with sexuality forms the fixed center around which Verlaine's badinage and verbal artifice circle in the next three poems. "Les Ingénus," "Cortège," and "Les Coquillages" first offer exciting glimpses of the woman's body: "Parfois luisaient des bas de jambes ... c'étaient des éclairs soudains de nuques blanches" (Sometimes bare ankles twinkled ... white napes suddenly flashed). These voyeuristic thrills are associated with specious words. In "Cortège" such glimpses become more overtly sexual, but they are not offered from the viewpoint of a poetic "nous"; instead, they are attributed to the lyric self's dissociated, projected primitivism and animality in the form of a monkey and of a "négrillon." The female object's going up- and downstairs in this poem represents sexual intercourse with an archetypal symbolism of regular movement and increasing breathlessness as one "mounts" the stairway. As in a series of dreams where the inadmissible repressed moves gradually toward direct expression, in this series of poems the lyric self at last becomes a "je." In "Les Coquillages" as in "Dans la grotte" the setting is again a cavern, but now the sexual symbolism—the lyric self enters the cave as a penis enters a vagina— is no longer masked by the reversal whereby the poet figure overtly imagines piercing himself with his sword rather than penetrating the desired woman. And the specious rhetoric of female "cruelty" (rejection) has disappeared. The cavern "où nous nous aimâmes" (where we once loved) is studded with shells. Each suggests part of the woman's complexion or body; one, particularly disturbing, suggests her vagina and thus reduplicates the entire rupestral setting. As the next poem, "En patinant," implies with its scornful concluding cacophony "—quoi qu'on caquette!" (p. 113: whatever they may cackle!), only nature remains meaningful, and culture in the form of words may be dismissed entirely.

Here, midway into the collection, Verlaine moves beyond disparagement, mockery, cliché, hyperbole, and erasure to more radical ways of subverting words. Cacophony, the intimate enemy of lyric, gains reinforcement from structural incoherence, the enemy of context already apparent in "Sur l'herbe." Each of the nine stanzas of "Fantoches" and "En bateau" introduces a different set of characters. Such composition by juxtaposition becomes pictorial rather than narrative or syntactical. "Fantoches" attributes no words to its human characters, only gestures and body movements. A nonhuman being assumes the task of verbal communication: on behalf of a lovesick Spanish pirate, "un langoureux rossignol / Clame la détresse à tue-tête" (p. 114: a languorous nightingale / Yells out distress at the top of its lungs). Any musical delights the mention of the dreamy nightingale might lead us to anticipate are promptly canceled by the excessive loudness and harshness of its song, described with six stop consonants within eight syllables. Similarly, in "Le Faune" inhuman noises shatter the momentary serenity surrounding the silent humans. The sinister laughter of a terra-cotta faun ushers them in, and the clattering of tambourines making noise without players escorts them out.

The sounds of nature become agreeable in the next poem, "Mandoline," only further to devalue faithless love and its empty words by contrast. Maids and swains "échangent des propos fades / Sous les ramures chanteuses" (exchange trite remarks / Beneath the singing branches). While the trees sing, the promiscuous multiplicity of the human messages voids them of meaning. Damis "pour mainte / Cruelle fait maint vers tendre" (writes many a tender verse for many a cruel lady). The characters, portrayed as "donneurs de sérénades" and as "écouteuses," have no functions other than these idle diversions (p. 115). They are stock characters from pastoral, so familiar—like the "éternel [i.e., predictable and boring] Clitandre"—that they pall.

Insubstantial as these phantoms already are, they will be further reduced: to their clothes, to their mood, and finally to their limp shadows, which whirl until they in turn are absorbed into the moonlight.
The last word applicable to human speech in this poem, "jase," refers
to the empty background chatter of the mandolin. Not only the signifying power of the speakers' words but even the speakers themselves
have been erased.

The major transition of the *Fêtes galantes* occurs when the next
poem, "A Clymène," shifts from presenting lovers in general, as the
previous pieces have done, to dramatizing the lyric self as lover. This
self thus becomes directly involved in the failure of love language to
signify. When the phrase "romances sans paroles" (borrowed, of
course, from the title of Mendelssohn's musical composition) denotes
the effect that the beloved woman has on the poet, words have been
altogether deleted from the love relationship. Described as an
"étrange / Vision," the woman's very voice is metaphorically robbed
of sound as well as of words. The stripping away of its capacity for
rational communication is represented by the violent enjambment that
shatters the phrase placed in opposition to "voix."

The six concluding poems in the *Fêtes galantes* call into question the
signifying abilities of words even more thoroughly and explicitly than
any of the preceding poems. Through incongruous juxtaposition,
through a diaphoric alternation of mutually incompatible tones,[17]
"Lettre" presents a devastating critique of lovers' language which anticipates Roland Barthes or Nathalie Sarraute's satire of literary criticism in *Les Fruits d'or*. The verses in rhyming couplets (which in and
of themselves suggest banality) begin by protesting the lover's total
physical dependence on the presence of the beloved: "Je languis et
me meurs, comme c'est ma coûtume / En pareil cas" (I'm languishing
and dying, as my habit is / In such a case). The platitudinous iterative
of the last three words promptly undercuts the melodramatic sin-
gulative. Undaunted by, and apparently unaware of, the breakdown
of the illusion of devotion he is attempting to create, this unreliable
narrator/lover continues with a pseudo-Platonic turn:

> enfin, mon corps faisant place à mon âme,
> Je deviendrai fantôme à mon tour aussi, moi,

17. See Philip Wheelwright, *Metaphor and Reality* (Bloomington: Indiana University
Press, 1962), pp. 78–86.

....

Mon ombre se fondra pour jamais en votre ombre.   [p. 117]

(Finally, my body giving way to my soul, / I too will become a ghost in
my turn,.../ My shade will melt into yours forever.)

But this lofty assertion of selfless love is vitiated by the prosaic self-
emphasizing disjunctive pronoun of the second line cited (*moi*); and
in the line immediately following, the respectful distance of the "vous"
is canceled by the presumptuous "tu" appearing in the flattest of homage clichés: "En attendant, je suis, très chère, ton valet" (Meanwhile,
dearest, I am your humble servant). The typography itself emphasizes
this presumption and triteness by isolating the line. The total effect
is like that of the dialogue in a French classical play when the discourse
of the master is interwoven with that of the servant, the master typically representing the superego and idealistic love, the servant embodying the id and the domination of bodily, materialistic impulses.

The third group of typographically distinct lines deploys the deliberate anticlimax (or, to use the more evocative French term, "rechute
dans la banalité") of inquiring prosaically about the beloved's pets and
friends (the conjunction implying their shared animality), particularly

cette Silvanie
Dont j'eusse aimé l'oeil noir si le tien n'était bleu,
Et qui parfois me fit des signes, palsambleu!   [p. 117]

(That Sylvania, / Whose dark eyes I would have liked if yours had not
been blue, / And who sometimes signaled to me, my word!)

By successfully tempting the poet to contemplate infidelity, Silvanie's
nonverbal communication retrospectively nullifies all the exalted protestations of passionate fidelity that he had broadcast in his letter.

The fourth block of lines returns to the tone of exalted homage.
The lyric self, more amorous than Caesar or Mark Anthony with
Cleopatra, claims that he plans to conquer the whole world so as to
lay its treasures at the beloved's feet as an unworthy token of his
devotion. (That the woman as object of devotion is compared to a
promiscuous historical figure, however, implicitly transforms her
from a guiding star to a "femme galante" who is no better than she
should be.) But then the last three lines intervene, impatiently breaking off the rhyming couplets in the middle of a pair. After repeating

the mundane "très chère" of the isolated line, they blatantly dismiss as trivial and otiose all that has gone before,

> Car voilà trop causer,
> Et le temps que l'on perd à lire une missive
> N'aura jamais valu la peine qu'on l'écrive. [p. 117]

(For that's too much chat, / And the time you lose reading a missive / Will never have been worth the trouble to write it.)

What we have learned from reading this poem, according to the lyric self, is that we should not have wasted our time on it in the first place. Rather than guide us to unknown heights of love, it has cast us down. By situating his metalanguage in final position, Verlaine has canceled his statement *en bloc*.

In the demonic world of the *Fêtes galantes*, the ultimate realities are lust and death. Such an interpretation may sound melodramatic, but it is borne out by the text of "Le Monstre," a poem composed at the same time as the poems in this collection:

> et les victimes dans la gueule
> Du monstre s'agitaient et se plaignaient, et seule
> La gueule, se fermant soudain, leur répondait
> Par un grand mouvement de mâchoires. [p. 128]

(And the victims in the maw / Of the monster struggled and lamented, and only / The maw, suddenly closing, answered them / With a great movement of its jaws.)

In this Dantesque inner circle of Hell, the only response to words is annihilation. Words themselves, however, are false lust and false death, since they postpone both the gratification of lust and the consummation of death. In "Dans la grotte," for example, the despairing homage of a promise of suicide functions to defer death; in "Les Indolents" the male's proposition of a suicide pact delays the fulfillment of lust until his practical lady friend interrupts: "Mais taisons-nous, si bon vous semble" (But let's stop talking, if you like). The implied author's mocking "Hi! hi! hi!" of conclusion then echoes the earlier laughter of the lady and of the watching fauns who serve as wordless advocates—so to speak—for the claims of nature against antinature.

Even the absence of words, however, does not guarantee sincerity

in Verlaine's eyes. The false promises of a flash of exposed flesh are
enough to dupe "Les Ingénus." "Colombine" accords a more extensive
treatment to the motif of the unreliability of nonverbal communication. The heroine of that poem, "une belle enfant méchante" (a beautiful, wicked child), leads her flock of gulls on to no one knows where.
The etymological sense of "enfant"—"without speech"—is clearly relevant in this poem. The level of communication has already been
reduced to nonsense when the antics of the clowns who try to impress
Colombine are summed up by a series of musical notes: "Do, mi, sol,
mi, fa." But it degenerates further to an exchange among metaphorical animals. The tacit sexual promises made by Colombine's provocative clothes and seductive body are contradicted by her perverse
feline eyes, which transmit the tacit command "A bas / Les pattes!"
(Down, boy!).

The ominous title of the following poem, "L'Amour par terre,"
announces at once the overthrow of the ideal of love. And it concludes
with an unheard, unanswered question addressed to the lyric self's
distracted female companion, who is engrossed in following the flight
of a butterfly, itself an emblem of her inconstant attention. The twofold
frustration of desire and art symbolized in the poem leaves her unaffected. She does not see the fallen statue of Cupid or the phallic
pedestal standing sadly alone beside it, a pedestal on which the lyric
self can scarcely decipher the sculptor's name. The topos of *exegi
monumentum* has been superseded by that of *disjecta membra poetae*. And
in each of the last three quatrains the lyric self's "c'est triste" contrasts
jarringly with the playful, heedless mood of his insouciant female
companion.

A rhetorical framework of six imperatives in "En sourdine," the
next-to-last poem, strains for a possible moment of happiness in love:
"Pénétrons ... Fondons ... Ferme ... Croise ... Chasse ... Laissons-
nous persuader" (Let us imbue ... melt together ... close your eyes
... fold your arms ... banish every plan ... allow ourselves to be persuaded). But in the final analysis the best these lovers have to hope
for is the successful accomplishment of a speech act—in other words,
that they will be persuaded. Paradoxically, they can achieve even that
tenuous, imaginary triumph only by completely forswearing all verbal
communication and, indeed, all purpose whatsoever ("tout dessein").
The couple's relationship survives only in the deep silence of a dark
wood; there it is the gentle breeze rather than their own words that
will "persuade" them to abandon themselves to languor; and when

night falls, it must be the nightingale's song rather than their own voices that will convey their despair.

The final poem of the *Fêtes galantes*, "Colloque sentimental," deploys an oxymoronic title to oppose feeling with debate. In French, moreover, the first word can convey an ironic nuance, suggesting a conversation whose participants exaggerate the importance of what is being discussed. The verbal exchange occurs between two specters in the icy wasteland of a deserted park. Four times in succession, one of them tries to evoke the love and ecstasy that they shared in the past, only to be flatly refuted by the other with retorts such as "Non" and "C'est possible." Translating Baudelairean spleen into dialogue, this conclusion creates a verbal exchange at cross-purposes, like those in the theater of the absurd. By offering no scope for expansion or development, the eight isolated couplets of this poem reveal that there is no hope of escaping back into the past or forward into a happier future. Further, in the framework of the conversation, the partial repetitions of the first couplet in the third and the second in the last, instead of creating the reassuring effect of the stability of repetition, underscore the poem's drift toward entropy. "Two shapes" reappear as "two ghosts"; "you can hardly hear their words" in the last line becomes "and only the night heard their words" as the void engulfs them.[18] As a country-and-western song says, "If love can never be forever, what's forever for?" Discourse and love perish together.[19] Verlaine's greatest originality and achievement in the *Poèmes saturniens* and the *Fêtes galantes* was to combine the conventional Romantic motif of loss of faith in the permanence of love with the Symbolist's crisis of doubt regarding the transcendental permanence of any signified.

From this perspective *La Bonne Chanson* (1870), published the year

18. For sources see Bornecque, *Lumières sur les "Fêtes galantes,"* pp. 179–83.

19. Claude Cuénot, who also considers the *Fêtes galantes* to be Verlaine's masterpiece, comments on their conclusion: "The frail decor of these painted canvasses is torn apart at the end, no doubt deliberately, by the two pieces called 'En sourdine' [the renunciation of love in the ecstasy of the void] and 'Colloque sentimental' [the excruciating memory of a dead love]": see "Un type de création littéraire: Paul Verlaine," *Studi francesi*, 35 (May–August 1968), 229–45; the quotation appears on p. 235.

In an interesting overview of Verlaine, R. A. York concludes: "Above all, Verlaine subverts the idea of a coherent and fully intended speech act. Hence his love of inapt register, of excessive pedantry, of implausible personae, of pastiche and irony. Hence his liking for disguised speech acts, most often for utterances which purport to be explanations or justifications of some previous remark, but which prove to be no more than rephrasings of it" (*The Poem as Utterance* [London and New York: Methuen, 1986], p. 77; see also pp. 61–78).

after the *Fêtes galantes,* seems retrogressive.[20] In the two earlier collections the poet, lacking faith in love, had also lacked faith in language. *La Bonne Chanson,* in contrast, represents a transient episode during which love and language are glorified together. The certitude of being loved restores and enhances the imagined value of all the ways in which the lyric self can communicate with the beloved. During this phase words, rather than being experienced as a source or token of spiritual impoverishment, become pregnant with promise. The eighth poem of the collection, "Une Sainte en son auréole," for example, celebrates

> Tout ce que contient la parole
> Humaine de grâce et d'amour;
> ....
> Des aspects nacrés, blancs et roses,
> Un doux accord patricien:
> Je vois, j'entends toutes ces choses
> Dans son nom Carlovingien.   [p. 147]

(Everything that human speech contains of grace and love; ... Pearly prospects, white and pink, / A sweet patrician harmony: / I see, I hear all of these things, / In her Carlovingian name.)

One detail in the text, however, makes this apparent triumph of signification seem suspect, transient, and unstable: an enjambment dissociates "parole" from "humaine" and introduces the latter term as if it expressed a limitation.

As the earlier collections have done, *La Bonne Chanson* establishes throughout a dichotomy of sincerity/insincerity, but places the lyric self squarely in the camp of sincerity, representing him as

> témoignant sincèrement,
> Sans fausse note et sans fadaise,
> Du doux mal qu'on souffre en aimant.   [II, p. 143][21]

(sincerely bearing witness, / Without a false note or insipidity, / To the sweet sickness one suffers from in loving.) And again he exclaims:

---

20. J. S. Chaussivert, however, eloquently defends its artistic merits: see *L'Art verlainien dans "La Bonne Chanson"* (Paris: Nizet, 1973), pp. 7–8, 31–33, 115, and passim. Chaussivert provides a helpful diagram of the collection's structure (p. 31).

21. The roman numerals that appear in citations from *La Bonne Chanson* refer to the numbers of individual poems.

> ah! c'en est fait
> Surtout de l'ironie et des lèvres pincées
> Et des mots où l'esprit sans l'âme triomphait.   [IV, p. 144]

(ah! It's done with, / Especially the irony and the pursed lips / And words where wit used to triumph without soul.)

Bathed in the aura of a harmony of shared sentiments, the lovers will find that communication is assured: "elle m'écoutera sans déplaisir sans doute; / Et vraiment je ne veux pas d'autre Paradis" (IV, p. 144: No doubt she will listen to me without displeasure; / And truly I want no other Paradise.) When the poet finds himself flooded by the vertiginous impressions of the howling noise, acrid odors, and rushing movement of a railway carriage, he no longer feels, as he did before, that his being is dissolving,

> Puisque le Nom si beau, si noble et si sonore
> Se mêle, pur pivot de tout ce tournoiement,
> Au rhythme [sic] du wagon brutal, suavement.   [VII, p. 146]

(Because the Name, so lovely, so noble and so resonant / Mingles, the pure hub of all this turning, / Sweetly, with the rhythm of the rough carriage.)

The untitled tenth poem refutes "Lettre" in the *Fêtes galantes*. Like its precursor, it is written in alexandrine rhyming couplets and divided into five blocks of lines. But in this poem the lyric self receives a letter rather than sends one. His tone remains consistent, and he is deeply moved. Even when at first glance his conversation with the loved one seems banal, the poet can read her expressions of love beneath the surface of the words (XIII). Her words and gestures are all-powerful (XV); the characteristic description of nonverbal communication, even here, represents an element of antilogocentrism that never entirely disappeared from Verlaine's poetry. The last five poems depict the poet and his fiancée united against the world. The couple is posited as a core of meaning (XVII, XVIII); the wedding day is eagerly anticipated (XIX), and the poet experiences exhilaration at the prospect of his union with his Ideal (XX, XXI). The beloved, in short, has become a signifier whose signified is the transformation of the poet: "tous mes espoirs ont enfin leur tour" (XXI, p. 155: all my hopes finally have their day). For the historical Verlaine, however, this attempt to metamorphose appears to have been an act of desperation. "So," observes Jacques Borel, "it seems that Verlaine must have rushed into marriage, so to speak, largely in order to ward off his tendency toward homosexuality."[22]

In the *Romances sans paroles,* whose original title was *La Mauvaise Chanson,* Verlaine's underlying sense of the inadequacy of the signifier reerupts. He is not just writing about being bad; writing itself is bad. These poems represent not only a rebellion against conventional social expectations but also the cancellation of Verlaine's recent praise of the "chanson" as verbal artifact. He now achieves the summit of his art by freeing himself from the former excesses of metalanguage, specifically from the continual need to depreciate words verbally, a need that had pervaded the *Fêtes galantes.* He now can evoke the indefinable without needing to dismiss the definable. But as a result, the poems in *Romances sans paroles* lack the thread of narrative continuity which had linked the various *Fêtes galantes* together into a progressive drama of the disintegration of the word.

The three section titles, "Ariettes oubliées," "Paysages belges," and "Aquarelles," all denote a transposition of the arts which reinforces the word-canceling gesture of the collective title, *Romances sans paroles.* The nine poems of the first section are untitled; thus the ostensible pretext, which titles so often convey, has been suppressed in favor of impressionistic drift. In the *Romances sans paroles* as in the *Fêtes galantes,* words, removed from human beings and ascribed instead to natural entities, no longer provide a mocking, jarring contrast to human aspirations. We have returned to an elegiac mode wherein nature appears to echo human hopes and desires. The satiric edge of the *Fêtes galantes* is lacking.[23]

The pathetic fallacy impregnates the nine "Ariettes oubliées" with anthropomorphism. In the first one, the choir of little voices in the branches expresses the plaintive, humble anthem of two human lovers' souls (p. 191). A murmur of unspecified origin in the second of these poems allows the lyric self to intuit "le contour subtil des voix anciennes" (the subtle contour of ancient voices); "les lueurs musi-

---

22. In Verlaine, *Oeuvres poétiques complètes,* p. 136 (editor's note).

23. One would expect the contrary, owing to the constant presence of Verlaine's lover Rimbaud—whose own poetry is preeminently satiric—during the composition of *Romances sans paroles.* But cf. Charles Chadwick, *Verlaine* (London: Athlone, 1973), p. 51, who claims that Rimbaud's influence on Verlaine's poetry was negligible. More likely, sexual satisfaction made Verlaine lose his edge.

ciennes" (the musical gleams) reveal to him a future dawn. The subtle synesthesias (a singing voice compared to an outline drawn by an artist, light compared to music) imply an overarching network of horizontal correspondences of sense impressions that ultimately derive from the organic unity of nature. The poet's heart and soul become a double eye reflecting "l'ariette... de toutes lyres!" (p. 192: the arietta of every lyre!). In the third poem the rain on the town corresponds to the weeping in the speaker's heart. By dispensing with a human verbal message Verlaine restores the harmony of self and externality that had been shattered in the *Fêtes galantes,* although of course he must use words to do so.

Considered as a group, the "Ariettes oubliées" are what John Porter Houston percipiently identified as "mood poems" when he characterized them as the one clear innovation of French Symbolism.[24] This innovation, however, has its ties to the past; it represents a further deterioration of the vestiges of the religious sentiment that survived, in degenerate form, in the lyric worldview of Romanticism. When at the turn of this century Romanticism was condemned as "spilt religion," the accusation meant that Romanticism presented free-floating, invertebrate religious sentiment without any doctrinal, institutional, or dogmatic support. But Verlaine's "Symbolism" in these poems further debases the Romantics' material/spiritual correspondences to material/sentimental ones, to a harmony between the order of physical nature and the poet's feelings. Unlike the Christian and the Romantic modes of sensibility, moreover, Verlaine's lacks a social context and therefore entails no revelation, no "message," nothing useful for humanity:

> O que nous mêlions, âmes soeurs que nous sommes,
> A nos voeux confus la douceur puérile
> De cheminer loin des femmes et des hommes,
> Dans le frais oubli de ce qui nous exile! [IV, p. 193][25]

(O let us mingle, kindred spirits that we are, / With our uncertain hopes the boyish sweetness / Of traveling far from women and men, / Newly oblivious of what is exiling us!)

---

24. John Porter Houston, *French Symbolism and the Modernist Movement: A Study of Poetic Structures* (Baton Rouge: Louisiana State University Press, 1980), pp. 19–40, esp. 22–23; reviewed by Laurence M. Porter in *Comparative Literature,* 36 (Winter 1984), 94–96.

25. The roman numeral iv refers to the number of this poem in the series of "Ariettes oubliées."

The dreamy swoon so characteristic of the "Ariettes oubliées," where the poet's feelings are in harmony with his surroundings, recalls the infantile bliss of being fed and cradled. These poems are indeed deeply regressive. "Le contour subtil des voix anciennes" in the second poem clearly evokes the voice of the mother recalled from infancy. And in the same poem, the "escarpolette" "balançant jeunes et vieilles heures!" (the child's swing, swaying young and old hours to and fro!) represents not—or at least not only—an alternation between homosexual and heterosexual feelings, as many critics have claimed. Instead, it reflects Verlaine's desire to move back and forth between a remembered infantile relationship with the loved woman and his present involvement with his wife Mathilde. What the poet weeps for in "Il pleure dans mon coeur" is the loss of this blissful past. The predominance of the infantile over the homosexual becomes apparent in the fifth poem when the "air bien vieux" in the "boudoir longtemps parfumé d'Elle" (p. 193: the ancient melody . . . the boudoir filled for a long time with her scent) is metaphorically transformed into "ce berceau soudain / Qui lentement dorlote mon pauvre être" (p. 193: that sudden cradle / Which slowly coddles my poor being). A tune from former days which elicits memories of the poet's past momentarily consoles him. More playfully and subtly, the same motif recurs in the sixth "Ariette" through the mediation of medieval and fairy-tale literature. There the "petit poète jamais las / De la rime non attrapée!" (the little poet who is never weary / Of chasing the rhyme he will never catch!) is a self-image, and rhyme figures the relationship between two separate entities, the first of which engenders the second as a mother engenders a child. The primordial loss of fusion with the mother is the source of the sense of exile and sadness in the seventh poem. This mood also generates the impression of the death of the moon (as a figuration of the mother-imago) and, in the ninth poem, the death of the shadows of trees and of smoke, which figure memories:

> Combien, ô voyageur, ce paysage blême
>   Te mira blême toi-même,
> Et que tristes pleuraient dans les hautes feuillées
>   Tes espérances noyées! [p. 196]

(How much, O traveler, this pale landscape / Caught sight of you, pale yourself, / And how sadly among the high foliage were weeping / Your drowned hopes!)

Language disappoints because it reminds us of the need to earn and to sustain in adult relationships the positive regard the mother unconditionally grants to the infant. Therefore the "Ariettes oubliées" attempt to create the semblance of a regression to a preverbal state, an impression that contrasts sharply with the ostensible modernity of the short, unusual line lengths and the synesthetic network of associations with the other arts. "Regression in the service of the ego" this poetry may be, but it also foreshadows a historical forward movement, away from the antiverbal crisis that marks the first phase of French Symbolism to the second Symbolist generation, characterized by a renewed aspiration to found a unity of the arts and to invent a cosmic, totalizing discourse.

From this point on *Romances sans paroles* deteriorates. Superficially the "Paysages belges" section appears to offer an impressionistic series of vignettes in rapid movement, but in fact these vignettes gravitate as a group around the fixed center of a happy home—inn, nest, or château—explicitly mentioned by the first three poems of the group. One could characterize the impossible return to infancy as centripetal, the demands of adult life as centrifugal (in the absence of a coherent sense of identity), and the resulting movement as circular. This motion appears in the next two poems in the form of a merry-go-round and of weathervanes. "Malines" combines the poles of movement and immobility in the image of railway cars speeding through the night but each providing at the same time an intimate home:

> Chaque wagon est un salon
> Où l'on cause bas et d'où l'on
> Aime à loisir cette nature... [p. 201]

(Each railway car is a living room / Where you talk in low tones and from which you can / Love this nature at leisure.)

These first two groups of poems are dated from May through August 1872; the last seven poems of the collection, dated from September 1872 through April of the next year, revert to an anecdotal, self-justifying confessional tradition characteristic of Verlaine's later verse and illustrated here most starkly by "Birds in the Night" and "Child Wife."

Written in prison in 1874 after Verlaine's drunken brutality and his escapades with Rimbaud had irrevocably ended his marriage, "L'Art poétique" reintroduces a corrosive subversion of the word through incongruous juxtaposition, self-contradiction, disunity of tone, pleonasm, and hyperpoeticism.[26] Robert Mitchell has pointed out that, except for the nine-syllable lines corresponding to Verlaine's recommendation to use imparisyllabic meters, "the form of the poem is basically unfaithful, and even antithetical, to its substance."[27] Verlaine advocates weaving an airy creation "sans rien en lui qui pèse ou qui pose" (without anything in it that weighs down or comes to rest), but he creates a strongly didactic statement in which twelve exhortations to the reader fill up all but three of the nine stanzas. Repeated and therefore heavy-handed commands to seek "nuance" (the word occurs three times among the twenty-seven words of stanza 4) strikingly subvert the desired effect of delicacy.[28] And from that point on the text is invaded by a decidedly antipoetic diction as in stanzas 5 and 6 the poem evokes that which it wishes to destroy: "tout cet ail de basse cuisine!...tords-lui le cou!...en train d'énergie...elle ira jusqu'où" etc. (all that greasy-spoon garlic!...wring its neck!...getting energetic...how far will it go). Condemning the mechanical repetition of rhyme (i.e., of the same sounds), stanza 7 itself accumulates six *ou*'s in lines 2 and 3, and four *s*'s and *f*'s each in lines 2 through 4. The last two stanzas return to enunciating a "poetical" statement of the ideal described as a free ramble through the fresh morning air "vers d'autres cieux à d'autres amours" (p. 327: toward other skies, to other loves). But even here—if we are to assume that this concluding image of an aimless stroll corresponds to the "music" that Verlaine recommended "above all else" in his first line—Verlaine's putative "musicality" amounts to precisely the opposite of what a musician would understand by that word: the absence of structure and direction.

The jarring incongruity of prescribing a light touch in "L'Art poétique" in a language coarsened by pedestrian diction and crude excesses of alliteration and assonance not only conveys an ironic reflection on the claims of poetry but also betrays an inner conflict between faith

---

26. See Carol de Dobay Rifelj, *Word and Figure: The Language of Nineteenth-Century French Poetry* (Columbus: Ohio State University Press, 1987), esp. pp. 120–25.

27. Robert Mitchell, "Mint, Thyme, and Tobacco: New Possibilities and Affinities in the *Artes poeticae* of Verlaine and Mallarmé," *French Forum*, 2 (September 1977), 238–54. On "Images d'un sou," also from the "Jadis" section of *Jadis et naguère*, cf. Zimmermann, *Magies de Verlaine*, p. 133.

28. Mitchell, "Mint, Thyme, and Tobacco," pp. 240–43.

in poetry and disdain for it as a vehicle for aspirations.[29] Through the *Romances sans paroles* Verlaine's poetry—based on a fantasized relationship to an Other whose domain is language—alternates between vulnerable openness and wary mistrust. The losses of his wife Mathilde and of his lover Rimbaud, the shock of these failures of love, robbed love of its justification for Verlaine. No longer having the energy to mistrust, he regressed into a relationship with himself. For a time he tried to aggrandize himself through a religious conversion that seemed to hold the promise of associating his self with a greater self. But transcendence eluded him. Throughout his later collections of verse he remained inextricably entangled in self-justifications of various kinds. He tried to have something to show for his past; he yielded to the rhetoric that must accompany such a stance and sank back into a dilute reworking of the confessional strain of late Romantic elegiac poetry. As Jacques Borel observes, by the time of *La Bonne Chanson* Verlaine was already beginning to retreat from the full originality of his personal vision: "He will be impelled forward by Rimbaud, called on in a sense to pursue down to its ultimate consequences an experiment that he had been the first to initiate by having a presentiment of the liberating power of the dream, but away from which, suspecting the dangers that 'Crimen Amoris' and then 'Mort!' will denounce, he had already turned into the elegiac comfort of 1870."[30]

Our faith in the referentiality of language—that there exists a real link between the signifier and a signified—depends upon our faith in intersubjectivity, the belief that we share a common code and that each signifier means the same thing to us as to the significant others in our lives. Once Verlaine had experienced "l'incommunicabilité," the impossibility of communication, he attacked the belief in referentiality in three distinct ways in his poetry. At times, as in the theater of the absurd, he depicted a dialogue of the deaf, as in "Colloque sentimental," where each signifier has different referents for different people. At other times he exalted "musicality" over verbality: thus he was attracted to the libretti of Favart, which he studied with Rimbaud, because they provided the model for a form intermediate, so to speak,

---

29. See Michel Grimaud, "Questions de méthode: Verlaine et la critique structuraliste," *Oeuvres et Critiques*, 9 (1984), 125–26, for detailed comments.
30. Verlaine, *Oeuvres poétiques complètes*, p. 171 (editor's introduction).

between language and music, insofar as the importance of the words was minimized by the necessity of tailoring them to the prepotent musical form. Verlaine's marked choice of unusual rhythms augmented the ostensible importance of the "musical"—that is, the rhythmic—dimension of his verse by calling attention to its rhythms so they could not be taken for granted. As Verlaine, like the other Symbolists, was not himself musical and was in fact rather unfamiliar with music, the inspiration that music could provide for his verse had to remain limited.[31] Yet his fascination with musicality represented a positive response to the experience of the emptiness of language, for it implied that one can shift out of an unreliable system into another system that is self-contained. When you name musical notes, for example, your referents are elements of a preexisting structure independent of language; their "meanings" are precisely nonreferential, consisting as they do in internal relationships between the parts of a musical composition.

The pessimistic mode of Verlaine's assault on signification, the one with which he ended, was the specular, narcissistic short circuit in which all signifiers voiced by the poet refer back to the poet himself. In his earlier collections of verse, images of the moon symbolize this condition. The heavenly body corresponds to the poet's body (e.g., the Pierrot's white face explicitly mimics the appearance of the moon), and the moon also recalls the fantasized maternal breast, surviving in the preconscious as the dream screen and existing only to gratify the needs of the imperial self.[32] In the weaker later verse, the confessional tradition back into which Verlaine sinks narrativizes this pessimistic solution of narcissism. If you cannot communicate with others, then you must commune with your own emptiness.

31. See once again Peyre, "Poets against Music," cited in n. 4 above.

32. See Jeanne Bem, "Verlaine, poète lunaire: Mythe et langage poétique," *Stanford French Review*, 4 (Winter 1980), 379–94. For a recent discussion of the "Isakower phenomenon" (adult hallucinations of the mother's breast) and the related "dream screen" and "blank dream" experiences, plus a valuable bibliography, see Philip M. Brombert, "On the Occurrence of the Isakower Phenomenon in a Schizoid Disorder," *Contemporary Psychoanalysis*, 20 (1984), 600–601 and 623–24; see also chap. 2, n. 40.

Chapter 4

Baudelaire's Fictive Audiences

I

"Fictive audiences," as I use the term here, are those which can be inferred from the texts. They are the counterpart of the "implied author" or personality that appears coextensive with the text, that embraces its contradictions, and that in poetry we call the "lyric self." I focus on the problematics of the period from 1851 to 1858, when Baudelaire turns away from social commitment and commentary in order to dramatize his sense of isolation and the difficulty he experiences in establishing contact with an audience. Thus my analysis might be said to complement the work of Walter Benjamin, who examines Baudelaire's art as shaped by its grounding in an urban, capitalist, and imperialist world. (In the brief second and fifth sections of this chapter, however, I too consider the setting in which Baudelaire's Symbolist crisis occurred, its roots in his psychological make-up and in his social situation.)

A brief explanation of the terminology I use is necessary by way of preamble. Literary critics traditionally distinguish between the empirical audience actually, physically reading or hearing a text—the addressee of a real letter, or you and I with a volume of Baudelaire's poetry in our hands; the virtual audience suggested by and sometimes personified in the text; and the ideal audience of the "happy few" whom the author imagines as perfectly understanding his or her message, or as gradually trained to understand, in some hypothetical future, by the experience of the text. My term "fictive audience" includes both the virtual and the ideal audiences as opposed to the empirical audience. But the conventional notion of virtual audience must be refined. Its character obviously varies in Baudelaire's poetry. He creates satiric audiences whom he denounces and insults; didactic audiences whom he wishes to enlighten and instruct; and idealized audiences whom he praises or implores for attention, assistance, and love. The idealized audience consists of a single object of desire who seems to offer the hope of filling a void in the lyric self. The type of virtual audience conspicuously missing in Baudelaire's poetry is what we can call the "solidary audience," one that seems to share the poet's values and is addressed, for example, in the mutual celebrations of the ode or in Mallarmé's optimistic late poetry.

But once any of these categories of fictive audiences is applied to the examination of a particular poem, complexities and contradictions immediately arise. The dedicatees whose names were added to several poems between the publication of the first (1857) and the third (1861) editions of *Les Fleurs du Mal* initially seem to be solidary with the poet, but when we examine the context, we discover that his identification with them is specious. Often the poet will initially attack his didactic addressees by satire, as if to jolt them into paying attention. Often, too, idealized addressees will fail to be ideal: they may respond to the poet with indifference or incomprehension. He in turn seems to yearn for attention and broadcasts futile appeals that more often than not turn into violence. Through vehemence and violence, the poet attempts to regain control, to promote himself from *destinataire* (in A. J. Greimas's sense of one whose fate will be decided by another) to *destinateur* (one who decides another's fate).

The question that concerns me is not who reads Baudelaire (quite pertinent for the socially committed literature of his early and late periods) but who he imagines is reading him. In my opinion the critical categories of object-relations psychology afford the most suggestive understanding of the poet's relationships to his fantasized audiences. This psychoanalytic school focuses on the mother or primary caregiver as every child's "first object" (of love feelings and dependency) and then examines how "transitional objects" and other mother-surrogates gratify our needs when the primary caregiver is no longer available. I claim that Baudelaire's fictive audiences often function as mother-surrogates and as objects of a fearful neurotic desire that frustrates itself by secretly denying to itself what it most craves. The poems that constitute *Les Fleurs du Mal,* of course, are shaped by a psychodynamics far more complex and labile than simple self-denial. Frustrated in his quest to regain contact with the mother, Baudelaire's lyric self at times turns to the father instead (e.g., in "Bénédiction") or else assumes the maternal role vis-à-vis the audience (as in "Le Soleil"), offering it (metaphorical) food.

As André Gide observed, Baudelaire's poetry is marked throughout by a "curious desire to get closer to the reader (whereas Leconte de Lisle, Mallarmé, Valéry resolutely withdraw from him or her)."[1] But during his "Symbolist crisis" of 1851 to 1858, Baudelaire's lyric selves flee from what they profess to desire. For an adult, infantile contact with an all-powerful mother figure is tantamount to engulfment. If his ostensible wish for intimacy with her is gratified, he fears being drained of his independent identity (the motif of vampirism pervades Baudelaire's verse). The proffered breast then becomes a "bad breast," a hollow, an abyss, a void. Threatened with annihilation, the lyric self evades the threat by taking control of the bad breast and thrusting it at the audience so the plenitude of the latter turns to emptiness. Satiric denunciation and the macabre, prominent in the poems added to *Les Fleurs du Mal* between 1857 and 1861, effectively force the reader rather than the poet to play the role of victim. Satan in "Au lecteur," Love in "L'Amour et le crâne," and everywhere the invisible worm of original sin rob us of our vital essence if we come in contact with Baudelaire's text.

The solution that predominates during Baudelaire's crisis period, however, is an ultimately self-defeating narcissism. The narcissist reasons, If the Other won't love me, I'll love myself. (The Other's response, in any event, could never compensate for the loss of the infant's sense of oceanic bliss during total communion with the mother.) But since I still need the Other, and since she, like me, must be a narcissist, perhaps I can bribe her to pay me attention by offering her a flattering image of herself in my poetry. Then the poem becomes a mirror in which either she or I will contemplate ourselves.

If Baudelaire's lyric self is so severely neurotic, what is the interest of his poetry? How is it "Symbolist," and how does Baudelaire differ from any other neurotic? The answer is that Baudelaire, unlike others, manages to sublimate a self-defeating, maladaptive concern for con-

---

1. André Gide, *Anthologie de la poésie française* (Paris: Gallimard, 1949), pp. xli–xlii.

tacting the audience into a rich symbolic system, into a strikingly personal network of associations whose coherence and ingenious variety make them instantly recognizable as his and those of no one else. (Perhaps the closest nineteenth-century parallel to the emotional climate of Baudelaire's poetry appears in the novels of Dostoevsky, whose characters alternate between self-abasement and fierce pride.) Baudelaire's keen sense of original sin, of the irremediable corruption and corruptibility of human nature, alternates with an arrogant rebellion against God. Integrated into an artistic structure with multiple resonances, these attitudes create an intricate depiction of our all-too-human vacillations between autonomy and dependence.

I I

The difficulty of making contact with his empirical audience preoccupied Baudelaire as soon as he began to write. Among his earliest letters, addressed to the half brother who was sixteen years his senior, two-thirds appeal desperately for a reply or refer to hindrances to communication such as lost addresses. "Je te prie dans toutes mes lettres de me répondre," he laments; "le silence que tu gardes depuis longtemps me prouve que tu n'es pas content de moi" (I beseech you in all my letters to answer me; your protracted silence proves to me that you're dissatisfied with me). After leaving home in 1839, he adopts a similar tone in writing to his mother, bemoaning "le parti pris chez toi de ne plus m'écouter" (your fixed resolve not to listen to me any more). Near the end of his life, his relationships with others continue to reproduce these childhood frustrations: "J'écris tant de lettres auxquelles on ne répond pas. Si tu savais quelle colère on éprouve quand on est complètement isolé, enfermé dans un milieu hostile, sans conversations, sans aucun plaisir possible, et quand personne de qui vous avez besoin ne vous répond!" (I write so many letters that remain unanswered. If you only knew how angry one feels when one is completely isolated, imprisoned in a hostile social setting, with no conversations, with no possible enjoyments, and when none of the people you need will answer you!).[2]

2. Charles Baudelaire, *Correspondance*, 2 vols., ed. Claude Pichois (Paris: Gallimard, 1973); hereafter cited in text and notes as *Corr.* Quotations in the preceding passages are from Baudelaire to his brother, Alphonse, May 17, 1833, and February 26, 1834 (I, 17, 27), and Baudelaire to his mother, summer 1844 and July 31, 1864 (I, 108, and

This painful lifelong pattern of isolation and incomprehension forms the basis of Baudelaire's self-dramatization as an author confronting his audience. Baudelaire's ambivalent struggle for contact with his audiences passes through three main phases: optimistic solidarity, pessimistic withdrawal, and ironic, self-parodying assurance undermined at times by an excess of allegorization. In other words, two periods of socially committed literature (the allegorical impulse being a didactic one) frame a middle period of narcissistic aestheticism. Although I will examine each phase of Baudelaire's literary evolution in turn, I devote most attention to the middle period of desperate isolation because it corresponds to Baudelaire's Symbolist crisis, when he produced his greatest masterpieces and when his subversion of the communicative process becomes most apparent.

First, under the visionary socialist influence of Charles Fourier, Baudelaire optimistically works for a reconciliation of artist, bourgeois, and worker in the *Salons* (reviews of the official, national, annual art exhibition in Paris) of 1845 and 1846, in the early poems on death and wine, and in the first six of the eighteen "Tableaux parisiens" in *Les Fleurs du Mal*. Irony soon tinged his hope of replacing injustice and alienation with social equity and brotherhood, but in the late 1840s Baudelaire actively committed himself to the left-wing socialism of Louis-Auguste Blanqui and Pierre-Joseph Proudhon and to armed insurrection on the barricades of 1848. In this period he believes his individual actions can help change society, and his writing is dominated by the essay, a genre that presupposes the writer is able to reach and persuade an audience. (Contrary to his oft-quoted statement that the imperialist coup d'état of December 1851 had "physically depoliticized" him, Baudelaire, by his own testimony, remained passionately interested in political issues and true to his egalitarian convictions in economic and political affairs until his death.)[3]

II, 390–91); see also Baudelaire's letters to his mother: I, 147, 168, 324–25, 345, 349, and 353.

   3. On Baudelaire's social commitment see Marcel Ruff, "La Pensée politique et sociale de Baudelaire," in *Littérature et société: Recueil d'études en l'honneur de Bernard Guyon* (Paris: Desclée de Brouwer, 1973), pp. 65–74; and the more limited studies by Richard D. E. Burton, "Baudelaire and the Agony of the Second Republic: 'Spleen' (LXXV)," *Modern Language Review*, 81 (July 1986), 600–611; Graham Chesters, "A Political Reading of Baudelaire's 'L'Artiste inconnu' ('Le Guignon')," *Modern Language Review*, 79 (1984), 64–76; and Hartmut Stenzel, "Les Ecrivains et l'évolution idéologique de la petite bourgeoisie dans les années 1840: Le Cas de Baudelaire," *Romantisme*, 17–18 (1977), 79–91.

In these early years Baudelaire appears confident of his potency as a producer and communicator. This attitude appears clearly in the portrait of the market-wise writer of "Comment on paie ses dettes, quand on a du génie" (How you pay your debts, when you're a genius), even though the anecdote is a facetious parody of Balzac's self-aggrandizing puffery. Baudelaire may well have feared and envied the overwhelming competition of Balzacian hubris. But if so, he conceals his self-doubts well, for example, in the epilogue to the "Salon caricatural de 1846," where, shifting to the first person, he evokes

le public nouveau qui se presse à la porte,
Et...
Va me choisir encor pour son cicerone.
....
Je me suis efforcé d'avoir, en quelques pages,
Plus d'esprit, de talent, plus de verve et d'images
Qu'il n'en faut pour toucher le plus rogue lecteur.[4] [II, 523–24]

(The new public who is crowding through the doorway, / And...is going to choose me as its guide. /...In the scope of a few pages, I have made efforts to have / More wit, talent, verve, and imagery / Than you would need to reach the most cantankerous of readers.)

Such self-mockery reflects both self-assurance and a sense of complicity with the public. Complicity in turn depends on Baudelaire's optimistic faith in the possibility of reconciling opposing social classes. The introduction to the *Salon de 1845* exemplifies this position.[5] It defends the Romantic artist's traditional enemy, the bourgeois, as an inoffensive being who would like nothing better than to appreciate good painting if artists could produce it and critics explain it (II, 351). Baudelaire's attitude here foreshadows the more specific Fourierism of the *Salon de 1846*, in which he seems to aspire to a union of the

4. For a subtle discussion of how Baudelaire's self-dramatizing "I" evolves from the locus of certitude in the early poems to a tangle of questions and doubts in the later ones, see Ross Chambers, "*Je* dans les 'Tableaux parisiens' de Baudelaire," *Nineteenth-Century French Studies*, 9 (Fall 1980–Winter 1981), 59–68, esp. 59–62.

5. Marcel Ruff finds a mixture of base flattery and insolence in the tone of both early *Salons* ("Pensée politique et sociale de Baudelaire," p. 66). But I do not find it in the *Salon* of 1845. On Baudelaire's ironic (and, I would add, probably two-edged) deconstruction of the opposition artist/bourgeois, see Gretchen Van Slyke, "Les Epiciers au musée: Baudelaire et l'artiste bourgeois," *Romantisme*, 55 (1987), 55–66.

proletariat and petite bourgeoisie, not only through democratic and republican institutions but also through a shared appreciation of art.[6]

Working within the limits of a shared cultural code in the 1845 *Salon*, Baudelaire attempts to communicate with his audience on its own aesthetic terms. In his words, he "arrays artists according to the place and rank that public esteem has assigned them" (II, 353). That is, to structure his essay he espouses the Neoclassical hierarchy of genres in painting. This hierarchy ranks subjects according to the twin criteria of social importance (decisive events in the lives of nations outrank portraits of important personages, which in turn outrank the "genre painting" depicting the working classes) and anthropomorphism (human subjects outrank still lives, and these—devoid of a human presence but reflecting the ordering activity of a human intelligence—outrank landscapes). But Baudelaire then reveals affinities of genius that cut across all these divisions. He praises Delacroix, Daumier, and Ingres as the supreme draughtsmen of his time. Delacroix and Daumier—the one with his grand mythological and historical tableaux, the other with his caricatures—stand at the opposite extremes of the hierarchy of social importance. And Delacroix and Ingres had been the foci for the prolonged, vehement quarrel between Rubénistes and Poussinistes, advocates respectively of the primacy of color and of line in painting (II, 356). By praising the mastery of line in all three artists, Baudelaire reveals an unexpected confraternity of greatness that makes the hierarchy of genres seem trivial by comparison. The initial concession to established canons of taste aims to facilitate an eventual reconciliation between opposing camps of art criticism.

"Taste" for art implies a taste for food as well (the French *goût* has the same double meaning as its English equivalent), and Baudelaire takes the pun more seriously than many people would do. He equates love with food, and in his relationships with his public he is concerned with being fed and with "feeding the hungry heart" (this catchphrase is used in psychotherapy to explain one motivation underlying compulsive eating and substance abuse). In his didactic writings, therefore,

---

6. Stenzel ("Ecrivains et l'évolution idéologique," pp. 80–83) summarizes Marx's perceptive analysis of the petite bourgeoisie in nineteenth-century France as a living contradiction between capital and labor, hoping for a reconciliation of these two opposite extremes. After the 1851 coup d'état, the petite bourgeoisie either joined the new dominant power of the haute bourgeoisie or resigned itself to that power as a historical fatality.

the alimentary metaphor is common. It appears in the 1846 article "Le Musée classique du Bazar Bonne-Nouvelle," where Baudelaire's didactic addressees are those unscrupulous, commercially oriented artists who, like bad mothers, feed their aesthetically infant bourgeois audience unnourishing food: "Il [le bourgeois] vous demande tous les jours son morceau d'art et de poésie, et vous le volez. Il mange du Cogniet,[7] et cela prouve que sa bonne volonté est grande comme l'infini. Servez-lui un chef-d'oeuvre, il le digérera et ne s'en portera que mieux!" (II, 414: He [the bourgeois] asks you every day for his ration of art and poetry, and you cheat him. He consumes Cogniet, and that shows he has infinite good will. Serve him a masterpiece; he will digest it and will be all the healthier in consequence!). Baudelaire himself functions as the good, nurturant mother when in the opening passage of the *Salon de 1846* he addresses the bourgeois: "Vous pouvez vivre trois jours sans pain;—sans poésie, jamais" (II, 415: You can live three days without bread; without poetry, not at all).

Until late in 1851 Baudelaire maintains a nurturant stance toward his fictive audiences and remains confident of the effective force of his messages: he thinks art can improve the world. In "Le Soleil," for example (first published in 1857 but held to be one of the earliest poems),[8] the sun serves as the poet's ego-ideal. The revivifying message of its rays—analogous to the poet's verses but prepotent—cannot be ignored. The sun knocks forcefully on every door and makes a royal entrance into every hospital and palace. This detail fulfills a threefold function: it insists on the irresistible universality of the message; it enforces social solidarity by juxtaposing mutually disaffected classes; and the final homonymic pun ("palais" = palace or palate), to say nothing of the final rhyme, a homonym for "lait" (milk), reinforces the alimentary metaphor that runs through the latter two sections of the poem. In these sections the sun orders harvests (of

7. Léon Cogniet (1794–1880), a pupil of Jean-Baptiste Guérin (1783–1855), won acclaim with his portraits hung in the Salons of 1845 and 1846.
   8. Charles Baudelaire, *Oeuvres complètes*, ed. Claude Pichois, 2 vols. (Paris: Gallimard, 1975–76), I, 83. For the prose and verse poems, all of which appear in volume I, subsequent citations consist of page number only. For Baudelaire's other works, citations include both volume number and page number. The abbreviation *OC* is included wherever needed to avoid ambiguity.
   The sun's pervasive light implies that the poet's vision not only transforms but also unifies. Illumination—shared knowledge—bridges the gap between author and audience and evokes the chimera of universal mutual intelligibility, analogous to the vision of the total decipherability of natural phenomena presented in "Correspondances."

inspiration) to ripen in the heart; it fills hives and minds alike with honey; and as an androgynous "père nourricier," it resembles the poet, thus assimilating writing poetry to giving the breast, and reading to suckling.

This strategy of a benevolent, paternalistic approach to the didactic addressees already shows signs of strain in the *Salon de 1846*. The clash of ironic and sincere tones in this work seems to derive from the coexistence in Baudelaire's mind of a tenacious hope for social harmony together with a skeptical self-mockery about that hope, to conceive which requires an almost religious leap of faith. The shift toward an uncompromising position appears first in Baudelaire's aesthetics rather than in his social theory. From then on he sides with the Rubénistes, rejecting the arbitrary boundaries of the intact draughtsmanly outline just as, shortly thereafter, he rejects social stratification and the unequal distribution of wealth and power.[9]

Baudelaire's 1851 article on his worker-poet friend Pierre Dupont expresses his last hope of harnessing poetry to the cause of social reform. Dupont as exemplary figure is the "symptom" (a somewhat disparaging term, since it implies the ascendancy of the involuntary) of a "popular sentiment" he echoes. Baudelaire seeks to exorcise the unclean spirits of Romantic confession, elegy, and lament in favor of "the poet who puts himself into permanent communication with the men of his time and exchanges with them thoughts and feelings translated into an elevated, absolutely correct language.... Any true poet should be an incarnation." Poetry should never repine but should be utopian, aspiring always for a more just world (II, 27–35). The many lines of Baudelairean verse that Dupont inspired indicate that Baudelaire responded to the working man sincerely and without condescension.[10] By presenting the model poet as a figure other than himself, however, Baudelaire may be suggesting that he has begun to lose confidence in his ability to shape his social destiny and to transform the world through poetry.

9. See David J. Kelley, "Deux aspects du *Salon de 1846* de Baudelaire: La Dédicace aux Bourgeois et la Couleur," *Forum for Modern Language Studies*, 5 (October 1969), 331–46. See also Laurence M. Porter, "Reflections on the World-View of Romantic Painting: Baudelaire's Critical Response to Delacroix's Painterly Style," *Centennial Review*, 16 (Fall 1972), 349–58, with plates; and Porter, "The Anagogic Structure of Baudelaire's 'Les Phares,'" *French Review*, Special Issue no. 5, "Studies on French Poetry" (1973), 49–54.

10. See Jean Dominique Biard, "Baudelaire et Pierre Dupont," *Nineteenth-Century French Studies*, 16 (Fall–Winter 1987–88), 111–19.

Baudelaire's ironic essay, "Conseils aux jeunes littérateurs," written in 1846, had preserved a note of paternalistic optimism about the artist's power to determine his destiny. Advancing a sort of catastrophe theory of reputation, Baudelaire claimed that the sudden, startling success of certain artists had always been long prepared for by many previous, unobserved lesser successes. There was no "guignon" (jinx) but simply, in less prominent writers, a lack of patience and hard work. At the end of 1851, however, Baudelaire wrote "Le Guignon." Graham Chesters points out that the drawings on the sheet on which Baudelaire transcribed this poem show that he was trying to renounce despair and embrace a life of action; but his use in "Le Guignon" of only the pessimistic lines from Longfellow's "Psalm to Life" and his addition of the phrase "dans l'oubli" suggest "a lost or unheeding audience.... The poem is one of disengagement, conveying Baudelaire's realization of the limits of his own poetic action. It is a denial of the optimism of the Dupont article."[11] The poem further departs from its model by depicting a central figure *conscious* of a lack of contact with any potential audience, Baudelaire rewriting "Mainte fleur épanche *en secret* / Son parfum doux" as "Mainte fleur épanche *à regret* / Son parfum doux" (pp. 17, 859, 861: Many a flower *secretly* [*reluctantly*] gives off its sweet perfume [emphasis added]). And Baudelaire's August 1851 letter to his mother similarly reveals that he has come to believe himself a victim of bad luck, of social upheaval that had distracted attention from his poetry (*Corr.* I, 178). A few months later, in his first long essay on Poe (March 1852), Baudelaire generalizes the idea of the "poète maudit" (i.e., unduly neglected): he says that Vigny's *Stello* shows that no form of government, be it absolute monarchy, constitutional monarchy, or republic, has a place for the poet (II, 250).[12]

III

During his ensuing Symbolist crisis, Baudelaire wrote the Poe translations and most of the later *Fleurs du Mal*. His poetic practice now

11. Chesters, "Baudelaire's 'L'Artiste inconnu,' " pp. 65–66, 74, 76. Cf. Paul Bénichou, "A propos du Guignon: Note sur le travail poétique chez Baudelaire," *Etudes baudelairiennes*, 3 (1973), 232–40.

12. Baudelaire, *OC* I, 859–62. For a general overview of this topic, see the special issue of the journal *Oeuvres et Critiques* (vol. 9 [1984]) devoted to the legend and the reality of the "poète maudit" in mid-nineteenth-century France.

becomes patently regressive. Losing hope for improvement in the political sphere, he withdraws inside himself. In aesthetic terms, from 1851 through 1858 Baudelaire reaches the height of his achievement as a Symbolist lyric poet, but in psychodynamic terms he abandons his outward-looking stance and his attempts to inculcate aesthetic and humanitarian sensitivity in the bourgeoisie, a didactic, idealistic position characteristic of the socially committed writings of the late 1840s and the early 1860s.

Fantastized and remembered relations with his mother in childhood and infancy now shape his relations with the Other—including the fictive audiences—in the present. The lyric self simultaneously desires communication with the Other with infantile urgency and dreads contact with the Other. This middle period poetry reflects Baudelaire's keen anticipations of the two major assumptions of classical psychoanalytic theory: our relations with significant others in childhood shape our later life by providing an enduring unconscious model for all adult relations; and our mental life frequently is directed by unconscious forces over which we have little control.

Baudelaire needed an appropriate poetic mold in which to cast the expression of his loss of faith in progress, his retreat from involvement in public affairs, and the quasi-confessional introspection that replaced political commitment. He found a suitable vehicle in the traditional genre of the elegy, which had recently been revived by the Romantics.

The elegiac tradition is the most ancient of the Western lyric.[13] It runs from parts of the Iliad (Andromache's lament) through Bion and Moschus to Tibullus and Propertius; from Clément Marot and Joachim Du Bellay through André Chénier and Alphonse de Lamartine to Baudelaire, Verlaine, Apollinaire, and Jacques Prévert. Rhetorically, the elegy consists in an appeal to a superior being. The lyric self, unlike the speaker in the traditional genres of the ode or the satire, remains uncertain of securing a response. The intended audience may not even listen to him. So the initially plaintive tone may shade into frustration, anger, and invective. Whereas the ode depicts an unequivocally positive object of praise, and satire a wholly negative object of blame, the elegy portrays an object that is positive

---

13. For a characterization and capsule history of the elegy, see Laurence M. Porter, *The Renaissance of the Lyric in French Romanticism: Elegy, "Poëme," and Ode* (Lexington, Ky.: French Forum, 1978), pp. 21–29.

insofar as it is desired but negative insofar as the lyric self blames it for its frustrating indifference or absence. Such emotional ambivalence and affective lability make the psychodynamics of even traditional elegies difficult to characterize; but the problem of untangling clashing feelings in the love lyric becomes acute in Baudelaire, who weds the extremes of primal regression and rhetorical sophistication in his powerful creations.

The elegy's traditional pretext is the loss of a beloved object or the narcissistic losses of illness or imminent death. To these Baudelaire adds the loss of creative power and of religious faith. To regain contact directly or indirectly with what has been lost—at least by finding consensual validation for the poet's suffering—the elegy adopts one of three main strategies. It may make an anxious appeal for attention from the lost object or for sympathy from intermediaries or replacements; frustrated, it may verbally assail the lost object or the obstacles separating the latter from the lyric self (a strategy typical of Propertius); and finally, disheartened, it may altogether withdraw cathexis (i.e., a focus of desire) from the outside world, sinking into apathy, ennui, and self-destructive impulse. This last condition can ordinarily be remedied only if material losses can be recouped on a spiritual plane. In any event, the elegy adopts a dominantly retrospective stance. It looks toward the happier but vanished past; and its major trope is the apostrophe, discourse directed toward an audience that is nonhuman, remote, or dead. Referring to the audience *in* the text rather than to the audience *of* the text, we can define the elegy as the genre that postulates the absence of this audience and then strives to regain contact with it.

Charles-Augustin Sainte-Beuve's *Poésies de Joseph Delorme* was the model of elegiac rhetoric most immediately available to Baudelaire. For the sake of economy, I shall limit my discussion to this one privileged source among many. Sainte-Beuve's collection of verse occupied a much more prominent place in Baudelaire's imagination than we could readily guess today, owing to Sainte-Beuve's fame as the leading nineteenth-century French literary critic and to Baudelaire's great admiration for him as a poet as well.[14] Sainte-Beuve in turn

---

14. Baudelaire dedicated a youthful untitled *épître* to Sainte-Beuve (*OC* I, 206); see also the *Correspondance*, passim, for expressions of his admiration. Baudelaire may have derived an added satisfaction from an unconscious identification with Sainte-Beuve because the latter, as lover of Hugo's wife, had been the successful sexual rival of the

believed that he was continuing the elegiac tradition of Chénier and
Lamartine, and he considered the elegy to be unduly neglected in his
own time.[15] The prose introduction to *Joseph Delorme* adopts the hoary
device of the found manuscript: through the mediation of Sainte-
Beuve, an unknown sufferer who felt that he could not find "union
with another soul" on earth posthumously finds sympathizers. This
device is a variant of the *sta viator* topos frequently found in the elegy:
the passer-by is invited to contemplate the tomb and fate of an unknown person, typically one who has died young. Sainte-Beuve does
not fail to make this topos explicit with an "editorial" metaphor comparing Delorme's volume of verse to a stone inscribed with the dead
youth's name and brought forth to help construct the doorway of the
temple to the Muses.[16]

The *sta viator* topos mediates the relationship between the public
and the lyric self through a piece of foregrounded commemorative
writing (the inscribed epitaph) inserted as an internal reduplication
within the writing of the main text. In contrast, Baudelaire's verbal
appeals are more urgent and direct. His lyric self often speaks from
beyond or even from within the tomb. Like Baudelaire, however,
Sainte-Beuve frequently dispenses with the archaic mediation of the
inscription and provides a model for his successor when he directly
addresses the implied audiences of his texts. He employs at least 44
apostrophes and 195 rhetorical questions (frequently used in pairs)
in 126 poems—coincidentally the same number of poems as in Baudelaire's 1861 edition of *Les Fleurs du Mal*. Occasionally the subdued
mood typical of Sainte-Beuve erupts in Baudelairean explosions of
violence: "Que si tu m'oubliais jamais, —je te poignarde!" (If you were
ever to forget me, I'll stab you!). In both Sainte-Beuve and Baudelaire,
the vocal appeal of the elegiac enterprise generates rich, manifold
stylistic emphasis in the text. Like Sainte-Beuve, Baudelaire frequently
uses rhetorical questions. These questions are always also non-
questions that feign to invite a response that they actually discourage.
They seek genuine contact with both the empirical and the fictive
audience in other ways. By casting a statement in the linguistically
marked (unusual) form of a question, they add a phatic element, an

---

dominant father figure in nineteenth-century French poetry, a figure toward whom
Baudelaire himself felt strong ambivalence.

15. Charles-Augustin Sainte-Beuve, *Vie, poésies et pensées de Joseph Delorme* (Paris: Levy,
1863 [1829]), p. 169.

16. Ibid., p. 20.

effort to attract attention. At times these questions name the interlocutor, and especially in Baudelaire, they frequently link the audiences to the author through their aphoristic, generalizing force.

Again like Sainte-Beuve, Baudelaire often adopts apostrophes to
create a virtual audience. So strong is his predilection for this rhetorical device that, as Ross Chambers has pointed out, nine poem titles
function both as dedications and as apostrophes (e.g., "A une Malabaraise"), as addresses "to an absent illocutionary partner."[17] Less
specifically, Baudelaire exploits personal pronouns and adjectives to
foreground the transmission of a message. In communicative acts the
third person is neutral, whereas the first person highlights the sender,
and the second person highlights the receiver. Jean Hytier, among
others, has remarked on Baudelaire's frequent use of *tu, toi, vous,* and
vocatives; Margaret Gilman finds either the first or second person in
all but eight of the *Fleurs du Mal;* Alison Fairlie comments on "Baudelaire's frequent substitution of the personal for the general." She
refers in particular to possessive adjectives of the first and second
person, which inscribe one of the illocutionary partners in the poem.[18]
More revealing than the mere statistical preponderance of such words,
however, is the *mouvement général* of Baudelaire's imagination, de-
tectable both in his manuscript variants and in the way that his finished
poems unfold. He characteristically begins a poem with third-person
description but concludes it with an apostrophe or prosopopoeia
dramatizing the presence of an audience and moving the *énoncé* into
closer contact with its intended receiver.

When introduced by the vocative "O," a word found only in lyric
poetry and highly rhetorical prose, the apostrophe fulfills simultaneously the contrary needs for intimacy and for distance. While turning away from the empirical readers (who no longer can imagine
themselves as being addressed), the apostrophe creates a virtual addressee who is also kept at arm's length. For "O" means both "what
follows is addressed to an audience that is elsewhere, nonhuman, or
dead" and also "this is a poem" (a discourse without referents sub-
sisting in the here and now of the communicative situation). "O" is

17. Ross Chambers, "Baudelaire et la pratique de la dédicace," *Saggi e ricerche di
letteratura francese,* 24 (1985), 119–40.

18. Jean Hytier, "*Les Fleurs du Mal:* Evénement poétique," *Romanic Review,* 59 (1968),
249–66 (p. 261); Margaret Gilman, *The Idea of Poetry in France from Houdar de la Motte
to Baudelaire* (Cambridge: Harvard University Press, 1958), p. 240; Alison Fairlie, *Imagination and Language* (Cambridge: Cambridge University Press, 1981), pp. 248–49.

self-canceling as a vocative and phatic device. But when repeated in final position, it serves aesthetic if not pragmatic needs (i.e., for influencing the audience). Such repetition creates the effects of symmetry and closure. When repeated, the vocative acquires a new meaning, not as a prelude to direct address, but as a marker of emphasis and intensity which again foregrounds the speaker rather than the audience—as at the end of "Le Balcon" or "A une passante"—while resealing the poetic discourse into its speaker's subjective world.

Baudelaire chooses the archaic vocative "O" to initiate an apostrophe in one poem out of nine. Thirteen of the eighteen examples of the apostrophes beginning in this manner are addressed to abstractions or inanimate objects. Thus at first glance they appear to function even at the beginning of the poems as "O" normally functions at the conclusions of poems: they connote emotional intensity rather than any plausible act of communication, in the same way as the intensifying apostrophe (without a vocative "O") functions near the end of "Un voyage à Cythère": "Ridicule pendu, tes douleurs sont les miennes" (p. 119: Ridiculous hanged man, your sufferings are mine). The "O" appears then to serve ultimately as a flavoring device, adding connotations of formality and general allegorical significance as well as emotivity.

The fundamental meaning of all direct address in Baudelaire's lyrics, whether apostrophe or not, is revealed by a related device that may or may not be presented in the form of an apostrophe. Baudelaire employs the imperative of verbs denoting mental—and more specifically, imaginative—experience to invite the addressee to share the vision of the poem:

1. Contemplons ce trésor de grâces florentines ["Le Masque: statue allégorique dans le goût de la Renaissance," p. 23].
2. Rappelez-vous l'objet que nous vîmes, mon âme ["Une charogne," p. 31].
3. Songe à la douceur / D'aller là-bas vivre ensemble ["L'Invitation au voyage," p. 53].
4. Vois sur ces canaux / Dormir ces vaisseaux ["L'Invitation au voyage," p. 53].
5. Imaginez Diane en galant équipage ["Sisina," p. 60].
6. Avez-vous observé que maints cercueils de vieilles ["Les Petites Vieilles," p. 89].
7. Contemple-les mon âme; ils sont vraiment affreux ["Les Aveugles," p. 92].

8. Connais-tu, comme moi, la douleur savoureuse ["Le Rêve d'un curieux," p. 128].

(1: Let us contemplate this treasure trove of Florentine grace; 2: Do you recall the object that we saw, my soul; 3: Think of the rapture of going there to live together; 4: See those vessels sleeping on those canals; 5: Imagine Diana in elegant array; 6: Have you noticed that many old women's coffins; 7: Contemplate them, my soul; they are truly frightful; 8: Are you familiar, as I am, with the savory pain).

All these examples are syntactically congruent (except 6 and 8, which, as rhetorical questions, constitute attenuated forms of the imperative). But 1, 5, 6, and 8 are directed to the virtual reader, whereas 2, 3, and 4 are addressed to a female companion. Examples 2 and 7 use an identical form of address, "mon âme," but the first is technically not an apostrophe, since it designates the present female companion, while the second is, since it designates a part of the poet. This convergence of form and function despite the variety of illocutionary situations and addressees suggests that all forms of direct address in the lyric fulfill the role that Jonathan Culler has attributed to apostrophe alone. On one level of reading, Culler explains, the apostrophe serves as a rhetorical intensifier; on a second, it constitutes an *I–Thou* relationship; on a third, "the vocative of apostrophe is a device which the poetic voice uses to establish with an object a relationship that helps to constitute him. The object is treated as a subject, an *I* which implies a certain type of *you* in its turn."[19] Specifically, in Baudelaire's love poems, as in those of his precursors in the Western tradition, the poet, according to Arden Reed, "assures his beloved that he will preserve her memory in his verse. The genre is complex and ambiguous, because it creates a potential conflict between the aim of perpetuating the woman's identity—which implies a self-effacement of the poet [—] and the aim of self-promotion since success in this genre testifies to the power of the artist."[20]

The elegy has endured for two millennia, however, because it expresses concerns far more primordial than artistic self-consciousness and relations with an audience. Psychodynamically, it depicts a helpless lyric self, who sometimes regresses to the state of a child depen-

19. Jonathan Culler, *The Pursuit of Signs: Semiotics, Literature, Deconstruction* (Ithaca, N.Y.: Cornell University Press, 1981), p. 142 (and compare all of chap. 7, "Apostrophe," pp. 135–54).

20. See Arden Reed, *Romantic Weather: The Climates of Coleridge and Baudelaire* (Hanover, N.H.: University Press of New England, 1983), p. 305.

dent on a parent. The elegy reflects the fear of losing love and the
hope of regaining it, emotions reaching back to infancy, when being
nurtured by one's primary caregiver was literally a matter of life and
death. It taps the powerful survival instincts that we share with animals
but which can easily become confused with the adult human's yearn-
ings to be loved and cared for, giving such desires a peculiar urgency
and vesting those who might fulfill them with extraordinary importance. To be more specific, many of the attempts to restore contact
with a lost love object in the traditional elegy and in Baudelaire are
artistically elaborated variants of behaviors common to the higher
animals, to children, and to bereaved adults.[21] Three typical phases
of response may be observed across many species. The first consists
of summoning cries. Predictably, such cries can be heard in *Les Fleurs
du Mal*:

> —Mais le vert paradis des amours enfantines,
>
> L'innocent paradis, plein de plaisirs furtifs,
> Est-il déjà plus loin que l'Inde et que la Chine?
> Peut-on le rappeler avec des cris plaintifs,
> ["Moesta et errabunda," p. 64]

(But the green paradise of childhood loves, // The innocent paradise,
full of furtive pleasures, / Is it already farther away than India and
China? / Can we recall it with plaintive cries.)

"Les Phares" generalizes the lonely infant's sobs to all humanity when
Baudelaire compares all artistic creation to an "ardent sanglot," a
passionate appeal rising wavelike to break upon the shores of eternity
next to an apparently indifferent God.

The second phase of reaction to bereavement is a restless, wandering search, also a hallmark of Baudelaire's elegies. This search
may be attributed to the lyric self ("Mais je poursuis en vain le Dieu
qui se retire" [But I pursue in vain the retreating God] in "Le Coucher
du soleil romantique," p. 149); to kindred but benighted spirits
("Ombres folles, courez au but de vos désirs; / Jamais vous ne pourrez
assouvir votre rage" [Crazed shades, run after the goal of your desires;

---

21. See John Bowlby's classic study *Attachment and Loss*, 3 vols. (London: Hogarth,
1969–80). The more popular pioneering work by Elisabeth Kübler-Ross, *On Death and
Dying* (New York: Macmillan, 1969), identifies five successive stages in the human
reaction of grief: denial, anger, bargaining, depression, and acceptance. Kübler-Ross's
ideas have been widely applied to help therapists and their clients understand emotional
reactions to all kinds of losses. My own research to date, however, has convinced me
that her schema is not readily applicable to literature.

/ Never will you be able to assuage your passion] in "Femmes damnées. Delphine et Hippolyte," p. 155); or to humanity in general:

> Singulière fortune où le but se déplace,
> Et, n'étant, nulle part, peut être n'importe où!
> Où l'Homme, dont jamais l'espérance n'est lasse,
> Pour trouver le repos court toujours comme un fou!
> ["Le Voyage," p. 130]

(A curious destiny with a shifting goal, / Which, being nowhere, can be anywhere at all! / Where Man, with his indefatigable hopes, / Rushes about like a madman in order to find repose!)

Baudelaire represents the third phase of the bereavement reaction, indifference, by the condition of "Spleen," a state of clinical depression familiar, though in a milder form, from such classics as Lamartine's "L'Isolement," whose lyric self characterizes himself as forgotten and having no consolation other than his own company.

Like the poems of his precursors, Baudelaire's respond not only to the loss of significant others but to the self-losses of aging, death, and damnation. Baudelaire also follows the traditions of spiritualizing the loved object and eliminating anecdotal and autobiographical detail (the elegy is quite an impersonal genre and yields little information to those who wish to learn about the life of the author). He reduces the frequency of periphrasis and mythological (as opposed to allegorical) personifications found in Lamartine. Like Hugo, Baudelaire balances the subjective with the didactic and adds elements of physical and social realism (e.g., illness and poverty). But he decreases the prominence of the overt rhetoric of anaphora and parallelism found in Hugo. And unlike Hugo, whose preference for the ode reflects his confidence in making contact with an audience that shares his values, Baudelaire makes contact with his audience problematic by reviving a lyric genre, the elegy, that is more thoroughly grounded than the ode in the interplay of appeal and response. By abandoning the use of pseudonyms in 1851 (see *OC* II, 1095), he expresses a desire for greater intimacy than he had previously enjoyed with his public.

The intimate tone in Baudelaire's elegies is more marked than in those of his precursors, because to self-disclosure (of feelings, not of autobiographical anecdote) he adds a new and pervasive climate of shame and guilt which will be rivaled in French poetry only by Apollinaire. For the first time in French poetry since François Villon, Baudelaire depicts an elegiac self who is not merely the victim of circumstance but a sinful creature torn between soul and matter, good and evil.[22] His entire collection of 1857 (a spiritual autobiography like Hugo's ode cycle Les Contemplations, published the year before) is arranged as a desperate drama of the loss of faith in art, love, the possibility of evasion from reality (through sexual perversion or drugs), and the efficacy of revolt, after which disillusionments the possible novelty of a life after death remains as his only hope.

The elegiac repertory of conventional subjects which Baudelaire adopted is dominated by an opposition between intimacy and separation, with ancillary polarities of home and exile, warmth and cold, family and strangers, grace and sin. The lyric self of Baudelaire's middle period experienced an existential exile whose fundamental source as he perceives it is original sin, a break with our divine origin.[23] This degradation is aggravated in Baudelaire's view by the progressive blunting of our sensitivity as we age and lose the imaginative keenness of childhood.[24] "Bénédiction" combines these motifs of our collective and our individual fall by stating that mortal eyes even at their fullest radiance "ne sont que des miroirs obscurcis et plaintifs!" of the "foyer saint des rayons primitifs" (p. 9: are only dimmed and plaintive mirrors of the sacred hearth of the primordial rays).

The simplest dramatization of the lyric self's loss of contact with the maternal figure or her replacement is her withdrawal in time and space. The joy of symbiotic union that she inspired, and the idyllic past that she inhabited, withdraw along with her, as in the passage from "Moesta et errabunda" cited above. In "Le Balcon," with obvious phallic undertones, the happy past becomes a "gouffre interdit à nos sondes" (p. 37: an abyss our leads are forbidden to sound). As if to counteract loss in these same poems, the versification becomes an icon of regression: Baudelaire adopts a five-line stanza whose fourth line repeats the second and whose fifth line repeats or nearly repeats the

22. See Marcel Ruff, L'Esprit du mal et l'esthétique baudelairienne (Paris: Colin, 1955), p. 143; and Georges Poulet, La Poésie éclatée: Baudelaire-Rimbaud (Paris: Presses universitaires de France, 1980), pp. 66–73.

23. Thus he prepares the Catholic sensibility of the religious renaissance in French letters which was introduced by the later Verlaine. Continued by Joris-Karl Huysmans, this renaissance endured throughout the first half of the twentieth century. Whereas Hugo externalized the opposition of good and evil in the forms of spirit and matter, darkness and light, Baudelaire internalizes this opposition through allegory so that it becomes part not of God's creation but of our own.

24. See Baudelaire, "Morale du joujou" (1853), I, 582–83.

first. After the midline of each stanza, the reader reverses direction and returns to the starting point. This stanzaic pattern A-B-C-B-A appears as well in the remorseful "L'Irréparable" (pp. 54–55). In "Moesta et errabunda" the Latin title regresses in linguistic history as well as in human history through its allusion to the exiling of Adam and Eve.

Baudelaire's own family situation and his affective response to it predisposed him to an unresolvable fixation on his mother. Not long after the beginning of what we would now call the latency period, his indulgent father, who was much older than Baudelaire's mother, died. The recently suppressed Oedipal attachment to the mother could then be revived. Baudelaire the child enjoyed a few months of special closeness with his mother, feeling that he possessed her without a rival. Years later, near the end of his short life, he recalled this period with delight. On May 6, 1861, he wrote his mother that at that time "tu étais uniquement à moi. Tu étais à la fois une idole et un camarade. Tu seras peut-être étonnée que je puisse parler avec passion d'un temps si reculé. Moi-même, j'en suis étonné" (You belonged to me alone. You were an idol and a companion at the same time. Perhaps you will be astonished that I can speak passionately of a time so long ago. I am astonished by that myself [*Corr.* II, 153]).[25] But unknown to the child, his mother soon became secretly pregnant by a new lover, General Aupick. Her confinement was disguised as an illness. Her baby girl was stillborn, and Baudelaire probably never learned the truth. But as soon as his mother returned home she promptly married Aupick.

The sudden, unexpected appearance of a new rival for his mother's affection appears to have intensified the child's attachment to her while ensuring his continual frustration. His yearning scarcely abated with age. In the same May 1861 letter to his mother he invokes their symbiotic bond: "toi, le seul être à qui ma vie est suspendue. . . . Après ma mort, tu ne vivras plus, c'est clair. Je suis le seul objet qui te fasse vivre" (You, the only being on whom my life depends. . . . After my death, you could not survive; that's clear. I am the only thing you have to live for [*Corr.* II, 150–51]).

Baudelaire's dependency was so acute not only because of the early

25. For an eloquent survey of Baudelaire's mother-fixation, often discussed since François Porché's pioneering biography in 1945, see Sima Godfrey, "'Mère des souvenirs': Baudelaire, Memory and Mother," *L'Esprit Créateur*, 25 (Summer 1985), 32–44.

death of his biological father but because God, a possible father surrogate, did not answer the poet's appeals. As the same letter explains, "je n'ai que le portrait de mon père, qui est toujours muet"; "Je désire de tout mon coeur (avec quelle sincérité, personne ne peut le savoir que moi!) croire qu'un être extérieur et invisible s'intéresse à ma destinée; mais comment faire pour le croire?" (I have only my father's picture, and it never speaks; With all my heart [and how very sincerely, no one but I can know] I long to believe that an invisible, external being takes an interest in my fate—but what can I do to make myself believe that? [*Corr.* II, 152, 151]). Yet he felt his mother could never understand him: "Je t'aime de tout mon coeur; tu ne l'as jamais su. Il y a, entre toi et moi, cette différence que je te sais par coeur, et que tu n'as jamais pu deviner mon misérable caractère" (I love you with all my heart; you've never discovered that. Between you and me, there is this difference: I know you by heart, and you have never been able to guess what my wretched personality is like).[26] In the verse poems, "la servante au grand coeur" (p. 100) seems the only woman who spontaneously feels maternal solicitude for the poet-persona. Baudelaire imagines her returning from the dead to weep over him, because he fancies that if she saw him as an adult, she would be heartbroken with disappointment. After General Aupick died in 1857, however, Baudelaire did not take advantage of the opportunity to live with his mother. He frequently promised to move in with her at Honfleur as soon as he had paid his debts or finished current business in Paris—and he worked productively when he visited Honfleur in 1859[27]—but throughout the remaining decade of his life he never managed to settle permanently with her.

Baudelaire's lifelong financial difficulties sustained his association between his mother and his disapproving, withholding empirical audiences, both of which in turn contributed to the images of his fictive audiences. After he had squandered nearly half his inheritance within two years, Baudelaire lost control of his finances to a family council. Although its members were themselves rich, they doled out only small allotments for the rest of the poet's life. As a prominent member of this council, Baudelaire's mother remained until his death associated

26. Baudelaire to Mme Aupick, October 11, 1860, *Corr.* II, 99.
27. Richard D. E. Burton, *Baudelaire in 1859: A Study in the Sources of Poetic Creativity* (Cambridge: Cambridge University Press, 1988), describes the poet's visit to Honfleur in 1859. A period of intense productivity, this visit marked the end of the crisis of 1851–58.

with the frustration that had originated in his "loss" of her to her second husband. His unappreciative audiences ensured that Baudelaire's other source of income, literary royalties, would remain meager. And as soon as Baudelaire had published his masterpiece in 1857, he was placed on trial for outraging public morals. In other words, the expression of his most intimate yearning (he said that he wrote to be loved ["Epigraphe pour un livre condamné," p. 137]) was labeled as a criminal act in a dramatic fashion that must have revived Baudelaire's most painful affective memories of his punishing childhood superego.

Both the poetic and the historical Baudelaire long for acceptance. The poetry is filled with appeals, entreaties, and prayers. The man often aspired to official recognition such as the medal of the Legion of Honor, the directorship of a state-sponsored theater, a seat in the Académie Française.[28] He thus appears to have secretly courted rejection by asking for honors that all his contemporaries, however sympathetic they might have been, realized that he would never receive. For he had also been inviting social disapproval by living for years with a mulatto sometime prostitute; by publishing a then scandalous volume; and finally by spreading rumors that he was a criminal, a pervert, a police spy.[29] His poetic focus on social and religious outcasts expressed his sense of having been rejected, but it also allowed others to reject him unjustly by associating him with the victims he depicted. By exploring moral corruption, he constantly risked the condemnation of his readers, who saw his choice of subjects as an involuntary confession of depravity. Self-assumed degradation seemed to afford him masochistic pleasure because it confirmed his self-condemnation. He announced, "I have one of those fortunate personalities that derive enjoyment from being hated and that exalt themselves in the midst of others' scorn" ("Projet de préface pour Les Fleurs du Mal," OC I, 185).

Baudelaire, however, for all his apparent martyr complex, was far from being merely self-defeating and self-destructive. What distinguishes him and other creative artists from the ordinary character-disordered person is the successful ego-defense of sublimation, which directs some of the energies of infantile yearning toward regression in the service of the ego. In other words, an imaginative return to

---

28. A pithy discussion of Baudelaire's ambitions appears in OC I, xii.
29. Baudelaire to Mme Paul Meurice, January 3, 1865, Corr. II, 437.

infancy puts Baudelaire in touch with primitive contents of the psyche. Then self-contemplation allows him to achieve sufficient detachment from these contents so that they can be freely exploited to provide materials for art.[30] And Baudelaire is keenly aware of this procedure. In "Le Peintre de la vie moderne" he claims that "le génie n'est que *l'enfance retrouvée* à volonté" (II, 690: genius is no more than *childhood recaptured* at will [emphasis in original]).

And he proves himself keenly aware of infantile sexuality. In a letter to his publisher in which he explains the work of imagination that he has accomplished in his verse poems, and where the *"intelligent"* (i.e., *comprehending* [emphasis in original]) reader should follow him, Baudelaire characterizes the kind of childhood his genius has recaptured: "qu'est-ce que l'enfant aime si passionnément dans sa mère, dans sa bonne, dans sa soeur aînée? Est-ce simplement l'être qui le nourrit, le peigne, le lave et le borde? C'est aussi la caresse et la volupté sensuelle. Pour l'enfant, cette caresse s'exprime à l'insu de la femme, par toutes les grâces de la femme" (What is it that the child loves so passionately in his mother, in his nanny, in his older sister? Is it merely the being who feeds him, combs him, washes him, and tucks him in? It's also caresses and sensual delight. For the child, those caresses are given unknown to the woman, by all of her womanly graces).[31] Elsewhere he unequivocally states that poetry and regression are inseparable: "Tout poète lyrique, en vertu de sa nature, opère fatalement un retour vers l'Eden perdu" (By virtue of his very nature, every lyric poet inevitably accomplishes a return toward the lost Garden of Eden.[32] More rigorously "Symbolist" in the tropological sense than Verlaine or Rimbaud, although less so than Mallarmé, Baudelaire stages regression by organizing a tightly coherent system of metaphors around his breast-fixation so as to create masterpieces of original poetry. He transports infantile and neurotic attitudes from the do-

30. For the most recent authoritative discussion of character disorders (forms of psychopathology more severe than neurosis although not frankly psychotic), see the *DSM-III-R (Diagnostic and Statistical Manual of Mental Illness,* 3d ed. rev. [New York: American Psychoanalytical Association, 1987]). On "regression in the service of the ego," see Ernst Kris, *Psychoanalytical Explorations in Art* (New York: International Universities Press, 1952), pp. 60–63, 197–99, 220–22. On ego-defenses see Anna Freud, *The Ego and the Mechanisms of Defense,* rev. ed. (New York: International Universities Press, 1966), updated and greatly expanded in Henry P. Laughlin, *The Ego and Its Defenses* (New York: Appleton-Century-Crofts, 1970).

31. Baudelaire to Auguste Poulet-Malassis, April 23, 1866, *Corr.* II, 30.

32. Baudelaire, "Théodore de Banville" ([1861], II, 165).

main of deeply unconsious fantasies—which we all share—to the domain of lyric action. And in his poetry, the crux of these fantasies is the phantasmal image of a woman.

Indeed, no adult experience can ever quite match the infant's joy in intimacy with its mother; no later response can ever be as gratifying as hers: such is the psychological deep structure of Baudelaire's elegy. He calls to our attention the regressive tendencies inherent in the elegiac situation, but presented in only a sketchy, haphazard fashion by his precursors. Compare, for example, the latent motif of mother-fixation in Sainte-Beuve's *Joseph Delorme*, less intense and elaborately wrought than in Baudelaire, although it is already quite noticeable. Delorme explains "Moi je chantais pour être aimé!" (*I* sang to be loved!) By whom? The poem with the unwittingly punning title "Premier Amour" (the love of the infant for his mother, as well as the love of a lad for a maid) calls on the beloved "tel un fils orphelin invoque encor sa mère" (as an orphaned son still calls out for his mother). Attachment to the loved woman focuses on her breasts: "Oh! qu'à ce sein je puisse... Clouer mon front brûlant" (Oh! might I glue [literally: nail] my burning forehead to that breast). More tellingly, Delorme equates enforced separation from the beloved with being weaned (see the untitled "Non, je ne chante plus" and the "Ode au soir").[33] But in Sainte-Beuve this motif remains undeveloped.

Far more boldly than Sainte-Beuve, Baudelaire elaborates a network of regressive oral symbolism focused on the breast as the first object and on suckling. He brings out the child's perspective by depicting many of his ideal women as colossi in every sense of the word: statuesque and important as well as huge. In "La Géante," for example, he dreams of crawling like an infant over the woman's body: "Parcourir à loisir ses magnifiques formes; / Ramper sur le versant de ses genoux énormes" and then after presumably being satiated at her breast, "Dormir nonchalamment à l'ombre de ses seins" (p. 23: To range over her splendid forms at leisure; / To crawl upon the slope of her enormous knees... To sleep nonchalantly in the shadow of her breasts). Other poems are more subtle, simply suggesting the presence of a woman's body far larger than the poet's; in "Je t'adore à l'égal de la voûte nocturne," he says, "Je grimpe aux assauts" (p.

33. The lines from Sainte-Beuve quoted in this paragraph appear in *Joseph Delorme*, pp. 189, 285, 29, and 199–200 respectively. Apropos of the last quotation, cf. pp. 36, 200, 201, and 202.

27: I clamber upward to the assault). At still other times Baudelaire explicitly presents relations with a woman as a means of returning to his childhood—"et revis mon passé blotti dans tes genoux" ("Le Balcon," p. 37: and I relive my past huddled between your knees)—or even to the womb itself: "Je veux longtemps... Dans tes jupons remplis de ton parfum / Ensevelir ma tête endolorie" ("Le Léthé," p. 155: I want for a long time... in your skirts filled with your scent / To burrow my wounded head). Often he is more anatomically precise. "Je veux m'anéantir dans ta gorge profonde," he has a female character declare in "Femme damnées. Delphine et Hippolyte" (p. 154: I want to annihilate myself in your deep bosom). And he concludes "Le Léthé" by evoking the oceanic symbiosis of nursing mother and the poet as nursling:

> Je sucerai, pour noyer ma rancoeur,
> Le népenthès et la bonne ciguë
> Aux bouts charmants de cette gorge aiguë,
> Qui n'a jamais emprisonné de coeur.   [p. 156]

(I will suck, to drown my bitterness, / [A magical Greek beverage said to dispel sorrow and anger] and the kindly hemlock / From the charming tips of those pointed breasts, / Which never imprisoned a heart).

In the untitled juvenilium, "Je n'ai pas pour maîtresse une lionne illustre," he makes the connection between poet and infant explicit: "Ainsi qu'un nouveau-né, je la tête et la mords" (p. 203: Like a newborn, I suckle and bite her). In one of the uncommon instances in *Les Fleurs du Mal* in which the woman takes the initiative in lovemaking, the crucial transition from the poet's indifference to arousal is marked by the poem's focus on "votre gorge nue" ("Causerie," p. 56: your naked breasts). Indeed, his quest for the nipple—always a darker color than the surrounding bare breast,[34] and especially so during pregnancy or lactation—is implicit in the condemnation of decadent modern beauties: "Car je ne puis trouver parmi ces *pâles* roses / Une fleur qui ressemble à *mon rouge idéal*," and he longs for "appas façonnés aux *bouches* des Titans!" ("L'Idéal," p. 22: For among these *pale* roses I cannot find / A flower that resembles *my ideal red*... charms shaped for the *mouths* of Titans! [emphasis added]). Via a double apophany,

---

34. See Frank Patalano, "Color in Dreams and the Psychoanalytic Situation," *American Journal of Psychoanalysis*, 44 (Summer 1984), 183–90.

the last word can become *tétons*, both noun and verb (breasts/let us suckle).

Both Baudelaire's friends and his critics noted his breast-fixation. As early as 1842, Ernest Prarond, an intimate companion at the time, pointed it out in a poem addressed to Baudelaire.[35] And an early review of *Les Fleurs du Mal* in *Le Figaro* fifteen years later exploded: "the odious rubs elbows with the ignoble, the repellent joins forces with the foul. You never saw so many breasts bitten and even chewed in so few pages."[36] What is unacceptable about carrying infantile behavior over into mature sexual encounters is of course that childhood "innocence" then risks being retrospectively tainted by adult sexuality. From the adult perspective, in turn, fantasies of suckling are no longer innocent; they have become bound up with the incest taboo. Triumphing in the Oedipal rivalry, the poet as nursing infant comes between his father and his mother literally as well as figuratively. Ingesting the moon's tear/milk in "Tristesses de la lune," he places it in his heart "far from the eyes of the sun" (the rival father).

The temptation of narcissistic regression appears in disguised form as early as "Don Juan aux enfers" (first published in *L'Artiste* of September 6, 1846). This poem was only the second that Baudelaire signed with his own name. The stoical, unrepentent hero ignores all the claims others make on him. The poem functions as an anti-elegy, stubbornly cutting off possibilities for communication rather than striving to create them. In each of the five stanzas alternating between male and female accusers, the intensity and the formidable quality of the accusations of the messages increase.

Male Accusers	*Female Accusers*
st. 1: Beggar	st. 2: Miscellaneous victims
st. 3: Valet; Father	st. 4: The betrayed wife Elvire
st. 5: Elvire's father, slain in a duel with Don Juan	

35. I am indebted to Sima Godfrey for showing me this prescient caricature, which can now be found in the municipal library at Amiens.

36. "L'odieux coudoie l'ignoble, le repoussant s'y allie à l'infect. Jamais on ne vit mordre et même mâcher autant de seins en si peu de pages." Cited by François Porché, *Baudelaire: Histoire d'une âme* (Paris: Flammarion, 1945), pt. IV, chap. 5, p. 2 (sections are paginated separately).

Within this scheme, however, the vigorous gestures of the first two stanzas (seize, writhe) undergo a diminuendo (the father points with trembling finger) and finally freeze into immobility (the statue of Elvire's father merely stands erect), while the loud vocalizations of stanzas 2 and 3 cease in stanzas 4 and 5. The resulting silence endows the calm, disdainful hero of the last two lines with a monumental stasis. But Baudelaire's regressive obsession with suckling appears even in this presentation of a character who does not share it, for he added to his manuscript the anatomical detail that the women seduced by Don Juan appear "montrant leurs seins pendants" (p. 20: displaying their pendulous breasts [perhaps a sign that he has impregnated them before abandoning them]).

The supreme independence of Baudelaire's hero depends upon the presence of people to whom he is *not* paying attention. Moreover, he finds oblivion only in death. Similarly, the autonomy asserted pridefully but with a suspect vehemence in "Le Mort joyeux," "Obsession," and "Le Goût du néant" is achieved only at the cost of accepting self-destruction. "Horreur sympathique" likewise asserts autonomy by making every element of the setting into a reflection of the poet's pride; and the first quatrain is addressed by the poet to himself. Rhetorically as well as thematically, the motif of self-sufficiency thus rejoins that of the secondary narcissism in "a heart become its own mirror" ("L'Irrémédiable"); as well as the motifs of the poet's emotions reflected by his surroundings in "La Musique" and of the poets mesmerized by their own reflections in the mirror eyes of "La Beauté." To define itself, the ego depends on the presence of others. Total isolation is equivalent to psychic death. Then the self becomes a prison, as in "Le Mauvais Moine" or in "Obsession," which evokes "nos coeurs maudits, / Chambres d'éternel deuil!" (p. 75: our accursed hearts, chambers of eternal mourning!). Throughout his Symbolist crisis, Baudelaire simultaneously cries out for release from his prison of selfhood and fearfully retreats further into that prison whenever he encounters the possibility of relatedness to others. The pose of stoical self-mastery attempts to promote a neurotic defense into a principle of moral excellence.

The point, of course, is not that depth psychology "explains" Baudelaire, but rather that much of the greatness of Baudelaire consists in the rich, intricate sensitivity with which he anticipates and illustrates depth psychology. He is not offering us an involuntary spectacle; instead, he tries to offer us the gift of reviving the lost childhood freshness of our imagination. In poems such as those of the initial, "aesthetic" section of *Les Fleurs du Mal* or "Tristesses de la lune," Baudelaire attempts to implicate us in his fantasy by describing the mother-surrogates in the third person. For a third person implies a second. When I write "you" in reference to an entity in the poem, the empirical readers "overhear" the discourse of the poem, ostensibly not intended for them. But when I write "she," you as empirical reader become at least potentially included among an audience of "you's." Then that audience becomes an accomplice to the regressive vision. More radically, since it is within an oral-regressive framework that Baudelaire foregrounds the process of transmitting the poetic message and emphasizes the difficulty of making verbal/affective contact with the indifferent Other, the ultimate result is that successful contact with any audience may well entail speaking and suckling simultaneously.

Vis-à-vis the loved woman, Baudelaire's persona feels simultaneously the desperate need and the frustrated fury of the infant; adult sexual attraction; and the stern prohibition of the father-imago which has been internalized and then reprojected outward onto a supernatural or cosmic decor. To evade the unconscious Oedipal taboo, the lyric self seeks a nonprohibited opposite of the loved woman,[37] as in the untitled sonnet that begins

> Une nuit que j'étais près d'une affreuse Juive
> ....
> Je me pris à songer près de ce corps vendu
> A la triste beauté dont mon désir se prive. [p. 34]

(One night when I was next to a hideous Jewess...I started to muse, next to that bartered body, / About the sad beauty of whom my desire deprives itself).

In Freudian psychology, the German term for "frustration" (*Versagung*) can refer to either external or self-imposed denials of desire. In these lines it is the latter; the prohibition has become internalized.

At the end of this sonnet, the interdependency of the return of the maternal imago, of the urgency of making contact, and of the equal and opposite force of self-denial becomes obvious. After the quatrains

---

37. Sigmund Freud, "Contributions to the Psychology of Love I–III" (1910–17), *Standard Edition of the Complete Psychological Works of Sigmund Freud,* ed. and trans. James Strachey, 24 vols. (London: Hogarth Press, 1953–74), XI, 163–208, esp. 165–73 and 185–86.

the poetic discourse shifts: the speaker no longer refers to the loved woman in the third person; he addresses her directly, in an apostrophe. The phatic element becomes still more emphatic in the penultimate line with its "O" of lyrical address and its exclamation point. Fantasies of caressing the woman are reported hypothetically with the "second form" of the conditional perfect (a pluperfect subjunctive more tentative than an ordinary hypothesis; this nuance is lacking in English). The requested contact amounts to a symbolically displaced form of nursing.[38] The poet appeals to his lady to respond with a secretion of fluid, an analogue of lactation; to moisten with a tear of emotion her "froides prunelles" (cold pupils). In the unconscious, precoital fluid = milk = tears, and in Baudelaire's symbolic system all secretions of fluid represent a response from the Other (compare "Le Masque," p. 24).

Ironically, the "triste beauté" referred to in this early poem presumably was Jeanne Duval, the mulatto woman soon to become Baudelaire's longtime mistress. Some critics are shocked that later Baudelaire allegedly had her prostitute herself in order to help support him in Lyons, but her degradation appears to have been a psychic necessity for Baudelaire, a condition that made sexual concourse with her permissible.[39] It was inevitable that after becoming the historical

38. The definitive recent biography of Baudelaire by Claude Pichois and Jean Ziegler, *Baudelaire* (Paris: Julliard, 1987), does not tell us whether Baudelaire had a wet nurse.

39. See Baudelaire, *OC* I, 893, citing his friend Ernest Prarond. At a deeper unconscious level, the degradation of the poet's object serves not to distinguish her from the mother-imago but to associate her with it. Oedipal rivalry entails the "rescue fantasy" in which the son rescues the mother from the clutches of the oppressive, unworthy father. The fantasy can be acted out through attempts to "redeem" a prostitute by detaching her from her pimp and clients. Crudely wish-fulfilling versions of the fantasy commonly provide the subject for productions of popular culture such as the films *Never on Sunday* and *Klute*. High art offers disguised forms such as Verdi's *La Traviata* and Shaw's *Pygmalion*, or sophisticatedly open-ended versions such as Jacques-Stéphen Alexis's novel *L'Espace d'un cillement*. In real life, however, the acted-out strategy must fail in order for the ego to remain defended: if the despised object is really "redeemed," she comes too uncomfortably close to the idealized mother. Thus the compelling need to maintain the neurotic equilibrium of a frustrating relationship. This psychic dynamism is patent in Baudelaire's letter to his mother in which he describes Jeanne Duval as a person "avec qui il est impossible d'échanger une parole politique ou littéraire, une créature qui ne *veut rien apprendre*.... J'ai épuisé dix ans de ma vie dans cette lutte" (Baudelaire to Mme Aupick, March 27, 1852, *Corr.* I, 193–94: [a person] with whom it is impossible to exchange a word about politics or literature, a creature who *wants to learn nothing*.... I've drained away ten years of my life in this struggle [emphasis in original]).

poet's mistress, Jeanne should in due course become his despised object,[40] contrasted in turn with another idealized (although kept and promiscuous) woman, Apollonie Sabatier. Baudelaire's growing distaste for Jeanne and his announced intention to break with her antedates only slightly the first anonymous love poem sent to "Madame" Sabatier.[41]

The result of internalized prohibition is that the self retreats from the object because the self desires it. Psychic projection transforms this situation into one in which the object apparently withdraws because it is desired; it thereby preserves its ideal status and redoubles its fascination through its distance, as in these lines from "Je t'adore à l'égal de la voûte nocturne":

> Et t'aime d'autant plus, belle, que tu me fuis,
> Et que tu me parais, ornement de mes nuits,
> Plus ironiquement accumuler les lieues
> Qui séparent mes bras des immensités bleues.   [p. 27]

(And I love you all the more, my beauty, as you flee from me, / And all the more as you seem to me—adornment of my nights / —Ironically to accumulate the leagues / That separate my arms from the blue vastnesses.)

Following an ancient tradition of love poetry, Baudelaire depicts his lyric self as reading meaning in or into a woman's eyes, but by not responding, by neither accepting nor rejecting the poet, she retains her allure (as do similar idealized women in, for example, "La Beauté," "La Géante," "Hymne à la Beauté," "Parfum exotique," "La Chevelure," "Sed non satiata," "Le Chat," "L'Invitation au voyage," and the untitled poems XXIV, XXV, XXVII).

Such self-imposed frustration redounds to the poet's credit through a complicated dialectic. Since he believes himself to be worthless, he imagines that the loved woman ignores or rejects him (that is, through psychic projection, he transposes responsibility for his unconscious or

40. See, e.g., Baudelaire to Mme Aupick, cited in n. 39 above (*Corr.* I, 190–97); Baudelaire's disenchantment with Jeanne Duval coincides with his enthusiastic discovery of an ego-ideal, Edgar Allan Poe.

41. After Apollonie Sabatier discovered her admirer's identity and slept with him at the end of August 1857, Baudelaire became disillusioned with her in turn as an ideal: "il y a quelques jours, tu étais une divinité, ce qui est si commode, ce qui est si beau, si inviolable. Te voilà femme maintenant" (A few days ago, you were a goddess, which is so convenient, which is so beautiful, so inviolable. And here you are a woman now [Baudelaire to Apollonie Sabatier, August 31, 1857, *Corr.* I, 425]).

semi-conscious flight from her). Her fantasized rejection of him reaffirms her value, since she will not become debased by contact with his worthlessness. But as a paradoxical result, her rejection also confirms the merit of the poet who adores her. He is worthy insofar as the object of his adoration is worthy. On the rhetorical plane, direct address and second-person possessive adjectives or pronouns reinforce the poet's defensive maneuvers: they compel the Other to be present as an idea, while suggestions of her absence or her superhuman status preserve her inaccessibility.

This equilibrium of presence and absence, desire and prohibition in Baudelaire's poetry remains precarious. The beloved risks becoming either too inhuman or all too human. Excessively abstract idealization of the beloved may literally turn her into a statue (obstensibly immune to change or corruption) and thereby endow her with a phallic rigidity that ultimately threatens to castrate the poet, as in "La Beauté," where each lover in turn is bruised by the woman's breasts of stone (p. 20). Yet without the poet's arduous, unrelenting exercise of control in his depiction, the loved woman may reveal through her facial expression or her words that she is just as vulnerable as he (see "Confession" and "Le Masque"). Once the poet learns that she shares the suffering of the human condition, he can no longer vest in her his hope of ultimate redemption through association with a superior being. (This hope is explicitly named in the love poem "Réversibilité," referring to the Catholic dogma that the supererogatory merit of the saints can be applied toward the salvation of ordinary people.)

The total Baudelairean constellation of regression, fixation on the mother-imago, Oedipal prohibition, and narcissistic self-recuperation via the female intermediary is richly illustrated in "A une passante" ([1860], pp. 92–93), despite its superficial conformity to the aesthetics of "le beau moderne," the spontaneous sketch snatched from the cityscape which Baudelaire extolled in his essay on Constantin Guys (II, 683–724). This poem ostensibly recounts an enchanted moment of communicative plenitude. Typically, it moves from the third person in the quatrains to an intimate apostrophe (beginning "fugitive beauté") in the tercets. (I have schematized the presentation of this text in order to highlight the pervasive quality of the Oedipal fixation dramatized by the poem, and the thick web of associations that this fixation generates. The parenthetical numbers added to the text of the poem correspond to the numbered statements in the commentary that follows it.)

La rue assourdissante autour de moi hurlait (1).
Longue (2), mince (4), en grand deuil (4), douleur majestueuse (2),
Une femme (2) passa, d'une main fastueuse (4)
Soulevant (4), balançant (4) le feston (5) et l'ourlet (4);

Agile (4) et noble (2), avec sa jambe (4) de statue (5).
Moi, je buvais (6), crispé [var.: tremblant, 6] comme un extravagant (7),
Dans son oeil, ciel livide (3) où germe l'ouragan (2, 4),
La douceur qui fascine (6) et le plaisir (7) qui tue (7).

Un éclair... puis la nuit (7) —Fugitive beauté
Dont le regard m'a fait soudainement renaître (6) [var.: souvenir et renaître],
Ne te verrai-je plus que dans l'éternité (8)?

Ailleurs, bien loin d'ici! trop tard! *jamais* peut-être!
Car j'ignore où tu fuis, tu ne sais où je vais (8, 9),
O toi que j'eusse aimée, ô toi qui le savais! (9)   [pp. 92–93]

(The deafening street was howling around me. / Tall, slender, in deep mourning—a majestic sorrow— / A woman passed, with a sumptuous hand / Raising her flounces and eyelets and making them sway; // Lithe and noble, with her statuesque leg. / I drank in, contorted [trembling] like an eccentric, / From her eyes, a livid sky where the hurricane germinates, / The gentleness that fascinates and the pleasure that kills. // A flash of lightning... then darkness—Fleeting beauty / Whose glance made me be suddenly reborn [remember and be reborn] / Shall I never see you again except in eternity? // Somewhere else, far from here! Too late! *Never* perhaps! / For I know not where you are fleeing, you know not where I go, / O you I would have loved, O you who knew it!)

(1) At the beginning of the poem, the lyric self is deprived of love, and his archaic memories unconsciously associate this state with the condition of the infant deprived of the breast, crying with discomfort and frustration. Since this affective memory remains powerful but is unrecognized, it must find expression in a disguised form. It is projected on the poet's surroundings: the "howling" cityscape is an *état d'âme*. The resulting tumult dazes the poet, erasing conscious meanings from the scene and leaving the mind blank, a slate on which the unconscious may inscribe messages by selecting them from among the manifold impressions offered by the crowded street. (2) A woman appears, anonymous like most figurations of the mother in our fantasy life. Like a mother seen by her child, she is tall ("longue") and seems endowed with the authority vested in a superior social rank ("majestueuse, noble"). (3) Baudelaire's frequent meteorological metaphors

convey the remembered omnipotence of the parents, whose unpredictable moods can determine the child's emotional world. (4) Yet now the woman has become sexually available, set free by the death of the rival ("en grand deuil") and not pregnant with another potential rival ("mince"). (We should note that Baudelaire's step-father had died three years before the publication of this poem.) The hypallage of "fastueuse" applied to her hand rather than to the fabric that it raises suggests the keen pleasure that her touch could bring. As such movement always is for Baudelaire, her agile swaying is sexually provocative. He becomes aware of her as a physical being ("jambe") whose clothing suggests the fetishistic appeal of displaced symbolic substitutes for the sexual organs ("ourlet"). Raising her skirts to keep them clear of the mud of the streets, she calls to mind the gesture she would make if she were to begin to disrobe,[42] and the hint of a storm in her eye (cf. Verlaine's "la bonne tempête") foreshadows the turbulence of lovemaking.

Prohibition cohabits with desire. (5) The words "statue" and "feston" (which can mean not only "embroidered draped cloth" but also the decorative stone swags of architecture) give the woman an air of impenetrable monumentality. The second syllable of "statue" migrates through other terms that also connote a taboo ("majes*tue*use," "fas*tue*use," "*tue*"). This syllable is located prominently at or just before the rhyme, and finally it is reechoed in the double designation of the loved woman herself ("tu" twice in line 13), as if to associate her intimately with the idea of inaccessibility. "Statue" brings to mind the phallic rigidity of perfection. It ends a line that breaks the rhythm of the stanzas (the libidinal flux of the lyric self); and like "feston" it connotes a memorial to the past and is thus analogous to the mother-imago itself. The woman's generic designation, "une passante," recalls the word "passé." (6) The codes of orality and intense physical response reduce the poet once more to the condition of a nursing infant; the telltale variant "souvenir et renaître" implies a return to that state in memory. (7) In and of itself, however, such a physical response already seems tantamount to transgression, as the etymology of "extravagant" (wandering too far) suggests. Sexual enjoyment ("le plaisir") calls forth immediate punishment ("qui tue"). The lightning flash

42. This image is a cultural cliché. See Michael Riffaterre's comments on the "jupe soulevable/insoulevable" (the liftable/unliftable skirt) in "Flaubert's Presuppositions," in *Critical Essays on Gustave Flaubert*, ed. Laurence M. Porter (Boston: G. K. Hall, 1986), pp. 76–86.

("l'éclair") not only denotes a discharge of sexual electricity from the stranger's eye, but it also and primarily functions as a synonym for "tue," for it is the bolt of fire thrown by a vengeful Father God. The ensuing night represents not merely the woman's absence but also death.[43]

(8) Lines 11–13 reinstitute the Oedipal prohibition, restating seven times the absolute barrier between the lyric self and his object: he never will see her again, unless in another life, elsewhere, far away, too late, or perhaps never. Neither of the two knows how to find the other again. Yet as soon as their separation has been announced ("la nuit"), the poet vigorously tries to regain contact through the rhetorical device of a threefold apostrophe (lines 9 and 14) whose first phrase, "fugitive beauté," sums up the clash of desire and frustration. Only when the poet is at some distance from his object does he seem to feel safe enough to address her directly rather than in the third person. (9) But in a sense she has never left him. Line 13 iconically represents the fact that he contains her ("je...tu...tu...je"), since she has emanated from his unconscious; and if she can read his thoughts, as the last line claims, it is because she is part of him. "A une passante," in short, demonstrates that Baudelaire can recruit an ideal audience (the opposite of the noisy, indifferent crowds in line 1) only by summoning it from idealized memories of a happier past. More accurately, his initial attempt to contact an audience is incited by regressive fantasies that, in the course of the act of communication, remove the poet from the plane of the present where real communication might be possible.

Baudelaire achieves the perfect synthesis of desire and prohibition in "Harmonie du soir," part of the Apollonie Sabatier cycle of poems to the idealized woman. On the literal level, this poem describes a garden where (1) the scent of flowers fills the still evening air; (2) the

---

43. Compare the sequence of desire and punishment in Mallarmé's "L'Après-Midi d'un faune," whose eponymous character imagines raping the mother-surrogate Venus: "Je tiens la reine!...ô sûr châtiment" (I hold the queen!...O certain punishment). Ross Chambers calls the woman herself in "A une passante" "a figure of death"; see "The Storm in the Eye of the Poem: Baudelaire's 'A une passante,'" in *Textual Analysis: Some Readers Reading* (New York: Modern Language Association, 1986), ed. Mary Ann Caws, pp. 156–66. Chambers's analysis of the complex illocutionary situation of the poem emphasizes the "noise" (interferences with communication) in the street, the street being the channel of communication for the message passed in the wordless glances between poet and woman. I would add that from a psychodynamic perspective, the howling crowd suggests the demands and distractions of adult life which interfere with the exclusivity of the mother-child relationship.

sun sets, filling the sky with brilliant colors that suggest drying blood; (3) the moon rises. On the figurative level (1) the fragrant smoke from a censer purifies the place of sacrifice before High Mass; (2) the ritual sacrifice of the sun/son (I do not claim that Baudelaire was thinking of this English homonym) is accomplished; (3) commemoration is achieved ("Ton souvenir en moi luit comme un ostensoir!" [The memory of you shines in me like a monstrance!]). The unusual rhyme-words "encensoir," "reposoir" (a portable altar used in outdoor processions), and "ostensoir" sketch the ceremony of the Mass. At its culmination, the priest raises the pale disk of the consecrated host. In context (the garden setting) this gesture implies the rising of the full moon suddenly prominent after sundown. During a real Mass, after the Elevation the priest places communion wafers in the communicants' mouths; they consume the divinity in a ritualized situation and with the sanction of the Father. In this poem, however, the Father who prohibits and the object that is desired are conflated by the image of the monstrance, the round metal object with rays that suggest the sun and with a transparent door on the front which reveals the relics of the saints—or a consecrated host—within while preventing anyone from touching them. Baudelaire does not consummate his ceremony, because *his* round white object is the mother's breast. The moon as a memory of the departed sun (another heavenly body perceived as about the same size and reflecting the sun's light) is analogous to the round, pale communion wafer that recalls the departed Christ and also the Isakower phenomenon (adult hallucinations of the vaguely remembered maternal breast) in psychopathology.[44]

Such extraordinary overvaluation of the loved woman proves exceedingly difficult to sustain, as we learn only too plainly from Baudelaire's disillusioned letter after a night with Apollonie Sabatier (for whom "Harmonie du soir" was written); from his association of sexuality with the bestial; and from the frequent manifestations of the Madonna-Prostitute complex in Baudelaire's poems, which either venerate or despise their female subjects. For one brief period from mid-1854 through 1855, however, Baudelaire's lyric appeared to achieve emotional equilibrium. Composed at that time, the ten poems of the cycle inspired by Marie Daubrun (an actress to whom Baudelaire was then strongly attracted) provisionally manage to resolve the stress

---

44. Compare the diatribe of Saint Peter, the disappointed lover "abandoned" by Christ in "Le Reniement de saint Pierre."

caused by the polarization of the love object (evident as early as 1842–
43 in the Jeanne Duval cycle) and to eliminate the concomitant instability of that object in its idealized mode (in the Apollonie Sabatier
cycle of December 1852 to May 1854). In these ten poems (which are
numbered XLIX through LVIII in the 1861 edition) and in the related "Hymne à la Beauté" in the initial, aesthetic cycle of *Les Fleurs
du Mal* (I through XXI), the equivocal woman transcends and thus
subsumes both good and evil, sexuality and spirituality. Proffered in
abundance, the fluids of emotional and sexual response no longer need
to be solicited from the beloved, but in accepting them, the now guilty
poet becomes aware of his transgression: "ton regard, infernal et divin,
/ Verse confusément le bienfait et le crime" (p. 24: your gaze, infernal
and divine, / indiscriminately pours forth kindness and crime). The
delicate balance of infantile desire and paternal prohibition finds a
meteorological correlative in these poems via evocations of a hazy sky
that mingles feminine fluids with the fatherly sun:[45] "un soleil couchant
dans un ciel nébuleux" ("Le Poison," p. 48: a sun setting in a misty
sky); "les soleils des brumeuses saisons…un ciel brouillé" ("Ciel
brouillé," p. 49: the suns of the cloudy seasons…a troubled sky); and
of course

> Les soleils mouillés
> De ces ciels brouillés
> Pour mon esprit ont les charmes
> Si mystérieux
> De tes traîtres yeux
> Brillant à travers leurs larmes.   ["L'Invitation au voyage," p. 53]

(For my mind, / The damp suns / Of those troubled skies / Have the
ever so mysterious enchantments / Of your treacherous eyes, / Gleaming
behind their tears.)[46]

45. Cf. "La Géante," in which the poet as voyeur spies on a feeling inspired by
another, thus symbolically intercepting it. He longs to guess "si son coeur couve une
sombre flamme / Aux humides brouillards qui nagent dans ses yeux" (p. 220: whether
her [the giantess's] heart is brooding a somber flame [of passion] / From [studying] the
damp fogs swimming in her eyes).

46. As if by contagion, "Sisina," the first poem following the Marie Daubrun cycle,
does not allow the punitive flames of the male rival to dry up the symbolic breast: "son
coeur, ravagé par la flamme, a toujours, / Pour qui s'en montre digne, un réservoir de
larmes" (p. 61: her heart, ravaged by flames, has always / For he who shows himself
worthy, a reservoir of tears). Baudelaire's conflation of desire, guilt, and punishment
produces a curiously feminized Satan figure in "Au lecteur": "*Sur l'oreiller* du mal c'est
Satan Trismégiste / Qui *berce* longuement notre esprit enchanté" (p. 5: *On the pillow* of
evil it is Satan the thrice-great / Who *cradles* at length our beguiled minds [emphasis

Elsewhere than in the Marie Daubrun cycle, the rare moments of perfect happiness in *Les Fleurs du Mal* occur only when the lyric self falls asleep and once again encounters the dream screen, that unconsciously remembered backdrop of maternal flesh which is the last thing the nursing infant sees as she or he falls asleep. The speaker projects exotic images of warmth and plenitude upon it:

> Quand, les deux yeux fermés, en un soir chaud d'automne,
> Je respire l'odeur de ton sein chaleureux,
> Je vois se dérouler des rivages heureux...
> ....
> Une île paresseuse où la nature donne
> ...des fruits savoureux;   ["Parfum exotique," p. 25]

(When, having closed both eyes, on a hot autumn evening, / I inhale the scent of your warm breast, / I see happy shores unfold their vistas ... / A languid isle where nature offers / Savory fruits [symbolic breasts].)

As in "L'Invitation au voyage," where ships "sleep" on the canals before the entire poetic world drops into slumber in a warm light, in "Parfum exotique" the landscape resembles the woman, deprived of the power of making distracting remarks; the prose version specifies that the ships are the poet's thoughts, resembling infants "qui dorment ou qui roulent sur ton sein" (p. 303: who sleep or who roll on your breast). On several occasions in Baudelaire's poetry, the breast serves unequivocally as a synecdoche for the woman ("La Muse malade," p. 14, ll. 9–10; "Le Balcon," p. 37, l. 8; "La Beauté," p. 21, ll. 2–4). Associated with the naked woman as symbolic breast and representation of the nocturnal dream screen, the round white moon of "Tristesses de la lune" communicates with the poet via a "good feed." She secretes a tear, a drop of pearly fluid which the poet catches in his hand and then literally absorbs. Baudelaire also implicitly equates visual contact with the moon with suckling, for example, in "Chanson d'après-midi": "tu mets sur mon coeur / Ton oeil doux comme la lune" (p. 60: on my heart you place / Your eye as gentle as the moon).

Transformed into an infant, however, the lyric self soon threatens his own happiness. His outbursts of infantile impatience repeatedly assail his fragile self-validating structures. In their simplest form they destroy the object, as in the phallic-aggressive knife woundings of "A

---

added]). Consider, too, the comforter and consoler in "Les Litanies de Satan" and the hermaphroditic Eros in the prose poem "Eros, Plutos, et la Gloire."

une Madone" or "A celle qui est trop gaie." That the onanistic pseudo-
rape depicted in the latter was a figurative representation of a moral
dilemma (as Baudelaire protested in an "editorial" note) does not
negate the self-defeating quality of the lyric self's ambivalence,
through which hate cancels love: "Je te hais autant que je t'aime," he
declares in that poem (p. 157). "A une Madone" achieves the desired
response—making blood flow forth from the heart like abundant
milk—only by destroying the beloved (p. 59).[47] Likewise, in "L'Héau-
tontimorouménos" achieving violent contact with the object initially
seems to promise gratification:

> Et je ferai de ta paupière,
>
> Pour abreuver mon Saharah,
> Jaillir les eaux de la souffrance.   [p. 78]

(And from your eyelid, / To slake my Sahara, / I shall cause the waters
of suffering to spurt.)

But the poet thus shatters the female mirror that had covertly reflected
his own idealized self-image; he then comes to embody the dishar-
mony between humanity and the cosmos, to be "le sinistre miroir /
"Où la mégère se regarde" (p. 78: the sinister mirror / In which the
shrew [Irony] looks at herself).[48]

Even when the lyric self manages provisionally to preserve the object, his regressive drive toward orality frequently reduces his contact
with the object to mere cannibalism, which once again ultimately destroys the object. Speaking is replaced by suckling and suckling by
devouring. He can imagine himself partaking of the object's merits
only through the primitive ego-defense of incorporation (the fantasy
that we become morally as well as physically what we eat). In "Remords
posthume," for example, the poet begins with the traditional terrorism
of the Western male "love" lyric: he has the tomb speak for him to

47. The implicit breast symbolism of this concluding detail is corroborated nine lines
earlier by the evocation of a white, round elevation surrounded by fluids: "Et sans cesse
vers toi, sommet blanc et neigeux, / En Vapeurs montera mon Esprit orageux" (And
ceaselessly toward you, white, snowy summit, / My tempestuous mind will rise like
Mists). Note the capital "V" on the word designating the site where desire and its object
coalesce in a cathexis.

48. Like the mirrors of Renaissance painting which symbolize the vanity of worldly
things, the mirrors of Baudelaire's poetry combine the illusion of plenitude with the
reality of the void.

threaten the loved woman with remorse if she will not have sex with him. But he concludes by saying that after her death "le ver rongera ta peau comme un remord" (the worm will gnaw your skin like a pang of remorse). "Ver" as homonym for "vers" (a line of poetry) metonymically associates the poet with the devourer—an identification that becomes blatant by the end of "Je t'adore à l'égal de la voûte nocturne." Oral-sadistic behavior appears implicitly even in the insistent questioning of "Réversibilité." The title implies that the loved woman is a saint whose holiness might help to win salvation for the speaker. But in this instance contact does not purify the poet; it degrades his beloved. In the first and last lines of each *quintain* he asks his "angel" whether she is familiar with the sufferings that are diametrically opposed to her perfections: anguish, hatred, illness, and aging. Finally, he asks for her prayers, but they will be efficacious only if her thoughts have become tainted with her awareness of the poet's deformities, which have been thrust at her through rhetorical juxtaposition.

When Baudelaire more fully develops his conversational exchanges with the idealized woman, they shade into an anal sadism that defiles her. The poet as infant, but with the full knowledge of what he is doing, symbolically smears his symbolic mother and her surroundings with excrement. As the repellent, rejected child, he achieves revenge by forcing himself on the mother-imago. In "Confession," this strategy becomes particularly apparent, although distanced by a simile. For one moment the "angel" accompanying the poet drops her guard to reveal the secret flaw in her apparent happiness, her long-concealed fear of being abandoned and forgotten, a fear which suddenly appears "comme une enfant chétive, horrible, sombre, immonde, / Dont sa famille rougirait" (p. 45: like a wretched child, horrible, somber, foul, of whom her family would be ashamed).

More openly anal-sadistic in "Une charogne," the poet addresses his beloved as "mon âme," a Romantic cliché but one that suggests she exists as a mental image rather than as a real person. For nine stanzas he describes to her the rotting carcass that they encountered on a summer's walk. The first details immediately associate the dead animal "sur un lit... / ...comme une femme lubrique" (on a bed... like a lascivious woman) with the woman looking at it. Near the end of the loathsome description, a metaphor implies that the corpse has its origins in the archaic regions of the poet's own psyche:

Les formes s'effçaient et n'étaient plus qu'un rêve,
Une ébauche lente à venir,
Sur la toile oubliée, et que l'artiste achève
Seulement par le souvenir.　[p. 32]

(The shapes blurred and were no longer any more than a dream, / A sketch slow to arrive / On the forgotten canvas, and which the artist completes / From memory alone.)

The past is the poet's own as well as that of the dead animal when it was still alive. The bitch hiding behind a rock and impatiently waiting to be able to return to devour the carcass connotes time halting in the present moment of narration as the poet revives his memories, as well as the animal nature and thus the physical vulnerability of the loved woman. Directly addressing her once more the poet concludes,

—Et pourtant vous serez semblable à cette ordure,
A cette horrible infection,
Etoile de mes yeux, soleil de ma nature,
Vous, mon ange et ma passion!　[p. 32]

(—And yet you will be like that filth, / Like that horrible infection, / Star of my eyes, sun of my nature, / You, my angel and my passion!)

Three stanzas in a row, each constituting a separate sentence, strive to complete contact; the last two are both reinforced by an expletive, the "O" of formal lyric address, and by three more exclamation points. Oral and anal sadism converge in the final metaphor as the poet literally devours the beloved, now a decaying corpse, by assuming the form of "ver[s]-mine."[49]

In the irrational world of the unconscious, where adult experience and infantile urges combine, such rage on the part of the poet is entirely understandable. From the conflated adult/infantile viewpoint, the Mother cannot come into being without always having already been unfaithful to her male child, by having had sex with another male. But from the viewpoint of the infant, whose archaic understanding survives deep in our psyche, it is with the breast (the only

49. See Georges Blin's famous study of *Le Sadisme de Baudelaire* (Paris: Corti, 1948), pp. 13–47. Blin's remarks on Baudelaire's masochism are an indispensable complement to my discussion here. Blin, however, does not discuss Baudelaire's anal-sadistic tendencies (i.e., literally or figuratively smearing the Other with one's excrement), whose allegorical extension is of course the *danse macabre* (in over a dozen poems, Baudelaire "rubs our nose" in the fact that our bodies will rot away).

sexual object that he initially knows) rather than the vagina that she betrays him. So it is via the breast that Baudelaire contrasts the good symbolic mother with the bad real mother in "La Lune offensée" when the moon (the idealized mother as metaphoric breast) tells him:

> —Je vois ta mère, enfant de ce siècle appauvri,
> Qui vers son miroir penche un lourd amas d'années,
> Et plâtre artistement le sein qui t'a nourri!   [p. 142]

(—I see your mother, child of this impoverished age, / Who is leaning toward her mirror a heavy load of years, / And artfully plastering with make-up the breast that nurtured you!)

Breasts, then, may become synecdoches not only for the woman but for the allure of all transgressions. In the desert Baudelaire's saint Antoine "a vu surgir comme des laves / Les seins nus et pourprés de ses tentations" ("Femmes damnées," p. 114: Saint Anthony saw, surging forth like lava, the bare crimson breasts of his temptations). More indirectly, in "Tout entière" the poet gives himself away when the Devil tempts him to betray his ideal and reduce the idealized beloved to a sexual object by declaring which part of her body he prefers. The poet ostensibly resists by declaring "tout en elle est dictame." The normal and abstract meaning of this rare last word is "consolation," but the concrete referent is a plant with healing properties which belongs to the family of "labiacées," so-called because their petals resemble lips (in English, "heal-all" or "carpenter plant" from the mint family). To borrow a term from Raymond Courrèges in François Mauriac's *Fleuve du feu,* everything about Baudelaire's women becomes "comestible."

If the only difficulty encountered by Baudelaire's lyric personae was their yearning for the inaccessible maternal breast, their fictive existence would remain relatively simple. But his phantasmal breasts are dangerous temptations not only because they are forbidden by the rival, punishing Father but also because they might empty, not fill, whoever sucks them. The nursing infant who is fed too seldom or not enough attributes his or her pangs of hunger to the frustrating "bad breast." Unconsciously, the infant must then distinguish the notion of the bad breast from that of a gratifying "good breast" in order to preserve the belief in a reliable source of relief and satisfaction. Combined with the experience of mature sexuality, in the adult male

the unconscious image of the bad breast may generate what is known
to psychoanalysts as "the draining fantasy." This primordial fear, not
uncommon in schizophrenia, consists in the unconscious belief that
one's vital essence will be drawn out through the penis during orgasm
and lost.[50] In the form of the fantasy which usually reaches consciousness, the secondary defense of symbolic displacement substitutes for
sperm the blood or vital organs reduced to a fluid—for example, the
brain tissue transformed into soap bubbles and then blown away
through a pipe by a demonic Cupid in Baudelaire's "L'Amour et le
crâne." Synthetic modes of the suckling/draining fantasy, in which
desire and its punishment are telescoped into a single representation,
are the empty breast, the poisoned breast, or the symbolic form of
the latter as a flask filled with a deadly beverage. Frequently in *Les
Fleurs de Mal*, the cathexis of desire and the anxiety generated by an
unconscious prohibition are thus presented in rapid alternation.

Predictably, then, assuming the form of a seductive woman, Satan
uses "philtres infâmes" (foul philtres; i.e., bad breasts engorged with
venom) in "La Destruction" (p. 111). The prose poem "Les Tentations" associates the bad breast with the phallic mother who wears a
living serpent as a belt; from it hang the artificial breasts of "fioles
pleines de liqueurs sinistres" (p. 308: vials filled with sinister liqueurs).
Even "l'amour véritable" offers us only "fioles de poison" in "Le Vin
de l'assassin" (p. 108). The transition from good breast to bad breast
to none appears dramatically in "Les Métamorphoses du vampire."
In this poem the demonic woman's most striking feature is her jutting
breasts. While the poet has sex with her, she sucks the very marrow

50. On the "draining fantasy" in psychopathology see Bertram P. Karon, *The Treatment of Choice for Schizophrenia* (New York: J. Aronson, 1981). An unpublished paper
by Edward Gibeau (1988) illustrates how frequently this fantasy is encountered in
therapy. The fear of being drained of one's vital essence (popularized in the film *The
Dark Crystal*) has created a social institution among the aborigines of New Guinea. There
the adult males carry off male children who have reached the age of five or six and
oblige them to perform fellatio on the adults until the children have reached puberty.
The rationale is that there is a limited, nonrenewable quantity of sperm in the world.
Once it belonged to a single great god, from whom it was stolen to be distributed
among men. To avoid depleting the supply, men should waste as little of it as possible
on women and instead recycle it among themselves.

When fluids are abundant in Baudelaire's poetry, they are generally bad fluids: the
verb "verser" (to pour) becomes sinister in two "Spleen" poems (LXXV and LXXVIII)
and in "Rêve parisien" (pp. 72, 74, 103); what is poured upon humanity is "un froid
ténébreux," "un jour noir plus triste que les nuits," "des ténèbres" (a shadowy cold
[LXXV], a dark [or sinister] light more lugubrious than the nights [LXXVIII], shadows
["Rêve parisien"]).

from his bones. Afterward he turns toward her to see "une outre aux flancs gluants, toute pleine de pus" (p. 143: a wineskin with sticky sides, filled up with pus); when he dares steal a second glance, he finds only "des débris de squelette" (remains of a skeleton) whose empty ribcage here connotes the barren breast.[51] The allegorical impulse of these macabre poems, simultaneously providing the poet with a protective multiplicity (because he is identified with all humanity) and warranting the claim of his verses to our attention (because they apply to us as well), is strongly presented from the outset by the abstract nouns in the titles of the first two poems cited above ("La Destruction" and "Les Tentations"). The definite articles of all four titles reinforce the allegorical mode, transforming these personal nightmares into universally valid representations of human experience. And the didacticism that allows the poet to externalize his anguish also removes it to a more comfortable distance.

As one might expect given the artistically self-conscious mode of Symbolist poetry, verbal analogues of the draining fantasy are not lacking in Baudelaire. His lyric self strives in vain to interest "La Béatrice" in the "chant de ses douleurs." An ironic antiphrasis, the title itself (referring to Woman as guide toward spiritual perfection) is "poisoned," and the vital fluid of the poem (imagined as a container of words) is evacuated to be replaced by a mocking prosopopoeia from the swarm of demons attending the adored but evil woman. The alien discourse of the Other has a parasitical function: it feeds on the poet rather than feeds him with love. Instead of finding an audience, the poet becomes a captive audience for his enemies. The vampiristic connotations are reinforced by the obvious intertext, Charles Nodier's "Smarra," where the witch-lover as "Terrible Mother" brings minions who suck out her lover-victim's blood and eventually tear out his heart. "La Béatrice," then, clearly associates the demonic reversal of suckling with a failure to contact the desired audience.

"Le Goût du néant" illustrates how pervasive are the indirect resonances of the suckling/draining motif:

> Et le Temps m'engloutit minute par minute,
> Comme la neige immense un corps pris de roideur;
> Je contemple d'en haut le globe en sa rondeur   [p. 76]

51. The apparent intertexts are Charles Nodier's (semi-plagiarized) "Aventures de Thibaud de la Jacquière" and Jacques Cazotte's *Le Diable amoureux*.

(And Time swallows me up minute by minute, / As the vast snow engulfs a numbed body; / From above, I contemplate the globe in its roundness.)

The poet looks down on the symbolic breast ("le globe en sa rondeur") that empties itself upon him, but its white fluid (snow/milk) freezes instead of giving life. The accumulation of sterile whiteness progressively obliterates the poet's identity. (The incoherent spatial notation, situating the poet both above and below, reveals that this scene occurs in the theater of the *imaginaire*.) Through a sort of hysterical conversion symptom, the poet's numbed body expresses the psychic suicide of a withdrawal of cathexis from the outside world. Needless to say, the poem's title itself condenses Baudelaire's dominant obsession by oxymoronically juxtaposing gratified orality ("le goût") and its demonic opposite, emptiness ("le néant").

The draining fantasy appears repeatedly in both the intimate and the allegorical poems. In the titles of two of the love poems the word "vampire" refers to the desired woman (compare the association of vampirism and fellatio in Lautréamont's *Chants de Maldoror*). "Tu mettrais l'univers entier dans ta ruelle" equates woman in general with a "buveur du sang du monde" (p. 27: one who drinks the blood of the world). The poet imagines that he is slowly bleeding to death through an invisible wound in "La Fontaine de sang" (p. 115). In "La Cloche fêlée" his blood also leaks away as he lies crushed beneath a heap of dead soldiers, a metaphorical representation of past failures (with possible homoerotic undertones). "Au lecteur" dramatizes the same fantasy symbolically: there Satan sublimates "le riche métal de notre volonté" (the rich metal of our willpower), presumably leaving a hollow in its place. The same poem generalizes to and therefore imposes on all humanity a frustrating "bad feed" at a withered breast:

Ainsi qu'un débauché pauvre qui baise et mange
Le sein martyrisé d'une antique catin,
Nous volons au passage un plaisir clandestin
Que nous pressons bien fort comme une vieille orange.   [p. 5]

(Like an impecunious libertine who kisses and eats / The martyred breast of an ancient bawd, / We steal clandestine pleasures on the wing / And squeeze them quite hard like withered oranges).

Meanwhile our vices suck our blood like parasites, devouring us from within.[52]

On a universal scale, the *gouffre* or *abîme* represents the Baudelairean bad breast, the embodiment of cosmic irony. This essential motif became the subject of at least one scholarly book. Its true prominence in Baudelaire's poetry has nevertheless been obscured by the way that scholars conventionally estimate the relative importance of various motifs in literature. They simply count up how often each key word appears in a text or body of texts and then claim that the most common words reveal the dominant preoccupations of the author. Such a procedure, when applied to Baudelaire, yields an unsurprising list of the nouns most commonly found in *Les Fleurs du Mal: oeil, coeur, ciel, beau* (as both noun and adjective), and *âme*, in that order, with the verbs *faire* and *voir* also figuring among the ten most common noninstrumental words.

Charting the frequency of Baudelaire's key words not in isolation but in relation to their occurrence in a half-million-word corpus drawn from ordinary language produces an altogether different picture. From this perspective, the words Baudelaire uses most often are *gouffre* (which does not appear at all in the control group of words), *pleur, Satan, coeur,* and, in ninth position, *sein*. Fluids other than tears— *sang, mer,* and *vin*—also appear among the thirty terms most characteristic of Baudelaire. Far down the list, the most disproportionately frequent verbs are *chanter* and *dormir*, in forty-third and forty-eighth positions. Associated with the bad father *(Satan)* and the bad breast *(gouffre)*, the complex of orality and regression thus comes into its rightful prominence.[53]

The word *gouffre* itself derives from the Greek *kolpos*, which means among other things the breast, the lap, a gulf, a fold, the vulva, the womb (in poetry), and the grave (figuratively speaking). Its Vulgar Latin form *colpus* means the vulva, an ulcer, or a gulf. Since Baudelaire

---

52. Compare the symbolic empty breast and loss of vital essence in "Le Jeu," whose self-destructive gamblers are depicted "fouillant la poche vide ou le sein palpitant" and "courant avec ferveur à l'abîme béant" (p. 96: rummaging in their empty pockets or their trembling bosom [and] rushing fervently to the gaping void). They become intoxicated from drinking their own blood. Note also the draining of Christ's blood in "Le Reniement de saint Pierre."

53. See N. F. Cunen, "Le Gouffre et l'abîme de Baudelaire: Thèmes fondamentaux de Baudelaire," *Travaux de linguistique et de littérature*, 15 (1977), 109–39. Cunen, however, does not comment on Baudelaire's orality, its connection with the *gouffre*, or the etymology of the latter.

does not appear to have been versed in Greek, and since *colpus* does not appear in the Latin authors he was most likely to have read—Vergil, Horace, and Ovid—the connection in his mind between breast and *gouffre* remains at best speculative.[54] The metonymic connection between breast and *gouffre* in his poetry, however, is clear. His *gouffre* externalizes the insatiable existential thirst for love that for him marks the human condition. It is the symptom of which the loss of the breast is the cause. As he specifies in "L'Horloge," "Le gouffre a toujours soif" (p. 85: The abyss forever thirsts).[55]

By using allegory, Baudelaire extends the breast fixation of his lyric self to all poets and all humanity—frustrated, as in "La Beauté" (p. 21), or fulfilled, as in the primitive times of "J'aime le souvenir de ces époques nues" (p. 11), when the goddess of Nature, "louve au coeur gonflé de tendresses communes, / Abreuvait l'univers à ses tétines brunes" (a she-wolf whose heart swelled with tenderness for all and sundry suckled the universe at her brown nipples). He sees school as a place "où l'enfant boit, dix ans, l'âpre lait des études" ("Epître à Sainte-Beuve," p. 206: where for ten years the child drinks the tart milk of his studies). The poem titled "Allégorie" describes innocent, bestial Woman thus: "Et dans ses bras ouverts, que remplissent ses seins, / Elle appelle des yeux la race des humains" (p. 116: And with her eyes, she summons the human race into her opened arms, filled with her breasts). Nursing their infants as they wander, the gypsies of "Bohémiens en voyage" find that their loving mother, Cybèle, has

54. See Albert Dauzat, *Nouveau dictionnaire étymologique* (Paris: Larousse, 1964), p. 348, col. 2; Henry George Liddell and Robert Scott, *Greek-English Lexicon* (Oxford: Clarendon Press, 1983); the *Thesaurus Linguae Latinae*, 9 vols. (Leipzig: Teubner, 1907), III, 1726, col. 2; and standard concordances to the Roman authors cited. *Colpus*, however, appears several times in the New Testament.

55. According to both Jean Chevalier, *Dictionnaire des Symboles* (Paris: Robert Laffont, 1969), and Juan E. Cirlot, *A Dictionary of Symbols* (New York: Philosophical Library, 1962), the abyss in archetypal symbolism can represent both the mother and the return to childhood. Baudelaire hints at this connection in "L'Aube spirituelle" by stating that the remote Ideal draws one like a *gouffre*. His obsession with the word is betrayed by its awkward repetition in lines 16 and 17 of "Le Flacon," a negligence uncommon in Baudelaire's poetry.

Certain words related to *gouffre* through an affinity of sound—*souffre, goût* (with its oral resonance), *couler, écouter, gouge*—seem to have a special affective significance for Baudelaire. To justify his choice of the last (in its pejorative sense of "camp follower") in "Danse macabre," in which he calls death an "irrésistible gouge" (p. 98), he writes: "Couleur, antithèse, métaphore, tout est exact" (coloration, antithesis, metaphor, everything is precise) and then develops his defense at length in his letter of February 11, 1859 to Calonne, *Corr.* I, 546–47.

in effect offered *them* her own breasts since she "fait couler le rocher" (p. 18: makes springs gush from the rock). And elsewhere poet and reader, allegorically linked as "l'Humanité," suckle together from the enormous breasts of "La Douleur" and "l'austère Infortune." Allegory reestablishes the poet's contact with the audience by transforming personal obsessions and weaknesses into wisdom, into insights with a general validity. It implies that by learning about Baudelaire's poet-persona, we are learning about ourselves.

Baudelaire does not erase his frustrated orality by sublimating it through writing poetry. Instead, he creates a phantasmic world where suckling and communication are one. If oral communication is assimilated to suckling, regaining contact with the maternal breast is implicitly figured as gaining an illocutionary partner's attention. Or *sometimes* as listening to the Other's words. Most of the prosopopoeias to which Baudelaire's lyric self serves as an involuntary audience are menacing, spoken by entities that represent draining and death. But when in "L'Ame du vin" such a discourse is enunciated by a beverage, it consoles rather than horrifies. The equation of listening with suckling appears more patently in "Le Chat," where the creature's voice fills the poet like a fluid, and in "Le Serpent qui danse," where at length the lyric self draws liquid from the creature's female mouth. Conversely, the symbolic empty breast is linked to failed communication: "Le gouffre infranchissable, qui fait l'incommunicabilité, reste infranchi" ("Mon coeur mis à nu," *OC* I, 1290: The unbridgeable abyss, which makes communication impossible, remains unbridged).

Since Baudelaire's persona constitutes itself by assimilating adult relationships with women to infantile relationships with the mother, and infantile relationships with her to his rapport with the fictive audience, rejection of the poet by the empirical public recalls rejection of the child by the mother. As he tells his audience in the "Epigraphe pour un livre condamné," "If,"

> Ton oeil sait plonger dans les gouffres,
> Lis-moi, pour apprendre à m'aimer;
> . . . .
> Plains-moi! . . . Sinon, je te maudis!   [p. 137]

(Your eye is able to plumb abysses, / Read me, in order to learn how to love me; / . . . Pity me! . . . If not, I'll curse you!)

Outside the Spleen poems, however, rarely does the lyric self completely lose contact; rarely is he quite forgotten. In the Spleen poems
he is totally isolated; his appeals go unheard. Elsewhere, by addressing
messages, he designates and creates virtual audiences. But unlike the
conventional elegiac poet, Baudelaire does not ask aspects of nature
to deliver messages to a third party. He approaches the intended
recipient without intermediaries. Often he uses apostrophes to ask
various entities to explain their mysteries. And often he directs prayers
to either God or Satan. Since he receives no response, we cannot
determine whether these prayers are apostrophes to an absent or
nonexistent being, or direct discourse to an indifferent one. Either
alternative remains possible if we take into consideration Baudelaire's
famous statement in "Mon coeur mis à nu" that we find "en tout
homme, à toute heure, deux postulations simultanées, l'une vers Dieu,
l'autre vers Satan" (I, 682: in every man, at every hour, two simultaneous appeals, one to God, the other to Satan). In French, "pos-
tulation," a speech-act noun, means "appeal" or "invitation."

Overall, Baudelaire is by turns a frustrating *destinateur* (sender), a
nurturant *destinateur*, a frustrated *destinataire* (receiver), and a satisfied
destinataire. That is, he alternately delivers and receives an unwelcome
message. He swings from a regressive self-absorption that appears to
exclude any audience to an allegorical mode that makes his lyric self
a representative of mankind. (I use the gender-specific noun advisedly
here, for Baudelaire's poetry, like that of French Symbolism in general, is dominated by the male imagination portraying woman as the
Other, as the feared and desired object.) In allegory, any message
addressed to the lyric self concerning human sinfulness and corruptibility will implicitly be directed to us didactic addressees as well.
From one poem to another or even within one poem, the idealized
addressees—the loved woman, God, Satan, the illustrious dedicatees
of 1859 and 1860—may instead become satiric targets of a sly or
sadistic assault. And when Baudelaire assumes the tone of a moralist
or preacher, his didactic addressees become satiric targets as well, a
condition in which the lyric self may or may not be implicated.

Whether impelled by desire for the idealized addressee, scorn for
the satiric target, or concern for the didactic audience, however, the
poem requires the silence of the Other in order to preserve the in-
tegrity of the lyric self. If the idealized addressee speaks, the rest of
the poem becomes a mere framework for revelation. The resulting
effacement of the lyric self by the discourse of the idealized addressee

can be demonstrated empirically. How many readers or critics remember that "Beauty is truth, truth beauty" was spoken not by Keats's lyric persona but by his Grecian urn and that the former (ventriloquist though he may be) does not necessarily endorse the discourse of the latter? If the satiric addressee speaks, the remainder of the poem becomes contaminated with its inferiority.

To attenuate the dissolving influence of the Other, the poem can:

1. Merely report but not cite the Other's enunciation.
2. Allow the Other only nonverbal expression (such as, significant looks).
3. Multiply or generalize the Other.
4. Allow the Other to be present only through allusion.
5. Erase the Other from the poem.

This drastic final solution, however, would deprive the lyric self of any basis of comparison upon which to found its superiority, be it scornful or nurturant. Apostrophe becomes the compromise solution of choice. It means that the Other is either present but unable to speak or present only through allusion.

The poet uses direct discourse only with the loved woman, and even rhetorical devices establish a curious pseudo-communication, a one-sided conversation dominated (as often occurs in lyric poetry generally) by imperialistic devices for absorbing or silencing the discourse of the Other. "Et bien que votre voix soit douce, taisez-vous!" the poet declares in "Semper Eadem" (Always the same), whose very title denies autonomy to the love object (p. 41: And though your voice be sweet, be still!). Baudelaire repeatedly claimed that loving another (or even sharing oneself through writing) meant being untrue to oneself, prostituting oneself. Ultimately he writes not to commune with others but to distinguish himself from them: "Seigneur mon Dieu! accordez-moi la grâce de produire quelques beaux vers qui me prouvent *à moi-même* que je ne suis pas le dernier des hommes, que je ne suis pas inférieur à ceux que je méprise!" (My Lord God, grant me the grace of producing some beautiful lines of verse that will prove to *myself* that I am not the basest of men, that I am not inferior to those whom I despise!)[56]

56. Baudelaire, "A une heure du matin," *Le Spleen de Paris*, X (I, 288 [emphasis added]). In "Mon coeur mis à nu," Baudelaire defines love variously as "le besoin de sortir de soi" (I, 692: the need to get outside oneself); "le besoin d'oublier son *moi* dans la chaire extérieure" (I, 700: the need to forget one's *self* in external flesh). Loving is

The primary rule of Baudelaire's poetry seems to be that whoever takes the initiative in a communicative exchange will encounter only rejection or indifference.

Baudelaire's narcissistic economy requires a delicate equilibrium. The Other as object must be deprived of speech so that it will not acquire too much individuality to function as a reflection of the Self: "sois charmante, et tais-toi" (be charming, and be still), Baudelaire exhorts the beloved. But if the Other loses too much of its substance to the vampirish self-absorption of the poet (inflicting on others what he most fears himself), the illusion of alterity will dissipate, and the Self will be left to confront its own unmediated image, the horrifying ugliness and torment of ungratified desire:

> Dans ton île, ô Vénus! je n'ai trouvé debout
> Qu'un gibet symbolique où pendait mon image...
> —Ah! Seigneur! donnez-moi la force et le courage
> De contempler mon coeur et mon corps sans dégoût!
> ["Un voyage à Cythère," p. 119]

(On your isle, O Venus, I found nothing standing / But a symbolic gallows from which my image hung /...—Oh Lord! give me the strength and the courage / To look upon my heart and my body without disgust!)

When the mother-imago proves unavailable as a source for narcissistic supplies, the symbolic father as ego-ideal must be invoked to provide them. This move appears twice in succession in "Bénédiction." Horrified at having given birth to a poet, the mother of the first five stanzas curses him and expresses her particular loathing at having to offer him her breast: "Ah! que n'ai-je mis bas tout un noeud de vipères, / Plutôt que de nourrir cette dérision!" (Oh! Why didn't I give birth to a whole tangle of vipers, / Rather than having to nurse this mockery!). But then an angel guides the child to a surrogate parent, the sun, whose good paternal breast both literally and figuratively restores the lost maternal milk:

---

prostitution, and thus God is the supreme prostitute (I, 692). "Le vrai héros s'amuse tout seul" (I, 682: The true hero entertains himself all alone), Baudelaire adds, and he insists: "*Avant tout, Etre un grand homme et un Saint pour soi-même*" (I, 691: *Before all else,* to be *a great man* and a *saint* in one's own eyes [emphases in original]).

L'Enfant déshérité s'enivre de soleil,
Et dans tout ce qu'il voit et dans tout ce qu'il mange
Retrouve l'ambroisie et le nectar vermeil. [p. 7]

(The disinherited Child becomes drunk from the sun, / And in all that
he sees and in all that he eats / Rediscovers ambrosia and rosy nectar.)

Meanwhile the hostile public offers the symbolic bad breast by mixing
ashes and spittle with the poet's food. His wife drains him rather than
fills him, tearing his heart from his chest. The simile linking this heart
to "un tout jeune oiseau" (a fledgling) recalls that identity of poet and
child. But in the last five stanzas the poet's prayer anticipates a celestial
reparation of idealized milk offered by the second surrogate parent,
God the Father; he imagines a mystical crown "puisée au foyer saint
des rayons primitifs" (p. 9: drawn [like a fluid] from the holy hearth
of the primordial rays). Mortal eyes are simply "miroirs obscurcis et
plaintifs" (dimmed, plaintive mirrors) of this brightness. The narcissistic short circuit, in other words, ensures that the poet no longer
needs to seek love—a flattering reflection of himself—in the eyes of
others. Love has become part of him. By the end of this process, even
the symbolic father can be obliterated.

The ostensible female objects of the love poems, then, serve as
vehicles for projected self-love. Sexual union with them in the present
is not an ultimate goal but at best a preparation for another sort of
union, that of the poet with his past. The three main cycles of love
poems in Les Fleurs du Mal show that Baudelaire idealizes neither love
experienced (Jeanne Duval) nor love anticipated (Marie Daubrun) but
love remembered (Apollonie Sabatier). Metaphorically transformed
into a repository for memories (like the monstrance in "Harmonie du
soir"), the idealized woman becomes the site of privileged meeting
between the poet and himself.[57]

The one time the loved woman does enunciate an inspiring message
in the virtual present of Baudelaire's poetry ("You should love
beauty"), it is her *fantôme* (the poet's projected fantasy using her image
as a prop) that speaks in a prosopopoeia (XLII). "Le Poison" gives
this strategy away: in the last two stanzas, following two generalizing
stanzas on the transforming powers of wine and opium, the shift to
a direct address mimes the establishing of contact with an audience.

57. See Barbara Johnson, *Défigurations du langage poétique* (Paris: Flammarion, 1979),
p. 45.

The intimate second-person singular form of the possessive adjectives ("tes ... tes ... ta") retrospectively reveals the entire poem to have been direct address. That this locutionary situation is masked in the beginning betrays an ambivalent combination of amorous approach (the movement from third to second person) and narcissistic withdrawal. The Other serves only as the instrument of the lyric self's ecstasy:

> Tout cela ne vaut pas le poison que découle
> De tes yeux, de tes yeux verts,
> Lacs où mon âme tremble et se voit à l'envers...
> Mes songes viennent en foule
> Pour se désaltérer à ces gouffres amers.
>
> Tout cela ne vaut pas le terrible prodige
> De ta salive qui mord,
> Qui plonge dans l'oubli mon âme sans remords,   [p. 49]

(All that is not worth the poison distilled / By your eyes, by your green eyes, / Lakes where my soul shudders and sees itself upside down. / ... My dreams arrive in hordes / To slake their thirst at these bitter abysses. / All that is not worth the terrible wonder / Of your biting saliva, / Which plunges into oblivion my remorseless soul.)

The repetition in the second line quoted above iconically anticipates the mirroring of poet and Other in the third line; and the outcome of the encounter, oblivion, represents the final triumph of narcissism in which self-absorption erases a self-consciousness always dependent on the presence of the Other.

Personified projections of the poet's libido can communicate a wealth of wordless meaning during the "découverte amoureuse de soi" (fond discovery of oneself), as we observe in "Le Chat":

> Dans ma cervelle se promène,
> Ainsi qu'en son appartement,
> Un beau chat, fort, doux, et charmant
> ....
> Pour dire les plus longues phrases,
> [Sa voix] n'a pas besoin de mots.   [p. 50]

(In my brain there strolls about, / As if in its apartment, / A handsome cat, strong, gentle, and charming. / ... To utter the longest sentences, / [Its voice] requires no words.)

The poet's heart responds to this voice more intensely than to any musical instrument and as profoundly as if his heart itself had become an Aeolian harp. The cat is the familiar spirit of the place (of the poet's psyche); perhaps it is a god, Baudelaire speculates. Magnetically drawn to the cat's eyes, he discovers that "je regarde en moi-même" (I'm looking into myself). Typically, he elaborates upon this self-discovery with allegorical extension. Speaking of man in general contemplating the ocean (L'Homme et la mer" [mère]), he explains: "La mer est ton miroir"; "Tu te plais à plonger *au sein de ton image;* / Tu l'embrasses" (p. 19: The sea is your mirror; you enjoy plunging *into the depths* [literally, "breast"] *of your image;* you embrace it [emphasis added]).

In the psychic economy of Baudelaire, love can come only from the parent of the opposite sex. Since that object is forbidden, love can come only from the self. So he imagines that, like him, women too love only their own image. In Baudelaire's belated version of the mirror stage, young women form a mediated image of their own selfhood by contemplating "les fruits murs de leur nubilité" (the ripe fruits of their nubileness [i.e., their breasts]; "Epître à Sainte-Beuve," p. 207). The gigantic naiads of "Rêve parisien" pass their time contemplating their reflections as well. In retrospect, we can see that the mother artfully applying make-up to her breasts in "La Lune offensée" is being unfaithful to her child, not ultimately with another man, but with herself.

To please his female addressees, Baudelaire tenders them a flattering image of themselves:

> Je veux te raconter, ô molle enchanteresse!
> Les diverses beautés qui parent ta jeunesse;
>   Je veux te peindre ta beauté   ["Le Beau Navire," p. 51]

(I wish to tell you, O indolent enchantress, / About the varied beauties that adorn your youth; / I wish to depict for you your beauty).

The beauty is mirrored iconically (by the repetition of the word "beauté[s]" as well as paraphrastically (by the descriptive relative clause in the second hemistich of the second line). In both the verse and prose "Invitation au voyage" the ultimate seduction is the promise to journey to an idyllic land "qui te ressemble." In the flesh (as opposed to dreams and reverie), the poet sees himself as powerless with women because he is not one of them:

Hélas! et je ne puis, Mégère libertine,
Pour briser ton courage et te mettre aux abois,
Dans l'enfer de ton lit devenir Proserpine!   ["Sed non satiata," p. 28]

(Alas, and I cannot, lascivious shrew, / To break your spirit and put you at bay, / Become Persephone in the hell of your bed!)

To the metamorphosis of man (the speaker) into woman (Persephone, but one who still magically possesses the phallus, "la pine,"[58] as the last syllable of her name) the play of the signifier adds the transformation of verse (the verbal medium that the poet uses to address his lover here) into "Prose." In becoming attractive to the woman, in other words, the poet would lose his lyric enchantment for himself. For since the narcissist has only a tenuous sense of self, in the presence of the wishes or needs of others he actually fears losing a part of himself.

Although the poet's flattery may provide woman with a verbal image of herself, only a lesbian lover can incarnate that image. Thus Baudelaire's fascination with the Sapphic, which affords him vicarious gratification in imagining a person who can receive a woman's love. He fancies the legendary isle of Lesbos as a mythical paradise of gratified desire, where both thirst and its verbal analogue, the sigh of longing, find instant satisfaction:

Lesbos, où les baisers sont comme les cascades
Qui se jettent sans peur dans les gouffres sans fonds,
....
Où jamais un soupir ne resta sans écho.   ["Lesbos," p. 150]

(Lesbos, where kisses are like waterfalls, / Fearlessly hurling themselves into bottomless abysses, / . . . Where never was a sigh that did not find an echo.)

Both partners in a lesbian relationship possess the breast, and in contemplating such relationships as well as heterosexual ones, Baudelaire repeatedly equates love with a fluid, with a variant of mother's milk. He feels sympathy for the lesbian "Femmes damnées" not only because of the "soifs inassouvies" (unslaked thirsts) he shares with them but also because of "les urnes d'amour dont vos grands coeurs sont pleins" (p. 111: the urns of love with which your great hearts are filled). Thus his early plan to call Les Fleurs du Mal "Les Lesbiennes" stemmed not so much from a desire to shock as from a richly over-

58. This slang word is attested in Baudelaire's correspondence.

determined complex of associations. These associations link that title to the other alternative he considered, "Les Limbes": the unbaptized infants who were denied the saving fluid versus the lesbians who possess the saving fluid (milk) in abundance but are still not saved.

The lyric self of Baudelaire's crisis period himself remains in limbo, misunderstood and unloved. He knows that his appeals for contact are foredoomed, since even ideally attentive fictive audiences cannot assuage his yearning or comprehend him. In the Spleen poem "Je suis comme le roi d'un pays pluvieux," the inability of the people and animals surrounding the ruler to entertain him or please him or even elicit a response from him is ironically underscored by the abundant presence of "wrong" fluids, rain and blood rather than mother's milk. And in "La Vie antérieure" the hapless speaker inhabits a paradise of narcissistic mirroring: his eyes reflect the sea and sky, which reflect each other. Perfumed, naked slaves surround him, and their "unique soin était d'approfondir / Le secret douloureux qui me faisait languir" (p. 18: their only concern was to fathom the painful secret that made me languish). It is precisely this incommunicable secret that is missing from Baudelaire's probable sources for this poem, Mademoiselle de Maupin and the hashish vision in Le Comte de Monte-Cristo (see OC I, 862–63).

The continual frustration of the poet's attempts to communicate leads to emotional exhaustion, to the state of "Spleen." This is a state of entropy: not the opposite of the Ideal but the opposite of attempts to attain to the Ideal—withdrawal rather than compliance or revolt. The "flat calm of my despair" ("La Musique," p. 68) makes the poet feel keenly "the fearsome futility of explaining anything whatsoever to anyone at all."[59] Like the other great French Symbolist poets, Baudelaire thus expands to the dimensions of entire poems the age-old topos of inexpressibility. But in a way peculiar to him, he centers this topos on the question of creating and sustaining relations with the audience.

IV

Baudelaire concluded the 1857 edition of Les Fleurs du Mal with "La Mort des artistes," first published in April 1851. The original version (pp. 1090–91), composed at the end of his optimistic period, declares

59. Baudelaire, [Projets de préfaces]. "Préface des Fleurs," OC I, 182.

that some poets may be doomed never to glimpse their ideal but that
he knows constant effort will at least reveal his personal ideal to him.
The poet's destiny is in his own hands. The pessimistic 1857 version
of "La Mort des artistes," however, no longer distinguishes between
those poets who strive and those who repine, longing only for death.
Now all poets are seen as ridiculous, inadequate clowns; for them any
encounter with the Ideal would be situated in an uncertain future.
And in the 1861 edition Baudelaire adds three poems about the death
of humanity in general after the original conclusion. The effect is to
transform the frame of the entire collection. In 1857 this frame focuses our attention on the life cycle of the individual artist from his
birth ("Bénédiction") to his death ("La Mort des artistes"). The frame
of the 1861 edition focuses our attention on an allegorical statement
about us all, from the moment that we first achieve moral awareness
by being constituted as Baudelaire's readers (in "Au lecteur") until
our death (in "Le Voyage"). "Le Voyage," the new conclusion to the
1861 edition, enhances the significance of "Au lecteur" by reintro-
ducing at the end the personified reader who has already appeared
at the beginning of *Les Fleurs du Mal* in 1857. Thus Baudelaire gives
the entire volume a more pragmatic, less expressive slant.

The first of the concluding poems added in 1861, "La Fin de la
journée," (tentatively dated fall 1860) describes the vision of one allegorical poet who sees all effort as useless:

> Sous une lumière blafarde
> Court, danse et se tord sans raison
> La Vie, impudente et criarde.   [p. 128]

(In a wan light, / Life, impudent and shrill, / Runs, dances and writhes
senselessly.)

Initially Baudelaire had thought that the poet's contact with the reader
could guide the reader; in his pessimistic middle phase, he hopes that
contact will bring the poet consolation, although he realizes that only
the interlocutor's silence will preserve the illusion on which all hope
depends. The final phase finds consolation only in the ironic detachment that is expressed through allegory and generalizations.

As Baudelaire emerges in 1858 from his Symbolist crisis, he begins
to efface the sharp division he had earlier established between the
lyric self and its virtual audience. The latter loses its parental prestige,

and the poet's veneration gives way to insult. Yet Baudelaire actually draws closer to his readers in the very act of assailing them. Notably, his masterful use of dramatic dialogue becomes prominent in his poetry only from 1858 on. With this device he objectifies and thereby absorbs the virtual reader, who as a speaker becomes incorporated into the verbal texture of the poems.[60] That is, the poems no longer depict a passive recipient of a message but rather a partner in conversation.

Two examples of Baudelaire's later use of pronoun shifters may make this process more comprehensible. These shifters and similar transitional devices in literature often provide a major clue to the dynamics of an author's imaginative universe because they preserve an equilibrium between two dominant opposing forces. In Austen, Flaubert, or Goethe, for example, the use of represented discourse (*style indirect libre*) stakes out an ambiguous ground between the discourse of the narrator and the discourse of the character. By partaking of both, represented discourse facilitates movements from one register to the other, thus balancing the objective and the subjective. Similarly, in both French and English the first-person plural pronoun and adjective are doubly ambiguous because they may or may not include third parties or the addressee: "nous/we" may mean "I and they/she/he" or "I and thou/you" or "all of us." In "Duellum" ([September 1858], p. 36), for example, the first quatrain describes two dueling warriors in the third person (ll. 1–2). Their noisy battle is an allegorical representation of "*une jeunesse* en proie à l'amour vagissant" (a youth preyed on by wailing love; ll. 3–4 [emphasis added here and hereafter in the discussion of this poem]). In the second quatrain, the weapons break in the fray "comme *notre jeunesse,* / Ma chère!" (like *our youth,* my dear! ll. 5–6). The vocative "Ma chère!" retrospectively transforms the first quatrain into direct address as well. The repeated "jeunesse" now links relations between the speaker and the just personified female auditor to those between the duelists of the allegorical tableau. A manuscript version of the first tercet changed the impersonal "les héros" to "*nos* héros" (l. 10; cf. I, 895). While maintaining the intimate connotations of "poet and his beloved," the possessive adjective simultaneously reflects a formal authorial stance through

---

60. See Russell King, "Dialogue in Baudelaire's Poetic Universe," *L'Esprit Créateur,* 13 (Summer 1973), 115–18; and Henri Peyre, *Connaissance de Baudelaire* (Paris: Corti, 1951), p. 132.

which both the woman and we as empirical audience become implicated as didactic addressees. This ambiguity is preserved but modu-
lated toward the restoration of an atmosphere of intimacy when the
abyss into which the fighters roll is described as "l'enfer, de *nos* amis
peuplé" (Hell, peopled by our friends; l. 12). At the conclusion of the
sonnet, however, when the speaker invites the woman to struggle with
him and roll downhill after the first couple "afin d'éterniser l'ardeur
de *notre* haine!" (so as to render eternal the ardor of our hatred!), the
possessive adjective *notre* recollapses the virtual audience to the com-
pass of an *I-Thou* relationship. The instability of the personal referents
in this poem reflects Baudelaire's vacillation between fight and flight,
intimacy and detachment.

By using *on* instead of *notre*, Baudelaire achieves a smoother transition from a distant to an intimate audience in "Les Aveugles" (1860)
than in "Duellum" two years earlier.[61] Like *nous/nos/notre*, *on* functions
as an *embrayeur* (a device for "shifting gears" in language and literature), but *on* is less abrupt than the first-person plural because it is
even more all-encompassing. It becomes a discreet vehicle for the
captatio benevolentiae (appeal for the reader's sympathy) analogous to
the role of the frame narrator in fiction (e.g., in *Manon Lescaut* or
L'Immoraliste) who provides a model for a sympathetic response to the
central story. By subsuming both *vous* and *je*, *on* allows the poet to
move from the former (stated or implied) to the latter so as to create
a bond with his audience. Thus pronomial movement proceeds in this
fashion in the last three stanzas of "Les Aveugles": "*On* ne les *voit*
jamais"; "O cité!" "autour de *nous* tu chantes"; "*Vois!* je me traîne
aussi" (*You* never *see* them; O city! . . . you sing around *us; Look! I* too
drag myself; p. 92 [emphasis added]). Here the poetic function (the
heedless singing of the city) is associated with blindness, and physical
blindness is associated with spiritual insight. Ending with an uncomprehending question, the poet assimilates himself to the didactic object
of an implied message. The ambiguous *nous* hovering between *je* and
on allows us empirical readers the choice of identifying either with
the spiritually blinded satiric object "éprise du plaisir jusqu'à l'atrocité"
(infatuated with pleasure to the point of atrocity) or with the didactic
addressee susceptible of enlightenment.

---

61. See Ross Chambers's perceptive essay "Seeing and Saying in Baudelaire's 'Les
Aveugles,'" in Robert L. Mitchell, ed., *Pretext. Text. Context. Essays in Nineteenth-Century
French Literature* (Columbus: Ohio State University Press, 1980), pp. 147–56.

Expressed through allegory, however, the impulse to inclusiveness ultimately undermines itself and marks the beginning of Baudelaire's poetic decline. This process is evident in two poems from 1861, "Le Couvercle" (p. 141) and "Recueillement" (pp. 140–41). Consider "Le Couvercle," with its iconic title sitting atop the text like a lid on a pot. In the quatrains, seven tedious, facile oppositions attempt to encompass all humanity ("on land or sea," "in prayer or lust," etc.). Then the tercets accumulate metaphors for heaven to the point of incoherence: it is the wall of a burial vault, a brightly lit stage ceiling, a dark lid. All the antitheses of the quatrains are finally exposed as otiose when what the lid covers is characterized as "l'imperceptible et vaste Humanité" (p. 141: vast, undiscernible Humanity).

The "very careless" and "indisputably weak" lines that Valéry denounced in *Les Fleurs du Mal*[62] all come from the middle of the sonnet "Recueillement." Here are the first nine lines (the parenthetical numbers correspond to the comments below; the emphasis is mine):

> Sois sage, ô ma *Douleur* (4), et tiens-toi plus tranquille.
> *Tu* (4) réclamais le Soir; il descend; *le voici* (3):
> Une atmosphère obscure *enveloppe la ville* (1),
> *Aux uns* (1) portant la paix, *aux autres* (4) le souci.
>
> Pendant que *des mortels la multitude vile* (1),
> Sous le fouet du *Plaisir, ce bourreau sans merci* (2),
> Va cueillir des remords dans la fête servile,
> *Ma Douleur, donne-moi la main* (4); viens *par ici* (3),
>
> Loin d'eux ... (3)

(Behave yourself, O my *Suffering*, and do not be so restless. / *You* were asking for the Evening; it's coming; *here it is.* / A dim atmosphere *is covering the town,* / Bringing relief to *some,* to *others* bringing care. // While *the vile horde of mortals,* / Beneath the whip of *Pleasure, that merciless torturer,* / Goes to glean remorse at their feast of slaves, / *My Suffering, give me your hand;* come *over here,* // Far from them.)

Addressed to the poet's suffering, the poem as a whole is an apostrophe. Although in the traditional elegy apostrophe bridges the gap between the poet and a lost object, here it links the poet to an allegorical personification of his own pain. He invites this entity to retreat

---

62. See Paul Valéry, "Situation de Baudelaire," in *Oeuvres*, ed. Jean Hytier, 2 vols. (Paris: Gallimard, 1957), I, 598–613 (p. 610). The lines Valéry attacks appear in Baudelaire, *OC* I, 140.

with him far from the madding crowd, but the dense concentration of a totalizing discourse (1) reattaches him—as a perceptive representative—to all humanity. Such an ambivalent gesture, combining allegorical approach with literal withdrawal, is a Baudelairean hallmark.

Thus far the allegorizing seems tolerable. But when Baudelaire embroiders upon it by introducing a second personification, Pleasure as an executioner or torturer (2), the additional associative/dissociative movement makes the poem incoherent. The pleasure felt by hoi polloi contrasts with the poet's pain and inflicts pain at the same time. The cumulative effect resembles that of a sentence with two successive oppositional clauses (but . . . but), both of which, in Baudelaire's text, clash with the general context of totalizing discourse. According to line 4, moreover, as dusk envelops the town some people feel relief and others anxiety, but none of them are clearly associated with either the poet or the horde of pleasure-seekers he scorns. Further, the prosaic spatial deictics "le voici" and "par ici" (3) strain to connect the poet's pain with the soothing evening, thus setting themselves at odds with "loin d'eux," a phrase expressively enjambed to function as an icon as well as a sign of separation. The second vocative naming "ma Douleur" appears superfluous, and the poet's dramatized physical contact with this entity in the phrases "donne-moi la main; viens" (4) seems superfluously concrete, since the intimate "tu" of the apostrophe has already established close virtual contact. The vehement rhetoric of willed isolation generates a hidden countervailing drive toward relatedness, betrayed by the exuberance of the allegorical impulse through which the poet seeks things in common with his readers.

Even as Baudelaire addresses the reader more directly in the later verse poems with the unwelcome message of the *memento mori* topos (remember that we all must die), he distances that message and weakens its impact, first, through its very conventional quality and, second, by foregrounding his own rhetorical control of that message. The confrontation with horror is palliated for us by formality, generalization, and abstraction, in a revival of the techniques of *klassische Dämpfung*.[63] Accordingly, in "Danse macabre" the threatening apparition draws nearer as four stanzas of description of a skeleton in ball

---

63. This term and its definition come from Leo Spitzer's famous essay on Racine's "récit de Théramène" (*Phèdre* V, 7) in *Linguistics and Literary History* (New York: Russell & Russell, 1948), pp. 105–15, 123–25.

dress modulate into a seven-stanza apostrophe (the skeleton is now next to the poet) and then to a fourteen-line prosopopoeia beginning "Dis donc à ces danseurs" (So tell those dancers) and dictated to the skeleton by the poet. The speech in the poem having become the speech of the poem as well, we too are now among the addressees and are ourselves in the skeleton's presence. But the alliteration of the *d*'s in the phrase just cited and the poet's overt role as morbid puppeteer highlight an artificiality that diminishes the terror of death. And by the end of the prosopopoeia the addressee has become not only "these dancers" and (by implication) us but all humanity, in an allegorical dilution that further depersonalizes the transmission of the message. More generally, the many scenes in Baudelaire in which Death in person confronts the lyric personae are distanced by being identified as engravings or statues.

The poet becomes our representative in the late poems when he depicts himself not as the sender of menacing discourse but as its unwilling recipient: "Comme tu me plairais, ô nuit! sans ces étoiles / Dont la lumière parle un langage connu!" ("Obsession," p. 75: How pleasing you would be to me, O night, without those stars / Whose light speaks a familiar tongue!). Messages the poet does not want to perceive or understand haunt him in "Obsession." After he retreats from the forest, the sea, and the night, his unwelcome memories remain:[64]

> Mais les ténèbres sont elles-mêmes des toiles
> Où vivent, jaillissant de mon oeil par milliers,
> Des êtres disparus aux regards familiers.   [p. 76]

(But the shadows themselves are canvases / Where, spurting in thousands from my eyes, / Live vanished beings who gaze at me as if they knew me).

"Correspondances" also employs the phrase "aux regards familiers," but here the reassuring gaze originates in the self rather than in the external world. The poet's eye has become a breast; from it personal memories like jets of luminous milk gush onto the murky backdrop of the shadows (a detail that reminds us this setting is phantasmic,

---

64. Paul de Man provides an excellent comparison of the motif of universal analogy in "Correspondances" and its reworking in "Obsession"; see *The Rhetoric of Romanticism* (New York: Columbia University Press, 1984), chap. 9, pp. 252–62. Cf. Baudelaire, *OC* I, 839–44.

not real). Through this gesture of narcissistic projection, "we retrieve," as Paul de Man explains, "what was conspicuously absent from 'Correspondances,' the recurrent image of the subject's presence to itself as a spatial enclosure, room, tomb, or crypt in which the voice echoes as in a cave."[65] De Man goes on, however, to characterize the phrase "par milliers" as a "reassuring indeterminacy," when in fact it expresses the demonic fragmentation of the self, conveyed through the motifs of *effritement* (crumbling away) and incoherent heaping (of clothing, cards, dead soldiers, snowflakes, etc.) elsewhere in the Spleen poems. But the rhetorical ornament of the sonnet decreases the intensity of the confrontation between the poet and his thoughts. Each of the first three stanzas proffers a separate apostrophe to an aspect of Nature. As we move from one to the next, the tone becomes increasingly emphatic, exclamation points multiply, and the formal lyric "O" opens the last apostrophe. The point is that although thematically "Obsession" (as de Man has shown) represents a profoundly pessimistic reworking of "Correspondances," whose organic worldview and synesthesia promised the artist transcendent visions, from a rhetorical standpoint this poem counterbalances its pessimism with an accumulation of artifice and phatic pressure absent from "Correspondances."[66] The later poem contains three apostrophes, five exclamations (yet another was added in 1868), and four intimate second-person pronouns or adjectives; the earlier poem has none of these.

This strategy of balancing the immediacy of annihilation with the distancing of rhetoric becomes clearer still in "L'Horloge." A thousand voices repeat the warning that the poet's life is draining away. The image of vampirism is invoked (ll. 11–12). The text breaks into a prosopopoeia: "Le gouffre a toujours soif; la clepsydre se vide" (The abyss is always thirsty; the water clock drains dry). The water clock combines the menace of passing time with the emptying of the symbolic breast. Within this prosopopoeia a second, proleptic one is embedded: at the hour of death, the poet anticipates, "Tout te dira: Meurs, vieux lâche! il est trop tard!" (p. 81: Everything will tell you:

65. De Man, *Rhetoric of Romanticism*, p. 256.

66. For a qualification of the view that "Correspondances" does indeed promise transcendence, see Laurence M. Porter, "The Invisible Worm: Decay in the Privileged Moments of Baudelaire's Poetry," *L'Esprit Créateur*, 13 (1973), 100–113, in which I argue that the poem (like "Elévation," and like all poems by Baudelaire) reflects a steady descent away from the ideal.

Die, old coward! It is too late). But such supererogatory artifice as the doubly embedded discourse weakens the force of the warning, as does a dense accumulation of rhetorical ornament that reminds us that a dying poet remains a poet for all that: "Qualis artifex pereo!" In stanza 1, for example, the prosopopoeia is framed by an initial apostrophe to the "Horloge! dieu sinistre," whose "finger" (clock hand) "tells" us that we must remember. That Baudelaire makes part of a clock "speak" reveals how rhetorical and artificial the transmission of the message is in this poem; the fact that anything the poet designates now has an imperious claim on our attention shows that the problem frantically dramatized in earlier poems, attracting the attention of an indifferent audience, has disappeared. A cluster of fifteen voiced and unvoiced plosive consonants in only two lines of the clock hand's discourse imitates the impact of the "arrows" it describes: "Les vibrantes Douleurs dans ton coeur plein d'effroi / Se planteront bientôt comme dans une cible" (p. 81: In your heart full of dread, quivering Sorrows soon will lodge as if in a target). The hammering insistence of these sounds also suggests the prepotent communication of a voice raised too loud and words scanned too emphatically to be ignored. This emphasis is reinforced repeatedly in "L'Horloge" by an extraordinary concentration of rhetorical devices (simile, allegory, anaphora, exclamation, and additional prosopopoeia), together with a peremptory, aphoristic tone and self-contained generalizations.

By stanza 4, the clock's "finger" has acquired a "throat" as well, and it pauses to indulge in some self-conscious metalanguage with an ornamental display of three languages: "Remember! Souviens-toi, prodigue! Esto memor! / (Mon gosier de métal parle toutes les langues.)" (Remember! Remember, prodigal! Remember! / [My metal gullet speaks all languages.]). Not only is Baudelaire's persona now confident of reaching French audiences but it has received the apostolic gift of tongues as well and can speak to all. Ordinarily, prosopopoeia in the lyric (such as this discourse of the clock hand) creates an internal reduplication that provides a privileged moment of revelation, often uttered by a second, supernatural voice.[67] But here the effect becomes diluted because the main prosopopoeia has been expanded beyond the normal limits of internal reduplication, over more than twenty-

67. See Laurence M. Porter, "Internal Reduplication in the Lyric," in *Poetic Theory*, ed. Claudio Guillén, Proceedings of the Tenth Triennial Meeting of the International Comparative Literature Association, vol. 2 (New York: Garland, 1985), pp. 192–98.

two of the twenty-four lines of the poem. The remainder of the poem thus becomes a mere frame rather than a believable setting representing ordinary human experience deprived of insight. And the three embedded secondary prosopopoeias (revelations within a revelation) uttered by "la Seconde" (with a fussy specification of how many seconds there are in an hour), by "tout," and by "maintenant" seem parasitical and anticlimactic.[68]

At first glance, in the year 1859–60 Baudelaire appears to have found a partial solution to the impasse of communication: to nine poems he appends dedications to various artists and writers among his contemporaries. Thus he creates the image of a "fit audience... though few" superseding the inadequate general public to whom the *Salons* had appealed fifteen years earlier. Ross Chambers points out, however, that it would be an error "to read the dedicatee [in these cases] as a figure for the reader" since the dedication itself, and thus the person to whom it refers, is an object of reading. Given the alienation and incomprehension that Baudelaire's unprecedented texts were sure to provoke, Chambers explains, Baudelaire had no choice—in 1859 as in 1846 when he dedicated his *Salon* to the bourgeois—but to select unsuitable dedicatees. Then by inviting a comparison between the poetry of those honored and Baudelaire's own, the dedications would deviously denounce Gautier's superficial aestheticism, Hugo's bombastic paternalism, and Arsène Houssaye's lack of finesse.

Chambers adds the reservation that the titles "Au lecteur" and "Aux bourgeois" are not dedicatory but, rather, phatic devices, since those addressed have not yet been transformed by the experience of the text into the ideal audience that could understand the message directed to them and could therefore merit the poet's approbation.[69] This interpretation appears true of the 1846 *Salon*, but I see no reason to distinguish "Au lecteur" from the other, added dedications. In Baudelaire's poetic world, once a dedication has situated a figure in the circuit of inspiration → message → reception, then that figure first serves as Muse before contemplating itself in the mirror provided

---

68. The editorial note in Baudelaire, *OC* I, 990–93 offers a valuable discussion of the sources and analogues of "L'Horloge." Note the rhetorical sobriety of Baudelaire's sources in contrast to his own hypertrophied rhetoric. Gautier's forty-eight-line poem "L'Horloge," for example, limits its internal inscription to one line: "Chaque heure fait sa plaie et la dernière achève!" (Each hour leaves its wound and the last gives the coup de grâce!), a translation of the Latin commonplace "Vulnerant omnes, ultima necat."

69. See the lucid and provocative discussion in Chambers, "Baudelaire et la pratique de la dédicace."

by the poem. In "A une Madone," for example, the recipient is invited to contemplate the process of her own idolization, which then degenerates into a sadistic assault.

Similarly, just as the 1859–60 dedicatees were attacked aesthetically (insofar as Baudelaire's poems prove superior to rather than derivative of the works of their dedicatees), the "lecteurs" of 1861 will be attacked existentially. For Baudelaire effects two major changes in the overall tone and content of *Les Fleurs du Mal* as he reworks the 1857 edition into the definitive version of 1861. First, the oral- and anal-sadistic macabre is powerfully reinforced by fifteen added poems: "Le Masque," "Duellum," "Le Possédé," "Un fantôme," "A une Madone," "Le Revenant," "Sépulture," "Une gravure fantastique," "Le Mort joyeux," "Le Tonneau de la Haine," "Le Goût du néant," "L'Héautontimoroumenos," "Les Sept Vieillards," "Le Squelette laboureur," and "Danse macabre." Such an insistence on death interjects into the collection yet another disruption of the exchanges between poet and audience: as Chambers shrewdly observes, "Death's most pervasive manifestation, in 'life' as in 'art,' is as that which problematizes human communication."[70] Second, Baudelaire's expansion of the unmasking motif in the added poems "Le Masque," "L'Amour du mensonge," "Rêve parisien," and "Le Voyage" obliges the audience to confront the macabre motifs and consequently to face the desperate human condition that it must share with the poet. Through the vicarious channel of the poet's sensibility, the audience of the late "Tableaux parisiens" is also obliged to share the desperation of the old, the sick, and the poor.

From the beginning, the ambiguous title of the collection of verse, *Les Fleurs du Mal*, had concealed a trap for the reader which is analogous to the unmasking motif. Seen paradigmatically—that is, as denoting a set of related objects—the title suggests the possibility of finding beauty amid evil, if only by transmuting the moral mud of Paris into poetic gold (Baudelaire's metaphor in one of his "Projets de préface"). Thus it appears optimistic. And more distantly, but in the same vein, it suggests the implied audience as didactic object, transformed by the experience of the text into an ideal audience. But considered syntagmatically—that is, as a connected sequence (first there are flowers, then there is evil)—the title invites us to infer that

70. See Ross Chambers, "Baudelaire's Street Poetry," *Nineteenth-Century French Studies*, 13 (Summer 1983), 244–59 (p. 247).

the first term is the cause of the second, that the alluring flowers have produced evil. They can be seen as meretricious. The beauty of the poems themselves is thereby unmasked as specious and dangerous. So with one hand the title snatches away what it has offered with the other.[71]

A similar movement of thought occurs on the level of the poet's relations with the audience. The liminal poem "Au lecteur" literally incorporates the addressee into the world of poetry by speaking to her or him in verse. (In contrast, Hugo's prose preface to the *Contemplations* told but did not show the resemblance between poet and reader.) The poem then denounces the readers' emptiness with a sadistic relish. The readers become filled with a bad fluid: "quand nous respirons, la Mort dans nos poumons / Descend, fleuve invisible, avec de sourdes plaintes" (p. 5: when we breathe, Death descends into our lungs, / An invisible river, faintly moaning). Their parasitical remorse serves only to drain them of energy, and their greatest vice, "l'Ennui," robs them of the capacity for enjoyment and threatens to devour them along with everything else.

In terms of the relations between author and audience, the way "Le Voyage" echoes the imperious tone of "Au lecteur" in concluding the 1861 edition of *Les Fleurs du Mal* shows that for Baudelaire communication with his public has become easy (he can attract attention) but futile (his hearers remain too naive to understand). He can only turn on them with sarcasm. "Le Voyage" reintroduces the personified reader of "Au lecteur" as an eagerly questioning group, entirely unenlightened and unimproved by the experience of having read the previous 125 poems. Asked about his travels in exotic lands, the poet replies that everywhere on earth one finds "le spectacle ennuyeux de l'immortel péché / ... —Tel est du globe entier l'éternel bulletin" (p. 133: the tedious spectacle of undying sin / ... Such is the everlasting news bulletin of the entire globe). Critics have repeatedly pointed out

71. The preliminary titles Baudelaire planned for the collection reveal his ambivalence toward his public. Should he seek love or independence? "Les Limbes" suggests that art may be the isolated poet's cry for attention; "Les Lesbiennes" implies that art is self-sufficing perfection. Such ambiguity becomes telescoped into the definitive title, which combines two confessional stances: Rousseau's self-justifying stance ("Fleurs"— my sins are really worthy of your love) and the Augustinian unmasking stance ("du Mal" discloses these flowers' true nature, and if you don't profit from my moral insights, so much the worse for you). For an illuminating discussion of the final title from the perspective of literary topoi ("timeless" subjects), see Philip Knight, *Flower Poetics in Nineteenth Century France* (Oxford: Clarendon Press, 1986), pp. 93–98.

the willful, anticlimactic platitude of this summarizing statement, but they have not specifically noted its radical intrinsic emptiness. In French the secondary meaning of a "globe" is a hollow crystalline sphere, and the etymology of "bulletin" is *bulle* or bubble. In short, the poet confronts us with the empty breast. We have only ourselves for sustenance, the poem soon explains, but we are always already tainted. The spectacle of the world forever "nous fait voir notre image: / Une oasis d'horreur dans un désert d'ennui!" (p. 133: shows us our image: / An oasis of horror in a desert of boredom!). We appeal for vicarious experience to the traveler's "yeux profonds comme les mers!" ("eyes deep as seas," suggesting the fantasized full breast, and the dilated pupils of the nursing mother in tune with her child as it gazes into her eyes), but only death, the empty breast or *gouffre* evoked in the penultimate line (p. 134), will answer.

V

The irony and detachment of *Le Spleen de Paris* show Baudelaire fully emerged from the Symbolist crisis of *Les Fleurs du Mal*. From the dramatization of desperate but futile attempts to contact an audience, he has passed into resignation and bitterness. The title *Les Fleurs du Mal* was designed to please and shock. In contrast, the titles Baudelaire gave his collected prose poems reflect his emotional dissociation from his public during the last phase of his poetic production: consider the aesthetic emphasis of the first two ("Poèmes nocturnes," 1857–61, and "Petits Poèmes en Prose," used irregularly and with uncertainty from 1861 to 1866) and the collectivist emphasis of the last ("Le Spleen de Paris," the title from 1866 on). The definitive title returns full circle to the early verse "Tableaux parisiens," but with an added nuance of pessimism.[72] This collection deserves a book to itself, but I treat it only briefly because it falls beyond the scope of my concerns with the crisis of the breakdown of faith in communication that in my view characterizes the first phase of the French Symbolist movement.

The early prose poems composed from around 1857 to 1859, still apparently reworkings of their verse equivalents, form a transition to the final phase of Baudelaire's career, from 1859 until his death. The 1857 doublets already betray ironic, deflating intentions toward their

72. The editorial note in *OC* I, 1296–1301 documents the history of these titles well.

verse originals (as the "odeur de cuisine," in both the literal and figurative sense, of the prose "Invitation au voyage" shows only too blatantly).[73] The products of this angry, oppositional phase were the 1859 *Salon*, the major article on Delacroix (1863), and the balance of the prose poems. Rather than hopelessly beg as before for contact with the Other, Baudelaire now builds such contact into the very rhetorical texture of his poems. He depicts situations in which it is easy to attract the attention of the Other or even in which the Other is eager to attract attention from him, only to then subject his lyric self to a higher sarcasm that denounces all communication as worthless. After his Symbolist crisis, however, Baudelaire's despair is mitigated vicariously by a recrudescence of the Emersonian optimism—particularly from 1860 to 1863—that had characterized his writing before 1852. From this Emersonian perspective, the Great Man, while seemingly at odds with his age, actually proves in retrospect to have reflected its inchoate aspirations. This long view gives Baudelaire the hope of being better appreciated by posterity and allows him to regain a measure of ironic detachment.[74]

The shift from Baudelaire's middle to his late period is reflected clearly in his Poe criticism. In 1852 he envies the American's confident ability to capture and to hold his reader: his envy occasions the only adverse criticism in the essay "Edgar Allan Poe, sa vie et ses ouvrages": "Le style est serré; *encaténé;* la mauvaise volonté du lecteur ou sa paresse ne pourront pas passer à travers les mailles de ce réseau tracé par la logique.... Il abuse du *je* avec une cynique monotonie. On dirait qu'il est tellement sûr d'intéresser, qu'il s'inquiète peu de varier ses moyens" (His style is taut; *concatenated;* the reader's ill will or laziness cannot slip through the meshes of this net that logic has woven.... He uses 'I' to excess, with cynical monotony. You'd say he was so certain of arousing [the reader's] interest, that he had little concern for varying his devices). At the conclusion of the essay, however, Baudelaire reaffirms his kinship with Poe as another superior but unappreciated artist. Published in 1856, "Edgar Poe, sa vie et ses

73. J. A. Hiddleston, *Baudelaire et "Le Spleen de Paris"* (Oxford: Clarendon Press, 1987), p. 70.

74. See Bernard Howells, "On the Meaning of Great Men: Baudelaire and Emerson Revisited," *Romanic Review*, 78 (December 1987), 471–89. A stimulating book that complements this chapter by placing Baudelaire's fictive readers in historical perspective is Susan Noakes, *Timely Reading: Between Exegesis and Interpretation* (Ithaca, N.Y.: Cornell University Press, 1988). The passages from Baudelaire's Poe criticism appear in *Oeuvres complètes*, ed. Marcel Ruff (Paris: Seuil, 1968), pp. 333, 345, and 347.

oeuvres" reflects the narcissism of Baudelaire's middle period. Poe's female characters, Baudelaire observes, are projections of Poe himself. (This observation is clearly akin to Baudelaire's famous comment about Flaubert's relation to his character Emma Bovary: in his 1857 essay on Flaubert's *Madame Bovary*, Baudelaire claimed Flaubert had endowed his heroine with his own masculine traits.) In contrast, the "Notes nouvelles sur Edgar Poe," published in 1859, display no such emotional permeability and vulnerability but instead praise Poe for the first time as a "farceur" (in context, a mocking jester) whose ironic stance reflects Baudelaire's own attitude in the prose poems.

In *Le Spleen de Paris* as in his verse poems, Baudelaire continues to declare his radical Otherness vis-à-vis society and feels himself superior to the rest of humanity. But his sense of superiority no longer depends on a masochistic acceptance of suffering (as in "Bénédiction" or many of the love poems); on the sanction of supernatural beings (the guardian angel of "Bénédiction," God in "Les Phares," Satan in "Les Litanies de Satan"); or on the superiority of such poet-surrogates as the Albatross, Don Juan, Saint Peter, or "les Phares." Society does not martyr "L'Etranger";[75] freed of all earthly ties, the title character feels a contemptuous independence and revels in imaginative contemplation. Like the lyric self of "Le Voyage," he rejects his interlocutor's naive, eager questions. But unlike the traveler at the conclusion of *Les Fleurs du Mal*, the Stranger can turn utterly away from human misery. He does not feel compelled implicitly to take upon himself the vanity and suffering of the world, as he would have had to do if he had denounced these defects.

In the corpus of prose poems as a whole, however, Baudelaire does not allow himself to take refuge in a permanent delusion of self-sufficiency. Even the serene contemplator of clouds in "L'Etranger" has an ironic counterpart later in the collection, the lyric self of "La Soupe et les nuages" (p. 350), who admires the clouds only *almost* as much as his idolized beloved's eyes. And to bring him down to earth and to the soup served on the table before him, his beloved strikes him violently on the back. It is she who has the last word in the poem, a word that reminds us of the commercial restraints of the poet's livelihood since she calls him a "marchand de nuages" (cloud salesman). Moreover, the expected process of communication is reversed.

75. This poem may date from as early as 1859: it is written on a manuscript page from the *Salon de 1859* (see the editorial note in *OC* I, 1311).

No longer is it the poet who tries to contact an elusive audience. And no longer can the unwelcome communication to which the poet becomes passively subject at least be distanced through the rhetorical ornament of prosopopoeia that shows him somehow still in control. Here it is another "real" person who makes contact with him and thus usurps his role, and he cannot resist because the Other's message is prepotent: a shout reinforced by a blow, it compels attention.

The beloved's interruption, to be sure, recalls the brusque conclusion to the verse "Rêve parisien." But when we compare this poem to *its* prose counterpart, "La Chambre double," we can see how greatly Baudelaire's self-depreciating irony has intensified in the prose. The verse poem devotes thirteen stanzas to elaborating the privileged vision, one controlled and directed by the poet. The vision is dispelled in only two concluding stanzas, isolated from the rest by an initial Roman numeral, and even the dissipation of the vision has been initiated by the poet: he opens his eyes. His consciousness is invaded by care, by a clock brutally striking noon, and by the gloomy sky; but because of the keenness of his suffering, he remains alone and still implicitly superior to his surroundings.

The prose version, in contrast, devotes exactly half of its lines to each phase, to dream and to reality respectively. Even in the dream, however, the loved woman appears in demonic guise to subjugate the poet's imagination. And here what interrupts the dream is not the poet's act of opening his eyes, but the action of another person, who knocks heavily on the door. In other words, the poet never escapes the hell of other people. Moreover, in the prose version the intruder could be any of three figures. This ambiguity suggests that the poem has been narrated in the iterative mode (more simply put, that the poet's concentration has been repeatedly shattered by interruptions). It describes a repeated Sisyphean failure, rather than a single privileged moment such as those we find in the verse. After the interruption, passing time invades the prose with two prosopopoeias that, juxtaposed with the ecstatic vision, undercut it with an irony even sharper than that of the interruption itself, with a competing voice that overwhelms the poet's.

No longer, indeed, can the poet of *Le Spleen de Paris* hover in ethereal regions. These poems frequently, ironically deflate his role. The lyric self of "Perte d'auréole" loses his halo in a muddy street and then is recognized in a brothel by a shocked acquaintance. "Le Joueur généreux" receives from the Devil the gift of the omnipotence of thoughts in exchange for his soul but then doubts whether the Devil will keep his word. "Le *Confiteor* de l'artiste" ("The Artist's Confession") shows the poet fallen so low that he betrays his artistic mission and begs to be allowed to forget about the ideal. And it appears that his wish is granted, for the next poem relates a trivial anecdote. In the "Dédicace" to *Le Spleen de Paris*, moreover, Baudelaire dispels a notion prominent in *Les Fleurs du Mal*, that writing poetry can either reveal or create organic unity; he characterizes the prose collection as a minor work without any particular order or plot, as a "tortueuse fantaisie" (p. 275: a tortuous fancy). And he adds, self-disparagingly, that we can stop reading when we please. We find none of the urgency of "Au lecteur," in which our salvation might depend on our attentiveness to the poet's message.

As source and substance of the poetry, idealized Woman is demoted as well. In the verse poems, any diminution of her transcendent status results from the poet's desperate yearning to make contact. He might inflict physical pain on her, but she remains spiritually superior to him. At other times, he might remove her immutable mask of perfection to show how she shares ordinary human emotional suffering, frustration, and fear. But aside from this vulnerability, she remains more exalted than the poet and the rest of humanity. Thus the poet can justify and celebrate his devotion to her. Even verse poems such as "La Jolie Rousse" or "A une Malabaraise," which present the woman as socially inferior to the poet, still affirm that she should have been, and in other circumstances would have been, worshiped by all.

By discerning latent ideal qualities where others see only a prostitute, beggar or slave, then, the poet of the verse poems glorifies his own insight. But in the prose poems, the poet's adoration becomes a patent delusion. His women appear irremediably physically flawed as well as socially inferior. One is "vraiment laide . . . usée" (truly ugly . . . worn out); another has a hysterical voice roughened by alcoholism; yet another is a self-described "fameuse canaille" (a first-rate low-life). When she tells the poet so, he screams, "Non! non! non!" and refuses to listen. A fourth is a hairy, howling geek in a cage.[76] In this last poem, "La Femme sauvage et la petite-maîtresse," the poet stresses to his perfumed, pampered female companion that her only supe-

---

76. These four descriptions refer to "Un cheval de race" (p. 343), "La Soupe et les nuages" (p. 350), "Laquelle est la vraie" (p. 342), and "La Femme sauvage et la petite-maîtresse" (pp. 289–90).

riority to the sideshow freak depends on her unmerited socioeconomic privileges. And her melancholy sighs are only the tedious affectations of one who has never really suffered, rather than the promise of an emotional depth that might ally her with the poet. By abandoning the pretension that his female love objects are intermediaries between himself and the ideal, however, the poet potentially regains the contact of human solidarity, insofar as he becomes better able to consider women as equals.

In the prose poems, the negative counterpart of the feminine ideal, the *gouffre,* itself loses its emotional charge. No longer does it symbolize the absence of the desired breast or the regressive womb that can be reentered only at the cost of self-destruction. As in the final verse poem, "Le Voyage," it now simply means death, as in the phrase "l'ivresse de l'Art est plus apte que toute autre à voiler les terreurs du gouffre" ("Une mort héroïque," p. 321: Art more than any other form of intoxication is suitable for veiling the terrors of the abyss). The result is that the now neutralized breast can be simultaneously present and absent, empty and full. With her boyish chest, the aging, experienced mistress of "Un cheval de race" is described as both "squelette" and "breuvage" (p. 343).

Except in a few socially conscious poems such as "La Fausse Monnaie" and "Les Yeux des pauvres," in the prose poems the impossibility of communication is no longer a pretext (the cause of desperation) or a climax (the sudden shock of alienation) but a topic—that is, a situation that had been intellectually apprehended before the poems began and that is contemplated with resignation. The attempt to communicate now is seen not as dramatic and urgent but rather as idle, frivolous, or even contemptible, "une prostitution...*fraternitaire*" (a *fraternalizing* form of prostitution) committed by "nos races jacassières" (our jabbering races: "La Solitude," pp. 314, 313 [emphasis in original]). Overwhelmed by indifference, the poet at length abandons even the attempt to contact his fellows ("Chacun sa chimère," p. 283). And his potential readers, instead of being fascinated as in the frame poems of *Les Fleurs du Mal,* are now repelled ("Le Chien et le flacon"). At least five prose poems clearly present self-absorption as a goal: "L'Etranger," "Les Projets," "A une heure du matin," "La Solitude," and "L'Horloge." Indeed, in this last poem the poet's "découverte amoureuse de soi" as he contemplates his own creation obliterates any desire for communication with his female companion: "En vérité, j'ai eu tant de plaisir à broder cette prétentieuse galanterie, que je ne vous demanderai rien en échange" (p. 300: Truth to tell, I had so much pleasure in embroidering this pretentious flirtation, that I shall ask you nothing in exchange).

But Baudelaire does not pretend that such narcissistic plenitude provides a lasting source of happiness. He sets it up for an ironic fall. The idealized, autonomous self-image constituted by the work of art loses its efficacy nearly as soon as it has been generated by the poet; it must be continually, arduously renewed ("A une heure du matin," p. 288). Paradoxically, Baudelaire thus recuperates a measure of optimism, for art can improve on nature. As a case in point, the prose "Invitation au voyage," unlike its verse counterpart does not seem to be a transposition from the paintings of the Flemish intimists or Vermeer. It becomes clearly identified as "ce tableau qu'a peint mon esprit"; "pays singulier, supérieur aux autres, comme l'Art l'est à la Nature, où celle-ci est réformée par le rêve, où elle est corrigée, embellie, refondue" (pp. 303, 302: This picture my mind has painted; a curious land, superior to others, as Art is to Nature, when the latter is reshaped by the dream, when it is emended, beautiful, recast).

Such an emphasis on individual inspiration in the prose poems would seem to widen the gap between the poet and his virtual audience. But Baudelaire's poetic vision in the prose poems is not presented as something remote from the audience, something that must gradually be made accessible through the apprenticeship of the literary experience. Instead, his vision in the prose poems has been rhetorically mediated from the beginning through the use of language that presupposes referents already shared by poet and audience in a domain of intersubjective convention. The verse "L'Invitation au voyage," for example, begins "Mon enfant, ma soeur, / Songe à la douceur" (My child, my sister, / Think of the sweetness). The phatic imperative designed to ensure contact reinforces the redoubled direct address, which has been further reinforced by the rhetoric of intimacy and by the invitation to an imaginative participation. In contrast, the prose version begins "*Il est* un pays superbe, un pays de *Cocagne, dit-on*" (*There is* a magnificent land, a land of *milk and honey, they say* [emphasis added]). The impersonal presentation formula ("there is a land") assumes that the magical place has an objective existence. The familiar name belongs to a cultural code shared by poet and audience, and it further objectifies the vision in the form of a specific country rather than as an abstract feeling of *douceur*. The untranslatable pronoun *on* primarily identifies the impersonal voice of authority but secondarily implies the collective voice of the poet, the audience, *and* their society participating in a shared act of enunciation.

In the prose poems, the most striking use of *on* as a device to unite poet and audience—not as allegorical representatives of humanity via the *nous* of "Au lecteur" but as observers—appears in paragraphs 3 and 13 of "La Chambre double." This poem, in fact, twice associates poet and audience *in the act of enunciation:* "on les dirait doués d'une vie somnambulique" (par. 3: you [people in general, including poet and audience] would say they were endowed with a sort of sleepwalker's vitality); "ce que nous nommons généralement la vie" (par. 8: what we usually call "life"). No longer peculiar to the poet, the *énoncé* is therefore no longer alien to the audience (pp. 280–81).

Rather than appeal for contact with his audience, in other words, Baudelaire now builds it into the prose poems through various rhetorical strategies. On the dramatic level of lyric personae, he achieves automatic communicability with his audience through a shared pity for his characters: a spate of surrogate victims who return to the prose poems after having first appeared in some of the post–1857 "Tableaux parisiens." In the prose poems Baudelaire initially postulates not a difference between himself and his audience ("I suffer; pity me") but a resemblance ("they suffer; let us pity them"). Thus the lyric self changes from subject to observer in "Le Désespoir de la vieille," "Le Fou et la Vénus," "Le Mauvais Vitrier," "Les Veuves," "Le Gâteau," "Le Vieux Saltimbanque," "Les Yeux des pauvres," "Une mort héroïque," "La Fausse Monnaie," "La Corde," "Les Fenêtres," "Les Bons Chiens," and ironically in "Assommons les pauvres!" At the same time Baudelaire now condemns forms of self-absorption in the Other— be they self-pity ("La Femme sauvage et la petite-maîtresse") or hypocritical solicitude ("La Fausse Monnaie" or "Assommons les pauvres!")—instead of fostering them in the Other and in the lyric self.

An ironic surfeit of communication from the Other to the lyric self in the prose poems supersedes the lyric self's extreme difficulty of making contact with the Other in the verse poems of the crisis period. No longer does Baudelaire's persona have trouble attracting attention: he receives more than he desires. To be sure, in the verse poems prosopopoeia often places humanity or its allegorical representative, the poet, in the position of an unwilling recipient of a threatening message from Death or from Time. But such transmission occurs object-to-person or abstraction-to-person and, owing to its sources, partakes of the grandiose. In the prose poems, however, unwanted messages pass person-to-person from the Other to the poet; the content is often just the Other's trivial preoccupations rather than an imposing *memento mori*.[77] Baudelaire dramatizes the ineluctable character of such unwelcome exchanges by showing that they are initiated via prepotent communication. In the verse, it was the lyric self who adopted this attention-getting tactic with the knife stabbings of "A celle qui est trop gaie" or "A une Madone," or less directly, with the anal sadism of subjecting his companion to the reek of a rotting animal in "Une charogne." But in the prose, "Mademoiselle Bistouri" forces herself on the poet by seizing his arm; his mistress in "La Soupe et les nuages" attracts his attention by hitting him; in "Assommons les pauvres!" the beggar beats the poet to show that he has understood him; a knock on the door dispels the poet's reverie in "La Chambre double"; and a whistle-blast shatters the concentration of the poet-surrogate in "Une mort héroïque."

When *Le Spleen de Paris* depicts reciprocal communication, however, it does so ironically, if not farcically. "Assommons les pauvres!" is the most obvious example of such an exchange. In "La Fausse Monnaie," the friend who appears generously to give a beggar a valuable coin echoes almost verbatim the narrator's admiring comment that, next to being surprised, the greatest pleasure consists in surprising someone. But the friend's agreement opens an abyss of alienation in the narrator's mind once he realizes that the coin was counterfeit. In "Portraits de maîtresses,"[78] the clubmen in their smoking room illustrate a perfect fusion of subject and object—that is, of artist and woman. Like artists, they compose verbal portraits; like conventionally depicted women, they gossip; and, indeed, the text describes them as being in a "male boudoir." Each of the four describes a former mis-

---

77. Prosopopoeia itself becomes edulcorated or trivialized in the prose poem. In "Enivrez-vous" the clock, which along with a number of other entities addresses humanity, benevolently offers a formula for how to escape the tyranny of time instead of demanding that we submit to it, as does the clock in the verse, "L'Horloge" (p. 137). When the dead speak to the living at the end of the prose poem "Le Tir et le cimetière" it is to complain that the uproar made by the living is disturbing them, not to threaten the living with imminent death (pp. 351–52).

78. See Nathaniel Wing's rich analysis of this prose poem in *The Limits of Narrative: Essays on Baudelaire, Flaubert, Rimbaud, and Mallarmé* (Cambridge: Cambridge University Press, 1986), pp. 28–29.

tress. The last, who murdered his, found her company intolerable because she understood him perfectly. As he explains, "L'histoire de mon amour ressemble à un interminable voyage sur une surface pure et polie comme un miroir, vertigineusement monotone, qui aurait réfléchi tous mes sentiments et mes gestes avec l'exactitude ironique de ma propre conscience" (p. 348: The story of my love is like an endless journey across a surface as smooth and polished as a mirror, dizzyingly monotonous, which would have sent back the reflection of my every act and feeling with the ironic precision of my own conscience). Such flawless communication proved unbearable because the woman's responsiveness revealed an accurate rather than an embellished image of the frustrated lover, for whom self-deception thus became impossible.

Nevertheless, the dream of union with others persists in the prose poems. "Les Foules" explains that "le poète jouit de cet incomparable privilège, qu'il peut à sa guise être lui-même et autrui ...il entre, quand il veut, dans le personnage de chacun... [et] tire une singulière ivresse de cette universelle communion" (p. 291: the poet enjoys this matchless privilege: he can be himself and someone else at will...when he wishes, he can penetrate the personality of everyone...and he derives a peculiar form of intoxication from this universal communion). In a manner that recalls Balzac's Vautrin, Baudelaire compares this delight to that of priests, missionaries, and the founders of colonies (pp. 291–92). He expresses a similar mood in "Les Fenêtres," feeling "fier d'avoir vécu et souffert dans d'autres que moi-même" (p. 339: proud of having lived and suffered in others besides myself).

But in practice this dream cannot be realized. When the poet actually attempts a nurturant gesture—leaving a coin for an impoverished old circus performer ("Le Vieux Saltimbanque," p. 296)—the crowd sweeps him away. Likewise, when he tries to give a slice of bread to a starving child, he merely causes a vicious fight between the intended recipient and another child; as a result, the bread is crumbled and lost ("Le Gâteau," p. 298–99). He finally rejects the dream of fusion with others when the Devil (in the form of Eros) offers him "le plaisir, sans cesse renaissant, de sortir de toi-même pour t'oublier dans autrui, et d'attirer les autres âmes jusqu'à les confondre avec la tienne" ("Eros, Plutos, et la Gloire," p. 308: the pleasure, ceaselessly renewed, of getting outside of yourself to forget yourself in others, and of attracting others' souls to the point of confusing them with yours). For he realizes these other souls are not superior to his own; merging with them, he would gain nothing. And with a final pirouette at the conclusion of the poem, he mocks his own rejection of the dream; his renunciation itself thus becomes comical rather than solemn.[79]

Baudelaire's hope of creating an ideally comprehending audience— a hope abandoned during the course of his Symbolist crisis—was a remnant of the Romantic dream of organic unity and paradise regained. For him, the last refuge of this dream was the aesthetic ideal announced in the preface to the prose poems: the marriage of "poetry" and "prose," of emotion and the concrete object of representation, "le miracle d'une prose poétique, musicale sans rythme et sans rime, assez souple et assez heurtée pour s'adapter aux mouvements lyriques de l'âme, aux ondulations de la rêverie, aux soubresauts de la conscience" (the miracle of a poetic prose, musical without rhythm and without rhyme, flexible and accented enough to conform to the lyrical movements of the soul, the undulations of revery, the sudden starts of the conscience).[80] But "La Chambre double" destroys even this dream, when Baudelaire realizes that "relativement au rêve pur, à l'impression non analysée, l'art défini, l'art positif est un blasphème" (p. 280: relative to the pure dream, to the unanalyzed impression, clearly defined art, actual art is a blasphemy). Having abandoned hope of a satisfying communicative interchange with others, the poet now despairs of attaining a narcissistic communion with himself via the

---

79. Compare Baudelaire's more overt affirmations of his desire for isolation in his intimate writings composed sometime between 1859 and 1865: "Quand j'aurai inspiré le dégoût et l'horreur universels, j'aurai conquis la solitude" ("Fusées," I, 660: When I shall have inspired disgust and horror in everyone, I shall have conquered solitude); "Pensons-y: un peu d'impopularité, c'est consécration" ("Peintres et aquafortistes," II, 741: Think of it: a little unpopularity is a consecration); "Goût invincible de la prostitution dans le coeur de l'homme, d'où naît son horreur de la solitude. Il veut être *deux*. L'homme de génie veut être *un*, donc solitaire" ("Mon coeur mis à nu," I, 700: [There is] an invincible taste for prostitution in the human heart, which gives birth to man's dread of solitude. He wants to be *two*. The man of genius wants to be *one*, therefore solitary).

80. Baudelaire, "A Arsène Houssaye" (I, 275–76). In her splendid essay on how Baudelaire's prose poems effectively deconstruct the difference between verse and prose, Barbara Johnson appears to "buy into" his project as stated hypothetically in this preface, proclaiming it as a triumphal synthesis rather than recognizing how the pervasive irony of its context acknowledges a regretful failure to effect any such *Aufhebung*. The true dominant tonality of the prose poems, so to speak, is dissonance. See Barbara Johnson, *The Critical Difference: Essays in the Contemporary Rhetoric of Reading* (Baltimore: Johns Hopkins University Press, 1986), chap. 3, pp. 23–51.

mediation of the work of art. Consequently, he can no longer see a specific artistic creation as anything other than the symptom of a delusion. And so the final word of the poem, defining the lyric self, is "damné."

Chapter 5

Artistic Self-consciousness in Rimbaud's Poetry

Rimbaud more than any other Symbolist poet strains against the limitations of language. He forever strives to "make it new." He affirms the willed, autonomous origins of his visions by occluding referents beyond the texts. Yet from the moment of their conception, these visions are bound by the systems of language required to embody them. Any paradigmatic explosion of metaphor promptly falls back toward the syntagmatic axis of convention. And the free associations of the poetic imagination which fuel metaphoric displacement ultimately reveal themselves to be the products of necessity.

The struggle against the inadequacy of words as vehicles of transcendence is not, however, the one that predominates in Rimbaud's texts. For poetry depends on its public as much as on its medium. We can say that, like a nova in a distant galaxy, poetry does not occur if no one is present to observe it. And Rimbaud wrote nearly all his poetry during five adolescent years when he needed others against whom to define himself. Superficially, he appears to seek autonomy through withdrawal from society and through the intellectual form of that withdrawal, hermeticism. He invents for himself a private theater, an inaccessible fantasy world where he can don masks to conceal himself from a harsh, unsympathetic society. Even in his first surviving composition, a prose piece probably dating from the year he was eleven, he invents fictive parents and imagines that he was born during the Renaissance.¹ Yet the Other constantly intrudes into his early poetry—secretly summoned, of course, by the poet himself—because he wants to consolidate his sense of identity through defiance without forfeiting the attention of an audience on which he ultimately depends for validation.²

By overlooking or being insufficiently sensitive to this fundamental trait of Rimbaud's creative imagination in his poems, his need to summon the unwelcome Other repeatedly, we risk sinking into speculative biographical anecdote. "Mon triste coeur bave à la poupe" (my sad heart is drooling on the rear deck), for example, may or may not represent a veiled account of homosexual gang rape in a Commune barracks, but it surely offers an emblem of the youthful poet's unwilling dependence on an audience (the same dependence that bound him to the alcoholic, weak, maudlin, and despised Verlaine). "Quand ils auront tari leurs chiques / Comment agir, ô coeur volé?" ("Le Coeur volé," p. 101: When their wads of chewing tobacco are dry / How shall we act, O stolen heart?) is routinely glossed as "What shall I do, now that they have sullied me?" but an equally plausible meaning, made more so by the future perfect tense, would be: "What shall I do, when they stop paying attention to me?" A variant title of this poem, "Le Coeur du pitre" (The Heart of the Clown), reveals Rimbaud's hidden agenda of willfully making himself bizarre in order to become a spectacle.³

In short, the limitations of the linguistic vehicle of poetry, frequently

---

1. Petre Solomon, "La Vision dramatique de Rimbaud," in *Rimbaud Multiple: Colloque de Cérisy* (1982), directed by Alain Borer, Jean-Paul Corsetti and Steve Murphy (Gourdon: Dominique Bedou and Jean Touzot, 1986), pp. 197–214. This information appears on p. 205. For the prose text in question, see the "Prologue" in Jean-Nicolas-Arthur Rimbaud, *Oeuvres*, ed. Suzanne Bernard and André Guyaux (Paris: Garnier, 1981), pp. 5–7. Unless otherwise noted, subsequent page references to Rimbaud are from this edition. I have chosen it because it is more recent than Antoine Adam's good Pléiade edition of the *Oeuvres complètes* (Paris: Gallimard, 1972), but both must be consulted because the Pléiade edition reproduces far more letters and variants and because the annotations in the two editions complement each other well. When it is necessary to distinguish the two, I identify them as Bernard and Adam respectively. See also Louis Forestier's informative edition of the poetry: *Poésies; Une Saison en enfer; Illuminations*, 2d ed. rev. (Paris: Gallimard, 1984); hereafter cited as Forestier.

2. For a sharply contrasting reading of Rimbaud as a metaphysical poet, particularly in the *Illuminations*, see Jacques Rivière's classic *Rimbaud: Dossier 1905–1925*, ed. Roger Lefèvre (Paris: Gallimard, 1977), pp. 147–62. Rivière himself, however, later retreated from his original position.

3. The variant titles of "Le Coeur du pitre" are discussed in more detail in n. 25 below.

stressed by Rimbaud's critics, pose no greater obstacle than the binding syntagm of the act of communication itself (a sender requires a message and the latter a receiver) called into existence each time one sets pen to paper. Ineluctably, the poetic voice through which the Self comes into being summons its hearer. And then the Other, turning toward the clamor of the poem, imprisons that self within the categories of that Other's own alien perceptions. Applied to Rimbaud's poetry, such a set of metaphors is not really overblown. For Rimbaud is a highly dramatic poet, introducing many speaking characters into his verse. This multiplication of personae becomes especially marked in the *Illuminations,* where it is reinforced by a theatrical vocabulary referring to scenes, comedy, spectacles, and the like.[4] The mode of drama that appears most frequently in Rimbaud consists of three phases: expression by the poet, attack by the public, and defense by the poet.

Poetic expression can be figured as writing, speaking, singing, or more generally as emanation. Since Rimbaud is more visual than aural as poets go, one would expect him to privilege the act of writing. And indeed the "Voyelles," whose colors he later boasted of having invented, are graphemes—the five letters *a, e, i, o, u* of the French alphabet—rather than the sixteen vocalic phonemes of the spoken language.[5] Rimbaud's major goal in this poem is not to play with synesthesia, the effect produced when an impression received by one sense (in this instance, the sound of a vowel) is experienced as an impression received by another (e.g., color), as in Gautier's "Symphonie en blanc majeur" (Symphony in White Major) or Baudelaire's "Correspondances." Rather, his goal is to be able to move from his

4. Solomon, "Vision dramatique," pp. 209–10. The primordial form of dramatization occurs through doubling. As Shoshana Felman observes, "Rimbaud's originality consists in his premonition of modernity as a problem concerning the couple: of the couple, on the levels both of desire and of language; the couple of lovers, or of the signifier and the signified, of the word and its truth" (*La Folie et la chose littéraire* [Paris: Seuil, 1978], p. 114). To these pairs one should of course add that of the writer and reader.

5. The most plausible source for the idea of associating vowels with colors in "Voyelles" would be the piano lessons Rimbaud's friend Etienne Cabaner gave him in Paris. Cabaner taught by associating a color and a vowel sound with each note; he even dedicated to Rimbaud a sonnet illustrating this system. See Pierre Petitfils, *Rimbaud* (Paris: Julliard, 1982), pp. 150–51. Concerning the prevalence of eye-rhyme in Rimbaud, a feature that demonstrates how the grapheme takes precedence over the phoneme in his verse, see René Etiemble, *Rimbaud: Système solaire ou trou noir* (Paris: Presses universitaires de France, 1984), pp. 44–46.

verbal inscription to a medley of sense impressions in a way that
attenuates as much as possible the rationalized intermediate steps of
description. Rimbaud thus weakens and fragments the decor bound
to a particular, recognizable place and time, whereas synesthesia den-
sifies and consolidates such decors by multiplying the sum total of
sense impressions associated with them. Because synesthesia is produced only when some elements of the setting incite two or more
simultaneous sense impressions, the device implies a riveting of the
attention, a coagulation of desire, and a hierarchy of desired objects,
as some are capable of eliciting more associations—more "meanings"—than others. This contemplative, static mode is alien to Rimbaud. He wants not focus but distraction. Writing seems to offer such
freedom since, unlike speech, it is not ordinarily scrutinized by the
Other while it is being produced.

But Rimbaud still requires the presence of the Other in order to
define himself, and writing, unlike speech, is difficult to dramatize.
Few authors are like Lautréamont, who imagined being struck by an
angry thunderbolt as he sat at his desk, subversive pen in hand. "Singing" (*chanter*, that is, the performer poet accompanying himself on
the lyre), in contrast, appears to combine the advantages of speech
and of writing, since it takes place before an audience but an audience
that presumably remains silent. It suggests a voluntary, unmediated,
spontaneous form of expression. And a potent one. The poet's song,
associated with myths of Amphion, Orpheus, and God, charms, sub-
dues, and creates. But the verb *chanter* itself has been too thoroughly
consecrated by tradition to be suitable for Rimbaud's purposes. So if
he uses it, he either does so mockingly to refer to the trite poetic
efforts of others or he ascribes to those of his poet figures who do
sing the harsh, strident voices of the raven or the wolf.

In general, when spoken expression in Rimbaud is marked (explicitly designated by a verb of discourse) it is satirized. In his early
poems, speech often assumes the routinized and debased form of
telling a rosary, of ritual prayers. Words used in this way stifle poetic
originality, since they function not for self-assertion but for self-
effacement. Prayer, having become instinctual, may even degrade us
to the level of beasts, as it has done to the people in "Les Pauvres à
l'église," "bavant la foi mendiante et stupide" (the poor people at
church, drooling out their stupid, mendicant faith). Nature itself, that
overworked source of inspiration for ordinary poets, does not sing to

Rimbaud but drools in "Les Douaniers" and in "Mes petites amoureuses." It becomes animalistic rather than exalting, like one of Circe's
swine, and so does the poet seduced into praising it. Rimbaud, in fact,
adopts the pseudonym "Alcide Bava [drooled]" to sign his sarcastic
hymn "Ce qu'on dit au poète à propos de fleurs." Yet with the verb
"baver" we return full circle from speech to writing, since the derived
noun "bavure" can refer to a blot in printing or in a schoolboy's
copybook: that is, to an illicit, condemned form of verbal expression
and, by extension, perhaps to the self-assertion of a refusal to
conform.

From around the time Rimbaud was sixteen, he invited disapproval,
growing his hair long and cultivating eccentricity.[6] Similarly, when
the tone of the poems he writes then is not enraged it is provocative.
By acting as if others were his enemies he makes them so—and then
needs to defend himself. The surest defense is detachment through
humor. Thus "Roman" invokes the inexperience and fickleness of
the youthful poet-persona, beginning and ending with the self-
depreciating verse "On n'est pas sérieux, quand on a dix-sept ans"
(You're not serious, when you're seventeen). In and of itself, such a
naive repetition precludes solemnity. The prose frame of "Un coeur
sous une soutane" adds to humor an additional layer of self-protec-
tion: a scapegoat surrogate distinct from the implied author—the
eponymous character—risks poetic self-expression that incites deri-
sion in his audience. "L'Eclatante Victoire de Sarrebruck" eliminates
the scapegoat but gives the implied author the stature of a judge by
transforming his text into the "reader" of another work of art rather
than presenting it as being read or heard by a personified audience.
The pretext is a "brilliantly colored Belgian engraving" that served
French propaganda in the disastrous Franco-Prussian War, transforming a routine skirmish into a heroic triumph. The poem itself
refutes the engraving's claims to military triumph and glory by exposing the irreconcilable gap between reality and pretense in the
incongruous juxtapositions of the details of the description: garish,
clashing colors; sublime mixed with grotesque tones; omniscient narration mixed with baby talk.

Such inconsistency of tone on the figural level has been named

6. Ernest Delahaye, *Delahaye témoin de Rimbaud*, ed. Frédéric Eigeldinger and André
Gendre (Neuchâtel: A la Baconnière, 1974), pp. 294–95.

"diaphor" by Philip Wheelwright, who gives as an example "My country 'tis of thee; / Higgledy-piggledy, my black hen."[7] Here the solemnity of patriotism has been undercut by association with part of a nonsense rhyme. Although discontinuity of tone characterizes Romanticism, which thereby calls accepted codes into question, postulating a simple opposition of serious and comic modes, or formal and familiar language, is too crude to account for what occurred in Romanticism and what Rimbaud inherited from his precursors. To characterize this legacy adequately one must consider at least three axes. On the first axis, which could be called the rhetorical, one can juxtapose a serious tone (or, in the language of I. A. Richards's and Max Black's theories of metaphor, a serious vehicle) and a trivial referent (or tenor), producing hyperbole. This comic inflationary mode is represented on the level of character by the *alazon* (the braggart) and on the level of genre by the mock-heroic. (Not surprisingly, one of the schoolboy Rimbaud's favorite works was Boileau's mock-heroic *Le Lutrin*.) "Les Assis" and "L'Eclatante Victoire de Sarrebruck" are written in this mode.

Alternatively, one can juxtapose a trivial tone with a serious subject, producing understatement, the deflationary skepticism of the *eiron* (the character traditionally paired with the *alazon* in ancient comedy), and the genre of Romantic irony (authorial intervention that dispels the illusion of the author's own work) represented notably in certain works by Alfred de Musset, Byron, and Heinrich Heine. In this mode heroic ideals, and particularly the dignity of artistic creation, are subverted by the primary voice in the work—that is, the voice of the commentator or narrator. Rimbaud, however, does not mention these precursors, with the exception of Musset, whom he finds particularly detestable (seeing only his weepy confessional side). He departs from them by attributing the deflationary voice to a character rather than to the lyric self—in "Les Reparties de Nina," for example—or by making the lyric antiself (the horrible example introduced to set off true values by contrast) into a companion rather than an enemy of the poet, as in the section "Délires I" of *Une Saison en enfer*. The poet then becomes deflated through association with an unworthy comrade. Both these examples illustrate how Rimbaud's dramatic turn of mind leads him

7. Philip Wheelwright, *Metaphor and Reality* (Bloomington: Indiana University Press, 1964), pp. 78–86 and passim.

to introduce the deprecating voice not on the level of metalanguage, as in the authorial interventions typical of Romantic irony, but rather on the level of personification. Romantic irony tries to forestall attacks on the work of art by making them first; the implied author becomes his or her own reader. This device generates a form of prolepsis (in the sense of an anticipation of the reader's arguments), characteristic also, for example, of Montaigne, Freud, and Stendhal. Rimbaud's personifications, in contrast, introduce the hostile or inadequate reader directly into the work on the same plane as the other lyric personae.

The second axis, the archetypal, juxtaposes contraries in order to prepare for the appearance of the archetype of inversion. The latter is widespread in Romanticism. In its more common, positive form this archetype transforms shame into glory, defeat into victory, ugliness into beauty, and madness into vision. Outstanding examples in the Western tradition are the Beatitudes or the Crucifixion followed by the Resurrection of Christ. Romantic defiance presents an embryonic form of inversion: the poet identifies with outcasts. In "Orgie parisienne ou Paris se repeuple," for example, Rimbaud condemns those who rejoiced in the French defeat in the Franco-Prussian War and claims that when order has been reestablished, "le Poète prendra le sanglot des Infâmes, / La haine des Forçats, la clameur des Maudits" (the Poet will take up the sobs of the vile, / The hatred of the Convicts, the clamor of the Accursed).[8] More truculently in "Oraison du soir," the poet, in a gesture typical of the blasphemous provocations in Rimbaud's poems near the end of 1870, prays by pissing high and far toward the dark sky in a ritual aspersion through which he assumes God's role.[9] The ultimate triumph of role reversal occurs in "Ce qu'on dit au poète à propos de fleurs," when the poet Banville's vigorous blooms (symbols for his poems themselves) turn on the bad reader who ordinarily could abuse them with impunity, "Pochant l'oeil fou de l'étranger / Aux lectures mal bienveillantes!" (Blackening the crazed eye of the stranger / Whose readings are ineptly wellmeaning!)[10]

8. Compare "Les Mains de Jeanne-Marie," in which the fierce revolutionary Marseillaise contrasts with weak Christian prayers ("les Eléisons") begging for mercy.

9. This interpretation is suggested by Louis Forestier in Forestier, pp. 248–49, nn. 3 and 5.

10. For a detailed treatment of this poem see Jean-Pierre Giusto, *Rimbaud créateur*

The third axis of tonal incongruity could be called the totalizing or organic axis. It reflects the ideal of a literature that strives to become all-inclusive in an attempt to simulate the richness of life itself. To believe that a reductive schema such as language could somehow encompass the whole of which it is merely a small part has always been a temptation. At the height of French Classicism, a movement supposedly based on an aesthetics of exclusion, critics rejected Aristotle's suggestion that tragedy should stand at the summit of the hierarchy of genres because of its intensity and concentration. Instead they exalted the epic for its abundance and variety. One hundred fifty years later, Victor Hugo, in his "Préface de Cromwell" (1827), urged writers to combine the sublime with the grotesque, not as a diaphoric or ironic statement typical of code-challenging mid-century Romanticism, but rather as a literary application of the Neoclassical worldview of *concordia discors*—that is, of a cosmic harmony arising from the necessary complementarity of opposites. Hugo's black-and-white moral vision sharpens the distinction between categories rather than blurs them as they are blurred by Romantic irony. A world of binary oppositions such as Hugo's reflects a faith in ultimate meaningfulness; situated in the gap between the poles, the literary work is nevertheless defined by them.

Rimbaud, however, comes to create a poetry not of structures but of beginnings. To be sure, his nostalgia for a totalizing vision is betrayed by his oft-stated desire to reinvent and recreate, by the hypothetical future tense in his poems, by his plurals of normally singular nouns, and by his frequent use of the adjective *tout*. But this nostalgia is not supported by Rimbaud's experience of the communicative exchange. The Romantics could salvage meaning from the very opposition between poet and audience. For Rimbaud, these two poles always threaten to merge.

The motif of the eye which eventually pervades his poetry allows Rimbaud to move beyond Romantic oppositional posturing to a Symbolist self-consciousness fraught with ambiguity. Like most key symbols, this symbol of the eye cuts two ways. In the frames of Rimbaud's poems—that is, near the beginning or ending—the eye tends to connote the presence of an Other who disapprovingly watches the

---

(Paris: Presses universitaires de France, 1980), pp. 146–53. I agree that this poem is not a parody of Banville but rather a challenge to him, to Verlaine, and to other poets to reject convention and join Rimbaud in his iconoclasm.

performer-poet, inhibiting him with warnings, rules, and strictures. But at the core of the poems, and particularly at privileged moments of lyric intensity, the Rimbaldian eye denotes the Natural Eye—mandala, sun, or flower—revealing a nonjudgmental sensibility with which the poet hopes to commune free from self-consciousness. At best the poet-persona may itself become assimilated to the uninhibited Natural Eye, as it does in "Tête de faune." Objectively the Rimbaldian eye remains a detail revealing the presence of a consciousness whose relationship to the lyric self must be defined by the context. But subjectively it represents a totality, since only through this eye can externality become known. The lyric self forever risks becoming alienated from this eye and becoming its object.

Although, paradoxically, it must always be reported in words, nonverbal communion with Nature in Rimbaud circumvents the hostile Other and assures a state of perfect passive happiness in which the poet becomes the receiver rather than the sender of the virtual message. Rimbaud's Nature offers unvarying and unconditional acceptance. The poet wordlessly unites with it, whereas he cannot seek to join society without uttering words that are always judged and that may be rejected and condemned. René Char sensitively characterized this Nature as "non-static..., not particularly valued for its conventional beauty or for its products, but associated with the flow of the poem where it frequently intervenes as the subject, a luminous backdrop, a creative force, a support for inspired or pessimistic enterprises—as grace."[11]

Abandoning himself completely to the womb of Nature, however, the poet risks being swept up and consumed by processes more rapid than the human life cycle. At times he expresses a suicidal desire for such union: "Je veux bien que les saisons m'usent. / A toi, Nature, je me rends" (I am willing to have the seasons consume me. / To you, Nature, I surrender myself).[12] But at other times he feels ambivalent. In "Le Dormeur du val," for instance, the description of the young soldier lying dead amid lush vegetation on the bank of a stream and cradled by Nature as an infant is cradled by its mother does not merely

11. This quotation is from Char's preface to Forestier, p. 11.
12. "Bannières de mai," p. 157. Elsewhere, "love" as Rimbaud conceives it often seems to connote a Romantic pantheistic idea of communion with Nature. For him, however, such communion is more clearly linked to the temptation of suicide (cf. Flaubert's *Tentation de saint Antoine*, published in 1874) than it was in such precursors as Goethe and Senancour.

express indignation at the way war intrudes on and brutally disturbs the bucolic setting. The hypogram of the poem must be Alfred de Vigny's line in "La Maison du Berger" which refutes our traditional notion of a consoling, solicitous Nature: "On me dit une mère, et je suis une tombe" (They call me a mother, and I'm a tomb).[13]

Rimbaud, then, generally does not allow himself to become overwhelmed by sensory impressions from Nature. In his response to such impressions, he remains aware of himself receiving them. Impressions that have thus become internalized via self-consciousness enrich rather than drown the perceiving self.[14] Self-contemplation can evade both the destructive energy of the natural cycle and the disapproving gaze of the Other. As Ross Chambers has pointed out, from some of his earliest poems on Rimbaud attempts to shield his vulnerability by including explicit designations that integrate him into these poems as a spectator. Sometimes he presents himself as an observer commenting on the spectacle ("Et le Poète dit" [And the Poet says] at the end of "Ophélie"), sometimes as both spectator and part of the spectacle. More subtly, in later poems such as "Mémoire" insistent metaphors of the eye transform an element of the decor into the pure gaze of the poetic consciousness.[15] By contemplating his own message, the poet transforms himself into its receiver, protects the message itself from a hostile or insensitive reception, and consolidates a desirable poetic autonomy.

Such self-sufficiency finds its spatial analogue in voluntary sequestration that may be associated with self-reading. In the last section of "Les Poètes de sept ans," the child protagonist savors the solitude of his room where he can pore over his own "roman" (tale) "sans cesse médité" (an unending subject of contemplation). Thus he dramatizes being the author as well as the observer of his fictive self. As such he escapes the limitations of tradition, inexperience, or lack of inspiration. "A une raison" in the *Illuminations* proposes the myth of an infinite poetic competence, of boundless possibilities: "Un coup de ton doigt sur le tambour décharge tous les sons et commence la nouvelle harmonie" (A tap of your finger on the drum releases all sounds

13. A hypogram is a condensed form appearing in a earlier intertext. For a discussion of this valuable concept see Michael Riffaterre, *The Semiotics of Poetry* (Bloomington: Indiana University Press, 1978), pp. 82–86, 109–10, 124–50, and passim.

14. For him, "sentir, c'est *se* sentir," as Georges Poulet strikingly puts it in *La Poésie éclatée: Baudelaire-Rimbaud* (Paris: Presses universitaires de France, 1980), p. 108.

15. See Ross Chambers, "Rimbaud et le regard créateur," *Saggi e ricerche di letteratura francese* 10 (1969), 199–208, esp. 217.

and inaugurates the new harmony). Totally dependent on this demiurgic poet, the fictive audience pleads with him to change their lives. But he can choose instead to remain unreadable. "Parade," for example, evokes a kaleidoscopic variety of performances about which the poet observes, "J'ai seul la clef de cette parade sauvage" (I alone have the key to this savage parade; cf. "je réservais la traduction" [I did not divulge the translation] in *Une Saison en enfer*). Even this subdued audience overwhelmed by the poet's virtuosity is made to disappear later in the *Illuminations*. In "L'Eternité" the lyric self breaks completely free from the mortal condition:

> Des humains suffrages,
> Des communs élans
> Là tu te dégages.   [p. 160]

(From human approbation, / From commonplace enthusiasms, / There you disengage yourself.)

Juxtaposed with the union of male and female principles and of sea and sun evoked both earlier and later in the poem, this statement conveys a plenitude of self-acceptance.

Our rapid overview of Rimbaud's strategies for dealing with the hostile audience shows his strategies becoming steadily less tentative, more effective, and more grandiose. Devices for circumventing the audience appear throughout Rimbaud's texts from the time of his first published French poem, "Les Etrennes des orphelins." The more prominent these devices, the more likely it is that the poem in question will have drawn criticism for being obscure.

In "Les Etrennes des orphelins," two four-year-olds huddle alone in an icy house: their mother has died, their father is absent.[16] The wakening birds who start singing at dawn and then "approach" the children suggest the dream of a warm nest that contrasts with their cold and lonely bed. The poem evokes a time of past happiness when the family exchanged Christmas gifts: "Ah! c'était si charmant, ces mots dits tant de fois" (Ah! How charming they were, those words so often spoken). There would in fact have been two or at most three times when the children could have understood those words: the hyperbole of "tant de fois" intensifies the sense of loss. They fall asleep

---

16. For a complementary essay that emphasizes the conventional, derivative qualities of this poem, see J. F. Massol, "Pratiques scolaires, visées littéraires: 'Les Etrennes des orphelins,'" in *"Minute d'éveil": Rimbaud maintenant*, Colloque de la Société des Etudes romantiques (Paris: SEDES, 1984), pp. 6–20. For a more complete list of the many obvious sources of this poem, see Bernard, pp. 360–62.

again, and a comforting angel brings a dream in which the family has
been restored:

> On dirait qu'une fée a passé dans cela!...
> —Les enfants, tout joyeux, ont jeté deux cris...Là,
> Près du lit maternel, sous un beau rayon rose,
> Là, sur le grand tapis, resplendit quelque chose...
> Ce sont des médaillons argentés, noirs et blancs,
> De la nacre et du jais aux reflets scintillants;
> Des petits cadres noirs, des couronnes de verre,
> Ayant trois mots gravés en or: "A NOTRE MERE!"
> .... [p. 38]

(You would think that a fairy had had a hand in that! / —All happy,
the children each shouted...There, / Next to the mother's bed, bathed
in a beautiful pink ray, / There, on the great carpet, something is
gleaming..../ It's medallions of silver, black and white, / Ivory and
ebony with sparkling reflections; / Little black frames, glass shields, / With
three words engraved in gold: "TO OUR MOTHER!")

One of the few critics to pay attention to this poem, Robert Greer
Cohn, reacts harshly. He finds that it ends awkwardly and anticli-
mactically; the emotional impetus is exhausted and the attempt at
closure is clumsy. By mentioning the engraved medallions, Rimbaud
seeks a "monumental finality" (they are metal funeral wreaths, combining memories of loss with memories of the joy of gift-giving).[17]
Cohn tries to demystify Rimbaud's career by demonstrating that his
early efforts were not works of incomparable genius, that he had to
learn his trade like anyone else. He implies that Rimbaud padded the
ending of his poem as he struggled to resolve it. But the line of dots
that concludes the printed text shows that such was not the case. The
editors of *La Revue pour tous* had told Rimbaud they would publish
his poem if he cut it by one-third. He removed two passages, one of
which was the original ending (now lost). The "couronnes mortuaires,"
in other words, represent a definitive final image freely and carefully
chosen by Rimbaud, a place in the poem he considered to be a strong
point. I believe that what Cohn experiences as awkwardness derives
from a clash between the mimetic (a plausible representation of what
four-year-olds might think and feel) and the thematic (a rendering

17. Robert Greer Cohn, *The Poetry of Rimbaud* (Princeton: Princeton University Press,
1973), pp. 36–37.

of the fifteen-year-old author's own feelings toward his mother and himself).

The children had seemed to murmur as they slept. Perhaps in their dreams they were making a yearning appeal to their mother, a plea hinted at by the engraved message at the conclusion of the dream. As frames for funeral wreaths, the medallions signify the mother's permanent absence and tinge the fantasy of happiness with irony. But the fact of this absence has blended with the children's wishes to communicate with her once more. The tenor of the final message, "A NOTRE MERE!" is simple and appropriate for the small children. The vehicle, engraved letters of gold, is not. These children could have neither written nor read the message. As a citation of a text created by someone other than the children, the golden words close the frame of depersonalization introduced in the opening line by the impersonal "on" who hears the children's whispering.

The discrepancy between the naive effusion of the message and its elaborate vehicle suggests that it is the adolescent poet who feels bereft and helpless as an orphan in the cold climate of maternal indifference. His poetry is a gift of love, refined into a verbal artifact that the precocious Rimbaud knows to be of beauty and value. Fear of rejection, combined with the guilt inspired by maturing sexuality, sublimates into chaste words the inchoate feelings inspired by being "near the maternal bed." The maternal body as desired object stimulates a physical response disguised as colored light ("a lovely pink ray"), a form of energy that like a cathexis calls attention to something. Then a movement of repression simultaneously cancels and preserves desire, transforming the colored ray and the unmentionable "quelque chose" that the ray illuminates into a metaphorical figuration: black words on the white page, a surrogate for the lost object, the presence of an absence. In the nineteenth century, of course, colored images were much rarer than they are today. Engravings were the norm. The mediated experience of works of visual art was a black and white experience. Therefore, the contrast between color (representing the natural) and black and white (representing the artificial: repression, denial, sublimation) was much more obvious and prominent in Rimbaud's time that it would be today (though we can compare it with a cinematic experience: the striking shift from Kansas to Oz in *The Wizard of Oz*). Once sublimation has occurred, however, light (represented in the phrase "aux reflets scintillants") and then color (in the word "or") can be restored to the desired object, since it is now embodied in the acceptably distanced mode of the engraved word "mother" rather than in the real person. Moreover, the glass cover above this word ("couronnes de verre") both reveals it and yet prevents a direct, profanatory contact.

Meanwhile, a repeated, three-layered chiasmic structure mimics the movement of desire back and forth between the unconscious and awareness, through the preconscious. We can schematize this structure as follows:

1. Light associated with feelings: "Près du lit maternel, sous un beau rayon rose"; "resplendit"; "argentés"
   2. Words (black): "noirs"
      3. On the white page: "et blancs"
      3. Whiteness: "de la nacre"
   2. Blackness: "et du jais"
1. Light as representation of feelings: "aux reflets scintillants"
   2. Words (black) framing thoughts: "des petits cadres noirs"
      3. Integrated with feelings, the page forms a transparent but protective barrier: "des couronnes de verre."
1. plus 2. Feelings effectively sublimated as words: "Avec trois mots gravés en or: 'A NOTRE MERE!'"

This layered structure suggests that of the psyche, in which the childhood and adult selves overlay the infantile self, which nevertheless remains dynamically active throughout life and communicates in disguised symbolic form with the other selves.

Thus Rimbaud affirms his artistic vocation by suggesting that his lyric self can step back far enough from his emotions (from the yearning expressed by the exclamation "A NOTRE MERE!") to use them as material for his craft. He transforms them into an ornate (here meaning traditionally versified) artifact. As part of a funeral wreath, the medallions show that the object of desire has already been irrevocably lost; but by way of compensation they afford a certain narcissistic gratification. Standing for the entire poem in which they occur, and like it representing both a gift of and an appeal for love, they form an internal reduplication, the emblem of the self-contemplating intellect.[18] The stiffness and formality of this symbolization derive from

18. For a formal definition of the concept of "mise en abyme" or internal reduplication, and a brief bibliography of criticism, see Laurence M. Porter, "Literary Structure

a defense against rejection by the mother, who functions as implied audience. She is the one who would judge the gift dedicated to her. Rimbaud will require more self-assurance as a poet before he can take the risk of dramatizing an audience that is present to hear or read his verse.

In the course of his development toward such assurance, Nature serves as a transitional object in his poems as the adolescent (recreating infancy at will in his imagination) moves from exclusive attachment to the mother to involvement with society. Signs of (defensive) self-contemplation are less overt in the early poems that follow. Rimbaud finds a provisional solution to the problem of reconciling the maternal and the sexual, or conciliating his desire for attention and his fear of rejection, by evoking a conventional personified Nature. She becomes not only the sexually receptive mother who is not forbidden to the poet but also an idealized audience for whom the poet's mere presence constitutes an acceptable, fully sufficient message as he rehearses in preparation for seeking relationships with others outside his family.

Perhaps the first of such people to constitute a true "public" insofar as he was not a teacher or other personal acquaintance of Rimbaud's was the poet Théodore de Banville. On May 24, 1870, Rimbaud sent him a letter that included the poems "Sensation," "Soleil et chair," and "Ophélie." "Sensation" (untitled in the letter, as if to convey the impressionistic absence of an analytic intellect) depicts a plenitude of communication eliciting the oceanic obliviousness of infantile, pre-verbal delight:

> Je ne parlerai pas, je ne penserai rien:
> Mais l'amour infini me montera dans l'âme,
> Et j'irai loin, bien loin, comme un bohémien,
> Par la Nature,—heureux comme avec une femme.   [p. 39]

> (I will not speak, I will not think: / But infinite love will rise up in my soul, / And I shall go far, very far, like a gypsy, / Through Nature—happy as if with a woman.)

---

and the Concept of Decadence: Huysmans, D'Annunzio, and Wilde," *Centennial Review,* 22 (Spring 1978), 188–200. For an overview of this topic see Porter, "Internal Redu-plication in Lyric Poetry," in *Poetic Theory,* ed. Claudio Guillén, Proceedings of the Tenth Triennial Meeting of the International Comparative Literature Association, vol. 2 (New York: Garland, 1985), pp. 192–98. In *Le Récit spéculaire: Essai sur la mise en abyme* (Paris: Seuil, 1977), Lucien Dällenbach applies the idea of reduplication to the French New Novel and provides an important theoretical introduction.

"Soleil et chair" similarly begins with an ecstatic union that, this time, implies a return to the womb:

> Et, quand on est couché sur la vallée, on sent
> Que la terre est nubile et déborde de sang:
> Que son immense sein, soulevé par une âme,
> Est d'amour comme dieu, de chair comme la femme,
> Et qu'il renferme, gros de sève et de rayons,
> Le grand fourmillement de tous les embryons!   [p. 40]

(And when you have lain down on the valley, you feel / That the earth is nubile and overflowing with blood: / That its immense breasts, swollen by a soul, / Are made of love like God, or flesh like a woman, / And that it encompasses, full of sap and rays, / The great swarming of all the embryos!)

At first it appears that Rimbaud has had to compensate for exposing his verse to the critical gaze of a stranger by sheltering his lyric persona to an extraordinary degree. But soon he acknowledges with regret that humanity can no longer suckle at Nature's breast, for modern scientific knowledge has led to a complacency that blunts our capacity to respond to Nature:

> Misère! Maintenant il [l'Homme] dit: Je sais les choses,
> Et va, les yeux fermés et les oreilles closes.
> —Et pourtant, plus de dieux! plus de dieux! l'Homme est Roi...
> L'Homme est Dieu!...   [p. 41]

(Misery! Now Man says, "I know things," / And goes along with closed eyes and stopped ears. / —And yet, there are no more gods! No more gods! Man is king... Man is God! [cf. Adam, pp. 845–46].

Rimbaud's poetry invites the audience to become aware of the transcendent reality of which that audience is part. By rejecting transcendence, the positivistic spirit of the late nineteenth century rejects poetry as well. Through subliminal reversal and transposition, the unwelcome realization that "she rejects me" (represented by the mother's absence in "Les Etrennes des orphelins") has become the defensive structure of "they reject her [Nature]; I accept her; by ceasing to reject her, they will cease to reject me." This movement of the unconscious creates a bond between the poet and his desired object (Mother/Nature), since both are rejected. So the presence of an uncomprehending or hostile audience ensures the fantasized union of the lyric self with his Ideal.

The second section of "Soleil et chair" affirms the speaker's faith in the mother-goddess. The variant title, which appeared in the letter to Banville, was "Credo in Unam" (I believe in One [Goddess]). The goddess combines maternal with sexual love. Here the poet's complaint is not that humanity has lost religious faith but rather that humanity, having been enslaved by the Christian god, has lost contact with the mother-goddess: "—Oh! la route est amère / Depuis que l'autre Dieu nous attelle à sa croix!" (Oh! How bitter is the road / Since the other God has harnessed us to his cross!). This flat contradiction of the first section arises from a cautious movement toward avowal, as the cloak of a historical perspective shifts to disclose a more frankly individual view. "L'autre Dieu," the father figure, emerges from an inner conflict between the lyric self's sexual development (which creates the potentiality for rivalry with the father) and the internalized prohibition of the superego which makes the child experience with guilt his formerly innocent attraction to the mother. Rimbaud protects himself from exposure by generalizing this experience: "—Oui, l'Homme est triste et laid, triste sous le ciel vaste, / Il a des vêtements, parce qu'il n'est plus chaste" (Yes, Man is a sad and ugly sight, a sad sight beneath the vast heavens, / He has clothes, because he is no longer chaste). Formerly the feminine ideal could inspire the "immense amour" that fuels a movement toward spiritual perfection: today, "La Femme ne sait plus même être Courtisane!" (Woman doesn't even know how to be a whore any more!). In the male child's unconscious, the mother is always a prostitute because she has shared her body; she has had sex with the father. But now, as a forbidden object, she denies even this sharing to the maturing (i.e., weaned) child, whose longing to reconcile the maternal and the sexual is mocked by the older, more experienced male rival: "et le monde ricane / Au nom doux et sacré de la grande Vénus!" (And the world sneers / At the sweet holy name of great Venus!).

The hypothetical future time of the poem's third section restores the lost paradise of childhood. Humanity will free itself of all gods and all fear. Aphrodite, the mother-goddess, will be reborn "au sein des grandes mers [=mères]" (in the bosom of the great seas). The figurative use of "bosom" in conjunction with the sea symbolizes the abundant mother's milk that forms the essence of the successful infant–maternal bond. Twenty-three lines further on, the implied concurrent equation of ocean and womb becomes explicit. In markedly Hugolian accents, Rimbaud celebrates the dissipation of the mysteries separating humanity from the soul of the universe. In an ecstatic movement concluding the section, Man finds an ideally sympathetic response from Nature when he emits his poetic message: "Il chante ... et le bois chante, et le fleuve murmure / Un chant plein de bonheur qui monte vers le jour!" (p. 44: He sings ... and the wood sings, and the river murmurs / A song full of happiness that rises toward the dawn!). Alienation from the audience is no longer at issue when such perfect reciprocity results in a narcissistic mirroring of one's own message. The poem's fourth and final section celebrates the restoration of paganistic pantheism. In the last line the gods—the reconciled superego—listen attentively to the commingled song of Man and Nature. Already presented in "Les Etrennes [plenitude] des orphelins [loss]," the Romantic master myth of paradise lost and paradise regained finds resolution here through the image of an audience at once idealized and passively receptive.

By invoking moonlight in the last block of lines in "Soleil et chair", Rimbaud, like the Romantics before him, creates a stage for the effortless transmission of the message that would have been incommunicable in the daylight of the present, fallen world. For despite the triumphal conclusion, the poet's hope of embracing reality (full sun) and the ideal at the same time remains unrealizable.

Starlight functions similarly in "Ophélie," creating a transreal setting for communication: "Un chant mystérieux tombe des astres d'or" (A mysterious song is falling from the golden stars). In an apostrophe to Ophelia, the poet explains that she could hear but not reproduce "le chant de la Nature," since in the real world "tes grandes visions étranglaient ta parole" (your great visions throttled your words). Here Rimbaud has combined the pantheistic vision of Hugo's poetry with the artistic self-consciousness of Romantic prose. In the latter, the mad person alone has access to the privileged vision, but in pursuing it he or she becomes lost to the real world.[19] Before disappearing, however, the mad person makes contact with a frame narrator who can thus attest both to the authenticity of the vision and to its inaccessibility. Rimbaud adapts this prose device of the frame narrator to lyric poetry. His "Poète" comprehends Ophelia via intuitive sympathy

---

19. Here, of course, the mad person is Ophelia. Two other examples are Balzac's Louis Lambert and the narrator of Gérard de Nerval's *Aurélia*. The frame narrator of *Aurélia* is the formerly mad protagonist "cured" by psychotherapy and recalling his past madness.

rather than through a rationalized, narrativized encounter and conversation.

In the last stanza, the Poet (capitalized in the text) sees Ophelia returning home, again by starlight, and speaks of having witnessed her suicide. This detail resembles several of Rimbaud's poetic closures during this period in which he seeks to make his poetic message self-sufficient by invoking a poet-persona, alluding to the raw materials of his art, or making himself into a spectator and part of the spectacle at the same time.[20]

During the summer of 1870, Rimbaud composed a series of "unmasking" poems whose tone is much more aggressive than that of the poems he had recently sent to Banville. He strips and assails the Other in "Bal des pendus," "Le Châtiment de Tartufe," "Le Forgeron," "Vénus Anadyomène," and "Les Assis," as he is still doing a year later in "Mes Petites Amoureuses" and "Accroupissements." The poem becomes a weapon rather than an evasion or an appeal.

"Bal des pendus" describes the skeletons of hanged men which Satan sets to dancing in the wind. At first glance this poem might seem merely derivative of Villon's "Ballade des pendus" and the macabre visions of Romanticism and Baudelaire. But unlike his precursors, Rimbaud does not identify with the dead. Instead, their performance amuses him. We find humor in every stanza: the poet cheers Satan on, and Satan is working for *him*, as the dative of interest in stanza 8 reveals ("secouez-*moi* ces capitans funèbres" [shake those funereal braggart warriors *for me*; emphasis added]). The dead are inferior users of language. The first noun of the descriptive phrase "au chant des ossements" associates the rattling bones with poetic activity, but the content of their message is incongruous and ineffectual. They "défilent, sournois, de leurs gros doigts cassés / Un chapelet d'amour sur leurs pâles vertèbres" (p. 49: are telling, craftily, with their thick broken fingers / A rosary of love on their pale backbones). Here, as in "Les Etrennes des orphelins" and "Le Châtiment de Tartufe," Rimbaud associates telling a rosary with a routinized, sterile form of verbal expression. Rimbaud's exceptionally keen artistic self-consciousness is evident in the way his use of the macabre contrasts with that of his precursors. Confronting death, they experienced a rage for life, a depressing sense of the emptiness of material existence, or both. But Rimbaud sees the dancing skeletons as symbols of his

20. Chambers, "Rimbaud et le regard créateur," p. 203.

poetic ancestors, as the dead hand of the past which he as a poet has triumphantly excelled.

This latent association will be spelled out clearly in Rimbaud's letter to Paul Demeny less than a year later: "Si les vieux imbéciles n'avaient pas trouvé de moi que la signification fausse, nous n'aurions pas à balayer des millions de squelettes qui, depuis un temps infini, ont accumulé les produits de leur intelligence borgnesse, en s'en clamant les auteurs!" (If the old imbeciles had not come up with only an inaccurate interpretation of my meaning, we wouldn't have to sweep away millions of skeletons who, from time immemorial, have accumulated the products of their half-blind intellect, while proclaiming themselves to be its authors!).[21] Shredding the flesh of his precursors and impelling them to violent motion prepares a cleansing disintegration more specifically enacted in "Les Assis," in which this purge is now associated with the library symbolizing (as does the ossuary in the passage just quoted) an oppressive accumulation of tradition by limited intellects.

As Rimbaud sets about aggressively defining himself as a poet, the two motifs that dominate his poems are the tearing away of the veils of pretensions and the forcible inscription of his own message on the Other. In "Bal des pendus," this message is figured by the involuntary dance. In "Le Châtiment de Tartufe" the hypocrite's punishment is to have his clothes torn off. The king's punishment in "Le Forgeron" is to be forced to wear, not the crown of superiority, but the revolutionaries' red Phrygian bonnet of equality. It is thrown upon his head, a humiliating symbol imposed on unworthy adult authority by the Promethean worker in fire. Even more aggressively, "Vénus Anadyomène" describes a fat, ugly woman rising from her bathtub. In this description the glass shield of repression that covered the medallions associated with the mother in "Les Etrennes des orphelins" has been lifted, as it were. The naked object of desire comes directly into view without the metonymic displacement of the earlier poem, which had substituted for the mother's body the bed on which it might be found.[22] Prohibition, however, has not disappeared: it manifests itself through repulsion, in the satiric enumeration of the loathsome physical features of this modern Venus. The final detail makes the

21. Rimbaud to Paul Demeny, May 15, 1871 (in Adam, p. 250).
22. Coincidentally or not, in French the word for bed, "le lit," is a form of the verb *lire* (to read) and so it assimilates the consumption of the mother's body to the consumption of the poem.

taboo explicit. The woman is "belle hideusement d'un ulcère à l'anus" (hideously beautiful from an ulcer on her anus). The infection bars the pathway to the Eden of infantile regression, like an angel with a flaming sword (compare the metaphor "Chanaan féminin" applied to the male rectum in "Les Stupra"). The words *Clara Venus* (illustrious Venus) are "engraved" above the woman's buttocks. This odd choice of words implies an artistic process and therefore the poet's imposition of his message: his ideal vision in written form refutes by contrast a wholly inadequate present reality. Such a direct confrontation with the compelling horror of the flesh seems to desensitize the poet, causing Oedipal guilt to ebb.

As he gains self-confidence, Rimbaud begins to experiment both with opposing an explicit discourse to his counterdiscourse and with imagining the gratification of his desires in the present rather than in the past. He now portrays real women who respond to him favorably. In "A la musique" the sprightly girls he follows laugh and turn their heads to look at him with eyes full of indiscreet messages. As this vignette suggests, the laughter of the Other in Rimbaud's poetry represents not a scornful belittling of the poet but an unself-conscious effusion that holds promise for further relations because it expresses the absence of a barrier. We find such laughter in a "fille aux tétons énormes, aux yeux vifs, / —Celle-là, ce n'est pas un baiser qui l'é-peure!" ("Au Cabaret-Vert: cinq heures du soir," p. 77: a girl with huge tits and lively eyes / —*That one* wouldn't be afraid of a kiss!) and in the "bon rire qui voulait bien" (the kind, willing laugh) of "Première Soirée" (p. 63).

This latter poem, like "La Maline" and "Rêvé pour l'hiver," inte-grates the woman's words with the poet's dream: the lyric self and its responsive desired object become fused. Indeed, in "Rêvé pour l'hiver" the female companion's "Cherche" orders the poet to satisfy his sexual curiosity. "Nous" in lines 1, 3, and 13 of this sonnet assim-ilate her to him. The couple is riding in a railway carriage, and the exploration of the landscape initially hints at the exploration of a body; the parallel becomes explicit through the verb "voyage" in the last line. Thus the woman's body becomes the world, while her closed eyes exclude potential hostile spectators—"populace / De démons noirs et de loups noirs" (a rabble of black devils and wolves)—on the outside.

Verbal fusion of the speaking lyric self and its object recurs in "Le Buffet." The piece of furniture initially functions as a Muse, inspiring an apostrophe addressed to it. The sideboard holds medallions, which, like those in "Les Etrennes des orphelins," merge the message with the object. Here the medallions are associated with generations of women, and they preserve memories of the past—that is, of the ideally loving and nurturant mother of infancy. Through a magical contagion, the container as well as its contents has acquired the air of kindly old people. Moreover, the sideboard could revive the past by assuming the poetic role: "—O buffet des vieux temps, tu sais bien des histoires, / Et tu voudrais conter tes contes" (O sideboard from days of old, you know a lot of stories, / And you would like to tell your tales).

Only in the domain of the imaginary, or course, can such a fusion of the symbolic and the real occur. As Rimbaud becomes more self-assured he acknowledges this limitation, and he becomes more playful, exposing his own illusions. "Ma Bohème," for example, echoes the Romantic cliché that material poverty is accompanied by spiritual riches. Hugo's "Le Mendiant" (*Contemplations* V, 9) is a typical expression of this commonplace: the poet, having invited a passing beggar to eat and warm himself at his fire, gazes at the poor man's tattered cloak drying before the fire. He imagines that the beggar is "full of prayers," and in the points of light gleaming through holes in the garment, the poet sees heavenly constellations. For Hugo the source of visionary insight is unquestioned. He speaks in the prophetic voice; what it says is true by virtue of being enunciated. In his text, the poor man himself has no personality. His social role is to obey three orders from the poet as he accepts charity; his visionary role is to serve as the passive, unwitting pretext for the poet's inspiration.

Rimbaud, in contrast, describes himself in torn and threadbare clothes, wandering beneath the night sky and sworn in fealty to the Muse. His past self is the object of his present contemplation. But the subtitle of "Ma Bohème," "Fantaisie," calls into question his inspired state. And whereas Hugo's rhetoric of spiritual enlightenment deploys unexpected sources of physical light everywhere to suggest a transcendent truth underlying the world of appearances, Rimbaud finds his inspiration in the "ombres fantastiques" (fantastic shadows) that surround him. He ridicules the way in which his poverty provides a source of poetry by rendering this idea in a grotesquely concrete form: he holds a ruined shoe next to his heart and produces poetry by twanging the laces as if they were the strings of a lyre. The archaic word "féal" (liege man) in his one-line apostrophe to the Muse ironically underlines how outmoded the remembered privileged moment now seems. What such a reading of this early poem indicates, then, is that Rimbaud's poetic development was continuous. *Une Saison en enfer* does not represent a sudden, unpredictable rejection of the career that had preceded it. Instead, it is consistent with a strain that appeared in Rimbaud's poetic practice nearly from the beginning, part of an ironic Romantic reevaluation of the dignity of inspiration and of the poet's calling which is absent from the high seriousness of Hugo.

The unappreciated, martyred poet was a commonplace in French Romanticism, dramatized notably in Vigny's *Chatterton* and *Stello*. Rimbaud subverts this commonplace when he suggests that perhaps the poet does not deserve to be taken seriously, or even more damaging for an exalted image of poetry, that when the desired audience *does* take the poet seriously, then that audience itself may prove quite unworthy, robbing the poetic act of any pragmatic value. Thus Rimbaud's long, idyllic invitation to a woman to partake of the pleasures of the country in "Les Reparties de Nina" is brusquely rejected by her rejoinder "—Et mon bureau?" (And what about my office?). As in "A la musique," this last word may refer by metonymy not to the responsibilities of office work but rather to a rival who works in an office, a quintessential antipoet. The critics' solemn suggestion that the woman's preference for such a rival would be a great betrayal of Poetry seems quite misguided:[23] it suggests that the remainder of the poem is an ethereal structure devised by Rimbaud and that the final line, "Et mon bureau?" constitutes a coarse, uncontrollable invasion by "reality," an involuntary upwelling of autobiographical detail. But whatever its source, the last line, like the rest, was chosen by the poet. He uses the contrast of the idyllic and the prosaic to stage an interaction between lyric self and fictive audience. That the latter—the poet's creation—understands the message but considers it irrelevant implies that the lyric self questions it too.

Conversely, the girl in "Roman" (note the antilyrical title) laughs at the poet's sonnets in her honor but finally condescends to write back. Instead of acting on this invitation to a relationship, the poet stops musing about her and returns to the cafés once more to drink with his friends. One must assume that her words failed to equal the dream

23. See Forestier, p. 242.

she had inhabited. A responsive as well as a dismissive audience, in other words, proves unassimilable by the daydream of the message addressed to it. Words cannot efface the alienness of the Other.

Having thus affirmed, reaffirmed, and called into question his identity as a Poet, sender of messages, Rimbaud feels confident enough to test this identity not only against the desired object but also against the rival. At first glance "Les Effarés" seems to recreate the situation of "Les Etrennes des orphelins." Children abandoned in winter yearn for maternal warmth. But this time center stage is occupied by the symbolic figure of the Oedipal father. A burly baker shoving loaves in and out of his oven (unrealistically, at midnight, the hour of secrets, rather than early in the morning) enacts the primal scene, which culminates in a procreation that fascinates the children watching outside: "ce trou chaud souffle la vie" (p. 70: that warm hole breathes out life). Variants of line 29 reveal both the function of these children as poet-surrogates and the progressive erasure of their poetic role from successive versions of the text. As they look on, the children pass the time, in the first version, "chantant des choses" (singing things); in the second version, "disant des choses" (saying things), and finally, "grognant des choses" (grunting things).[24] The first verb designates discourse that is definitely poetic; the second, discourse that might or might not be so; and the third, a verbalization that is clearly nonpoetic and may be noncommunicative as well. It seems that having imagined a confrontation between the helpless child-poet (the very division of this figure into several children tries to compensate for its frailty) and the rival, Rimbaud becomes progressively able to dissociate himself from it.[25]

24. The first version appears in a copy of the poem Rimbaud made for Paul Demeny (September 1870); the second, in a copy for Jean Aicard (June 1871); and the third, in a copy by Verlaine (after September 10, 1871).

25. Two powerful counterexamples are the child-poet figures in "Le Coeur du pitre" and "Honte." The title of the first poem underwent several metamorphoses. In his May 13, 1871, letter to Demeny, Rimbaud called it "Le Coeur supplicié"; elsewhere he refers to it as "Le Coeur volé." The present title appears in Rimbaud's June 10, 1871, letter to Demeny. This succession of titles shows a decisive growth in self-consciousness, as the idea of suffering pure and simple is superseded by the idea of the self as a performer who is ridiculous in the eyes of others. A hostile, mocking crowd of observers fills "Le Coeur volé." In "Honte" (one of the "Vers nouveaux"), their scorn has become internalized as self-condemnation. But in "Jeune Ménage," from the same period, it is allegorized and thus redistanced. In this poem the fairy-tale dwelling of the young couple has been invaded by hordes of meddlesome, inimical spirits. The explanation for the defensive distancing of condemnation from the lyric self in "Jeune Ménage" may be that Rimbaud was under stress at this time (in hopes that Verlaine's marriage

Therefore Rimbaud can now direct his energies toward a struggle against precursors and rivals other than the biological father. "Bal des pendus" adumbrated this move but without yet making an explicit contrast between the strong voice of the lyric self and the weak voices of other poets. Such a contrast does appear in the transitional poem "Les Corbeaux."[26] Here the poet appears in the multiple, fantastic guise of the dark, loud-voiced birds. Icy indifference still threatens them as it had threatened the orphan poets of "Les Etrennes des orphelins" and "Les Effarés": "Armée étrange aux cris sévères, / Les vents froids attaquent vos nids!" (Strange army with austere cries, / The cold winds are assailing your nests!). But their harsh cries resist without the weakness of an appeal. It is the human speaker of the initial apostrophe/prayer in stanza 1, addressed to the "Seigneur," who assumes the onus of that appeal. Quixotically he seeks God's blessing on the ravens' song that is designed to supplant "les longs angélus" of human worship. In stanzas 2 and 3, a second apostrophe addressed to the ravens thus associates them with the poet's words. And a third apostrophe in the final stanza completes the triumph of Nature over Culture by assimilating the ravens, "saints du ciel, en haut du chêne" (saints from heaven, at the top of the oak), to a new

---

could still be saved, Rimbaud's Paris acquaintances were asking him to break off his homosexual relationship with Verlaine and to leave town), and so he regressed to earlier attitudes.

To illustrate Rimbaud's growing sense of detachment from the hostile fictive spectator even at those times when he was under less pressure, one could cite the "Morts de Quatre-vingt-douze" of July 17, 1870, a poem nearly contemporaneous with "Les Effarés." Its epigraph, in which jingoistic servants of the empire insincerely invoke the glorious memory of the revolutionary freedom fighters, is Rimbaud's first poem to quote a counterdiscourse directly. His ability to insert an alien text in his poem reveals an enhanced sense of mastery.

26. The dating of this poem is controversial. Because of its regular versification, characteristic of 1871 and earlier, I agree with Bernard (pp. 386–87) and Henri de Bouillane de Lacoste, who assign it to 1871. (For an overview of the problems of dating Rimbaud's later poems and a set of tentative datings based on an analysis of his handwriting, see Bouillane de Lacoste, *Rimbaud et le problème des "Illuminations"* [Paris: Mercure de France, 1949].) Adam prefers 1872 (see pp. 874–75 and 929), but he seems unaware of how clearly the sharp struggle with tradition evoked in this poem belongs to the period preceding Rimbaud's stay in Paris.

By overlooking the importance of voice in "Les Corbeaux" (and in the lyric in general) and by placing this poem in the context of Poststructuralist criticism rather than in the context of Rimbaud's other poetry, Jefferson Humphries subjects it to a radical misreading in his otherwise impressive *Metamorphoses of the Raven: Literary Overdeterminedness in France and in the South since Poe* (Baton Rouge: Louisiana State University Press, 1985): "The *corbeaux* are synecdoches of the bleak, charred, ruinous defeat of knowledge, the loss of the totality of the sign" (p. 70).

holiness. The poem ends with a ritual expulsion of the "bons poètes," the weak, cloying voices of tradition:

> Laissez les fauvettes de mai
> Pour ceux qu'au fond du bois enchaîne,
> Dans l'herbe d'où l'on ne peut fuir,
> La défaite sans avenir. [p. 82]

(Leave the May warblers / For those chained in the depths of the wood, / In the grass from which you cannot flee, / By defeat without a future.)

The false decor of the social persona (*fauvettes* = faux-vêtes, "you clothe yourself in falsehood") is cast aside in favor of naked, spontaneous physical self-expression (*corbeaux* = corps beaux, "beautiful bodies").

Continuing Rimbaud's rivalry with the unworthy guardians of an outmoded tradition, "Les Assis" achieves a masterful equilibrium of fantasy and satire. The librarians alluded to by the title serve as sacrificial victims, as *pharmakoi*. Prominent in four of eleven stanzas, their half-blind, green-rimmed, venomous glance tries to master and objectify the young poet who disrupts their world not only by borrowing too many books but also by composing irreverent additions to the canon. They are defeated.[27] Enumerating their body parts, Rimbaud's mocking, luxuriant, neologistic description effectively dismembers them and then scatters them on the ground like the seeds of a new poetry. As Atle Kittang perceptively explains, here and in several other early poems a destruction of anthropomorphic unity encodes Rimbaud's destruction of syntactic and semantic unity and linearity. Thus emphasis shifts progressively from the signified to the signifying movement itself—to the writing.[28] A rhetoric of excess intensifies disruption: Rimbaud combines totalizing plurals of nouns found ordinarily in the singular with an abundance of metaphors for swelling, opening up, and excrescence. A creative, fecundating movement overmasters "Les Assis" and sweeps them up, transforming them willy-

---

27. But a poem written around the same time, "Les Poètes de sept ans," perpetuates the motifs of forced hypocrisy and the incomprehension of the child-poet's main audience, his mother. Written with a capital *M*, "Mother" acquires the symbolic meaning of all the forces that constrain a child (Bernard, p. 396, n. 2). Retrospection reanimates earlier helplessness.

28. Atle Kittang, *Discours et jeu: Essai d'analyse des textes d'Arthur Rimbaud* (Bergen: Universitetsforlaget, 1975), pp. 205–10.

nilly into artists and drunken boats. Like the skeletons in "Bal des pendus," they must play the master poet's tune and then dance to it:

> L'âme des vieux soleils s'allume...
> ....
> Et les Assis, genoux aux dents, verts pianistes,
> ....
> S'écoutent clapoter des barcarolles tristes,
> Et leurs caboches vont dans des roulis d'amour.   [p. 83]

(The soul of old suns flares.../ And the Sitters, moldy pianists, resting their teeth on their knees, /... Listen to themselves slapping out mournful barcaroles, / And their noggins drift off in the rolling troughs of love.)

"Clapoter," "barcarolles," "roulis," and in the next stanza "naufrage" incorporate these Sitters into the sea of the poetic experience. Not only does their involuntary adventure reflect the ecstasy of the writer caught up in his own creation;[29] Rimbaud, by making these Keepers of Culture share his delirium, cannibalistically absorbs them into himself.

The maturing Rimbaud now defiantly tries to liberate himself from artistic self-consciousness, from fear of disapproval by the Other, by deliberately provoking scandal. Excretion rather than words becomes the figurative vehicle of his communication. By way of evening prayer, he says, "Je pisse vers les cieux bruns" ("Oraison du soir," p. 87: I piss toward the brown heavens). Elsewhere, aspiring to beauty and "fantasque, un nez poursuit Vénus au ciel profond" ("Accroupissements," p. 94: Whimsical, a nose [an emerging turd?] pursues Venus in the deep sky [the third syllable of this title suggests urination as well]).

Toward the end of this rebellious period, in May 1871, celebrated metaphors in Rimbaud's letters to Georges Izambard and to Demeny also express the concept of the body as message, but with greater decorum: "Tant pis pour le bois qui se trouve violon.... Si le cuivre s'éveille clairon, il n'y a rien de sa faute" (pp. 346, 347: So much the worse for the wood that finds itself to be a violin.... If the brass awakens as a trumpet, that's not its fault at all). The body as message suggests a freedom from inhibition, but the strong dose of literary history in the "Lettre du voyant" reveals that the anxiety of influence

29. Ibid., p. 210.

remains with Rimbaud. He senses keenly that both the past and the present are watching him.[30] For all their power, Rimbaud's comparisons of his poetic self to musical instruments betray this limitation. For he describes his awakening as a poet as the transformation of inert matter into something that makes a noise—that is, into a language-using entity whose main function is the enunciation of messages, since its raison d'être is to be heard by others, on whom it therefore depends.

To achieve full artistic autonomy, Rimbaud must transform his body from an instrument playing for others into an audience for his own communications. So he begins to sign off with apostrophes addressed to parts of the body: "Comment agir, ô coeur volé?" ("Le Coeur volé," p. 101: How shall we act, O stolen heart?"). An apostrophe constitutes a choice of audience and thus a way of controlling who hears you in the virtual world of the poem. Making a part of your own body into your audience produces a solipsistic short circuit that frees the poetic message from the unwelcome contingency of disapproving human observers. And even a synecdoche that makes part of another's body into your audience reduces the Other to what he or she has in common with you—the body—instead of allowing the Other to relate to you through something that is alien, the mind: "On veut vous déhâler, Mains d'ange, / En vous faisant saigner des doigts!" ("Les Mains de Jeanne-Marie," p. 107: They want to make you lose your tan, Angel Hands, / By making your fingers bleed!").[31]

Once the poet has neutralized the Other by dismissal or dismemberment—albeit admiringly, as in the example just cited— he can imagine the poem flowing directly out from and back into himself without being deflected and distorted by an uncomprehending or inimical public. The resistance of the Other having been removed from the poetic circuit, poetic energy can accede to the ideal. Freed from the exigencies of self-defense, the lyrical impulse of the poem as a whole (an impulse embodied in miniature in the apostrophe) can

30. "He is still a performer," as Wilbur M. Frohock, who was quite insensitive to poetry but attuned to prose, demonstrated in shrewd detail in *Rimbaud's Poetic Practice: Image and Theme in the Major Poems* (Cambridge: Harvard University Press, 1963), pp. 70–92.

31. These lines imply that the "pétroleuse" (incendiary) of the Commune will be transformed into a well-behaved lady if her tan (sign of a working-class person exposed to the elements) is washed away by her blood.

concentrate itself in an unmediated movement toward transcendence. This new freedom is evident in several concluding lines of poems that Rimbaud wrote during this period, for example: "O Mort mystérieuse, ô soeur de charité" ("Les Soeurs de charité," p. 109: O mysterious Death, O sister of charity) and "—O l'Oméga, rayon violet de Ses Yeux! ("Voyelles," p. 110: O the Omega, the violet ray of Her/His Eyes). But such successes are short-lived, for Rimbaud's contemplation of his own ideals quickly recalls the debased ideals of others. Though provisionally repressed on the plane of the concrete, the alien audience returns, in later concluding apostrophes, on the plane of the abstract: "O Justes, nous chierons dans vos ventres de grès" ("L'Homme Juste," p. 114: O you Justified ones, we will shit into your stoneware bellies); "Christ! ô Christ, éternel voleur des énergies" ("Les Premières Communions," p. 126: Christ! O Christ, unending thief of energy). Once again the lyric impulse has been bound down to the constraint against which it rebels.

"Le Bateau ivre," Rimbaud's last poem before he left for Paris to embark on his adventures with Verlaine, develops to the fullest the struggle between constraint and expansion. Of its twenty-five quatrains, the initial four depict the opening out of space. In the first stanza the boat is being guided along a canal ("haleurs" refers to those pulling a barge from a tow-path); but as the word "fleuve" indicates, the canal is already being transformed into a river, a river, moreover, that is not a mere tributary ("rivière") but one that leads to a large body of open water. By capitalizing "Fleuves" and making it plural, Rimbaud transforms the poem from a literal depiction of movement toward the sea (during which one could descend only one river at a time) into a visionary drama outside known time and space.

The forces formerly restraining the poet become progressively immobilized. First, the haulers are seized by Indians, they are then nailed to stakes, and finally they are further transfixed by the weapons thrown and shot at them for target practice. Conversely, the boat becomes ever more free. By the third stanza it has reached the mouth of the river; the last extensions of the coast ("les Péninsules démarrées") fall rapidly astern, and the boat reaches the storm-swept open ocean. Rudder and boathook—the final instruments of external control—are washed away in the fifth stanza. "Et dès lors," the poet announces at the beginning of the sixth, "je me suis baigné dans le Poème / De la Mer" (And from that time on, I bathed in the Poem of the Sea). The boundless sea corresponds to the totally free poetic imagination, which can summon anything it wishes and which forms the poet while he shapes his vision.[32]

Critics stress that the comparison between poet and boat was a commonplace, and they correctly point out that *Le Parnasse contemporain* and other contemporary sources that Rimbaud read assiduously offered him many models of this topos.[33] But what distinguishes him from his precursors is the violence of his kinetic imagery, the forceful opening and closing and the turbulence of his spaces: "Des écroulements d'eaux au milieu des bonaces, / Et les lointains vers les gouffres cataractant!" (The waters collapsing in the middle of lulls, and the far-off places cataracting toward the abysses!). Distinctive too is the pervasive self-consciousness disclosed by recurring motifs of the voice, the eye, and literary tradition.

The yelling of the Indians in the first stanza is the objective correlative of the poet's discovery of his own voice, although, more literally, it represents Rimbaud's discovery of a literature of exoticism and savagery in the novels of James Fenimore Cooper and elsewhere, the literature that provides the pretext for this poem. Conversely, the impassiveness of the rivers in the first line reflects the poet's own original lack of self-awareness. He becomes liberated when his voice, broadcast through the Indians, has completely drowned out his former guides ("Quand avec mes haleurs ont fini ces tapages"). As the poet ventures forth into the open ocean (stanza 3), sound again conveys the conflict between land and sea, restraint and freedom. "Les clapotements furieux des marées" depicts the slapping noises of cross-chop against a hull—that is, the noise of the steep pyramidal waves produced by the clash of two contrary currents, here the flow of the river against the rising tide. But the poet/boat, now released from the countervailing force of inhibition, is deaf to this sound. He awakens to full awareness amid the waves "qu'on appelle rouleurs éternels de victimes" (that they call eternal rollers of victims) but which prove to be companions. He has rejected the timid, inauthentic voice of tradition.

Since the poet no longer heeds the alien voice but assumes his own,

---

32. As Poulet explains, "the boat's privilege of sailing through an element itself devoid of any reference point gives it the faculty of being able to summon all sorts of forms to life" (*Poésie éclatée*, p. 145). Cf. pp. 116–17 on Rimbaud's self-reflexive autonomy: "He's a creator and a creature at the same time."

33. Bernard, pp. 424–31; Adam, pp. 915–24.

since he becomes conspicuous by leaving the beaten track, he falls subject to the scrutiny of the Other's alien eye that disapprovingly inspects his message. This eye first appears in the form of the "oeil niais des falots," the lanterns placed (like "foolish eyes") along the shore to guide boats. When the poet leaves these lanterns behind him and enters the sea "infusé d'astres" (infused with stars), the eye of Otherness—the shining stars—has now become absorbed by "the poem of the sea." So any messages sent now return to the sender without passing through any other receiver. This communicative short circuit of self-sufficiency is embodied by a description of nature. Four stanzas later this short circuit is completed when the functions of singing poet and observer are even more intimately combined. In stanza 10 Rimbaud declares, "J'ai rêvé...l'éveil jaune et bleu des phosphores chanteurs!" (I have dreamed . . . the yellow and blue awakening of the singing phosphorous!). Glowing with their own light, these tiny jellyfish are autonomous; they do not require the sanction of the Other to be illuminated. And their status bears a hint of revolt insofar as the Greek roots of "phos-phorous" or "light-bearer" are semantically parallel to the Latin roots of "Luci-fer." The poem's visionary energy reaches its high point here. As early as the next stanza it begins to ebb: phosphorescence becomes associated with alien values (which are evoked through the very act of denying them) when Rimbaud says he never considered the possibility that the miraculous glowing feet of the holy Marys might rein in the panting ocean.[34] Now, self-generated light no longer illumines a chaotic theater for self-realization; instead, it derives from a conventional Catholic morality that sees divine intervention taming fallen and therefore sinful Nature. Self-consciousness has returned.

Self-consciousness, in fact, is wholly absent only in stanza 10. It is present subtly but consistently elsewhere. Even the visionary center of the poem, stanzas 6 through 16, harbors the phantom presence of the Other. Let us recapitulate. By stanza 6, Rimbaud seems to have detached himself completely from the past and achieved total immersion in the poetic experience. A transient validation of this fusion appears in the description of the sea as a place where "flottaison blême / Et ravie, un noyé pensif parfois descend" (pale and ecstatic flotsam, a thoughtful drowned man sometimes sinks). This phrase implies a

---

34. An allusion to the legend that the three Marys walked across the Mediterranean, calming the waters as they went, and set foot in the Camargue near Arles.

dual perspective. From the standpoint of convention, an imagination as unbridled as Rimbaud's is effectively dead, being lost to the world of acceptable communication. But the words "ravie" and "pensif," inapplicable to a truly dead person, reveal that from Rimbaud's standpoint his alter egos are "drowned in ecstasy" rather than literally drowned. Like him, they are absorbed in their experience. (By stanza 17 we know that the visionary episode has ended when "des noyés" sink back down through the boat's frail bonds of seaweed to sleep on the ocean floor.)

And yet, after the first ecstatic outburst in stanza 6, Rimbaud seems able to consolidate the affirmation of his imaginative discoveries only by contrasting them with tradition, which therefore promptly recontaminates the poem as it had done at the beginning. The visions in stanza 7 were "plus vastes que nos lyres" (vaster than our lyres): although authentic poetry has surpassed the false plenitude of convention ("nos lyres"), the latter must be mentioned as it will be again in "Et j'ai vu quelquefois ce que l'homme a cru voir" (And sometimes I saw what man believes to have seen).[35] "Pareils à des acteurs de drames très-antiques" (like actors in very ancient dramas), even the waves are grounded in tradition, although Rimbaud awkwardly tries to distance this tradition with the intensifier "très" and the choice of a hieratic art form (ancient Greek drama) as the element of comparison. In stanza 12, Rimbaud introduces a phatic element for the first time, as if the waning of poetic energy had made him fear losing his audience: "J'ai heurté, *savez-vous*, d'incroyables Florides" (*You know*, I bumped into incredible Floridas [emphasis added]). Such reinscription of the virtual audience in the poem dilutes the visionary experience. And "incroyables" is two-edged, since the word suggests that the vision is incommunicable as well as transcendent.

Because this stanza appears just halfway through the poem, one would expect the apogee of the visionary ascent to occur here or later. But other details in addition to the direct address to the audience reveal that the pure contemplative state of bathing in the poem of the sea has already become subject to certain restrictions. For example, the surrealistic fusion of tropical flowers with the eyes of panthers who have human skin at first appears as a manifestation of the free-ranging

---

35. Albeit in a sentence borrowed from Saint Paul. On Rimbaud's mysticism see Virginia La Charité, "Rimbaud and the Joannine Christ," *Nineteenth-Century French Studies*, 2 (Fall 1973–Winter 1974), 39–60.

creative vision. But the complex image also reimposes the human (the skin) upon the natural, uninhibited participant (the panther). Thus natural impulse comes to be restrained, as it is more overtly in the next two lines by the mention of bridles stretched from a rainbow to undersea "herds" of fish. In this latter image the union of sea and sky, earlier presented in the form of ecstasy (the stars reflected in the water), returns figured as the submerged id held in bondage by the heavenly superego. The same motif of great energies that have become landbound and paralyzed reappears in stanza 13, where a Leviathan lies rotting among the reeds. Stanza 13, moreover, begins with a return to the passive spectatorial verb "j'ai vu" following the crescendo of energy in the openings of the previous four stanzas: "J'ai vu" (stanza 9), "J'ai rêvé" (stanza 10), "J'ai suivi" (stanza 11), and "J'ai heurté" (stanza 12). The explosion of vicarious energy in the last two lines of the stanza describing the rotting Leviathan only postpones the decay of the vision. For in stanza 14 the stranding becomes multiple rather than single: one beached Leviathan becomes "échouages hideux" (hideous strandings).[36] The plural suggests that a disastrous, inglorious end to a sea adventure is the rule rather than an accident.

Since at the beginning of this poem the land represented conventions and contact with the land implied submission to those conventions, the poet's gradual approach to the land in stanzas 11–14 has a sinister quality. In stanza 11 he follows the ocean swells, which are compared to a herd of hysterical stampeding cattle assailing the reefs. The poet still affirms visionary freedom, but in a weakened way. Instead of describing himself as immersed in the experience of liberty, he now presents his liberty via what is in effect a double negative: "I am not unfree." The reefs (land, stasis, convention) invade the water (the theater of individual autonomy), although unrestrained instincts (the rampaging animals) attack them. Such a formulation reinscribes limitations amid limitlessness. And the outcome of the struggle remains in doubt. As we have seen, in stanza 12 the poet actually makes contact ("j'ai heurté") with the tropical lands; the marine animals he now sees have been bridled, and soon after he sees them beached. The light diminishes during the spectacle of the multiple strandings in stanza 14: within four lines, notations of color dim from "glaciers [blinding white]" to "argent [silvery]," "nacreux [pearly]," "braises

---

36. I read "échouages" as "beached boats" rather than with the possible alternative meaning of "places where boats can be beached," favored by Adam (p. 922, n. 1).

[glowing, but suggesting a light that will die]," "bruns [dull brown]," and finally "noirs [black/dark]." Context dictates that this final adjective be taken figuratively to mean "sinister," but secondarily its position at the end of a sequence of color words associates the seductive powers of the land (symbolized by serpents that, like Eve's, lurk in trees) with the loss of vision.

Exiled back onto the land, the poet regretfully says that he would have liked to show the singing fish of the sea (the untrammeled poetic voice) to children—the happy few, the fit, unspoiled audience. But he cannot, as the conditional perfect "j'aurais voulu" (I should have liked) implies. And as in the wording "Florides...fleurs" in stanza 12, the near-synonymy of the phrases designating the crux of the privileged vision here ("ces dorades...ces poissons d'or" [those dolphins ...those golden fish]) creates a multiple presentation of a unique revelation. This repetition produces fissures in the formerly seamless facade of the vision in the form of gaps between the synonymous phrases reporting it, thus transforming it into a tracery through which the leering face of banality can peer, as it can similarly peer through the temporal interstices created by the admission that contact with the vision has been intermittent, occurring only "sometimes" ("quelquefois" and "parfois," stanzas 8 and 16).[37]

After stanza 16 the land closes around the poet/boat itself, rather than merely around its defensive surrogates. Seaweed binds him; bird droppings cover him; he becomes "nearly an island" (stanza 17) and is then buried beneath seaweed on the beaches of coves ("les cheveux des anses," stanza 18). The next line shows him "jeté par l'ouragan dans l'éther sans oiseau" (cast by the hurricane into the birdless upper air). The storm has vomited him forth, expelled him from the sea. Here "l'éther" means not the quintessence that lies beyond the lower layers of the earth's atmosphere in ancient cosmology but rather that atmosphere itself. Rimbaud chose the poetic term "l'éther" because it is a homonym for "les terres"—lands that,

---

37. This self-deprecating practice amounts to the very opposite of the mechanism of transcendence in Mallarmé. Whereas Rimbaud's visions fray into a network that allows the external world to be glimpsed between the strands, Mallarmé's poems reduce materiality to a tracery—of lace, or smoke, or foam—that affords glimpses of the beyond. Rimbaud is obviously capable of implementing a strategy similar to Mallarmé's, and he does so in this very poem: "Je sais les cieux crevant en éclairs...Moi qui trouais le ciel rougeoyant comme un mur" (I know the skies splitting apart with lightning flashes ...I who used to smash through the reddening sky like a wall). But to a far greater extent than Mallarmé, he seems haunted by the anxiety of influence.

lacking vision, therefore lack birds (the farseeing poetic spirit). In context "l'éther sans oiseau" evokes Hell: "sans oiseau" is semantically parallel to the Greek *a-ornis*—the origin of the Latin Avernus, or Hades, referring to places avoided by birds because the air was filled with poisonous gases emanating from underground or from beneath the water. Such places were believed to be entrances to the nether regions.

Rejected by the sea, the poet cannot become reintegrated into society either. He says that neither military nor commercial ships ("les Moniteurs"; "les voiliers des Hanses") would deign to salvage his water-intoxicated hulk. The poetic experience has spoiled him for both war and trade—a notion repeated in the final stanza. Nevertheless, he is once more imprisoned: the ancient ramparts of Europe rise around him in the twenty-first stanza. By stanza 24 the only water to which he has access is a puddle that can accommodate nothing more than a toy boat.

As memories of the visionary experience flicker and fade in stanzas 15 through 22, Rimbaud presents a series of increasingly truncated flashbacks. Changes in the motif of the eye reflect increasing alienation. In stanza 20 the poet recalls having sped across the sea while "taché de lunules électriques" (spotted with little crescents of electricity)—variants of the self-contemplating eye. But by stanza 23 he has become alienated from Nature: "Toute lune est atroce et tout soleil amer" (Every moon is atrocious and every sun bitter). These heavenly eyes have now become inimical. The poet wishes for the twilight hour when neither is present. Two stanzas later, the poem closes with yet another evocation of the condemnatory gaze of the Other, in the form of the "yeux horribles des pontons" oppressively staring at the lyric self. These motionless hulks of prison ships seem to lower with social disapproval; they themselves are doubly horrible because they have been castrated, stripped of masts and rigging.[38]

---

38. Adam (p. 924, n. 5) seems to endorse the interpretation according to which the previous line of this stanza, "Traverser l'orgueil des drapeaux et des flammes" (To pass through the pride of flags and pennants), refers to the Nautilus in Jules Verne's *Vingt mille lieues sous les mers*, whose sharp bow sliced through a warship as a needle pierces cloth. But the enormous energy of that motif would clash with the resigned weariness of this stanza; similarly, the active search for the disapproving Other would clash with the spirit of the whole poem, a paean to withdrawal in the name of freedom. Rimbaud means that he can no longer pass among the haughty military men who think his duty is to soon become one of them. See Bernard, p. 430, n. 45: "The horrible eyes of the

Like a musical coda, stanzas 19–22 sum up the visionary escapade of stanzas 4–17. But the deliberately anticlimactic ending of stanzas 23–25 reveals that the poet has reached an impasse. He finds it impossible to return to the sea (stanza 23) or to childhood (stanza 24); nor can he accept the adult world (stanza 25).[39] Only an escape to Paris to seek a community of poetic kindred spirits appeared to offer a solution to Rimbaud's existential dilemma. But his persistent attempts to make himself into a negative counterpart of his rigidly disciplined mother through antisocial behavior, debauchery, and homosexuality made him an outcast even among poets. At the same time, the maternal values ironically survive in Rimbaud's insistence that "le dérèglement... de tous les sens" (freeing all the senses from rules) be *systematic*,[40] or that drug intoxication should be a "method" ("Matinée d'ivresse" in *Une Saison en enfer*).

"Mémoire" restates the motifs of "Le Bateau ivre" in concentrated, economical form. It reduces to one figure the earlier poem's multiple dramatizations of intrusive parental, literary, and religious traditions. The negative persona that this compression produces is called simply "Madame"—a name indicating reduction to a social function. She stands stiffly and rigidly; when she moves she destroys the flowers in bloom. In short, she represses and denies Nature. She contrasts with the yielding other woman, a personification of the stream in the landscape. The flowing water signifies simultaneously this positive image, its freedom, its desire, and its tears of loss. Its animation contrasts in turn with the dead pool at the end of the poem, like that at the end of "Le Bateau ivre." But here the poet, having already found his voice, can situate the visionary experience at the very beginning, in an explosion of intensely bright images that betoken his own heightened awareness. Described without verbs, the flood of light is thus placed outside time. Then a shift of the poet's gaze allows him to see beneath the water's surface the female *genius loci* uniting with its mate, the sun. This bright sun functions as the objective correlative of the poet's eye. But when the poet identifies himself with Nature, Nature's

---

prison ships recall the foolish eye of the beacons; by evoking a port, it's still a question of alluding to the routine, captive existence that the Boat rejects with horror."

39. In and of itself, "flache," the dialectal word for the puddle where he used to play with a toy boat as a child, embodies a return to childhood (antedating "standard French" in Rimbaud's experience among local playmates).

40. That is, "raisonné" in the French. See Rimbaud to Paul Demeny, May 15, 1871 (Bernard, p. 346). See also Alain de Mijolla, *Les Visiteurs du moi: Fantasmes d'identification* (Paris: Les Belles Lettres, 1981), p. 62.

rhythm, more rapid than that of the human life cycle, catches him up, and he becomes prematurely old. The sun fades and sets; the woman of the stream pursues him in vain; the light dims. Unable to follow them, the poet remains bound to the now lifeless eye of the water, which overlays only the mud of disintegration. The restricted scene of the poetic drama at the end of "Mémoire" does not suggest even the potentiality of childhood, as does the conclusion of "Le Bateau ivre"; all that remains is a weary, impotent, aged man. The poet's creative, visionary powers have departed with the sun.

Rimbaud's sense of relatedness to a potential audience evolved rapidly during the critical period of 1870–71. In his letter to Banville on May 24, 1870, he had beseeched indulgence and begged for publication in Le Parnasse contemporain. Nearly every paragraph awkwardly confessed his lack of self-assurance and his yearning for recognition: (par. 1) "pardon si c'est banal" (Excuse me if this is a cliché); (par. 2) "C'est bête, n'est-ce pas, mais enfin?" (This is stupid, isn't it, but still?); (par. 5) "Ne faites pas trop la moue en lisant ces vers" (Don't turn up your nose too much at these poems); (par. 6) "Ambition! ô Folle!" (O mad ambition!). The "Proses évangéliques" (of uncertain date, but I would situate them around the time of Rimbaud's departure for Paris in September 1871) still express anxiety about his acceptance by the poetic community, but he has distanced himself sufficiently from this concern to be able to express it indirectly and vicariously through comments on Christ's reception or reputation in various towns. The implied identification with Christ suggests that the Rimbaud who wrote this work, unlike the author of the letter to Banville, does not doubt his message is worth hearing, and it also suggests that he will offer French poetry revolutionary possibilities for transformation.

The editorially titled "Vers nouveaux" composed around 1872 in general express detachment and resignation rather than a struggle with a hostile audience. Rimbaud's desire for the absolute now appears mainly unmediated—that is, not conditioned by a reaction against literature and society.[41] Since he no longer feels such an imperative need to impose himself, he can moderate his claims: the absolute is described as sought rather than attained. He is no longer a Christ

41. René Etiemble underlines Rimbaud's playful parody of spiritualist lyrics by the Quietist Mme Guyon and by Marguerite de Navarre as he borrows from them the versification in pentasyllables and motif of bidding farewell to the world, combining these elements with non-Christian and sometimes obscene references to his liaison with Verlaine. See "Sur les 'Chansons spirituelles,'" in Etiemble, Rimbaud, pp. 28–46.

who possesses the truth others lack. To be sure, the first section of the "Comédie de la soif," titled "Les Parents," creates a dialogue of Culture versus Nature, tradition versus spontaneity. Rimbaud rejects the gratifications offered by family, literary legends, and Parisian friends. In the "Conclusion," however, rather than denounce these facets of culture, he identifies himself with the natural creatures of air, land, and water who, like him, thirst and long to "expirer en ces violettes humides / Dont les aurores chargent ces forêts" (p. 154: to expire amid these damp violets with whose dawns those forests are laden). In other words, he yearns to merge with the eyes of Nature, the flowers that simultaneously provide light (via their bright colors) and moisture. Here the mystical union of fire and water (also found in "L'Eternité" and "Mémoire") is not presented as it is in "Le Bateau ivre," as a spectacle or something whose superiority to conventional literature must be affirmed, but simply as the object of an unself-conscious aspiration.

This state of oblivious harmony with Nature appears again in "Bannières de mai," "L'Eternité," and "Age d'or" of the *Fêtes de la patience*. Rimbaud succinctly conveys the renunciation of his ambition to be recognized as a poet in the second of these poems.[42] The same withdrawal from any audience is restated in the "Chanson de la plus haute tour": "Je me suis dit: laisse, / Et qu'on ne te voie" (p. 158: I told myself: Drop it, and don't let them see you). Like an abandoned field, the poet ceases to be subject to exploitation. The Muses who surround the poet in "Age d'or," the last poem of this cycle, ask him to renounce intellectualizing, recognize his kinship with Nature, and abandon human society. He accepts this invitation from his inner "voix / Pas du tout publiques" (voices / [Which are] strictly private). Communing with these voices, and having become both source and spectator of his own inspiration, the poet accedes to a "nature princière" and feels himself surrounded with the "gloire pudique" (the chaste glory) of perfect self-acceptance.[43]

42. Cf. Adam, p. 935.

43. For Bernard (pp. 437–38), these poems express Rimbaud's desperate suffering following an enforced separation from Verlaine, who was seeking a reconciliation with his wife. For interesting speculations on "Entends comme brame" as a parody of Verlaine's verse, see Giusto, *Rimbaud créateur*, p. 186. See also Giusto's comments on the evolution of "O saisons, ô châteaux" from an obscene poem about Verlaine to a general statement about enslavement by the delusion of happiness in which Verlaine exemplifies the temptations that distract the *voyant* from his mission, as uxoriousness threatened to distract the medieval knight (p. 208). Cf. Etiemble, *Rimbaud*, pp. 28–46.

As Rimbaud changes strategies in the "Vers nouveaux" he attains the height of his artistic development. He no longer identifies himself with his goal but with his desire. Allowing himself to be caught up in the first spontaneous impulse, he nearly transcends artistic self-consciousness, becoming pure hunger, thirst, and desire for death. For him now, to drink is ultimately to dissolve, to become fully subject to the effects of what he desires. Or, to express this idea in the active mode, Rimbaud now tries to transform desire into an accurate description of the world.

Consequently, the homonymic title of the first "Fête de la faim" (fête/fêtes/faites/faîtes de la faim/fin: banquet/holidays/make/pinnacles of hunger/the end) identifies hunger, the symptom of lack, with a goal. The oxymoron of the title proper transforms unfulfilled desire into a feast. The refrain at beginning and end ("Ma faim, Anne, Anne, / Fuis sur ton âne"; pp. 169 and 170: My hunger, Anne, Anne, flee on your donkey) alludes to Charles Perrault's fairy tale, *Barbe-bleue* (Bluebeard). Threatened with death by her ogre-husband, the heroine asks her sister Anne to watch from the top of a tower for her rescuers. But Rimbaud significantly transposes the context. In Perrault, the heroine urges her sister to alleviate fear with reassurances. In Rimbaud, apposition identifies the sister with the painful sensation, hunger, rather than with what assuages that feeling. The cause of flight has become hunger rather than fear, seeking the positive rather than avoiding the negative. Anne as figuration of desire will range widely throughout the world, seeking satisfaction: desire has been implicitly transformed into a generative principle for the imagination.

In the first stanza, the barrenness of unfulfilled desire projects a desert world imagined nevertheless as capable of affording satisfaction: "Dinn! dinn! dinn! dinn! Mangeons l'air, / Le roc, les charbons, le fer" (p. 169: Dinn! Dinn! Dinn! Dinn! Let's eat air, stone, glowing coals, iron). The monotonous subverbal hammering of the first four syllables mimics barrenness while simultaneously implying its plenitude, since "dinn" can be read as a homonym for "dîne," "dine." (In a variant, "Je pais" [I graze] transforms the poet into a ruminant like the donkey of the refrain. By echoing this verb and by identifying the object of consumption with an element of language, the second stanza clearly shows that the poet *is* his hunger: "paissez, faims, / Le pré des sons!" [graze, hungers, on the meadow of sounds!]). By stating that "mes faims, c'est . . . L'azur sonneur" (My hungers, they're . . . the ringing blue [as in "way beyond the blue"]), the fourth stanza identifies

desire with the ideal ("L'azur"), which is both articulated ("sonneur")
and communicated. The pealing of a bell, which conventionally symbolizes a way of reaching toward the ideal—a prayer rising to heaven—
is here initiated by that very ideal itself. The desire that seeks has
been equated with its object. The result is a bounteous new harvest.
"Au sein du sillon je cueille / La doucette et la violette," the main
poem ends (p. 170). A hollow furrow in the bare earth, a redoubled
notation of absence and emptiness, produces both beauty (the violet)
and utility (the leaves of the *doucette* and of the violet can be eaten as
salad), which can both be gleaned there.

From a broader perspective, renouncing the world provides spiritual plenitude. This theme links the "Vers nouveaux" with the ensuing *Saison en enfer,* which ostensibly repudiates them. In both
collections, the act of bidding farewell makes Rimbaud feel ambivalent
toward his audience. He maintains contact and continues to transmit
his message in the very act of asserting that such contact no longer
matters. In this way he also evades disapproval and assures himself
the last word.

The untitled introduction to *Une Saison en enfer* explains how Rimbaud had been working toward such autonomy. His life at first had
seemed a joyous response to the possibilities of universal cameraderie,
"un festin où s'ouvraient tous les coeurs" (p. 211: a banquet where
every heart would open). Then he brusquely rejected the conventional
values of beauty and justice. He fled society, despaired, and defined
himself in masochistic opposition to others: "J'ai appelé les bourreaux
pour, en périssant, mordre la crosse de leurs fusils" (p. 211: I have
summoned the executioners in order to be able to bite the butts of
their guns as I die). His Hell is a place whose inhabitants have been
judged and irrevocably condemned.

Throughout *Une Saison en enfer* the self-mockery implicit in Rimbaud's ironic tone shows that he remains his own self-deprecating
audience. In the opening paragraphs he appears to adopt a flamboyant
Romantic rhetoric. He addresses an apostrophe to "Dear Satan,"
whom he hopes to please—along with the antibourgeois in his audience and the rebellious part of himself—through his "lack of descriptive and instructive capacity" as a writer.[44] Since this last phrase
designates recognizable physical and moral referents, it becomes clear
that Rimbaud wishes not simply to reverse the codes and contexts of

---

44. Giusto identifies this Satan with Verlaine (*Rimbaud créateur,* p. 348).

the audience in a counterdiscourse (as a Romantic would) but to renounce these codes and contexts.

The following section, "Mauvais Sang," dramatizes his renunciation.
He loathes not only the useful trades; even the ostensibly antisocial
occupations of begging and crime appear to him as forms of para-
sitism, as still all too depressingly dependent on society. Until now he
has been able to feign adherence to social values with a force of
conviction sufficient to allow him to live as a parasite: "qui a fait ma
langue perfide tellement, qu'elle ait guidé et sauvegardé jusqu'ici ma
paresse?" (p. 213: who has made my tongue so perfidious, that up
until now it has guided and protected my laziness?). He cannot, however, imagine any constructive role he or his accursed ancestors could
have played in history. Sharing no values with his contemporaries, he
has little hope of communicating with them: "Ne sachant m'expliquer
sans paroles paiennes, je voudrais me taire" (Not knowing how to
make myself understood without using the words of a pagan, I would
like to keep silence). The Good News of the Gospels has passed him
by. He hopes only for the loss of all awareness, for "un sommeil bien
ivre" (p. 215: a thoroughly drunken sleep).

The contradiction between his assertions that he belongs to a
damned race and his insistence on his personal innocence derives
from the distinction we must make between the social and the individual perspective.[45] The remainder of the section alternates between
paroxysms of submission to social imperatives, during which Rimbaud's own autonomous voice is obliterated ("J'aimerai mes frères....
je loue Dieu" [I will love my neighbor.... I give praises to God]) and
protestations that he has no moral sense as Christians understand it,
no code he shares with them. But society will seek out and try to
subdue the withdrawn, alienated person as well as the defiant rebel.[46]
Rimbaud's early conception of this section as a "livre nègre" (a nigger
book) and his metaphors of colonialization express the fear that a
peaceful but independent existence is impossible. In desperation, he
abandons all fantasized historical roles in order to become his own
absolute origin in the present moment. But he sees that this new quest
can lead only to farce, once he realizes that he cannot privilege his

45. See ibid, pp. 349–50.
46. If Rimbaud seems to equate damnation with madness (Giusto, *Rimbaud créateur*,
p. 348; cf. Felman, *La Folie et la chose littéraire*, pp. 108–11), it is because the oppressive
presence of someone else's reason is what defines madness, as the oppressive presence
of conventional moral values defines damnation.

origin in his own language over any other origin without merely repeating the deluded claims of the competing "origins" to be grounded in a metaphysical transcendence.[47]

"Nuit de l'enfer," the following section that was originally called "Fausse conversion," expresses a moment of weakness. Louis Forestier claimed that the hell described with an accumulation of conventional religious vocabulary in this section was constituted by Rimbaud's suffering when he found himself imprisoned in a tradition.[48] But the text shows the opposite. Hell is Rimbaud's nostalgia for tradition, at war with his desire for autonomy. At the beginning of *Une Saison en enfer*, Rimbaud allied himself with Satan, who was in turn associated with the absence of moral and descriptive faculties in an author, with withdrawal from the conventional expectations of an audience. Here, on the contrary, Rimbaud dramatizes himself as wanting desperately to communicate: that desire he sees as his weakness. Worse yet, the very act of composing the confessional *Saison en enfer* represents unfaithfulness toward Satan, his master. Rimbaud remains ambivalent about the total freedom from others which he supposedly seeks. Much as he fears loss of his poetic selfhood through a forced subservience to conventional values, he equally fears annihilation through the loss of all contact with the Other who, good or bad, makes self-definition possible. Hell ultimately appears to be the loss of communication: "Là-bas... J'ai un oreiller sur la bouche, elles [les âmes] ne m'entendent pas, ce sont des fantômes. Puis, jamais personne ne pense à autrui" (p. 221: Down there... I have a pillow over my mouth, they [the other lost souls] don't hear [secondary resonance: "understand"] me, they are phantoms. Then, nobody ever thinks of others). Desperately attempting to win the attention of an audience, he promises, "je vais dévoiler tous les mystères.... Ecoutez!" (p. 221: I am going to unveil every mystery.... Listen!). He tries to take everyone into his confidence. But Satan's magic dissolves him and isolates him from his surroundings. He yearns for any sensation, even a stab of the pitchfork or a scalding drop of liquid fire to convince himself he still exists. Finally, having exhausted all other recourses, he appeals to God.

The motif of a false conversion links "Nuit de l'enfer" to the following section, "Délires I. Vierge Folle." This companion in Hell makes

47. See Nathaniel Wing, *The Limits of Narrative: Essays on Baudelaire, Flaubert, Rimbaud, and Mallarmé* (Cambridge: Cambridge University Press, 1986), pp. 87–88. I highly recommend Wing's reading of *Une Saison en enfer*.

48. Forestier, p. 270, note to p. 131.

an ignominious confession and entreats forgiveness. Critics have hotly debated whether the Foolish Virgin's voice is a parody of Verlaine's voice or a dramatization of Rimbaud's weak, compliant side, divided against himself in inner debate. Certainly, the hysterical self-serving whining of the Foolish Virgin strongly suggests a parody, many of whose elements could have been inspired by Verlaine. The repentant attitude of this voice vis-à-vis conventional morality contrasts with the defiant attitude of the Infernal Bridegroom, as the Foolish Virgin names his/her companion. But it would be an oversimplification to say that the Foolish Virgin represents everything Rimbaud rejects whereas the Infernal Bridegroom illustrates everything he accepts. Both voices appear in the section titled "Délires" (self-deceptions). In opposite ways, both depend on conventional morality to define themselves. And the Foolish Virgin's voice, which receives narrative authority here, unwittingly parodies not only itself but the voice of the Infernal Bridegroom as well, quoted directly by the Virgin as the Bridegroom creates his own histrionic, grandiose self-image. In part, the Foolish Virgin's naive, uncritical admiration for the Infernal Bridegroom represents a higher sarcasm directed by Rimbaud against himself in the form of an adulatory but undiscriminating audience whose lack of discernment renders its admiration meaningless and the object of its admiration faintly comical. Through their disciples shall ye know them.

As "Délires I" depicts a delusional search for autonomous self-definition through love, "Délires II" describes the same attempt undertaken through writing. The juxtaposition of these two modes of the quest shows that language is simply another form of the presence of the Other as generator of desire (to be loved, read, understood). Though disguised by its ostensible impersonality, it is as alien to the desiring self as a personified object of desire would be.[49] The prose poem "Phrases" in the *Illuminations* will combine these two motifs. But here, verse figures the foreign objects of desire, embedded in the prose context emblematic of all that lies outside the self. "Délires II. Alchimie du verbe" incorporates seven verse poems into seven pages of prose. Appearing early in the history of French literature, this mixed prose and verse genre was known as the *chantefable*. The best-known example is *Aucassin et Nicolette*. The *chantefable* mode also appears in such works as Dante's *La Vita nuova*, Guillaume de Machaut's

49. Cf. Wing, *Limits of Narrative*, p. 90.

Le Voir Dit, Villon's *Le Grand Testament,* and John Ashbery's *Three Poems.* The form of the *chantefable* is analogous to the simultaneous staging of medieval and some modern theater, pointing to the co-existence of two or more levels of reality. The embedded verse poems typically represent privileged moments of more intense or purer emotion, of keener or deeper insight.[50] The prose frame serves to introduce, gloss, and endorse the poems.

But Rimbaud's prose setting is the contrary of an endorsement. He uses the prose frame to install himself as his own hostile audience. From the beginning, the section title "Délires" and the first line, "L'histoire d'une de mes folies" (the tale of one of my follies), dismisses what he has done. He then embarks on a proud statement of his past ambition to conceive a poetry capable of communicating everything but needing to communicate nothing: "Je me flattais d'inventer un verbe poétique accessible . . . à tous les sens. Je réservais la traduction. . . . je notais l'inexprimable. Je fixais des vertiges" (p. 228: I flattered myself [this verb constitutes him in the past as his own entirely approving but deluded audience] that I could invent a poetic Word accessible . . . to all the senses. I kept the translation to myself. . . . I noted down the inexpressible. I made still portraits of dizzying motion). Two examples of his neopastoral "vers nouveaux" follow, then a retrospective self-condemnation of such efforts as "la vieillerie poétique . . . mes sophismes magiques . . . le désordre de mon esprit" (p. 230: stale poeticism . . . my magical sophisms . . . my mental disorder).

Like a sorcerer's apprentice, Rimbaud has lifted the barriers of linguistic, prosodic, thematic, and generic convention at the cost of unleashing a deluge that threatens to overwhelm him. He sketches many broad gestures of taking possession of the concrete raw materials of poetic production and proclaims the hyperexpressibility of his art, only to then be seized by terror.[51] Self-mockery protects him by minimizing the gravity of his experience and ultimately refuting it. For example, he qualifies the poem "Elle est retrouvée! / Quoi? l'éternité" (p. 234: It's been recaptured! What? Eternity) by commenting that it was written with "une expression bouffonne et égarée au possible"

50. As my list of examples suggests, this hybrid genre tends to appear either in medieval or modern times. From the Pléiade through Romanticism, the concept of genre remained too rigid to encourage it. Giusto comments in some detail on the variants distinguishing the separate "Vers nouveaux" from the versions published in *Une Saison en enfer (Rimbaud créateur,* pp. 357–64).

51. Cf. Kittang, *Discours et jeu,* pp. 193–96.

([it was] expressed in the most clownish, misguided way possible). He condemns the system that produced such poems as "sophismes de la folie" (the sophistry of madness) and dismisses his entire poetic enterprise with a brusque "cela s'est passé" (that's over).

In the last three sections of *Une Saison en enfer*, Rimbaud continues to disparage himself. "Enfin," he announces in "Adieu," "je demanderai pardon pour m'être nourri de mensonge" (p. 241: Finally, I shall ask forgiveness for having battened on lies). He concludes by rejecting "ces couples menteurs" (p. 241: those lying couples) saying, "il me sera loisible de *posséder la vérité dans une âme et un corps*" (I shall be free to *possess the truth in one soul and one body* [emphasis in original]). The "couples menteurs" do not represent entirely or even primarily the illusion of romantic love, as one might at first suppose. Rather, they represent the quest evoked in "Délires I" for secrets that may transform life, secrets to be shared with others. In his letters to Izambard, Demeny, Banville, and Verlaine, Rimbaud, circumventing the ordinary, uncomprehending public, had tried to select for himself an elite audience of poets. His relationships with Verlaine and with Germain Nouveau constituted a more intense and sustained form of this appeal for understanding. For a poet, limiting one's audience and companions to one other poet offers the hope of achieving a narcissistic mirroring through the perfect mutual intelligibility of two kindred spirits. Having found this hope delusive, Rimbaud now plans to become self-sufficient. He ceases to write for the sake of winning attention, approval, love, and happiness and renounces his dependency on any audience whatsoever.

But he does not yet plan to stop writing entirely. His statement at the end of "Délires II," "Je sais aujourd'hui saluer la beauté" (Today I know how to pay my respects to beauty) has usually been taken as a declaration of his resolve to abandon poetry in favor of action. This interpretation of what was written in 1873 no longer seems viable, since recent critical findings suggest that a few of the *Illuminations* reflect some of Rimbaud's experiences from as late as 1876 and 1877, when he was in Java and in Stockholm. Rimbaud's statement probably refers to a decision to replace verse with prose poetry. For however original the chosen form of verse and stanza may be, it still constitutes a foregrounded pattern. Even "free verse" remains constrained by a fixed number of syllables per line and by the conventions of its *mise en page*. Prose, on the other hand, purges the poet's successive verbal gestures of any such traces of predetermination.

The second major transformation of Rimbaud's poetic practice in the *Illuminations,* announced in "Délires II," is related to the first. The "vers nouveaux" had gained a specious freedom by transforming desire into an accurate description of the poetic world. But making wish-fulfillment a given presents as great a risk of stagnation as does adherence to the conventions of verse. For yearning, or even gratification, when it becomes a constant, forms in its turn a new limitation and stasis as real as those of frustration. To forestall this aporia, in the *Illuminations* Rimbaud constantly transforms the objects of desire, adopting a kaleidoscopic, Protean theatricality. Thus he seeks protection against the congealing, conceptualizing force of language and undermines the ontological basis of the notion of a coherent self. The verb overpowers the noun. Each time that the freely desiring, evolving self reaches for the momentary object of its attention in the *Illuminations,* this object changes.[52] But as "Enfance IV" demonstrates, such autonomy creates its own difficulties.

"Après le déluge," the liminal poem of the *Illuminations,* is filled with cathartic tears of frustration and rage. They turn into a flood, a magically effective anger. This flood washes away a world in which the child has been unjustly condemned and punished by the loss of his father and the nurturant, affectionate mother.

Having purged the old, the lyric self entertains the new. The natural eye of the flowers (Nature as uncritical audience) is present from the outset. The unspoiled potentiality of children fills the world. To them, even the illustrations in books are marvelous. In this world where Nature is in harmony with Culture, the children can commune with both at once: "Sur la place du hameau, l'enfant tourna ses bras, compris des girouettes et des coqs des clochers de partout, sous l'éclatante giboulée" (p. 253: On the public square of the hamlet, the child rotated his arms, understood by the weathervanes and the roosters atop the bell towers everywhere, beneath the sudden burst of hail). Although both the weathervanes and the metal roosters are artifacts, they are still associated with Nature: the first are designed to respond to the natural force of the wind; the second simulate natural creatures. In the next episode the adults intervene awkwardly, insensitively, and

---

52. See Leo Bersani's fine discussion in Bersani, *A Future for Astyanax: Character and Desire in Literature* (Boston: Little, Brown, 1976), pp. 230–58. John Porter Houston also focuses on the *Illuminations* in his pioneering work *The Design of Rimbaud's Poetry* (New Haven: Yale University Press, 1963; reprint Westport, Conn.: Greenwood Press, 1978). This book remains indispensable.

imperialistically to superimpose Culture on Nature: they set a piano in the Alps and a luxury hotel at the pole (in cold, elevated domains of purity). Nymphs and other conventional figures from eclogues invade Nature. They interpret it, so that it can now be experienced only indirectly through their mediation: "Eucharis me dit que c'était le printemps" (p. 254: Eucharis [from François Fénelon's arch-didactic *Télémaque*] told me that it was spring). The natural eyes—gems, flowers, glowing coals—scatter, bury themselves, refusing any further communication with humans. And the potent supernatural women who remain, witches and queens, refuse to divulge the secrets that would restore the communion of humanity with Nature.

The second *Illumination*, "Enfance," relates the autobiographical cycle of the imagination.[53] Here, as in "Après le déluge," the imagination aided by desire summons worlds into being only to have them invaded by the Other in the form of cliché and prohibition. The drama begins on the beach and at the forest's edge—that is, at the border between consciousness and unconsciousness, where fantasies emerge to awareness (a form of birth symbolism slightly less overt than the image of the land uncovered by the receding flood in the first poem). The exotic idol evoked at the beginning suggests a child's toy.[54] Toys as small replicas of reality afford children an early experience of self-definition through the autonomous control of safe worlds of their own. The doll comes to life. Then, imaginatively subjected to three hyperbolic fields—exoticism, royalty, immensity—it shatters centrifugally into many women.[55] Each form that it assumes represents a possible new direction for desire. But by the end of section I (and again at the end of sections III and V) imaginative imperialism has conquered too much territory to hold against the intrusions of the conventional social world, whose values recontaminate the privileged vision: "Quel ennui, l'heure du 'cher corps' et 'cher coeur'" (p. 255: What a bore, the hour of "dear body" and "dear heart").

The second section begins anew by purging the landscape of human society; it evokes dead people and deserted homes and villages, the emotional void of the real world from which the poet's desire has become detached and which is supplanted by magical flowers and an-

---

53. Giusto calls "Enfance" a symbolic autobiography: "as in 'Larme,' the poet reviews his past, judges the results obtained inadequate, and sets himself new goals to which he cannot yet face up" (*Rimbaud créateur*, p. 269).

54. Cohn, *Poetry of Rimbaud*, p. 253.

55. Kittang, *Discours et jeu*, p. 229.

imals. The cleansing forces of anger and mourning for what has been rejected are imaged by the open sea, formed from an eternity of tears. Emotional effusions prepare a reign of freedom. Here Rimbaud sees grief as an instrument for the psychodynamic working-through of his passage between renunciation (in the "Vers nouveaux") and the new self.

The third section reintroduces self-consciousness through the presence of a bird whose song makes you stop short and blush. In other words, Nature itself, although cleansed of humanity, has become assimilated to the inhibiting audience. The lyric self attempts to free itself from this alien presence through rapid movement: it surveys its new world in a series of encounters reported with a sevenfold anaphora of "il y a." This recurring fixed element, followed by a variety of sentence endings, mimics the way the integral self moves through various settings, thus reconciling imaginative dispersion to the constancy of the self. This self becomes completely free when the superego has been drowned by desire, an event symbolized by the sinking cathedral (moral consciousness) and rising lake. But such a triumph can be only momentary, for "il y a quelqu'un qui vous chasse" (p. 257: there's somebody to drive you away). Renewed repression expels the poet from this exploratory, adolescent stage of his adventure.

He therefore counterattacks and reasserts his independence by re-transforming a temporal multiplicity of identities into one spatial identity. Like the simultaneous presence of various objects of desire in section I, the simultaneity of various possible roles for the self here emphasizes the voluntaristic strength of the new independent identity. Its center is not a fixed role but, rather, free choice. So the poet merges with a troupe of little (child) actors in costume. Their youth, their numbers, and the implied opportunities for changing costumes all enhance the promise of potentiality.

Section IV stages the poet's aspirations in a rising landscape that images desire. Adopting the successive roles of "saint," "savant," "piéton," "enfant" (saint, sage, pedestrian, child), the poet now wins through to a renewed childhood innocence. The plenitude of the child's possibilities antedates (as it were) language, whereas language, being a system of conventions, entails the death (fixity) of the language-using writer. But conversely, the triumph of a desire that would absorb all roles would similarly lead to death (extinction), since desire could then no longer find any object through which to define itself. Once a conquest is universal, it must cease to be, or, in Rimbaud's words, "Ce ne peut être que la fin du monde, en avançant" (p. 257: That can be only the end of the world, up ahead). Ceasing to be as an independent agent, the lyric self is once more overwhelmed by convention. Having futilely taken refuge in a whitewashed tomb in the final section,[56] he will be reimprisoned by the sterile literature of the Other: "Je m'accoude à la table, la lampe éclaire très vivement ces journaux que je suis idiot de relire, ces livres sans intérêt" (p. 257: I rest my elbows on the table; the lamp glares off those newspapers that I'm a fool to reread, those uninteresting books). Objective correlatives of an increasingly undifferentiated identity settle above him: city houses, fog, mud, night. In reaction, he conjures up symbols of the intact, self-sufficing personality: smooth, hard, gleaming things, gems and metal. But his control wavers: "Je suis maître du silence. Pourquoi une apparence de soupirail blêmirait-elle au coin de la voûte?" (p. 258: I am master of the silence. Why would a pale vent window appear in the corner of the vault?). The implied eye of the Other peers through in the form of a penetrating exterior ray, objectifying the poet. At last he confronts an insoluble dilemma. If he truly falls silent, he stops being a poet. But if he merely says that he is silent, the ruse fails. By using words, he inevitably summons the virtual Other immanent in any words as an observing, judging audience, since any words imply communication, connection, and exchange.

Jacques Rivière perceptively identified this sudden breach in Rimbaud's wall of solitude, and many similar events in Rimbaud's poems, as constituting the motif of an alien invasion of the poetic universe, always from above.[57] More specifically, the horizontal dimension figures the world; the vertical figures the self; a rising movement figures the harmony of self and world, as in "l'Aube exaltée ainsi qu'un peuple de colombes" (the Dawn exalted like a nation of doves); and a descending movement figures intrusion by the Other.

So in the next poem, "Conte," the whole work of evasion must begin anew. Here Rimbaud tries a new track, evasion on the plane of metalanguage. He will become the critic of his own solipsism. Metaphorically representing renunciation as destruction, he proposes a fable

56. Adam claims this setting was suggested by a basement apartment in London or by the subterranean walkway beneath the Thames (p. 981).

57. Rivière, *Rimbaud: Dossier 1905–1925*, pp. 138–45. For a contrasting view of this ending as a manifestation of prideful self-control, see Charles Chadwick, *Rimbaud* (London: Athlone, 1979), p. 84.

of giving up cherished possessions and relationships with other people. But the poem's title, "Conte," betrays a self-parodic intent, for it refers to the familiar popular genre that characteristically enacts naive wish-fulfillment and simultaneously announces itself as not real. (In French, "conte," or invented story, is opposed to "histoire," a true story.) A glorified self-image of the poet, the royal hero wishes to understand the ultimate truth of desire and its gratification. As in the traditional folktale, he performs three feats: the massacre of his mistresses, of his followers, and of his people. But the victims survive. The hero then meets the Genie, and despite the failure of his earlier efforts, he seems to experience perfect happiness from then on. The outcome of his life, however, finally proves quite ordinary. Thus the "Conte" fails to work as its title has led us to expect; it does not miraculously transform a life. The Genie, it turns out, has been merely the hero's reflection, a delusion created by psychic projection, rather than the proof of his transcendence. The passive acquiescence of all the Prince's subjects isolates him. Without opposition from Others, he has no ground beneath his feet from which to propel himself toward a beyond. He remains bound to the narcissistic reciprocity illustrated by the chiasmic pair of sentences: "Le Prince était le Génie. Le Génie était le Prince" (p. 260: The Prince was the Genie. The Genie was the Prince). The world of magical wish-fulfillment proves to be a void. Admitting defeat, Rimbaud then concludes: "La musique savante manque à notre désir" (p. 260: Our desire feels the lack of the wise music [the means to transform life through art]).[58]

"Parade," in contrast, expands the momentarily successful climax of section IV of "Enfance" into an entire self-contained poem of the liberation of multiple simultaneous identities. With a single stroke, it summons up a troupe of "maîtres jongleurs" (master jugglers [the word has connotations of performer-poets, circus performers, and people who can literally keep several things going at once]) and "des drôles très solides" (some very sturdy rascals) and then enumerates their powers. Since they are avatars of Rimbaud as performer, by naming and celebrating them he flaunts his own *vis poetica*, transformed during the course of the description into sexual and political dominion. Their theatrical multiplicity deconstructs the social self in order to create a new, overarching self built of poetic surges. Their gro-

58. Here I closely follow Hermann H. Wetzel, "La Parodie chez Rimbaud," in *"Minute d'éveil"* (see n. 16 above), pp. 79–90, esp. 87–89.

tesque vitality fascinates and repels.[59] On the figural level, a nest of oxymorons such as "le plus violent Paradis de la grimace enragée" (the most violent Paradise of furious grimaces) reasserts the performers' metaphoric energy, which Rimbaud refuses to dilute by submitting it to the conventions of communication: "J'ai seul la clef de cette parade sauvage" (p. 261: I alone hold the key to that savage parade). This undefined multiplicity has defensive undertones (a psychoanalyst would talk of warding off castration), suggested by a secondary meaning of the French "parade"—a parry. But by divorcing signifiers from their ordinary *designata*, Rimbaud makes the latter into places of indeterminacy that can be filled by the imagination of the reader; thus he creates the impression that he is using a system far richer than the mere linguistic code.[60] Maintaining this system at the level of suggestion, in "Vies" (Lives) Rimbaud preserves his autonomy as a person now "réellement d'outre-tombe" (really from beyond the grave) and consequently offering supernatural knowledge (p. 265). In "Matinée d'ivresse" the drug experience leads to similar autonomy: it transmutes mind and body into performers that only the self can observe while the self becomes totally free of "les honnêtetés tyranniques" (p. 269).

Such a sense of perfect control naturally generates fantasies of a subdued audience, as in "Royauté," with its "peuple fort doux" (very submissive subjects), or more clearly still, at the conclusion of "A une raison," where the audience pleads with the poet to transform their lives. And in "Vies" as in "Parade," Rimbaud further underlines supreme self-confidence through the motif of an infinite performing competence when he proclaims: "Exilé ici, j'ai eu une scène où jouer les chefs-d'oeuvre dramatiques de toutes les littératures" (p. 264: In

---

59. Cohn, *Poetry of Rimbaud*, p. 271n.
60. See Nathaniel Wing, *Present Appearances: Aspects of Poetic Structure in Rimbaud's "Illuminations"* (University, Miss.: Romance Monographs, 1974), p. 146. A fine reading of "Parade" appears on pp. 143–46. J. Marc Blanchard makes some interesting comments on "Après le Déluge" from a similar viewpoint, although, unlike Wing, he has been influenced by Harold Bloom as well as Jacques Derrida: see Blanchard, "Sur le mythe poétique: Essai d'une sémiostylistique rimbaldienne," *Semiotica*, 16 (1976), 67–86; and Harold Bloom, *The Anxiety of Influence: A Theory of Poetry* (Oxford University Press, 1973). In the light of these readings one would have to refine the conclusions of Douglas P. Collins and Herbert S. Gershman in "Romantic Irony in Rimbaud," *Texas Studies in Language and Literature*, 13 (1972), 673–90 (esp. 683–86). Collins and Gershman find Romantic irony in such "highly ambiguous closing sequences" in the *Illuminations*. Their essay, however, does provide a brief, useful background for that concept.

exile here, I have a stage on which I can perform the dramaturgical masterpieces of every literature; see also p. 268). The poet can work his will on language, and the result will subjugate his public.

A language freed from social conventions and expectations (a metonymy for the poet who employs it) reaches its acme of autonomy when Rimbaud personifies it and makes it speak. Then its role shifts from message to sender, from passive to active, from assistant to arbiter. This shift is what takes place in "Phrases," an unlucky poem that has drawn the critical thunderbolts "incoherent" and "irritatingly obscure" from expert readers.[61] Such criticism empirically demonstrates that Rimbaud has achieved his goal of liberating language from its referents. Indeed, too many nameless entities inhabit "Phrases" to permit a consistent interpretation. If we invoke the principle of Occam's razor, however, the only available antecedent for most of the feminine nouns and pronouns that pervade the poem in both the singular and plural is the title word itself. I would argue that a spokesperson for all the sentences speaks first as an individual ("je . . . celle") and then as a member of a collectivity ("nous"). A dangerous mistress, in the first section, she (the linguistic sentence who is speaking) promises a fidelity that threatens to restrict the poet's imagination fatally by actualizing all its dreams within the straitjacket of language: "Que j'aie réalisé tous vos souvenirs,—que je sois celle qui sait vous garrotter,—je vous étoufferai" (p. 270). Robert Greer Cohn translates "que" here as "even if," but it makes more sense to read it as "if and when" (If and when I have made all your memories real—if and when I be she who is able to pinion you—I'll smother you). Such a rendering does not create an opposition between the second and third clauses, both of which state negative outcomes contrasting with the specious fulfillment of the first clause.

The masculine plural adjectives of the second section suggest that the poet incited to speech by his Muse (the sentence) now speaks of himself and his "phrases" together as "forts, gais, méchants": "Quand nous sommes très forts,—qui recule? très gais,—qui tombe de ridicule? Quand nous sommes très méchants,—que ferait-on de nous" (p. 270: When we are very strong,—who draws back? Very joyful,—who is made ludicrous [or: who falls down laughing]? When we are very

61. See Frohock. *Rimbaud's Poetic Practice*, p. 190, and Cohn, *Poetry of Rimbaud*, p. 294, respectively. Neither of these critics knew that Rimbaud was probably the victim of a posthumous editorial construct that grouped together under the title "Phrases" two poems written at different times.

vicious,—what would they do with us). This questioning amounts to a rueful acknowledgment that even in concert the poet and his language cannot act upon the external world, and it explains the enigmatic pair of sentences that follows: "Parez-vous, dansez, riez—Je ne pourrai jamais envoyer l'Amour par la fenêtre" (p. 270: Adorn yourselves, dance, laugh—I'll never be able to send Love through the window [ambiguous: dismissed, or as a messenger]). The poet enjoys the antics of his language but realizes that its very independence has made it inscrutable.

After the dash beginning the third section, the poet turns to address the sentence who initially had spoken alone:

—Ma camarade, mendiante, enfant monstre! comme ça t'est égal, ces malheureuses et ces manoeuvres, et mes embarras. Attache-toi à nous avec ta voix impossible, ta voix! unique flatteur de ce vil désespoir. [p. 270]

(—My female companion, beggar woman [soliciting the flesh of words], monstrous child! How little you care about those poverty-stricken women and those workers [visible through the window on the street; the preceding words, "par la fenêtre," have focused the poet's gaze on the outside world. One hears a clear anti-Baudelairean resonance here.], and my difficulties [in expressing myself.] Attach yourself to us [to me, to other poets, to all humanity] with your impossible voice, that voice! Sole consolation in this base despair.)

The next five sections that are traditionally printed after this passage seem to have been composed at another time and as five discrete fragments, as they are written in a hand dissimilar to that of "Phrases" proper. But these fragments do partake of the self-confidence of both "Phrases" and of "Royauté" (written in a similar hand); they also exalt imaginative potentiality. And the last of these sections once more clearly refers to the sentences summoned by the poet. When the feast of the imagination ends, and odors revive in the evening damp, a gentle rain of black powder (the dried ink from which the sentences have been formed) gathers like darkness around him:

Avivant un agréable goût d'encre de Chine, une poudre noire pleut doucement sur ma veillée. —Je baisse les feux du lustre, je me jette sur le lit, et, tourné du côté de l'ombre, je vous vois, mes filles! mes reines! [p. 271]

(Reviving an agreeable taste of India ink, a black powder rains gently down on the vigil. —I lower the flames of the chandelier [i.e., the intensity of poetic creativity diminishes], I throw myself on the bed [*lit*, homonym of the present singular of the verb *lire*, suggests that the poet actually rereads—if not literally, then through remembrance], and, turned toward the shadows [again, these also figure the dark ink from which new sentences might be born], I see you [again], my daughters! My queens!).

Worshiping his own offspring, Rimbaud engages in a narcissistic ecstasy.

The emphasis on the inkiness of the poet's sentences in "Phrases" (a title, moreover, that commits one to neither prose nor verse) shows that they are still inchoate. Remaining fluid, so to speak, they offer infinite potentiality free from scrutiny. Once reified as the bearers of specific meanings, they would lose their charm. Precisely this loss is dramatized in "Les Ponts," the poem immediately following "Phrases" in the Lucien Graux manuscript of the *Illuminations*.[62]

The "ciels gris de cristal" (the gray crystal skies) at the opening of "Les Ponts" postulate an imaginary setting from which the eye of the sun as potentially critical audience has been cut off ("ciels" is the plural form used for skies in painting, as opposed to the natural "cieux"; we may be inside London's Crystal Palace, looking up at its girders and panes).[63] So the bridges are not so much literal, spanning a river at intervals and always parallel, never able to join with each other, as figurative, linking meanings and thus able to intersect to form the complex network of the text: "Un bizarre *dessin* de ponts, ceux-ci droits, ceux-là bombés, d'autres descendant ou *obliquant en angles sur les premiers*, et *ces figures se renouvelant* dans les autres circuits" (p. 273: A bizarre *pattern* of bridges, some straight, some arched, and others coming down to the first or *joining them at oblique angles*, and *these forms renewing themselves* in the other circuits [emphasis added]. They are laden with structures and *signaux*. Their "cordes" (ropes/strings of musical instruments) rising to them from the banks (their referents) become a source of harmonies in minor keys—that is, they generate artistic expression. But before the precise nature of this expression

62. This manuscript, named after the man who collected it, is now in the Bibliothèque Nationale.

63. The entire poem may have initially been inspired by the spectacle of the network of metal girders—"tellement longs et légers" (so long and delicate)—framing the Crystal Palace, a striking novelty in Rimbaud's day and only a stone's throw from the Thames. The water and canals mentioned in the text of the poem may be the glass panes seen under an overcast sky, as if they were beneath rather than above the poet. The sunbeam at the conclusion would "annihilate that comedy" because it restores a sense of orthodox vertical orientation.

can be identified—"Sont-ce des airs populaires, des bouts de concerts seigneuriaux, des restants d'hymnes publics?" (p. 273: Are those popular tunes, snatches of concerts for lords, scraps of official anthems?)— a shaft of light falling from above erases the performance. In other words, the gaze of the Other destroys the autonomy of Rimbaud's tissue of relationships; since the basis of all communication is intersubjective, what subsists from the poetic vision is only that which can be taken on the Other's own terms.

The next poem, "Ville," dramatizes the ultimate consequence of this impasse of creativity. It depicts a nightmare community "crue moderne parce que tout goût connu a été éludé" (p. 274: believed modern because all known tastes have been eluded). All difference— or individual preference—has been leveled to achieve perfect comprehensibility at the cost of voiding messages of content. As in Orwell's *Nineteen Eighty-four*, "la morale et la langue sont réduites à leur plus simple expression, enfin" (p. 274: morality and language have been reduced to their simplest expression, finally). Like faceless insects, millions of humans lead identical lives. They have no need to know each other; they are all the same.

So Rimbaud seems to have reached a dead end. The more advanced society becomes, the more it seems to abolish distinctions. The attempt to recuperate difference necessitates a retreat from civilization and therefore from the refined resources for artistic elaboration which its codes provide. Like the beach unmarked by Friday's footsteps, domains uncontaminated by the Other remain blank.[64]

In response to this aporia, "Barbare" represents Rimbaud's supreme attempt to create a balance between communicability and novelty. The very title includes and excludes. It reflects at once the metaphoric and the anaphoric axes of lyric poetry, where the twin

64. Elizabeth Roberts reaches a different conclusion in two fine articles, "Artifice and Ironic Perspective in Rimbaud's 'Ville,'" *Australian Journal of French Studies*, 24 (January–April 1987), 41–56, and "Artifice and Ironic Perspective in Rimbaud's 'Villes II,'" *Australian Journal of French Studies*, 24 (May–August 1987), 175–92. Roberts claims that "Ville" reflects a move from rejection of the other to rejection of the limiting, artificial subjectivity of the self, once Rimbaud has abandoned the hope that anonymity in the great city could lead to an ontological expansion of the self. She comments that the repeated titles "Ville" (to which one could add "Métropolitain") in the *Illuminations* demonstrate the persistence of this delusive hope ("'Ville,'" pp. 53–54). She adds that in "Ville II," "the irony that effectively disparages the city's grandeur, exposing its *trompe-l'oeil* architectural effects, its melodrama and its empty opulence is ultimately self-focused, taking as its target the verbal illusionism that masquerades as significant poetry" ("'Villes II,'" p. 190).

generative principles of transformation and of repetition are always at war. As a designation of the defamiliarizing effects of metaphor "Bar-bare" means foreign, beyond the pale of civilization—and in Rimbaud's version, beyond time and the known. Yet the second syllable, by mirroring the first, reimposes sameness on variation.

The puzzling second sentence maintains the tension between the commonplace and the original, an opposition that persists throughout the poem, although it is often overlooked. Most critics impose as routinized a cultural code as possible on the stage-setting sentence "Le pavillon en viande saignante sur la soie des mers et des fleurs arctiques (elles n'existent pas)" (p. 292: The flag/tent of bloody meat on the silk of the seas and the arctic flowers [they (both seas and flowers) do not exist]). The most common explanation proposes that "pavillon" should be taken literally as "flag" and "viande saignante" figuratively as designating a raw red color such as the ground of Danish or Norwegian flags on ships in northern waters. But a bowdlerizing reading of this kind flies in the face of common sense. The flag would denote an outpost of civilization, an entity that Rimbaud suppresses throughout the poem and unequivocally in the preceding line, "Bien après . . . les pays." If "flag" is figurative and the "bloody meat" literal, we have a slab of flesh suspended in midair, Nature red in tooth and claw displacing Culture.[65] But the context provides no more support for this reading than for the first; and contextual support is a sine qua non in this particular poem in which the density of repetition becomes so great that it suggests incantation. Context does support two other readings. One takes both elements of "pavillon . . . viande" literally; the other takes both figuratively. In both readings the uniformity of the relationships between signifiers and referents—consistently figurative or literal—increases rather than reduces the typical Rimbaldian tension between meaning and communication.

A literal reading of "pavillon" as "tent" finds support throughout the poem in motifs of withdrawal and enclosure. "*En* viande saignante" suggests that the presence of bloody meat should be taken literally as well. To use the preposition *en* rather than the more ordinary *de* before the name of a material in French stresses the noteworthy quality of the substance used to form a particular object. A

---

65. Antoine Fongaro adduces a substantial amount of circumstantial evidence for equating this raw meat with the vulva and the white tears that appear later with sperm. See his "Obscène Rimbaud" in *Sur Rimbaud: Lire "Illuminations"* (Toulouse: Service des Publications de l'Université de Toulouse-Le Mirail, 1985), pp. 95–108.

tent made from bloody meat then suggests an emergency retreat for an explorer (taking shelter from extreme cold inside the abdominal cavity of a large, recently dead animal) as well as a return to the womb. Continuing with our literal reading, we can say that "the silk of the seas and the arctic flowers" suggests a smooth white material of which both seas and flowers are made, an ice floe where crystals of frost form virtual, not real, flowers and where the sea, frozen into immobility, has been erased as a changing, timebound phenomenon. But then a literal reading of "they do not exist" itself reduces the entire arctic landscape to a mental experience. Only the womb remains, or more precisely, it becomes subsumed by the white cocoon of the poet's private vision, the sort of "dream screen," or blank expanse derived from the infant's unconscious memories of the mother's breast, which, as we have seen, dominates the poetry of Baudelaire. In other words, the most pedestrian reading of the poem possible (in terms of external everyday objects that form part of our routine shared experience) creates a countervailing movement that forcefully draws us away from that experience into oblivion.

If one attempts the opposite move, a purely figurative reading of "le pavillon en viande saignante," one encounters the metaphor's manifold ties throughout the poem to an oxymoronic tissue of oppositions involving indoors/outdoors and fire/ice which suggests that the "pavillon" may be a plume of fire, trailing like a vast banner over the arctic landscape as it erupts from inside a volcano. Descriptions of the active Mount Hekla in Iceland may have provided a pretext for this vision in Rimbaud's poem, but its content is a transcendent mystical union of male and female principles. This visionary synthesis of red and white reappears at the exact midpoint of the poem, in the sixth of eleven blocks of words: "Les brasiers, pleuvant aux rafales de givre,— Douceurs!—les feux à la pluie du vent de diamants" (The fires of live coals, raining down in the squalls of frost,—Sweetnesses! [agreeable sensations]—the fires in the wind raining diamonds). Then the trance deepens; it is no longer the visionary experience that is bracketed, "(elles n'existent pas)," but rather the mundane one, "(Loin des vieilles retraites et des vieilles flammes qu'on entend, qu'on sent)" (p. 292: [Far from the old retreats and the old flames that you can hear, that you can feel]).

Next the oxymoronic synthesis of above and below is superadded to that of fire and ice. It had been implied earlier in "la pluie . . . jetée par le coeur terrestre" (the rain cast by the heart of the earth): some-

thing that would ordinarily fall from above now comes from somewhere underground. The ecstatic erasure of difference becomes
explicit in the climactic phrase "La musique, virement des gouffres
et choc des glaçon aux astres" (p. 292: Music, spinning of the abysses
and blocks of ice striking the stars). The phrase "virement des
gouffres" constitutes a periphrasis for "tourbillon," which itself means
both a whirlpool below and a whirlwind above. The last word, "astres,"
synthesizes "up" and "fire." The elemental metaphors (fire = male;
water = female) and the kinetic/spatial metaphors (rising motion =
poetic self-affirmation; downward motion = intrusion by the Other)
which had preserved the self-conscious distinction between Self and
Other in the earlier poems, making them mutually communicable but
also mutually vulnerable, appear to have been momentarily surpassed,
the dichotomy they pose resolved. The last full block of words recalls
the visionary explosion at the beginning of the poem.

> O Douceurs, ô monde, musique! Et là, les formes, les sueurs, les che-
> velures et les yeux, flottant. Et les larmes blanches, bouillantes,—ô dou-
> ceurs!—et la voix féminine arrivée au fond des volcans et des grottes
> arctiques. [p. 292]

> (O Sweetnesses, O World, music! And there, the shapes, sweats, heads
> of hair and eyes, floating. And the white, scalding tears—O sweet-
> nesses!—and the feminine voice reaching to the depths of the volcanoes
> and the arctic caves.)

But this vision's descent into moistness ("sueurs ... flottant ... larmes"
betrays a loss of energy only partially compensated for by the thermal
hyperbole "bouillantes." Repressed alterity returns when the phrase
"les formes ... les chevelures et les yeux, flottant" reinscribes in phantasmal form the "êtres" dismissed at the beginning. These forms, in
fact, had already reappeared, albeit under the sign of negation, in
the third and eighth blocks of words: "vieilles fanfares," "anciens
assassins," "vieilles retraites," "vieilles flammes" (old fanfares, former
assassins, old retreats, old flames).

Despite these four episodic intrusions by the past, the violent dis-
placements effected by the poem have satisfied the lyric self's need
for action and have therefore made contemplation possible. "La voix
féminine" that at the conclusion reaches the depths of both the vol-
canoes and the ice caves is densely polysemous: (1) it is a vehicle
of grammatical self-reference reflecting artistic self-consciousness

("la voix féminine" is a tautology insofar as "voice" in French is of the feminine grammatical gender); (2) it designates speaking/singing as contrasted with action, but its penetration into hidden places gives it a "masculine" quality as well; (3) it does not accomplish an intrusion such as the vertical descent/invasion of the self-critical consciousness in other poems; rather it echoes the "Elle" as idealized companion in the two previous poems of the *Illuminations*, "Angoisse" and "Métropolitain": as an anima figure, it complements the poet's conscious self with a capacity for instinctual expression.

Retreat itself, Rimbaud now seems to feel, can transform things. The last section of "Jeunesse," for example, conveys a triumphant sense of creative power exercised in solitude: "Ta mémoire et tes sens ne seront que la nourriture de ton impulsion créatrice. Quant au monde, quand tu sortiras, que sera-t-il devenu? En tout cas, rien des apparences actuelles" (p. 298: Your memory and your senses will be only the food for your creative impulse. As for the world, when you leave, what will it have become? In any case, nothing of [its] present appearances [will remain]). The following poem, "Promontoire," again celebrates the poet's power, spreading a starburst of creative possibilities before its noble travelers. Soon afterward, in "Soir historique," historical pessimism merges with optimism about the poet's creative powers, as it was to do among the Modernists half a century later.[66] Poetic megalomania now intensifies so much that even the Apocalypse "sera donné à l'être sérieux de surveiller" (p. 301: the serious-minded being will be put in charge of it). The poet's powers transcend all earthly events; he dominates them like a god.[67] Finally, "Génie," the poem traditionally published last in the *Illuminations* although its date remains unknown, presents a totalizing discourse whose title represents both the goal and the pathway to that goal. Rimbaud becomes not only his own audience but his own author.[68]

---

66. In this poem, as in "Conte," "Royauté," "H," and "Dévotion," Giusto sees Rimbaud's renunciation of all his hopes of discovering a transforming power in poetry and his dismissal of poetry as subjective and therefore irrelevant (*Rimbaud créateur*, pp. 325–27). This group of poems "probably reflects the moment when Rimbaud is erasing the visionary experience" whose language he then parodies in "Dévotion" (p. 330).

67. Compare Lautréamont's more timid spectator's role when he imagines the world devoured by a sea of lice: "Moi, avec des ailes d'ange, immobile dans les airs, pour le contempler" (*Les Chants de Maldoror*, II, 9: I with the wings of an angel, motionless in the air, in order to watch it [the spectacle of the destruction of humanity] at leisure).

68. "A self who creates rather than being created, such is the ideal Rimbaud proposes to himself from the outset of his poetic career," observes Poulet, *Poésie éclatée*, p. 111.

Hugo Friedrich neatly summed up Rimbaud's originality: the poet institutes the abnormal divorce of the poetic 'I' from the empirical self."[69] In both "Délires II" and "Phrases," Rimbaud clearly implies his Muse is no longer the conventional guide through the nether-worlds of language; she has become language itself. Rimbaud exploits her powers as Mallarmé had done, through the simultaneous pres-ence/absence generated by denial; but, like Baudelaire, he also mul-tiplies other oxymoronic linkings of contraries. Oxymoron functions like a hyperbolic form of metaphor. Just as the arbitrary juxtaposition of two discrete terms in a metaphor suggests a third term that tran-scends both of the others, so the juxtaposition of two clashing terms in an oxymoron suggests an averarching third term surpassing the conventional categories of intersubjective, consensual reality. And by minimizing the role of finite (conjugated) verbs, Rimbaud, like Ver-laine, engages in a sustained attempt to exalt the purified imagination above grammatical time. He thus aspires to a mode of expression akin to the verbless Latin aphorism.

For Rimbaud's personal situation as an adolescent outcast made him keenly conscious that the prime instrument of the oppressive Other is language. Knowing that he himself could realize the imagi-nation only in the form of language, always already contaminated by other users and debased by the imperative of communicability, he experiences an ultimately intolerable constraint. The apparent triumph of the ending of the *Illuminations* proves ephemeral.[70]

"Poor Arthur's" renunciation of poetry in favor of a preoccupation with making business profits in North Africa (a topic belabored in nearly all his letters from the end of 1878 on) has been interpreted as a total undoing of his revolt, as "his conversion into a money-grubbing son of his mother" after he had resisted her materialism for so long.[71] But this interpretation fails to tell the whole story. The myth

69. Hugo Friedrich, *The Structure of Modern Poetry: From the Mid-Nineteenth to the Mid-Twentieth Century* (Evanston, Ill.: Northwestern University Press, 1974 [German ed., 1956; rev. 1967]), p. 48.

70. Borrowing Hayden White's terms, we can say that Rimbaud's poetic odyssey ends not as a Romance, "a drama of self-identification symbolized by the hero's transcendence of the world of experience, his victory over it, and his final liberation from it," but as a tragedy, "the epiphany of the law governing human existence which the protagonist's [unsuccessful] exertions against the world have brought to pass" (*Metahistory: The Historical Imagination in Nineteenth-Century Europe* [Baltimore: Johns Hopkins Uni-versity Press, 1973], pp. 8–11).

71. Cohn, *Poetry of Rimbaud*, p. 7. Cf. Elizabeth Hanson, *My Poor Arthur: A Biography of Arthur Rimbaud* (New York: Holt, 1960), passim.

of his father guided him too. From a status analogous to that of his abandoned mother—someone limited to trying to influence others through words and dependent on others' responses—he promoted himself to the status of his father, an autonomous doer. Previously, his restless journeying in Europe and his domination of Verlaine had brought him only partial success in achieving this status. His hope of transforming the world through incantation, "l'alchimie du verbe," gave way in his psyche to an imitation of his father, who had been a soldier in North Africa.

At first Rimbaud had tried to join the adult male world of Parisian poets. After his break with Verlaine, his publication of *Une Saison en enfer* represented an attempt to win recognition independently. As he wrote Ernest Delahaye in May 1873, "my fate depends on this book."[72] But without Verlaine's protection, Rimbaud was rejected in the literary circles whose members he had provoked and insulted.[73] After the winter of 1873–74 his identity as a poet was gradually extinguished. Probably he worked briefly with Germain Nouveau to prepare a publishable manuscript of the *Illuminations* during the spring of 1874; and as noted earlier, he continued writing the occasional *Illumination* until after his visit to Stockholm in 1877.[74]

But he increasingly began to experience a delusional identification with his father. His enlistment in the Dutch Foreign Legion in May 1876 was a rehearsal for this assumption of the paternal, military role. He deserted in August, but on May 14, 1877, he attempted to enlist in the United States Navy. On this occasion his letter of inquiry regarding the conditions of enlistment reveals that he was confusing himself with his father. Inaccurately (and most inappropriately) he claimed he had deserted from the 47th Regiment of the French Army, his father's former unit. At the end of 1878 he went to work as a foreman at a quarry in Cyprus, and his father died while Rimbaud was on his way there (November 17, 1878), as he probably learned a few months later.[75] Throughout the second half of 1879 he suffered

---

72. See Adam, p. 268. In the immediate context, however, this statement refers primarily to his intense desire to escape the boredom of the country rather than to win fame; and in the event, he made no serious effort to publicize his printed work by sending copies and letters to influential critics. Perhaps he became convinced of the futility of his attempt during the very act of making it.

73. See Petitfils, *Rimbaud* (n. 5 above), pp. 136 and 144.

74. Ibid., p. 235, and see p. 235 above.

75. His father's death date has been omitted from the chronologies of both the

from typhoid fever, in what may have been a sympathetic identification with the death of his parent. From mid-1880 on, when he went to Alexandria to seek employment, he lived in the part of the world where his father had served. At the end of 1880, in Harar, he told his employer that he had been born in Dole—his father's birthplace, not his own. And during the last months of his life, the unconscious identification with the father resurfaced in Rimbaud's paranoid fear that he would be arrested and imprisoned for not having done his military service, even though his leg had been amputated and even though his older brother's service had exempted Rimbaud years before.[76]

Like all such behavior motivated by conscious or unconscious identification with an Other, Rimbaud's actions contained an element of competition. He tried symbolically to go his father-imago one better. He operated on the same terrain as his father and likewise as a leader of men. But as a merchant, he sold rifles rather than fired them. And as a sort of director of warfare rather than an actor, profiting no matter which side won, he situated himself on a level of control that could be considered higher than that which his father had occupied. In this context his reaction to society's neglect of the veterans of the humiliating Franco-Prussian War was telling. When his friend Delahaye protested because the public now shunned the maimed and wounded soldiers they had feted before the defeat, Rimbaud cynically observed: "Those guys were just tools of the dead regime. People fussed over them as long as they thought they would win. Today when they're half-dead in hospital wards, what do you expect people to do with them?"[77] By abandoning poetry, Rimbaud had escaped from the helpless "female" role involving mere verbiage rather than action; and by seeing war only as a question of profits, he also avoided the "male'" helplessness of the martyred soldier. But as readers we must regret that his Pyrrhic victory over poetry had to be won at the cost of its glory.

Pléiade and Garnier editions of Rimbaud's works, apparently on the erroneous assumption that physical and psychic absence are the same.

76. Since 1977, when I first speculated that Rimbaud's renunciation of poetry in the latter half of his life was associated with an identification with his father, much supporting evidence has been adduced by Alain de Mijolla: see "L'Ombre du capitaine Rimbaud," chap. 2 in *Visiteurs du moi,* pp. 35–80.

77. Cited by Petitfils, *Rimbaud,* p. 119.

Conclusion: Beyond Symbolism

What united the greatest poets in France between 1851 and 1875 was their sense of the difficulty of writing. Unlike the Romantics, they did not believe that one could discover ideas by manipulating words. Bound down to the material order, poetry could escape it only through vagueness or negation. For the poet, either of these solutions was a form of suicide.

Yet Symbolism paradoxically attempted to apprehend the unattainable by organizing it, by exploiting the topos of inexpressibility as a major source of poetic developments, notably through a series of allusions to the inadequacy of the communicative act, no aspect of which was any longer taken for granted. The Symbolist poet no longer felt entitled to the privileged priestly status (persisting anachronistically and unconvincingly in Baudelaire's "Bénédiction") of an elect mediator between the transcendent and the public—a signifier personified—but instead he assumed the sooty greasepaint of words as a kind of necessary defilement.[1] Appearances to the contrary, in Symbolism the poet and poetry have become desacralized.

The prose poems of Baudelaire, Rimbaud's *Une Saison en enfer*,

1. I allude to Mallarmé's "Le Pitre châtié" and more generally to the motif of the clown in nineteenth- and twentieth-century French painting and poetry, studied notably by Jean Starobinski in *Portrait de l'artiste en saltimbanque* (Geneva: Skira, 1970), pp. 83–99 and passim.

and Mallarmé's return to active poetic and critical production in the mid-1880s signal the mutually independent but parallel resolutions of these authors' Symbolist crises. Their prose exists in dialogic tension with the verse. It makes the message of the verse retrospectively explicit, unveiling its mystery with ironic discursive statements. In the earlier poems, the topic of the ineffable had attempted to transcend both the conventional codes of Neoclassicism and the countercodes of Romanticism. But to explain in prose the mechanisms of the ineffable and to admit that it partakes of the same arbitrary (and self-deluding) quality as other poetic subjects is to demystify it and thus to cancel the virtual transcendence effected through the negation of the familiar in the earlier poems. Furthermore, to move from verse to prose poem or prose betrays a loss of faith in Cratylism, in the attempt to suggest transcendent organic unity through what Baudelaire calls "the incantatory magic" of the conventions of verse (repetitions of rhythm, sound, and word), even though these same conventions have served as banal vehicles for earlier poets. Among the four major Symbolists, only Mallarmé eventually emerges at the far side of this strategic withdrawal to attain a new optimism.

He does so in "Un coup de Dés" and in his projects for "Le Livre" by introducing a middle term between his words and the "compte total en formation" (sum total in the process of being formed) which he evokes at the end of "Un coup de Dés." This mediator is the orderliness of mathematics (or more precisely where Mallarmé is concerned, arithmetic), ultimately superseding the disorder of the world and reflected in a new order of symbols.[2] Thus after all the major poets of France save Mallarmé have either died or become inactive, we

2. Lautréamont had addressed a prayer to mathematics, arithmetic, and geometry in the third of his *Chants de Maldoror* (1869), but in his work they serve merely as another metaphor for the frustratingly inaccessible absolute rather than as a signpost guiding us toward that absolute.

One way some Symbolists do anticipate Modernism is through a feature both movements share with certain Romantics: challenging accepted codes by emphasizing the unpleasant. Thus Baudelaire and Rimbaud, along with Lautréamont, Corbière, and Laforgue, de-euphemize metaphor, replacing its usual tendency to edulcorate experience (e.g., death is sleep) by doing the opposite (God is a snake, the poet is a gnat intoxicated by the fumes from a urinal, etc.). See Laurence M. Porter, "Modernist Maldoror: The De-euphemization of Metaphor," *L'Esprit Créateur*, 18 (Winter 1978), 25–34. On a broader scale, this process has been masterfully analyzed by Michael Riffaterre in his discussion of "conversion" in *The Semiotics of Poetry* (Bloomington: Indiana University Press, 1978), pp. 63–80.

encounter the "second Symbolism" of the later 1880s and the 1890s, a Neo-Romantic dream of organic unity that had been abandoned until it was taken up again by Mallarmé and by the confident synthesizers of Modernism: Rubén Darío, Rainer Maria Rilke, T. S. Eliot, Paul Valéry, and Paul Claudel.

If Romanticism is fundamentally a myth of revelation, Symbolism is ultimately a myth of reconstruction. Baudelaire, like Guillaume Apollinaire after him, evokes a fragmented self that can be reassembled only in the context of a new order. Gérard de Nerval had anticipated this motif with his personal myth of the shattered pantheon of pagan gods (of inadmissible impulses) reunited in a universal pardon. Verlaine seeks to replace the weak unity of discourse with the firmer unity of song. Rimbaud speaks of "reinventing love" and Mallarmé of a final summing up. For Mallarmé, indeed, "symbol" means "synthesis."[3] William Blake had anticipated this notion in *Jerusalem*, and Richard Wagner echoed it in his plans for combining the resources of all the arts. We can understand Mallarmé's grand ambition to compose an "Orphic explanation of the universe" only if we recall from Ovid that Orpheus simultaneously describes *and* creates the order he is describing. Confronting the immensity of this task, the first generation of Symbolists (Baudelaire, Verlaine, Rimbaud, and the Mallarmé of the early and middle periods) was haunted by a sense of doubt, sterility, inability to communicate, and in a word, failure. Paradoxically, of course, such a proclamation of defeat salvages another kind of victory. "In writing of the subversion of the author," Barbara Johnson observes, "[Mallarmé has] subverted in advance any grounds on which one might undertake to kill off an authority that theorizes the death of all authority."[4] But it was for the second generation of Symbolists, the late Mallarmé and his heirs in the twentieth century, to recapture faith in a totalizing discourse.

What then is the relationship of Symbolism to more recent poetry? One problem for students of French literary history is the lack of a single, generic label for early-twentieth-century French

3. See Henri Peyre, *Qu'est-ce que le Symbolisme?* (Paris: Presses Universitaires de France, 1974), p. 297.
4. Barbara Johnson, *"Les Fleurs du mal armé:* Some Reflexions on Intertextuality," in *Stéphane Mallarmé: Modern Critical Views*, ed. Harold Bloom (New York: Chelsea House, 1987), p. 219. This essay also appears in Johnson, *A World of Difference* (Baltimore: Johns Hopkins University Press, 1987), pp. 116–33.

poetry, a label equivalent to "Modernism," which serves as a catch-all description for British and American poetry of the same period. We can distinguish at least four major currents of innovation in France: the religious revival led by Charles Péguy and Claudel; the "modernism" with a small *m* fostered by Apollinaire; the Surrealism of the 1920s and after; and the poetry of Valéry. Let us briefly consider each in turn.

Catholic poetry such as Claudel's no longer calls into question the communicative act, because God provides the inspiration, the topics, the linguistic vehicle, the justification, and indeed the imperatives for communication. It is our duty to praise God to our fellows and to spread the Good News of the hope of redemption. It is the duty of the audience reverently to listen. By writing poetry, Claudel emulates God's Creation with a simulacrum of words and thus honors the Deity. One of the most striking features in Claudel's verse is his self-dramatization as a visionary seizing on inspiration and relating all things through his centralizing activity: "Que mon vers ne soit rien d'esclave! mais tel que l'aigle marin qui s'est jeté sur un grand poisson, / Et l'on ne voit rien qu'un éclatant tourbillon d'ailes et l'éclaboussement de l'écume.... Je partage la liberté de la mer omniprésente!... Je vous salue, ô monde libéral à mes yeux!... Je suis en vous et vous êtes à moi et votre possession est la mienne" (Let my verse partake of nothing servile! But like the sea eagle that has thrown itself on a great fish, / And let nothing be seen but a dazzling whirlwind of wings and splashing foam.... I share the freedom of the omnipresent sea!... Hail, O world bountiful in my eyes!... I am in you and you belong to me and your possession is mine).[5]

Apollinaire continues the elegiac tradition of Verlaine, declaring his unworthiness and his victimization by life, directly (e.g., in *Le Bestiaire ou cortège d'Orphée,* to say nothing of the better-known "Zone" or "La Chanson du Mal-Aimé") and indirectly (e.g., in *L'Enchanteur pourrissant*). His lyric self is torn between obsessive restatements of an unhappy past and centrifugal attempts to escape to a prelapsarian moment of blissful happiness. He recaptures coherence by regressing to the oral stage of development. The title *Alcools*, the pun on "palate/palace" in "Palais", and exclamations such as "Je suis ivre d'avoir bu tout l'univers" (I am intoxicated from having drunk the whole universe) in "Vendémiaire" presuppose ingestion of externality as the

5. Paul Claudel, *Cinq Grandes Odes* (Paris: Gallimard, 1957), pp. 22, 38, 44.

sole organizing principle. The picture-poems of *Calligrammes* transmute the form as well as the content of poetry into an assimilable object by transforming the set of words on the page into an icon that the eye can instantly consume. Apollinaire's insatiable curiosity about the new serves as the motivating force of his later productions and as a master trope of *divertissement*, a way of forgetting the past, despised self.

Surrealism, as André Breton defined it in his manifestos, makes the transcendent accessible by situating it within rather than beyond the self. The optimistic rhetoric of discovery, control, and triumph which he adopts reveals a radical departure from the pessimistic dissatisfaction of the Symbolist crisis. He affirms that Surrealism is "psychic automatism in its pure state, by which one proposes to express... the actual functioning of thought.... If the depths of our mind contain... strange forces capable of augmenting those on the surface... then there is every reason... first to seize them, then, if need be, to submit them to the control of our reason. ... Surrealism is the 'invisible ray' which will one day enable us to win out over our opponents."[6] A former medical student conversant with Freud and Pierre Janet, Breton hoped that through a Hegelian opposition of the thesis of consciousness and the antithesis of the unconscious he could achieve a higher synthesis of our mental faculties.[7] He had such a clear sense of Surrealist goals and orthodoxy that he did not hesitate to expel many close friends and associates from the movement whenever they deviated from what he considered to be the true path.[8]

The transition from Symbolism to later French poetry and to Modernism is best illustrated by the work of Valéry, often held to be Mallarmé's major disciple. In his early *Album de vers anciens* (1894), Valéry was quite unoriginal and struggled against his own sense of inadequacy by disparaging his forebears.[9] First he wrote "La Jeune

6. André Breton, *Manifestoes of Surrealism*, trans. Richard Seaver and Helen R. Lane (Ann Arbor: University of Michigan Press, 1969), pp. 26, 10, 47.

7. Ibid., p. 14.

8. For further discussion of Breton's doctrinaire rigor, see Laurence M. Porter, "'L'Amour fou' and Individuation: A Jungian Reading of Breton's *Nadja*," *L'Esprit Créateur*, 22 (Summer 1982), 25–34.

9. In *Paul Valéry's "Album de vers anciens": A Past Transfigured* (Princeton: Princeton University Press, 1983), Suzanne Nash describes Valéry's dismay when he returned to these poems twenty years later and found them appallingly derivative. Nash's excellent book is a welcome, solid, and sensitive study of how unoriginal Valéry was in his early

Parque" to praise and bury Mallarmé, then he began to revise the
Album so as to refute Symbolist idealism (of the second, or optimistic,
phase) with a poetry "claim[ing] autonomy through critical self-
reference."[10] Here, one should add, he fails to recognize in the prose
poems of Baudelaire, Rimbaud, and Mallarmé the prior achievement
of his own goal. But he also revives the Enlightenment notion that
philosophy is an activity rather than a system.[11] For him, the mind
can be active not only in criticizing its own products but also in exploring externality in order to bring back discoveries. Rather than
limit his mind to creating the solipsistic projections of the static Symbolist landscape, he imagines his mind as generating the materials for
poetry by creating connections among things in the outside world as
it moves among them. To describe the mind's activity, he uses the
term "passages" in the painterly sense of an area of color serving to
effect a transition between one plane and another in the virtual space
of the artistic composition. Valéry may even be implying that in his
poetic universe mental activity can reveal the structures of reality by
paralleling their movement, a notion that would suggest an unac-
knowledged atheistic reworking of Claudel.

So Valéry's "Air de Sémiramis," for example, presents that monarch
as a parodic avatar of a Symbolism that stridently demands autonomy
and would construct a monument from the elements of its own body,
although her reign is ironically shaped and doomed by the very externality she denies.[12] (Apollinaire, for one, in poems such as "Cortège," reverses that Symbolist process by literally constructing for
himself a body from the external world.) Valéry's own self-assured
poetry trembles with potentiality and a sense of creative power. Repeatedly and vehemently he rejects the notion of inspiration as a
limiting subservience to something imaginary and outside oneself; he
reiterates the Neoclassical ethic of self-control, unremitting effort, and
the merits of "la difficulté vaincue" (obstacles [deliberately introduced
to strengthen us through the necessary struggles through which they
are] overcome). He confidently names the collection of his mature

---

verse and how he struggled against his own sense of inadequacy by disparaging his
precursors. In particularly keen discussion (pp. 51–63), she explains how Valéry eludes
the Baudelairean lion in his path by dismissing him as derivative of Poe—after which
Valéry appropriates Poe as his own master.

10. Nash, *Paul Valéry's "Album de vers anciens,"* p. 15.
11. Ibid., pp. 90–92.
12. On "Air de Sémiramis," see ibid., pp. 254–74.

verse "Charmes" (magical spells), implying that in the role of a poet he possesses magical, Orphic powers. "L'Amateur de poèmes," the 1906 note that came to serve as epilogue for the *Album de vers anciens*, is perhaps the starkest expression of Valéry's hubristic optimism; if we assume that it applies at least in part to the creation of the texts that he himself has just written. In this note, Valéry, like Montaigne undertaking the composition of his *Essais*, confesses his shame at the disorder of his thoughts, "that plethora of projects whose very facility cuts them short" as one shades into the next through the transforming power of involuntary associations. But when he reads a poem, he says, he breathes in harmony with a law prepared in advance. The text has foreseen and imposed order on even his astonishment. He effortlessly encounters the language of certitude.

The French "second Symbolism" of the era of Wagnerian myth leads into Modernism through a resacralization of poetry and a re-newed confidence in its instrument, language. The Modernists, in short, dramatize the success rather than the failure of the poetic act. The result is a Neo-Romantic self-assurance that the poet can triumph over the natural cycle that consumes him (cf. Vigny's "La Bouteille à la mer") by apprehending it intellectually. Mallarmé's anguished seek-ing "dans le doute du Jeu suprême" (amid the uncertainty of the supreme Game) becomes the confident overview of Valéry's "Le Ci-metière marin": "Tout va sous terre et rentre dans le jeu" (Everything goes underground and rejoins the game). Valéry would not always be so sanguine. The 1939 Zaharoff Lecture at Oxford, "Poésie et pensée abstraite," characterizes language as a frail plank thrown over an abyss: unless you pass over quickly, it will collapse beneath you. But by that date the dark night of Hitlerism has rendered Modernist optimism difficult to sustain.[13]

René Wellek's essay "The Term and Concept of Symbolism in Lit-erary History" misleadingly claims that by the time the post–1914 avant-garde movements emerged, "faith in language ha[d] crumbled completely."[14] He oversimplifies. Symbolists tried to detach language from material reality so that they could use it as an instrument of transcendence. When they failed to achieve transcendence, they lost

13. Paul Valéry, *Oeuvres*, Jean Hytier, 2 vols. (Paris: Gallimard, 1962–65), I, 94–95 and 1314–39.
14. This essay appears in the *Actes du Ve Congrès de l'Association Internationale de Littérature Comparée*, (Belgrade, 1967), ed. Nikola Banasevic (Amsterdam: Swets & Zeit-linger, 1969), pp. 275–92.

faith in language. At the same time, they paradoxically used language
to evoke transcendence by lamenting the inaccessibility of the transcendent. Modernists, in contrast, rejected the hope that language
could serve to effect transcendence. But in the process of renouncing
such a hope, the Modernist once again grounded language solidly in
reality. Therefore the ability of language to signify could once again
be taken for granted. Then language could be held to constitute a
reliable data base. And, paradoxically, some Modernist poets believed
that the accumulation of linguistic data could in turn help, after all,
to liberate people from the limitations of materiality. The Surrealist
Breton, for example, confidently declared, "Language has been given
to man so that he may make Surrealist use of it."[15] The violent dis-
tortions to which some Modernist experiments subject language are
analogous to the chemist's processes designed to create a new product.
Again, Ezra Pound's mosaic of borrowed words and citations from
various tongues reflects a totalizing optimism that all words, put together, will mean *something*. (Ultimately, of course, Pound expressed
disillusionment with the hope that his *Cantos* could add up to a coherent whole.) The mode of this optimism already differs from that
of Mallarmé's later career, when the French poet hopes that *some*
words, put together, will mean *everything*.

Because the poetic message is no longer considered ephemeral and
tenuous, the poet no longer feels the need to defend it watchfully
and perhaps anxiously. Unlike the Romantics, the Modernists and
their French cousins did not regard the reader as an enemy or an
incorrigible ignoramus, but rather as an educable, pliant postulant.
Thanks to the extensive footnotes provided by T. S. Eliot, for example,
the common reader becomes initiated into the poetic universe and is
invited to interpret the poetry (now considered as something decod-
able) rather than contemplate it. Thus any mystery is not an inherent
quality of the poetic subject but the result of a conscious stratagem.
One recalls Mallarmé's alleged joke to a journalist who wanted to
interview him about a lecture the poet had just given: "Wait a minute,
I have to add some obscurity."

To understand the relationship between French Symbolism and
the poetic movements that followed it in other countries, one must
recognize that Symbolism does not simply evolve into Modernism,

15. Breton, *Manifestoes of Surrealism*, p. 32.

as critics usually assume; Symbolism stands in sharp contradiction to Modernism. The distinction between the two movements has been needlessly blurred by a widespread critical carelessness in the use of the terms "subject" and "theme." Subjects are mere raw materials; themes are topics and motifs that have been shaped by an evaluation. The topic of death, for example, may produce any number of themes when it is combined with reactions of grief, joy, hope, fear, pity, despair, defiance, disgust, and indifference. Similarly, to center existence on the creative act may generate elation or dismay.

Modernist poets repeatedly borrow Symbolist motifs: the creative act, the remoteness of the ideal, the fact of physical death evaded by the intellectual transcendence of our physical limitations, simultaneous presence and absence, the self-contemplating swan, the pool as mirror or repository of memories, autumn, Narcissus, the Muse, and so forth. And to confuse matters further, Modernists often adopt a Symbolist diction characterized by ambiguity, polysemy, auto-referentiality, and the coexistence of presence and absence.[16] But a Modernist could not produce a Symbolist poem even by combining all these elements, because Modernist optimism inevitably casts them in a different mold than that of Symbolist pessimism.[17] The Symbolists' audience is sought, the Modernists' given. The Symbolists dramatize the difficulties and defeats of the poetic act; the Modernists exalt creative power and potentiality. Even at their most pessimistic, the Modernists doubt prospects offered by the outside world rather than their own powers as poets. To imagine the world ending not with a bang but a whimper is still to glorify the imagination that contains that world.

Thus Modernism in poetry (as in architecture) proves essentially retrograde in comparison to early-twentieth-century music and painting. It is a commonplace to say that literature evolves more rapidly than and anticipates developments in these other arts, but the rise of nonrepresentational painting and collage, the "found object," and

16. See, e.g., Valéry, *Oeuvres* I, 1333.

17. For an important opposing view that sees Symbolism as developing smoothly into Modernism, see John Porter Houston, *French Symbolism and the Modernist Movement: A Study of Poetic Structures* (Baton Rouge: Louisiana State University Press, 1980). Peyre is another proponent of this view: see *Qu'est-ce que le symbolisme?* pp. 225–29. For Peyre, Rilke attains the apogee of European Symbolism with the seventh *Duino Elegy* of 1923.

twelve-tone music just before World War I transforms the medium
into the message, desacralizes the artist once again, and corresponds
in poetry to experiments that come to flower only well after World War
II, when the creative drama of the play of the poet is replaced by the
antidrama of the play of the signifier.[18]

18. Among the many studies of Modernism, those I find most relevant to the present
argument are Michel Foucault, *The Order of Things* (New York: Pantheon, 1971),
pp. 292–300; Matei Calinescu, *Five Faces of Modernity: Modernism; Avant-Garde; Decadence; Kitsch; Postmodernism* (Durham, N.C.: Duke University Press, 1987 [revised version
of the 1977 edition]), pp. 86–93, 240–55, 272–79, and 356–63; and Paul de Man's essay
on Modernism in *Blindness and Insight: Essays in the Rhetoric of Contemporary Criticism*
(New York: Oxford University Press, 1971), where de Man shows that no two critics
can agree on the meaning of the word.

Index

Library of Congress Cataloging-in-Publication Data

Porter, Laurence M., 1936–
    The crisis of French symbolism / by Laurence M. Porter.
    p. cm.
    Includes bibliographical references.
    ISBN 0-8014-2418-6 (alk. paper)
    1. French poetry—19th century—History and criticism.
    2. Symbolism (Literary movement)—France. 3. Mallarmé, Stéphane,
    1842–1898—Criticism and interpretation. 4. Verlaine, Paul,
    1844–1896—Criticism and interpretation. 5. Baudelaire, Charles,
    1821—1867—Criticism and interpretation. 6. Rimbaud, Arthur,
    1854–1891—Criticism and interpretation. I. Title.
    PQ439.P7 1990
    841'.70915—dc20
                                                    89-45976